A History of Art in Ancient Egypt Vol. 1 (of 2)
Charles Chipiez

FROM THE FRENCH
OF
GEORGES PERROT,
PROFESSOR IN THE FACULTY OF LETTERS, PARIS; MEMBER OF THE INSTITUTE
AND
CHARLES CHIPIEZ.

ILLUSTRATED WITH FIVE HUNDRED AND NINETY-EIGHT ENGRAVINGS IN THE TEXT, AND FOURTEEN STEEL AND COLOURED PLATES.

IN TWO VOLUMES.—VOL. I.

ISBN: 978-1-63923-951-1

All Rights reserved. No part of this book maybe reproduced without written permission from the publishers, except by a reviewer who may quote brief passages in a review to be printed in a newspaper or magazine.

Printed: March 2023

Published and Distributed By:
Lushena Books
607 Country Club Drive, Unit E
Bensenville, IL 60106
www.lushenabks.com

ISBN: 978-1-63923-951-1

PREFACE.

M. Perrot's name as a classical scholar and archæologist, and M. Chipiez's as a penetrating critic of architecture, stand so high that any work from their pens is sure of a warm welcome from all students of the material remains of antiquity. These volumes are the first instalment of an undertaking which has for its aim the history and critical analysis of that great organic growth which, beginning with the Pharaohs and ending with the Roman Emperors, forms what is called Antique Art. The reception accorded to this instalment in its original form is sufficient proof that the eulogium prefixed to the German translation by an eminent living Egyptologist, Professor Georg Ebers, is well deserved; "The first section," he says, "of this work, is broad and comprehensive in conception, and delicate in execution; it treats Egyptian art in a fashion which has never previously been approached." In clothing it in a language which will, I hope, enable it to reach a still wider public, my one endeavour has been that it should lose as little as possible, either in substance or form.

A certain amount of repetition is inevitable in a work of this kind when issued, as this was, in parts, and in one place[1] I have ventured to omit matter which had already been given at some length, but with that exception I have followed M. Perrot's words as closely as the difference of idiom would allow. Another kind of repetition, with which, perhaps, some readers may be inclined to quarrel, forced itself upon the author as the lesser of two evils. He was compelled either to sacrifice detail and precision in attempting to carry on at once the history of all the Egyptian arts and of their connection with the national religion and civilization, or to go back upon his footsteps now and again in tracing each art successively from its birth to its decay. The latter alternative was chosen as the only one consistent with the final aim of his work.

Stated in a few words, that aim is to trace the course of the great plastic evolution which culminated in the age of Pericles and came to an end in that of Marcus Aurelius. That evolution forms a complete organic whole, with a birthday, a deathday, and an unbroken chain of cause and effect uniting the two. To objectors who may say that the art of India, of China, of Japan, should have been included in the scheme, it may be answered: this is the life, not of two, or three, but of one. M. Perrot has been careful, therefore, to discriminate between those characteristics of Egyptian art which may be referred either to the national beliefs and modes of thought, or to undeveloped material conditions, such as the want or superstitious disuse of iron, and those which, being determined by the very nature of the problems which art has to solve, formed a starting point for the arts of all later civilizations. By means of well-chosen examples he shows that the art of the Egyptians went through the same process of development as those of other and later nationalities, and that the real distinguishing characteristic of the sculptures and paintings of the Nile Valley was a continual tendency to simplification and generalization, arising partly from the habit of mind and hand created by the hieroglyphic writing, partly from the stubborn nature of the chief materials employed.

To this characteristic he might, perhaps, have added another, which is sufficiently remarkable in an art which had at least three thousand years of vitality, namely, its freedom from individual expression. The realism of the Egyptians was a broad realism. There is in it no sign of that research into detail which distinguishes most imitative art and is to be found even in that of their immediate successors; and yet, during all those long centuries of alternate renascence and decay, we find no vestige of an attempt to raise art above imitation. No suspicion of its expressive power seems to have dawned on the Egyptian mind, which, so far as the plastic arts were concerned, never produced anything that in the language of modern criticism could be called a creation. In this particular Egypt is more closely allied to those nations of the far east whose art does not come within the scope of M. Perrot's inquiry, than to the great civilizations which formed its own posterity.

Before the late troubles intervened to draw attention of a different kind to the Nile Valley, the finding of a pit full of royal mummies and sepulchral objects in the western mountain at Thebes had occurred to give a fresh stimulus to the interest in Egyptian history, and to encourage those who were doing their best to lead England to take her proper share in the work of exploration. A short account of this discovery, which took place after M. Perrot's book was complete, and of some of the numerous art objects with which it has enriched the Boulak Museum, will be found in an Appendix to the second volume.

My acknowledgments for generous assistance are due to Dr. Birch, Mr. Reginald Stuart Poole, and Miss A. B. Edwards.

W. A.

CONTENTS.

		PAGE
	INTRODUCTION	i-lxi
	TO THE READER	lxiii-lxiv

CHAPTER I.
THE GENERAL CHARACTER OF EGYPTIAN CIVILIZATION.

§ 1.	Egypt's place in the History of the World	1-2
§ 2.	The Valley of the Nile and its Inhabitants	2-16
§ 3.	The Great Divisions of Egyptian History	16-21
§ 4.	The Constitution of Egyptian Society—Influence of that Constitution upon Monuments of Art	21-44
§ 5.	The Egyptian Religion and its Influence upon the Plastic Arts	44-69
§ 6.	That Egyptian Art did not escape the Law of Change, and that its History may therefore be written	70-89
§ 7.	Of the place held in this work by the Monuments of the Memphite Period, and of the Limits of our Inquiry	89-93

CHAPTER II.
PRINCIPLES AND GENERAL CHARACTERISTICS OF EGYPTIAN ARCHITECTURE.

§ 1.	Method to be Employed by us in our Study of this Architecture	94-96
§ 2.	General Principles of Form	96-102
§ 3.	General Principles of Construction.—Materials	103-106

§ 4.	Dressed Construction	106-113
§ 5.	Compact Construction	113-114
§ 6.	Construction by Assemblage	114-119
§ 7.	Decoration	119-125

CHAPTER III.
SEPULCHRAL ARCHITECTURE.

§ 1.	The Egyptian Belief as to a Future Life and its Influence upon their Sepulchral Architecture	126-163
§ 2.	The Tomb under the Ancient Empire	163-241
	The Mastabas of the Necropolis of Memphis	165-189
	The Pyramids	189-241
§ 3.	The Tomb under the Middle Empire	241-254
§ 4.	The Tomb under the New Empire	255-317

CHAPTER IV.
THE SACRED ARCHITECTURE OF EGYPT.

§ 1.	The Temple under the Ancient Empire	318-333
§ 2.	The Temple under the Middle Empire	333-335
§ 3.	The Temple under the New Empire	335-433
§ 4.	General Characteristics of the Egyptian Temple	434-444

LIST OF ILLUSTRATIONS.

COLOURED PLATES.

	To face page
The Arab Chain, from near Keneh	102
The Pyramids, from old Cairo	102
Karnak, bas-reliefs in the Granite Chambers	124
Seti I., bas-relief at Abydos	126
General view of Karnak	360
Perspective view of the Hypostyle Hall, Karnak	368
Thebes, the plain, with the Colossi of Memnon	376

FIG.		PAGE
1.	During the Inundation of the Nile	3
2.	Hoeing	4
3.	Ploughing	4
4.	Harvest scene	5
5.	The Bastinado	6
6.	Statue from the Ancient Empire	10
7.	The *Sheikh-el-Beled*	11
8.	Hunting in the Marshes	14
9.	Shadouf	15
10.	The White Crown	16
11.	The Red Crown	16
12.	The Pschent	16
13.	Seti I. in his War-Chariot	23
14.	Rameses II. in adoration before Seti	25
15.	Homage to Amenophis III.	26
16.	Construction of a Temple at Thebes	27

17.	Columns in the Hypostyle Hall, Karnak	28
18, 19.	Scribes registering the yield of the harvest	29
20.	Colossi of Amenophis III. 30	30
21.	Scribe registering merchandize	31
22.	Boatmen	32
23.	Cattle Drovers	33
24.	Bakers	33
25.	Women at a loom	34
26.	Netting birds	35
27.	Shepherds in the fields	36
28.	Winnowing corn	36
29.	Herdsmen	37
30.	From the tomb of Menofre	39
31.	Water Tournament	42
32.	Mariette's House	43
33.	Amenhotep, or Amenophis III., presented by Phré to Amen-Ra	45
34.	Amen (or Ammon)	51
35.	Ptah	52
36.	Osiris	53
37.	The goddess Bast	54
38.	Painted bas-relief	58
39.	Sekhet	59
40.	Isis-Hathor	60
41.	A Sphinx	61
42.	Touaris	63
43.	Rannu	64
44.	Horus	65
45.	Thoth	66
46.	Sacrifice to Apis	67
47.	Statue from the Ancient Empire	73
48.	Woman kneading dough	74

49.	The Scribe Chaphré	75
50.	The Lady Naï	76
51.	Ouah-ab-ra	79
52.	Sculptor at work upon an arm	81
53.	Sculptor carving a statue	83
54.	Artist painting a statue	85
55.	Isis nursing Horus	87
56.	Chephren	90
57.	Ti, with his wife and son	91
58.	Square building	97
59.	Rectangular and oblong building	97
60.	The Libyan chain, above the Necropolis of Thebes	98
61.	General appearance of an Egyptian Temple	99
62.	Temple of Khons, at Thebes	100
63.	Temple of Khons, Thebes	100
64.	Temple of Khons, Thebes	100
65.	From the second court of Medinet-Abou, Thebes	101
66.	Ramesseum, Thebes	101
67.	The Egyptian Gorge or Cornice	102
68.	Capital and Entablature of the Temple of the Deus Rediculus at Rome	104
69.	The Egyptian "bond"	107
70.	Double-faced wall	108
71, 72.	Elements of the portico	108
73.	Egyptian construction	109
74.	Element of an off-set arch	111
75.	Arrangement of the courses in an off-set arch	111
76.	Off-set semicircular arch	111
77.	Voussoir	112
78.	Arrangement of voussoirs	112
79.	Semicircular vault	112

80.	Granaries, from a bas-relief	113
81.	Modern pigeon house, Thebes	114
82.	Elements of wooden construction	116
83.	Wooden building (first system)	117
84.	Wooden building (second system)	118
85.	Seti I. striking prisoners of war with his mace	124
86.	Stele of the eleventh dynasty	131
87.	Mummy case from the eighteenth dynasty	137
88.	Man and his wife in the style of the fifth dynasty	138
89.	Sekhem-ka, his wife Ata, and his son Khnem, in the style of the fifth dynasty	139
90.	Stele of Nefer-oun	140
91.	Preparation of the victims and arrival of funeral gifts	141
92.	Table for offerings	144
93.	Another form of the table for offerings	144
94.	Labourers heaping up ears of corn	146
95, 96.	Sepulchral statuettes	147
97.	Vignette from a *Ritual* upon papyrus	149
98.	Arrival in Egypt of a company of Asiatic emigrants	152
99.	The tomb of Ti; women, representing the lands of the deceased, carrying the funeral gifts	154
100.	Lid of the coffin of Entef	158
101, 102.	Scarabs	159
103, 104.	Funerary amulets	159
105.	Pillow	160
106.	Actual condition of a Mastaba. The Tomb of Sabou	167
107.	Three mastabas at Gizeh	168
108.	Restoration of part of the Necropolis of Gizeh	169

109.	The Mastabat-el-Faraoun	170
110.	Entrance to a Mastaba at Sakkarah	171
111.	Lintel of the tomb of Teta	172
112.	Plan of the tomb of Ti	174
113, 114.	Mastaba at Sakkarah	174
115.	Western wall in the chamber of the tomb of Ptah-Hotep	175
116.	Plan of a Mastaba with four serdabs	178
117.	Longitudinal section of the same Mastaba	178
118.	Transverse section through the chamber	179
119.	Transverse section through the serdabs	179
120.	Figures in high relief, from a Mastaba at Gizeh	180
121.	The upper chamber, well, and mummy-chamber	181
122.	Double Mastaba at Gizeh	182
123.	Sarcophagus of Khoo-foo-Ankh	183
124.	Details of the Sarcophagus of Khoo-foo-Ankh	184
125.	Bas-relief from Sakkarah	185
126.	Head of a Mummy	188
127.	Plans of the temples belonging to the Second and Third Pyramids	193
128.	Plan of the Pyramid of Cheops	198
129.	The Great Pyramid and the small pyramids at its foot	199
130.	The Three Great Pyramids; from the south	201
131.	The Pyramid of Illahoun, horizontal section in perspective	205
132.	Section of the Pyramid of Cheops	206
133.	The southern Pyramid of Dashour	207
134.	Section of the Stepped Pyramid	207
135.	The Stepped Pyramid	208
136-142.	Successive states of a pyramid	209

143.	Section of the Stepped Pyramid at Sakkarah	213
144.	Construction of the Pyramid of Abousir in parallel layers	213
145.	Partial section of the Stepped Pyramid	214
146.	The Pyramid of Meidoum	215
147.	The Mastabat-el-Faraoun	216
148.	Funerary monument represented in the inscriptions	216
149.	Plan and elevation of a pyramid at Meroe	219
150.	Method of closing a gallery by a stone portcullis	220
151.	Portcullis closed	220
152.	Transverse section, in perspective, through the Sarcophagus-chamber and the discharging chambers of the Great Pyramid	221
153.	Longitudinal section through the lower chambers	222
154.	Pyramidion	230
155.	The casing of the pyramids	233
156.	Plan of the Pyramids of Gizeh and of that part of the Necropolis which immediately surrounds them	237
157.	The Sphinx	238
158.	Pyramid with its inclosure, Abousir	239
159.	The river transport of the Mummy	243
160.	Tomb at Abydos	244
161.	Section of the above tomb	244
162.	Tomb at Abydos	245
163.	Section of the above tomb	245
164.	Stele of the eleventh dynasty, Abydos	246
165.	Stele of Pinahsi, priest of Ma; Abydos	247
166.	Façade of a tomb at Beni-Hassan	250
167.	Façade of a tomb at Beni-Hassan, showing some of the adjoining tombs	251

168.	Interior of a tomb at Beni-Hassan	252
169.	Plan of the above tomb	252
170.	Chess players, Beni-Hassan	253
171.	General plan of Thebes	257
172.	Rameses III. conducting a religious procession, at Medinet-Abou	261
173.	Rameses III. hunting	265
174.	Rameses II. in battle	271
175.	Painting in a royal tomb at Gournah	273
176.	Amenophis III. presenting an offering to Amen	274
177.	Flaying the funerary victim	275
178.	Entrance to a royal tomb	277
179.	Plan of the tomb of Rameses II.	282
180.	Horizontal section of the same tomb	282
181.	The smaller Sarcophagus-chamber in the tomb of Rameses VI.	283
182.	Entrance to the tomb of Rameses III. 284	
183.	Hunting scene upon a tomb at Gournah	286
184.	The weighing of actions	287
185.	Anubis, in a funerary pavilion	288
186.	Plan and section of a royal tomb	292
187, 188.	Theban tombs from the bas-reliefs	294
189.	Theban tomb from a bas-relief	295
190.	A tomb of Apis	296
191.	The tomb of Petamounoph	297
192.	The most simple form of Theban tomb	299
193.	Tomb as represented upon a bas-relief	299
194.	Stele in the Boulak Museum, showing tombs with gardens about them	302
195.	The sarcophagus of a royal scribe	303
196.	Canopic vase of alabaster	305

197.	View of the grand gallery in the Apis Mausoleum	306
198.	Sepulchral chamber of an Apis bull	308
199.	Section in perspective of "Campbell's tomb"	312
200.	Vertical section in perspective of the Sarcophagus-chamber of the above tomb	312
201.	A Tomb on El-Assasif	313
202.	The Temple of the Sphinx	324
203.	Interior of the Temple of the Sphinx	325
204.	The Temple of the Sphinx, the Sphinx, and the neighbouring parts of the Necropolis	331
205.	Ram, or *Kriosphinx*	336
206.	Gateway and boundary wall of a temple	339
207.	Principal façade of the Temple of Luxor	345
208.	The Temple of Khons; horizontal and vertical section showing the general arrangement of the temple	349
209.	The *Bari*, or sacred boat	352
210.	Portable tabernacle of painted wood	354
211.	Granite tabernacle	355
212.	General plan of the Great Temple at Karnak	358
213.	Longitudinal section of the Temple of Luxor	361
214.	Plan of the anterior portion of the Great Temple at Karnak	363
215.	The Great Temple at Karnak; inner portion	367
216.	Karnak as it is at present	369
217.	Plan of the Temple of Luxor	371
218.	Bird's-eye view of Luxor	373
219.	Plan of the Ramesseum	377
220.	The Ramesseum. Bird's-eye view of the general arrangement	379
221.	General plan of the buildings at Medinet-Abou	381
222.	Plan of the Temple of Thothmes	382
223.	Plan of the Great Temple at Medinet-Abou	383

224.	Plan of the Temple at Abydos	387
225.	Seti, with the attributes of Osiris, between Amen, to whom he is paying homage, and Chnoum	390
226.	Plan of the Temple of Gournah	392
227.	Façade of the *naos* of the Temple of Gournah	393
228.	Longitudinal section of the Temple of Gournah, from the portico of the *naos* to the back wall	393
229.	Plan of the Temple of Elephantiné	396
230.	View in perspective of the Temple of Elephantiné	397
231.	Longitudinal section of the Temple of Elephantiné	398
232.	Temple of Amenophis III. at Eilithyia	401
233.	Temple of Amenophis III. at Eilithyia; longitudinal section	403
234.	The speos at Addeh	406
235.	The speos at Addeh; longitudinal section	406
236.	Plan of speos at Beit-el-Wali	407
237.	Longitudinal section of the speos at Beit-el-Wali	407
238.	Plan of the hemispeos of Gherf-Hossein	408
239.	Gherf-Hossein; longitudinal section	409
240.	Plan of the hemispeos of Derri	409
241.	Longitudinal section; Derri	409
242.	Façade of the smaller temple at Ipsamboul	411
243.	Plan of the smaller temple	413
244.	Perspective of the principal Chamber in the smaller temple	413
245.	Longitudinal section of the smaller temple	413
246.	Plan of the Great Temple	413
247.	Perspective of the principal Hall in the Great Temple	414
248.	Façade of the Great Temple at Ipsamboul	415
249.	Longitudinal section of the Great Temple	417

250.	Dayr-el-Bahari	419
251.	Restoration in perspective of Dayr-el-Bahari	423
252.	The ruins on the Island of Philæ	431
253.	The battle against the Khetas, Luxor	436
254.	Rameses II. returning in triumph from Syria	437
255.	The goddess Anouké suckling Rameses II., Beit-el-Wali	441

INTRODUCTION.

I.

The successful interpretation of the ancient writings of Egypt, Chaldæa, and Persia, which has distinguished our times, makes it necessary that the history of antiquity should be rewritten. Documents that for thousands of years lay hidden beneath the soil, and inscriptions which, like those of Egypt and Persia, long offered themselves to the gaze of man merely to excite his impotent curiosity, have now been deciphered and made to render up their secrets for the guidance of the historian. By the help of those strings of hieroglyphs and of cuneiform characters, illustrated by paintings and sculptured reliefs, we are enabled to separate the truth from the falsehood, the chaff from the wheat, in the narratives of the Greek writers who busied themselves with those nations of Africa and Asia which preceded their own in the ways of civilization. Day by day, as new monuments have been discovered and more certain methods of reading their inscriptions elaborated, we have added to the knowledge left us by Herodotus and Diodorus Siculus, to our acquaintance with those empires on the Euphrates and the Nile which were already in old age when the Greeks were yet struggling to emerge from their primitive barbarism.

Even in the cases of Greece and Rome, whose histories are supplied in their main lines by their classic writers, the study of hitherto neglected writings discloses many new and curious details. The energetic search for ancient inscriptions, and the scrupulous and ingenious interpretation of their meaning, which we have witnessed and are witnessing, have revealed to us many interesting facts of which no trace is to be found in Thucydides or Xenophon, in Livy or Tacitus; enabling us to enrich with more than one feature the picture of private and public life which they have handed down to us. In the effort to embrace the life of ancient times as a whole, many attempts have been made to fix the exact place in it occupied by art, but those attempts have never been absolutely successful, because the comprehension of works of art, of *plastic* creations in the widest significance of that word, demands an amount of special knowledge which the great majority of historians are without; art has a method and language of its own, which obliges those who wish to learn it thoroughly to cultivate their taste by frequenting the principal museums of Europe, by visiting distant regions at the cost of considerable trouble and expense, by perpetual reference to the great collections of engravings, photographs, and other reproductions which considerations of space and cost prevent the *savant* from possessing at home. More than one learned author has never visited Italy or Greece, or has found no time to examine their museums, each of which contains but a small portion of the accumulated remains of antique art. Some connoisseurs do not even live in a capital, but dwell far from those public libraries, which often contain valuable collections, and sometimes—when they are not packed away in cellars or at the binder's—allow them to be studied by the curious.[2] The study of art, difficult enough in itself, is thus rendered still more arduous by the obstacles which are thrown in its way. The difficulty of obtaining materials for self-improvement in this direction affords the true explanation of the absence, in modern histories of antiquity, of those laborious researches which have led to such great results since Winckelmann founded the science of archæology as we know it. To take the case of Greece, many learned writers have in our time attempted to retrace its complete history—England, Germany, and France have each contributed works which, by various merits, have conquered the favour of Europe. But of all these works the only one which betrays any deep study of Greek art, and treats it with taste and competence, is that of M. Ernest Curtius; as for Mr. Grote, he has neither a theoretic knowledge of art, nor a feeling for it. Here and there, indeed, where he cannot avoid it, he alludes to the question, but in the fewest and driest phrases possible. And yet Greece, without its architects, its sculptors, and its painters, without in fact its passion for beautiful form, a passion as warm and prolific as its love for poetry, is hardly Greece at all.

Much disappointment is thus prepared for those who, without the leisure to enter deeply into detail, wish to picture to themselves the various aspects of the ancient world. They are told of revolutions, of wars and conquests, of the succession of princes; the mechanism of political and civil institutions is explained to them; "literature," we are told, "is the expression of social life," and so the history of literature is written for us. All this is true enough, but there is another truth which seems to be always forgotten, that the art of a people is quite as clear an indication of their sentiments, tastes, and ideas, as their literature. But on this subject most historians say little, contenting themselves with the brief mention of certain works and proper names, and with the summary statement of a few general ideas which do not even possess the merit of precision. And where are we to find the information thus refused? Europe possesses several histories of Greek and Roman literature, written with great talent and eloquence, such as the work, unhappily left unfinished, of Ottfried Müller; there are, too, excellent manuals, rich in valuable facts, such as those of Bernhardy, Baehr, and Teuffel; but where is there, either in England, in France, or in Germany, a single work which retraces, in sufficient detail, the whole history of antique art, following it throughout its progress and into all its transformations, from its origin to its final decadence, down to the epoch when Christianity and the barbaric invasions put an end to the ancient forms of civilization and prepared for the birth of the modern world, for the evolution of a new society and of a new art?

To this question our neighbours may reply that the *Geschichte der bildenden Kunst* of Carl Schnaase[3] does all that we ask. But that work has one great disadvantage for those who are not Germans. Its great bulk will almost certainly prevent its ever finding a translator, while it makes it very tedious reading to a foreigner. It must, besides, be very difficult, not to say impossible, for a single writer to treat with equal competence the arts of Asia, of Greece, and of Rome, of the Middle Ages and of modern times. As one might have expected, all the parts of such an extensive whole are by no means of equal value, and the chapters which treat of antique art are the least satisfactory. Of the eight volumes of which the work consists, two are devoted to ancient times, and, by general acknowledgment, they are not the two best. They were revised, indeed, for the second edition, by two colleagues whom Herr Schnaase called in to his assistance; oriental art by Carl von Lützow, and that of Greece and Rome by Carl Friedrichs. But the chapters in which Assyria, Chaldæa, Persia, Phœnicia, and Egypt are discussed are quite inadequate. No single question is exhaustively treated. Instead of well-considered personal views, we have vague guesses and explanations which do nothing to solve the many problems which perplex archæologists. The illustrations are not numerous enough to be useful, and, in most cases, they do not seem to have been taken from the objects themselves. Those which relate to architecture, especially, have been borrowed from other well known works, and furnish therefore no new elements for appreciation or discussion. Finally, the order adopted by the author is not easily understood. For reasons which have decided us to follow the same course, and which we will explain farther on, he takes no account of the extreme east, of China and Japan; but then, why begin with India, which had no relations with the peoples on the shores of the Mediterranean until a very late date, and, so far as art was concerned, rather came under their influence than brought them under its own?

The fact is that Schnaase follows a geographical order, which is very confusing in its results. To give but one example of its absurdity, he speaks of the Phœnicians before he has said a word of Egypt; now, we all know that the art of Tyre and Sidon was but a late reflection from that of Egypt; the workshops of those two famous ports were mere factories of cheap Egyptian art objects for exportation.

Again, the first part of Herr Schnaase's work is already seventeen years old, and how many important discoveries have taken place since 1865? Those of Cesnola and Schliemann, for instance, have revealed numberless points of contact and transmission between one phase of antique art and another, which were never thought of twenty years ago. The book therefore is not "down to date." With all the improvements which a new edition might introduce, that part of it which deals with antiquity can never be anything but an abridgment with the faults inherent in that kind of work. It could never have the amplitude of treatment or the originality which made Winckelmann's *History of Art* and Ottfried Müller's *Manual of Artistic Archæology* so successful in their day.[4]

Winckelmann's *History of Art among the Ancients*, originally published in 1764, is one of those rare books which mark an epoch in the history of the human intellect. The German writer was the first to formulate the idea, now familiar enough to cultivated intelligences, that art springs up, flourishes, and decays, with the society to which it belongs; in a word, that it is possible to write its history.[5] This great *savant*, whose memory Germany holds in honour as the father of classic archæology, was not content with stating a principle: he followed it through to its consequences; he began by tracing the outlines of the science which he founded, and he never rested till he had filled them in. However, now that a century has passed away since it appeared, his great work, which even yet is never opened without a sentiment of respect, marks a date beyond which modern curiosity has long penetrated. Winckelmann's knowledge of Egyptian art was confined to the *pasticcios* of the Roman epoch, and to the figures which passed from the villa of Hadrian to the museum of Cardinal Albani. Chaldæa and Assyria, Persia and Phœnicia, had no existence for him; even Greece as a whole was not known to him. Her painted vases were still hidden in Etruscan and Campanian cemeteries; the few which had found their way to the light had not yet succeeded in drawing the attention of men who were preoccupied over more imposing manifestations of the Greek genius. Nearly all Winckelmann's attention was given to the works of the sculptors, upon which most of his comprehensive judgments were founded; and yet, even in regard to them, he was not well-informed. His opportunities of personal inspection were confined to the figures, mostly of unknown origin, which filled the Italian galleries. The great majority of these formed part of the crowd of copies which issued from the workshops of Greece, for some three centuries or more, to embellish the temples, the basilicas, and the public baths, the villas and the palaces of the masters of the world. In the very few instances in which they were either originals or copies executed with sufficient care to be fair representations of the original, they never dated from an earlier epoch than that of Praxiteles, Scopas, and Lysippus. Phidias and Alcamenes, Pæonius and Polycletus, the great masters of the fifth century, were only known to the historian by the descriptions and allusions of the ancient authors.

In such a case as this the clearest and most precise of verbal descriptions is of less value than any fragment of marble upon which the hand of the artist is still to be traced. Who would then have guessed that the following generation would have the opportunity of studying those splendid groups of decorative sculpture whose close relation to the architecture of certain famous temples has taught us so much? Who in those days dreamt of looking at, still less of drawing, the statues in the pediments and sculptured friezes of the Parthenon, of the Thesæum, of the temples at Ægina, at Phigalia, or at Olympia? Now if Winckelmann was ignorant of these, the real monuments of classic perfection, it follows that he was hardly competent to recognise and define true archaism or to distinguish the works of sculpture which bore the marks of the deliberate, eclectic, and over-polished taste of the critical epochs. He made the same mistake in speaking of architecture. It was always, or nearly always, by the edifices of Rome and Italy, by their arrangement and decoration, that he pretended to explain and judge the architecture of Greece.

But Winckelmann rendered a great service to art by founding a method of study which was soon applied by Zoëga[6] and by Ennio Quirino Visconti,[7] to the description of the works which filled public and private galleries, or were being continually discovered by excavation. These two *savants* classified a vast quantity of facts; thanks to their incessant labours, the lines of the master's rough sketch were accented and corrected at more than one point; the divisions which he had introduced into his picture were marked with greater precision; the groups which he had begun to form were rendered more coherent and compact; their features became more precise, more distinct, and more expressive. This progress was continuous, but after the great wars of the Revolution and the Empire its march became much more rapid, and the long peace which saw the growth of so rich a harvest of talent, was also marked by a great increase in the energy with which all kinds of historical studies were prosecuted.

But the widest, as well as the most sudden, enlargement of the horizon was due to a rapid succession of discoveries, some the result of persevering searches and lucky excavations, others rendered possible by feats of induction which almost amounted to genius. It seemed as though a curtain were drawn up, and, behind the rich and brilliant scenery of Græco-Roman civilization, the real ancient world, the world of the East, the father of religions and of useful inventions, of the alphabet and of the plastic arts, were suddenly revealed to us. The great work which was compiled by the *savants* who accompanied Bonaparte to Egypt first introduced the antiquities of that country to us, and not long afterwards Champollion discovered the key to the hieroglyphics, and thus enabled us to assign to the monuments of the country at least a relative date.

A little later Layard and Botta freed Nineveh from the ruins of its own buildings, and again let in the light upon ancient Assyria. But yesterday we knew nothing beyond the names of its kings, and yet it sprang again to the day, its monuments in marvellous preservation, its history pictured by thousands of figures in relief and narrated by their accompanying inscriptions. These did not long keep their secrets to themselves, and their interpretation enables us to classify chronologically the works of architecture and sculpture which have been discovered.

The information thus obtained was supplemented by careful exploration of the ruins in Babylonia, lower Chaldæa, and Susiana. These had been less tenderly treated by time and by man than the remains of Nineveh. The imposing ruins of the palace at Persepolis and of the tombs of the kings, had been known for nearly two centuries, but only by the inadequate descriptions and feeble drawings of early travellers. Ker-Porter, Texier, and Flandrin provided us with more accurate and comprehensive descriptions, and, thanks to their careful copies of the writings upon the walls of those buildings, and upon the inscribed stones of Persia and Media, Eugène Burnouf succeeded in reconstructing the alphabet of Darius and Xerxes.

Thus, to the toils of artists and learned men, who examined the country from the mountains of Armenia to the low and marshy plains of Susiana, and from the deserts which border the Euphrates to the rocks of Media and Persia, and to the philologists who deciphered the texts and classified the monumental fragments which had travelled so far from the scene of their creation, we owe our power to describe, upon a sound basis and from authentic materials, the great civilisation which was developed in Western Asia, in the basin of the Persian Gulf. There were still many details which escaped us, but, through the shadows which every day helped to dissipate, the essential outlines and the leading masses began to be clearly distinguished, and the local distinctions which, in such a vast extent of country and so long a succession of empires, were caused by differences of race, of time, and of physical conditions, began to be appreciated. But, in spite of all these differences, the choice of expressive means and their employment, from Babylon to Nineveh, and from Nineveh to Susa and Persepolis, presented so many points of striking similarity as to prove that the various peoples represented by those famous capitals all sprang from the same original stock. The elements of writing and of the arts are in each case identical. The alphabets were all formed upon the same cuneiform principle, notwithstanding the variety in the languages which they served. In the plastic arts, although the plans of their buildings vary in obedience to the requirements of different materials, their sculpture always betrays the same way of looking at living forms, the same conventions and the same motives. Every work fashioned by the hand of man which has been discovered within the boundaries given above, displays community of style and unity of origin and tradition.

The result of these searches and discoveries was to show clearly that this ancient civilisation had sprung from two original sources, the one in the valley of the Nile, the other in Chaldæa. The latter was the less ancient of the two, and was considerably nearer our own time than the epoch which witnessed the commencement of the long series of Egyptian dynasties by the reign of Menes. These two civilizations met and intermingled through the agency of the Phœnicians, and any active and prolific interchange of ideas and products began, traces of which are still to be found both in Egypt and Assyria.

It still remained doubtful, and the doubt has but lately been removed, how the influence of these two great centres of cultivation was extended to the still barbarous tribes, the ancestors of the Greeks and Romans, who inhabited the northern and eastern shores of the Mediterranean.

It is only within the last twenty years, since the mission of M. Renan, that Phœnicia has become well-known to us. Several English and French travellers, Hamilton, Fellows, Texier, among others, had already, in the first half of the century, described the curious monuments of Lydia, Phrygia, Cappadocia, and of the still more picturesque Lycia, whose spoils now enrich the British Museum; people vaguely conjectured that through those countries had progressed, stage by stage, from the east to the west, the forms and inventions of a system of civilization which had been elaborated in the distant Chaldæa. But it was not till 1861 that an expedition, inspired by the desire to clear up this very question, succeeded in demonstrating the *rôle* actually played by the peoples inhabiting the plateau of Asia Minor. As for Cyprus, it was but yesterday that the explorations of Lang and Cesnola revealed it to us, with its art half Egyptian and half Assyrian, and its cuneiform alphabet pressed into the service of a Greek dialect. These discoveries have put us on the alert. Not a year passes without some lucky "find," such as that of the Palæstrina treasure, in the immediate neighbourhood of Rome, or that made by Salzmann at Rhodes. These pieces of good fortune allow the archæologist to supply, one by one, the missing links of the chain which attaches the arts of Greece and Italy to the earlier civilizations of Egypt and Assyria.

While the remains of Oriental antiquity were being thus recovered piece by piece, secrets no less interesting and documents no less curious were continually coming to the surface to cast new light upon the history of classic antiquity. First came the marbles of the Parthenon, transferred by Lord Elgin to the British Museum in 1816. Both artists and connoisseurs, after a short pause of hesitation, agreed in asserting that the bas-reliefs of the frieze and the sculptures of the two pediments excelled anything which had previously entered into any European museum. Artists declared that they experienced a sense of beauty never felt before; they were face to face for the first time with the ideal of the Greeks, as it had been conceived and realised at that happy period of perfection which followed the disappearance of the last traces of archaic hardness. That period was but too short. It was comprised in a single generation, which was followed by one which made the first steps down the slope of the decadence. During a single lifetime a crowd of works were produced which, in spite of differences in material and subject, were all stamped with the same character of easy and frank nobility, of sincerity and elegant severity, of simplicity combined with grandeur. The death, or even the old age of the great men who had produced these works, was sufficient to lower the standard. Emphasis and a striving for effect took the place of nobility; under a pretence of sincerity, artists took to a servile imitation of nature, and mannerism, with all its weaknesses, began to disfigure their works. Art remained at a high level in Greece, however, longer than elsewhere. The word decadence can hardly be pronounced in connection with the admirable works produced in the fourth century before Christ, and yet it cannot be denied that, so long as we were without original examples from the great epoch of Pericles, we were without that most necessary material for a history of Greek art, a knowledge of the most masterly, the most pure, and the most elevated of her creations.

The literary historian might as well have attempted to trace the course of her poetry without having read Sophocles, without having heard of the *Electra* or the *Œdipus Rex*.

Attention being once turned in this direction, discoveries followed each other in rapid succession. The statues from the pediments at Ægina, so ably restored by Thorwaldsen, were bought to form the nucleus of the collection at Munich.[8] The study of these statues is very instructive in making clear to us the paths which sculptors had to follow in their progress from the stiffness and conventions of early periods to the ease and amplitude of classic perfection. As for the friezes from the temple of Apollo Epicurius, near Phigalia, they too are in the British Museum.[9] Thus brought into immediate propinquity with the marbles from the Parthenon, with which they are almost cotemporary, they afford us some curious information. They show us what the art of Phidias and Alcamenes became when those sculptors had to work in what we should call "the provinces;" how much they preserved and how much they lost of their complete excellence when employed upon buildings erected at less cost and with less care than those of the capital. So far as the composition is concerned, the consummate facility and the natural *verve* of the master who supplied the sketches and models is never absent, but the execution, which must have been left to local artists, betrays their inferiority by its inequalities and general weakness. The same may be said of the figures with which Alcamenes and Pæonius ornamented the pediments and metopes of the Temple of Zeus at Olympia. Even before the discoveries at Ægina and Phigalia, the results of the French expedition to the Morea and the beautiful fragments of sculpture brought to the Louvre from the banks of the Alphæus, had given us reason to suspect this inferiority of provincial art, and the excavations recently undertaken by Germany, after an interval of about half a century of inaction, have finally removed all doubts. Neither the statues nor the bas-reliefs, nor any other part of the decoration of the temple at Olympia, possess the nobility and purity which distinguish the great buildings on the Athenian acropolis. They show abundant power and science, but also perceptible inequalities, and certain signs of that exaggerated objectivity which we now call realism. Each fresh discovery helps us to comprehend, not without a certain sense of surprise, how much freedom and variety Greek art possessed during its best time. There is none of that dull uniformity which, with other races, distinguishes most of the works of a single epoch, none of the tyranny of a single master or school, none of the narrowness of mere *formulæ*.

The memorable exploration to which we have alluded, and many others which it would take too long to enumerate, have not only made known to us the most original and most fertile period of Greek sculpture, but have given us much information as to that art which, when combined with the statues of Phidias and Alcamenes, reared those splendid creations which have been reconstructed with such skill and care by the artist and the archæologist; we mean Greek architecture at its best, the purest and the most complete architecture which the world has yet seen. Every year sees the excellent example set by Stuart and Revett,[10] in the second half of the eighteenth century, followed by an increasing number of imitators. The smallest remains of ancient architecture are measured and drawn with religious care; their arrangements are explained, their elements are grouped, their *ensemble* is restored with a comprehension of their artistic conditions which steadily gains in certainty and penetration. Blouet's interesting restorations of Olympia and Phigalia, published in the account of the French expedition to the Morea,[11] excited the emulation of the young architects at the French Academy in Rome, and opened to them a new course of study. Until then they had been contented with the monumental buildings of Rome and its neighbourhood, of Latium and Campania; a few of the more adventurous among them had penetrated as far as Pæstum; but it was not till 1845 that they ventured to cross the sea and to study the ruins of Greece and Athens;[12] in later years they have travelled as far as Syria and Asia Minor in search of objects for their pencils.[13]

But the occupants of the Villa Medici were not alone in these researches. Doubtless, the invaluable publication which contains the results of their labours, forms the most ample and varied collection of documents open to the historian of architecture among the ancients. But many other architects of different nationalities have given their help to the work of patiently reconstructing the past.[14]

Examined thus closely, and by the trained eyes of professional artists provided with all the necessary instruments, the relics of antiquity yielded up secrets which would never have been suspected by the casual observer.

Thus Mr. Penrose discovered and explained that those walls of the Propylæum and of the Parthenon, which seemed straight to the eye, are in fact planned on a gentle curve;[15] he showed how this subtle variation was calculated to add to the beauty of the buildings, and to augment their effect. Hittorf arrived at still more important results through the minute examination of the Sicilian ruins. He was the first to describe the important part which painting played in the decoration of Greek architecture; he affirmed that in many parts of their buildings the stone or marble was painted over, and that the various members of the architecture were distinguished by differences of tint, which gave accent to the mouldings, and force to the figures in relief. These ideas were too strongly opposed to modern habits of thought to be received without strong protestations. Their partisans, too, did something to retard their acceptance by their absolute fashion of stating their convictions, and by certain unhappy applications of their system; but the polychromatic principles of the Greeks are now confirmed by too many facts to be denied.[16]

Of the three principal branches of ancient art, that of which we know least is painting, properly speaking; the art of Polygnotus, of Zeuxis, and of Apelles. Of this we have but few remains, and we are obliged to take our ideas of its excellence from the descriptions of ancient authors. We have indeed the wall-paintings of those Campanian cities which were so long buried under the ashes of Vesuvius; paintings which were uncovered in great numbers under the Napoleonic domination, and have in later times been added to every year, in spite of the indolent fashion in which the excavations have been conducted. Fragmentary mural paintings of the same kind have also been discovered in Rome and in a few other neighbourhoods. But after all, great though the interest may be which attaches to these works, it must not be forgotten that they are Italian rather than Greek, that they are the decorations for the most part of small provincial cities, and that even the best of them, when compared with the productions of the fifth and fourth centuries before our era, are examples of decadence. At the most they enable us to recall, with some approach to probable truth, the taste and technical methods of the Alexandrian school.

[17] Winckelmann and his immediate successors saw the ashes cleared from the first Pompeian wall-paintings. But they possessed no standards by which they could define the styles of those great schools of painting which flourished in Greece between the epoch of the Persian Wars and the beginning of the Macedonian supremacy; such a definition we may now however attempt with at least partial success. Since the time of Winckelmann hundreds and thousands of those painted vases of burnt clay, which the public persist in calling Etruscan, have been discovered, classified, described, and explained, in such a manner as to leave unsolved scarcely any of the problems upon which they could cast a light.

Gerhard led the way in 1831 with his famous report on the Volscian vases; [18] numerous *savants* have followed his example, and nearly every day the series which they have established are enriched by new discoveries. These vases, as we now know, were made in many places, at Athens, at Corinth, in the Greek cities of Africa and of Magna Græcia. They were eagerly sought after by some of the races whom the Greeks considered barbarous, by the Græco-Scythians of the Crimea, as well as by the Sabellians and the Etruscans; the latter imitated them now and then more or less awkwardly, but it is unanimously acknowledged that they are an essentially Greek product, the product of an art which sprang up with the first awakening of the Greek genius, and was extinguished about two hundred years before Christ, when the nation ceased to be creative and prolific. From analogy with all that has passed elsewhere we are justified in believing that, in each century, the painting of these vases, which would belong to what we call the industrial arts, followed with docility the example set by historical painters, and that it reproduced, so far as its resources would allow, the style and taste of their works. If we study each series of vases in the light of the judgments passed by the ancients upon the most celebrated painters of Greece, we may find, by a legitimate induction, traces now of the style of Polygnotus, now of that of Zeuxis, and again suggestions of the hands of Apelles or Protogenes; a vase here and there may have even preserved more or less faithful imitations of the actual works of those masters. These inductions and conjectures certainly demand both prudence and delicacy of perception, but their principle is incontestable, and the profit to be obtained from them is great. In the whole wreck of antiquity there is no loss which lovers of art find so hard to bear, as the complete annihilation of the works of those great painters whom the ancients put at least upon the same level as their most famous sculptors; and who would not rejoice to be able, by the remains of contemporary though inferior productions, to trace a reflection, distant and feeble perhaps, but yet faithful so far as it goes, of a whole art which has been lost to the world?

The archæologists of the eighteenth century never dreamt of such researches as these, still less of the results to which they might lead; few of them suspected what valuable aid might be afforded to the historian of art and of antique civilization, by the multitude of small objects—vases, gems, glass, mirrors, bronze plaques and figures, terra-cotta bas-reliefs, and statuettes—which are now so eagerly sought after, and which begin to form valuable collections in most of the great museums of Europe.[19] These objects, which were in continual use, were manufactured in prodigious quantities for thousands of years, and their vast numbers gave them a greatly increased chance of being preserved. In spite of the rough usage of man, and the slower progress of destruction due to the action of nature, a certain number of them were sure, from the first, to find means of escape, and, from so many examples, a few of each type have therefore come down to us. The small size of these objects also contributed to preserve them from destruction. In times of war and revolution the poor and humble ones of the earth easily avoid the catastrophes which overwhelm those who are richer, more powerful, and more conspicuous than themselves. So it was with these little memorials of antiquity. Their insignificance was their salvation in the overthrow of the civilisation to which they belonged. More numerous and better sheltered than the masterpieces of fine art, they survived when the latter perished. Thus it is that so many of the lighter and more fragile products of industry have survived to our time, and have made us acquainted with modes of thought and life, and with forms of plastic expression which we should never have known without them. The painted vases, for instance, have preserved for us more than one myth of which no trace can be found in poetry or sculpture; and as for terra-cottas, to which the Tanagra statuettes have directed so much attention, we may judge from the labours of M. Henzey of the value which they possess for archæologists, who, though unable, like some of our amateurs, to buy them with their weight in gold, may compare them one with another and study their smallest details.[20] Those statuettes, which are now classified in museums in the order of their production, have shown us how narrow and inadequate were the formulæ by which the early historians of the plastic arts attempted to define the genius of the Greeks. Even now, the most accomplished and well-informed critics are not always able to repress a feeling of astonishment when they examine a collection of terra-cottas. Some of these figures, no more than a span high, resemble the marbles of the Parthenon in dignity and grandeur, others are full of grace and playfulness in their outlines, and show a capricious *abandon* which disconcerts for a moment even those who are least insensible to their charm. At the bases of such works one is apt to look for the signature of some artist of the Renaissance or of the eighteenth century. In reality they have existed ever since the fourth or third century before our era, and yet there is something modern in their appearance. But an indescribable purity of taste suffices to betray their real origin to all those who possess knowledge and delicate perceptions. That origin is still Greece, but Greece in her lighter and more playful moments, when, leaving the representation of gods and heroes, she condescends to treat the familiar objects of domestic life, and does it with an ease of which her great writers, notably Plato and Aristophanes, had also found the secret, when they passed from epic tragedy to comedy, from the noblest eloquence to hearty expressions of enjoyment.

These little statues interest the historian for other reasons also. They sometimes give him, as at Tanagra, the most precise and accurate information as to dress and social customs: sometimes, as at Tegæa, they afford particulars of a famous though obscure form of worship, of a divinity and of rites which are but imperfectly described in the writings of classic authors.

This extension of knowledge and the great discoveries upon which it was based, naturally led those who were interested in the study of the remains of antique civilisation, to feel the necessity of organisation, of division of labour, and of the importance of ensuring a steady supply of the best and most trustworthy information. Societies were therefore founded in many different centres with the express object of meeting those wants. We cannot, of course, enumerate them here, nor attempt to estimate their various claims to our gratitude, but we may be permitted to allude to the good work accomplished, during fifty years of incessant activity, by the Association which has perhaps done more than any other for the progress of

archæology, we mean the *Instituto di Corrispondenza Archeologica*, founded in Rome in 1829, by Bunsen, Gerhard, and the Duc de Luynes. Thanks to the breadth of view which characterised its founders, this society has been, ever since its inauguration, an international one in the best sense of the word; it brings together for a common end the most eminent European *savants* and their best pupils; it finds fellow-labourers and correspondents in every country. With their aid it soon established a *Bullettino*, where, month by month, all discoveries of interest made at any point of the Mediterranean basin were registered; and volumes, called sometimes *Annali*, sometimes *Memorie*, in which really important discoveries, and the problems to which they give rise, were discussed. Some of these dissertations are so elaborate and so full of valuable matter as to have formed epochs in the history of science. They are accompanied by fine plates, which, by their size, permit the reproduction of objects of art on a grander scale, and with more fidelity, than had been previously attempted.
[21]

While the Roman *Instituto* was thus devoting itself to research, and assuring to its members the advantages of a regular publicity, these inquiries were daily attracting a more considerable share of attention from the other learned bodies of Europe. The *Académie des Inscriptions et de Belles Lettres*, the Academies of Berlin, Munich, and Vienna, devoted an ever-increasing portion of their programmes to such studies. Men began everywhere to understand that the writings of the classic authors, which had been so exhaustively studied ever since the Renaissance, were no longer capable of affording fresh information. In order to learn more of antiquity than the great scholars of the last three centuries, it was necessary to penetrate into the past by paths as yet unexplored; it was necessary to complement and control the evidence of classic authors by that of public and private inscriptions, engraved upon bronze, marble, or stone; it was above all necessary to seek for the expression, in their handiwork, of the wants and ideas, of the personal sentiments and religious conceptions, of the men of antiquity. There are, in fact, nations, such as the Etruscans, whose whole literature has perished, who are only known to us by the relics of their art. Others, like the Greeks and Latins, have indeed transmitted to us noble masterpieces of literature; but these masterpieces are few in proportion to those which time has destroyed. Of the thoughts which they expressed in their immortal languages, too many have been lost for ever with the fragile strips of papyrus to which they were confided.

With the ardour for knowledge and the heroic perseverance which are among the virtues of our time, curiosity has refused to resign itself to such a loss. It has determined to discover the unpublished, to draw into the light all that has not perished beyond recovery, to collect all that the spirit of antiquity has left behind it, either upon works hitherto unnoticed, or upon those which have been imperfectly understood. The treasures of epigraphy have been classified and shown in their full value by Bœckh, Borghesi, and others, and the world is now able to guess all that history may owe to them. The study, however, of those remains which bear figured representations is still more complex and formidable. The language of forms is, in itself, less definite than that of words, and it becomes very difficult to decipher when we have no words dealing with the same ideas to help us, when we possess the art of a people without a line of their literature. Another difficulty springs from the very abundance and variety of the materials to our hand. We feel oppressed by the ever-growing accumulation of facts, and can neither determine where to begin our work, nor how to leave it off: we cannot see the forest for the trees!

II.

In 1830, when the Roman Institute was founded, the time seemed to have come for the formulation of all the gathered facts and for their arrangement into groups, a task which had become much more difficult than in the time of Winckelmann. To conduct it to a successful conclusion a rare combination of faculties was required; breadth of intellect, aided by vast reading and a powerful memory; a philosophical spirit, capable of wide generalisation, joined to that passion for accurate detail which distinguishes the philologist; it demanded one whose taste would survive the trying labour of the cabinet, a *savant* and an artist combined in one person. Books do not teach everything. He who wishes to speak of art with intelligence must study art objects themselves, must cultivate an intimate acquaintance with them, and, within himself, a love for beautiful forms. Without the perceptive powers which such an educational process alone can give, no man can appreciate the subtle differences which distinguish styles and schools. He who possesses no ear, who is unable to perceive the intervals which separate one note from another, who knows that he can neither recognise nor remember an air, does not, unless he be both presumptuous and ignorant, dilate upon music, or attempt to write its history. In the art of design, as in music, no education can supply the place of natural aptitudes; but the latter are not by themselves sufficient to form a connoisseur. Something more is necessary to those who wish to form judgments upon which reliance may be placed, and to give reasons for them which will bear discussion. A special preparation must be undergone, the rules and technical processes—that is to say, the language of art—must be learnt. A connoisseur need not be able to compose an opera, or to chisel a statue, but he should be able to read a part, or to decide, for instance, by the appearance of a copy whether its original were of bronze or marble.

At the end of the last century there was born in Silesia a man who, while yet in his first youth, gave evidence of a rare combination of the gifts necessary for the successful accomplishment of the task which we have described; we mean Carl Ottfried Müller, who has been called, without any exaggeration, a "scholar of genius."[22] A disciple of Niebuhr and Bœckh, he excelled all his contemporaries in his efforts to embrace the whole of antiquity in one view, to trace out and realise for himself all the varied aspects of ancient civilisation. As a philologist, he took the greatest pleasure in the science which weighs words and syllables, which collates manuscripts. A poet in his hours of leisure, he appreciated both ancient and modern works of literature. As a young man he studied with passion the antiques in the Dresden Museum and the gallery of casts belonging to the University of Gottingen.

In the last year of his life he traversed Italy and Sicily with continual delight, and was like one intoxicated with the beauty of that Athens of which he caught but a glimpse, of that Greece whose sun so quickly destroyed him.

All this knowledge, all these experiences he hoped to make use of as the lines and colours for the great picture of ancient Greece which he meditated, for the canvas upon which he meant to portray the Greek civilization for the benefit of the moderns, with all its indivisible unity of social and political life, of literary and artistic production. In striking him down in his forty-second year, death put an end to this project, and the great picture, which would have been, perhaps, one of the capital works of our century, was never executed. But the preparatory sketches of the master happily remain to us. While he was employed in collecting materials for the work which he meant to be his highest title to honour, he was not shut up in silence and meditation, as a less prolific spirit might have been. His facility of arrangement and utterance was prodigious; all that he learnt, all new discoveries that he made or thought he had made, he hastened to make public, either by direct addresses to the auditors who crowded round his chair at Gottingen, or by his pen to the readers of the numerous philosophical periodicals to which he contributed. Like a man who has travelled much and who loves to tell of what he has seen, he was ever ready to take the public into his confidence when he embarked upon a new study. This he generally did by means of papers full of facts and ideas, written sometimes in German, sometimes in Latin. In his later years he issued short articles upon archæology and the history of art, in sufficient number to form five substantial volumes.[23] Besides this, he gave to the world learned editions of Varro, of Festus, of the *Eumenides* of Æschylus; or important monographs like his *Geschichten hellenischer Stämme und Städte*, including *Orchomenos und die Minyer* and *Die Dorier*, the most famous and most actively discussed of his works; and finally, *Die Etrusker*, a work which was suggested to him by one of the publications of the Berlin Academy. There was also *Prolegomena zu einer wissenschaftlichen Mythologie*, which has been fruitful for good even in its errors, and the *Geschichte der griechischen Literatur*, &c., which, incomplete as it is, has never become obsolete. Since the time of Ottfried Müller several other critics have attempted to rival his achievements, but they have all lacked his breadth of view and comprehensiveness of exposition, as well as the versatility with which he combined the most accurate scientific investigations with a delicate appreciation of the beauty and originality of the Greek authors.

But of all these works, that which has perhaps rendered the greatest service to the science of archæology is the *Handbuch der Archæologie der Kunst*, which was published in Breslau in 1830.[24] Translated into French, Italian, and English, it at once took its place as the indispensable guide for all those who wished to learn something of antique art.[25] In all the universities into which archæology had made good its entrance, this manual has formed the basis of the teaching, and also has enabled the pupils to supplement for themselves the lessons which they learnt from their professors. Even now it has not been superseded, and to all appearance it will long preserve its supremacy.

The form of a *handbuch* or manual, which Ottfried Müller gave to his work, was well and favourably known to cultivated Germans, but it was not so with the French. They had nothing of the kind but worthless epitomes made to facilitate the passing of University examinations. In this matter the Germans are better off than any other nation in Europe. They have manuals in which every branch of history and science is treated by competent writers with as much care and skill as the most ambitious publications, a few being original works by savants of the first order. The arrangement of the *Handbuch* is very simple. It opens with an introduction in which the author defines art—more especially the plastic arts—divides it into classes, and indicates the principal works to be consulted, namely, those to which he himself has had continually to refer during the progress of his book. Then comes the history of Greek and Roman art divided into periods, and the paragraphs which are devoted to Etruria and the East. To this historical epitome succeed the theoretical chapters.

He takes antique art as a whole, and studies its constitution, the materials and processes which it employs, the conditions under which it works, the characteristics which it gives to form, the subjects of which it treats, and the partition of its remains over the whole territory occupied by ancient civilization. Greece, in her best days, gave most of its care to the representation of those beings, superior to humanity and yet clothed with human forms, in which her glowing imagination personified the forces and eternal laws of nature and of the moral world; it was in striving to create these types, and to endow them with outward features worthy of their majesty, that Grecian art produced its noblest and most ideal works. It will, therefore, be seen that a comprehensive manual had to include a history of those gods and heroes which, with that of their statues, formed a whole mythology of art; and this mythology occupies the larger portion of the second part of the work.

This plan has been often criticised, but we need here make no attempt to repel or even to discuss the objections which have been brought against it.

It has doubtless the inconvenience of leading to frequent repetition; monuments which have been necessarily described and estimated in the historical division are again mentioned in the chapters which treat of theory; but a better plan has yet to be found, one which will enable us to avoid such repetitions without any important sacrifice. The chief thing in a work of the kind is to be clear and complete, merits which the *Handbuch* possesses in the highest degree. Things are easily found in it, and, by a powerful effort of criticism, the author has succeeded in classifying and condensing into a single convenient volume, all the interesting discoveries of several generations of archæologists. Not that it is a mere compilation, for previous writers were far from being unanimous as to the dates and significance of the remains which they had described, and it was necessary to choose between their different hypotheses, and sometimes to reject them all. In such cases Müller shows great judgment, and very often the opinion to which he finally commits himself had been previously unknown. Without entering into any long discussion he sustains it by a few shortly stated reasons, which are generally conclusive. The plan of his book prevents him from launching out, like Winckelmann, into enthusiastic periods; he makes no attempt at those brilliant descriptions which in our day seem a little over-coloured; but in the very brevity of his judgments and his laconic but significant phraseology, we perceive a sincere and individual emotion, an independent intellect, a pure though catholic taste. We need say no more to the objectors who attack the mere form of the book. Its one real defect is that it was written thirty or forty years too soon. The second edition, carefully revised and largely augmented, appeared in 1835; it was the last issued during the lifetime of Müller. From that moment down to the day but lately passed when the excavations at Olympia and Pergamus were brought to an end, many superb remains of Greek, Etruscan, and Roman art have risen from their temporary graves and ranged themselves in our museums. If, however, recent archæology had made no further discoveries, a few occasional corrections and additions, at intervals of ten or fifteen years, would have sufficed to prevent the manual from becoming obsolete. With a little care any intelligent editor could have satisfactorily performed what was wanted. For the Græco-Roman period especially Müller had erected so complete a historical framework that the new discoveries could find their places in it without any difficulty. Welcker, indeed, published a third edition in 1848, corrected and completed, partly from the manuscript notes left by the author in his interleaved copy, partly from information extracted by the editor from the lectures and other writings of Müller. But why does Welcker declare, in his advertisement to the reader, that but for the respect due to a work which had become classic, he would have modified it much more than he had dared. And why, for more than thirty years, has his example found no imitators? Why have we been content to reprint word for word the text of that third edition?

A few years ago one of the most eminent of our modern archæologists, Carl Bernhard Stark, was requested by a firm of publishers to undertake a new revision of the *Handbuch*. Why then, after having brought his materials together, did he find it more useful, and even easier, to compose an original work, a new manual which should fulfil the same requirements on a system of his own devising?—an enterprise which he would have brought to a successful conclusion had not death interrupted him after the publication of the first part.[26]

The answer is easy. The East was not discovered till after the death of Ottfried Müller. By the East we mean that part of Africa and Asia which is bordered by the Mediterranean, or is so near to that sea that constant communication was kept up with its shores; we mean Egypt, Syrian Phœnicia, and its great colony on the Libyan Coast, Chaldæa and Assyria, Asia Minor, and those islands of Cyprus and Rhodes which were so long dependent upon the empires on the neighbouring continents. It was between 1820 and 1830 that the young *savant* conceived the ideas which he developed in his works; it was then that he first took an important part in the discussion as to the origin of the Greek nation, upon which archæologists had long been engaged. What part had foreign example taken in the birth and development of the religion, the arts, the poetry, and the philosophy of Greece, of the whole Hellenic civilization? How much of it was due to suggestions derived from those peoples who had so long preceded the Greeks in the ways of civil life? No historian has answered this question in a more feeble and narrow spirit than Ottfried Müller; no one has been more obstinate than he in insisting upon the originality of the Greek genius, and in believing that the Greek race extracted from its own inner consciousness all that has made its greatness and glory.

When Müller first attacked this question, Egypt alone had begun to emerge from the obscurity which still enveloped the ancient civilization of the East. It was not until three years after his death, that Botta began to excavate the remains of Assyrian art; and nothing but the vaguest and most confused information was to be had about the ruins in Chaldæa. Now, however, we can follow the course of the Phœnician ships along the Mediterranean, from the Thracian Bosphorus to the pillars of Hercules. From the traces left by the commerce and the industries of the Syrians and Carthaginians, we can estimate the duration of their stay in each of the countries which they visited, and the amount of influence which they exercised over the various peoples who were tributary to them. Forty years ago this was impossible; the writings of ancient authors were our sole source of knowledge as to the style and taste of Phœnician art, and the ideas which they imparted were of necessity inexact and incomplete. Wherever they passed the Phœnicians left behind them numbers of objects manufactured by them for exportation, and these objects are now eagerly collected, and the marks of the Sidonian and Carthaginian makers examined and classified, and thus we are enabled to recognize and describe the industrial processes and the decorative motives, which were conveyed to the Greeks and to the races of the Italian peninsula by the "watery highway" of the Mediterranean. Fifty years ago the land routes were as little known as those by sea. The roads were undiscovered which traversed the defiles of the Taurus and the high plateaux of Asia Minor, to bring to the Greeks of Ionia and Æolia, those same models, forms, and even ideas, and it was still impossible to indicate their detours, or to count their stages.

Leake had indeed described, as early as 1821, the tombs of the Phrygian kings, one of whom bore that name of Midas to which the Greeks attached so strange a legend;[27] but he had given no drawings of them, and the work of Steuart,[28] which did not appear till 1842, was the first from which any definite knowledge of their appearance could be obtained. Müller knew nothing of the discoveries of Fellows, of Texier, or of Hamilton; while he was dying in Greece, they were exploring a far more difficult and dangerous region. A few years afterwards they drew the attention of European *savants* to the remains which they had discovered, dotted about over the country which extends from the shores of the Ægæan to the furthest depths of Cappadocia, remains which recall, both by their style and by their symbolic devices, the rock sculptures of Upper Assyria. The Lycian remains, which give evidence of a similar inspiration and are now in the British Museum, were not transported to Europe until after Müller's death.

The clear intellect of Ottfried Müller easily enabled him to perceive the absurdity of attempting to explain the birth of Greek art by direct borrowing from Egypt. He saw that the existing remains in both countries emphatically negatived such a supposition, but materials were wanting to him for a right judgment of the intensity and duration of the influence under which the Greeks of the heroic age worked for many centuries, influences which came to them partly from the Phœnicians, the privileged agents of intercourse between Egypt and the East, partly from the people of Asia Minor, the Cappadocians, Lycians, Phrygians, and Lydians, all pupils and followers of the Assyrians, whose dependants they were for the time, and with whom they communicated by caravan routes. We may thus explain the extravagance of the hypothesis which Müller advocated in all his writings; and, as the originality of the Greek intellect displayed itself in the plastic arts much later than in poetry, the partial falsity of his views and their incompleteness is much more obvious and harmful in his handbook than in his history of Greek literature.

In writing the life of any great man and attempting to account for his actions, it is important to know where he was born, and who were his parents; to learn the circumstances of his education, and the surroundings of his youth. The biographer who should have no information on these points, or none but what was false, would be likely to fall into serious mistakes and misapprehensions. He would find great difficulty in explaining his hero's opinions and the prejudices and sentiments by which he may have been influenced, or he would give absurd explanations of them. Peculiarities of character and eccentricities of idea would embarrass him, which, had he but known the hereditary predisposition, the external circumstances during infancy and adolescence, the whole course of youthful study, of the man whose life he was describing, he might easily have understood. It is the same with the history of a people and of their highest intellectual manifestations, such as their religion, arts, and literature.

It was not the fault of Ottfried Müller, it was that of the time in which he lived, that he was deceived as to the true origin of Greek art. The baneful effects of his mistake are evident in the very first pages of the historical section of his work, in the chapters which he devotes to the archaic period. These chapters are very unsatisfactory. Attempt, under their guidance alone, to study the contents of one of those museum saloons where the remains of Oriental art are placed side by side with those from Etruria and primitive Greece; at every step you will notice resemblances of one kind or another, similarities between the general aspects of figures, between the details of forms and the choice of motives, as well as in the employment of common symbols and attributes. These resemblances will strike and even astonish you, and if you are asked how they come to exist among differences which become ever more and more marked in the succession of the centuries, you will know not how to reply. In these archaic remains there are many traits for which those who, like Ottfried Müller, begin with the history of Greece, are unable to account. He wishes us to believe that Greece in the beginning was alone in the world, that she owed all her glory to the organic development of her unequalled genius, which, he says, "displayed a more intimate combination than that of any other Aryan nation of the life of sensibility with that of intelligence, of external with internal life." He goes no further back than the Greece described to us in the heroic poems; he never has recourse to such comparisons as we are now continually making; at most he lets fall at lengthy intervals a few words which seem to imply that Oriental civilization may have had something to do with the awakening of Greek thought and the directing of her first endeavours. He never formally denies her indebtedness, but he fails to perceive its vast importance, or to declare it with that authoritative accent which never fails him in the expression of those ideas which are dear to him, of those truths which he has firmly grasped.

This tendency is to be seen even in the plan of his work. There is nothing surprising in the fact that Müller, in 1830, or even in 1835, had but a slight acquaintance with the art of the Eastern Empires; but as he thought it necessary not entirely to ignore those peoples in a book which pretended to treat of antiquity as a whole, it would perhaps have been better not to have relegated them to a few paragraphs at the end of his historical section. He knew well enough that the Egyptians, the Babylonians, the Phœnicians, even the Phrygians and the Lydians were much older than the Greeks; why should he have postponed their history to that of the decline and fall of Græco-Roman art? Would it not have been better to put the little he had to tell us in its proper place, at the beginning of his book?

This curious prejudice makes the study of a whole series of important works more difficult and less fruitful. It prevents him from grasping the true origin of many decorative forms which, coming originally from the East, were adopted by the Greeks and carried to perfection by their unerring taste, were perpetuated in classic art, and thence transferred to that of modern times; and this, bad though it is, is not the worst result of Müller's misapprehension. His inversion of the true chronological order makes a violent break in the continuity of the phenomena and obscures their mutual relations. There is no sequence in a story so broken up, falsified, and turned back upon itself. You will there seek in vain for that which we mean to strive after in this present history of antique art—a regular and uninterrupted development, which in spite of a few more or less brusque oscillations and periods of apparent sterility, carried the civilization of the East into the West, setting up as its principal and successive centres, Memphis, Thebes, Babylon, Nineveh, Sidon, Carthage, Miletus and the cities of Ionia, Corinth and Athens, Alexandria, Antioch, Pergamus, and finally Rome, the disciple and heir of Greece.

Ottfried Müller saw clearly enough the long and intimate connection between Greece and Rome, but he did not comprehend—and perhaps in the then state of knowledge it was impossible that he should comprehend—that the bonds were no less close which bound the Hellenic civilization to the far more ancient system which was born upon the banks of the Nile, and crept up the valleys of the Tigris and Euphrates, to spread itself over the plains of Iran on the one hand and of Asia Minor on the other; while the Phœnicians carried it, with the alphabet which they had invented and the forms of their own worship of Astarte, over the whole basin of the Mediterranean. His error lay in his arbitrary isolation of Greece, in dragging her from the soil in which her roots were deeply imbedded, from which she had drawn her first nourishment and the primary elements of that varied and luxuriant vegetation which, in due time, became covered with the fairest hues of art and poetry.

III.

Thanks to the numerous discoveries of the last fifty years, and to the comparisons which they have suggested, thanks also to the theories for which they afford a basis, history has been at last enabled to render justice to certain nations whose activity had never before been properly understood, to give to them their proper place in the civilization of ancient times. But Greece—the Greece which Ottfried Müller worshipped, and for which he was too ready to sacrifice her predecessors and teachers, to whom she herself was more just in her early legends—has lost nothing by the more exact information which is now at our command. Served by her situation on the confines of Europe and Asia and not far from Africa, by the superiority of the genius of her people and the marvellous aptitudes of her language, Greece was able to arrange and classify previous discoveries and to bring them to perfection, to protect from destruction and oblivion the machinery of progress, the processes of art, the newly-born scientific methods, in a word, all the complex and fragile apparatus of civilization which was so often threatened with final destruction, and which has more than once been overwhelmed for a time in epochs of national conflict and social decadence.

This is not the place for insistence upon all that Greece has accomplished in the domains of pure thought, philosophy, and science, nor even for calling attention to her literature. We are writing the history of the arts and not that of letters, a history which we wish to conduct to the point where Müller left off, to the commencement of those centuries which are called the Middle Ages; and Greece will occupy by far the most important place in our work. We shall endeavour to bring the same care and conscience, the same striving after accuracy, into every division of our history; but the monuments of Greece will be examined and described in much greater detail than those of Egypt and Assyria, or even those of Etruria and Latium. It was our love for Greece that drove us to this undertaking; we desire and hope to make her life better known, to show a side of it which is not to be found in the works of her great writers, to give to our readers new and better reasons for loving and admiring her than they have had before. A combination of circumstances that is unique in the history of the world gave to the contemporaries of Pericles and Alexander the power of approaching more nearly to perfection, in their works of art, than men of any other race or any other epoch. In no other place or time have ideas been so clearly and completely interpreted by form; in no other place or time have the intellectual qualities been so closely wedded to a strong love for beauty and a keen sensibility to it. It results from this that the works of the Greek artists, mutilated by time and accident as they are, serve as models and teachers for our painters and sculptors, a *rôle* which they will continue to fill until the end of time. They form a school, not, as some have thought, to enable us to dispense with nature, the indispensable and eternal master, but to incite to such an ardent and intelligent study of her beauties, as may lead to the creation of great works, works capable, like those of the Greeks, of giving visible expression to the highest thoughts.

As the Greeks excelled all other nations in the width and depth of their æsthetic sentiments; as their architects, their sculptors, and their painters, were superior both to their pupils and their masters, to the orientals on the one hand, and the Etruscans and the Latins on the other, we need feel no surprise at their central and dominating position in the history of antique art. Other national styles and artistic manifestations will pass before the eye of the reader in their due order and succession; they will all be found interesting, because they show to us the continual struggle of man against matter, and we shall endeavour to distinguish each by its peculiar and essential characteristics, and to illustrate it by the most striking remains which it has left behind. But each style and nationality will for us have an importance in proportion to the closeness of its connection with the art of Greece. In the case of those oriental races which were the teachers of the Greeks, we shall ask how much they contributed to the foundations of Greek art and to its ultimate perfection; in the case of the ancient Italians, we shall endeavour to estimate and describe the ability shown by them in apprehending the lessons of their instructors, and the skill with which they drew from their teachers a method for the expression of their own peculiar wants and feelings and for the satisfaction of their own æsthetic desires.

The study of oriental art will really, therefore, be merely an introduction to our history as a whole, but an introduction which is absolutely required by our plan of treatment, and which will be completely embodied in the work. The history of Etruscan and Roman art will be its natural and necessary epilogue.

This explanation will show how far, and for what reasons we mean to separate ourselves from our illustrious predecessor. We admit, as he did, we even proclaim with enthusiasm, the pre-eminence of Greece, the originality of its genius and the superiority of its works of plastic art; but we cannot follow him in his arbitrary isolation of Greece, which he suspends, so to speak, in air. Our age is the age of history; it interests itself above all others in the sequence of social phenomena and their organic development, an evolution which Hegel explained by the laws of thought. It would be more than absurd in these days to accept Greek art as a thing self-created in its full perfection, without attempting to discover and explain the slow and careful stages by which it arrived at its apogee in the Athens of Pericles. In this history of ours of which we are attempting to sketch the form, we must, in order to get at the true origin of Greek art, penetrate far beyond its apparent origin; to describe the springing of Greek civilization, we must first study the early history of those races which surround the eastern basin of the Mediterranean.

The Greece which we call ancient entered late into history, when civilization had already a long past behind it, a past of many centuries. In this sense, the words which, as we are told by Plato, a priest of Saïs addressed to Solon, were perfectly true, "You Greeks, you are but children!" [29] In comparison with Egypt, with Chaldæa, with Phœnicia, Greece is almost modern: the age of Pericles is nearer to our day than to that which saw the birth of Egyptian civilization.

Appearing thus lately upon the scene, when the genius of man had, by efforts continued without intermission through a long procession of centuries, arrived at the power of giving clear and definite expression to his thoughts, by means either of articulate sounds and the symbols which represent them or by the aid of plastic forms, the Greeks could only have remained ignorant of all that had been achieved before their time if they had sprung into existence in some distant and isolated corner of the world, or in some inaccessible island. Their actual situation was a very different one. In the earliest epoch of which we have any record we find them established in a peninsula, which is on one hand upon the very borders of Asia, and upon another seems to hold out a hand to Africa by the innumerable islands which surround its shores. Between the shores of this peninsula and those of Asia, these islands are sprinkled so thickly over the narrow seas that nature seems to have intended them for stepping-stones which should tempt the least venturesome to cross from one continent to the other.

The Greek race thus found itself, by the accident of its geographical situation, in contact with the Egyptian, Assyrian, and Median empires, the masters of the Eastern Mediterranean; while the insular or peninsular character of most of the region which it inhabited, together with the numerous colonies attached to the surrounding coasts like vessels at anchor, had the effect of greatly multiplying the points of contact. The Greek frontier was thus one of abnormal extent, and was, moreover, always open, always ready to receive foreign ideas and influences. Her eyes were ever turned outwards; the Greek nationality was not one of those which remain for ages inaccessible to foreign merchandize and modes of thought.

Such being the situation of Greece, it could not but happen, that, as soon as the Greek race drew itself clear from primitive barbarism, the fertile germs of art,—examples, models, processes,—should penetrate into the country from the neighbouring East by all the channels of communication which we have mentioned. Seeing how far civilization had advanced, would it not have been absurd for the Greeks to have turned a deaf ear and a blind eye to the experience of their predecessors; to have begun again at the beginning? Was it not better to take up the work at the point where it had been left, and to make use, for future developments, of those which had already been established? Man progresses as fast as he can; as soon as he learns any new method of satisfying his wants and ameliorating his life, he makes use of it; he makes use of it at first in its original form, but with years and experience he improves it and brings it nearer to perfection.

Thus then, the more we study the past, the more surely do we recognize the truth contained in those myths and traditions which betray the influence exercised upon Greece by the people of Egypt, Syria, and Asia Minor. To confine ourselves to the plastic arts, the historian of Greek art discovers *survivals*, forms and motives which had been employed in previous centuries and earlier civilizations, in exact proportion to the accuracy of his researches, and to the number of his elements for comparison. He also finds that the Greeks borrowed from the same instructors those industrial processes which, although not in themselves artistic, are among the antecedent conditions of art; namely, metallurgy, ceramics, smith's work, glass-making, weaving, embroidery, stone-working and carving, in a word all those trades which seem so simple when their secrets are known, but which, nevertheless, represent the accumulated efforts of countless unknown inventors.

It was not only the material outfit of civilization that the Greeks borrowed from their predecessors; they obtained, together with that alphabet which represents the principal sounds of the voice by a few special signs, another alphabet which has been happily named the *alphabet of art*, certain necessary conventions, combinations of line, ornaments, decorative forms, a crowd of plastic elements which they had employed in the expression of their own ideas and sentiments. Even after Greek art had reached perfection and was in the full enjoyment of her own individuality, we still find traces of these early borrowings. Sometimes it is a decorative motive, like the sphinx, the griffin, the palm-leaf, and many others, which, invented on the banks of the Nile or the Tigris, were transported to Greece and there preserved to be handed down to our modern ornamentist. The nearer we get to the fountain head of Greek art, the more we are struck with these resemblances, which are something beyond mere coincidences. The deeper we penetrate into what is called archaism, the more numerous do those features become which are common to oriental, especially Assyrian, art, and that of Greece. We find analogous methods of indicating the human skeleton, of accenting its articulations, of representing the drapery with which the forms are covered. Greek taste had not yet so transformed the details of ornamentation as to prevent us from recognizing the motives which commerce had brought for its use over the waves of the Ægean or the mountains of Asia Minor. The marks of their origin are continually visible, and yet a practised eye can perceive that the Greeks were never satisfied, like the Phœnicians, with merely combining in various proportions the materials furnished by the artisans of Egypt or Assyria; the facilities of such a soulless and indiscriminating eclecticism as that could not satisfy the ambitions of a race that already possessed the poetry of Hesiod and Homer.

The art of Greece was profoundly original in the best sense of the word. It was far superior to all that went before it; it alone deserved to become classic, that is, to furnish a body of rules and laws capable of being transmitted by teaching. In what does its superiority consist? How does its originality show itself, and how can its existence be explained? These are the questions which we propose to answer; but in order to arrive at a just conclusion we must begin with the study of those nations to whom the Greeks went to school, and of whose art they were the heirs and continuers. We should be unable to grasp the exclusively Greek features of Greek art did we not begin by defining the foreign elements which have taken their part in the work, and that we can only do by going back to the civilizations in which they were produced; we must endeavour to penetrate into the spirit of those civilizations, to discover whence they started and how far they progressed; we must first define their ideas of the beautiful, and then show, by well-chosen examples, by what means and with how great a measure of success, they realised their own conception.

We undertake this long detour in order that we may arrive in Greece instructed by all that we have learnt on the way, and prepared to understand and to judge; but during the whole voyage our eyes will be turned towards Greece, as those of the traveller towards his long-desired goal. Our route will conduct us from the shores of the Nile to those of the Euphrates and Tigris, over the plains of Medea and Persia and Asia Minor to the shores of Phœnicia, to Cyprus and Rhodes. But beyond the obelisks and pyramids of Egypt, beyond the towers of Chaldæa and the domes of Nineveh, the lofty colonnades of Persepolis, the fortresses and rock-cut tombs of Phrygia and Lycia, beyond the huge ramparts of the cities of Syria, we shall never cease to perceive on the horizon the sacred rock of the Athenian acropolis; we shall see it before us, as our history of the past advances, lifting into the azure sky the elegant severity of its marble porticoes, the majesty of those pediments where live and breathe the gods of Homer and Phidias.

When we have crossed the threshold of the Propylæa, and have visited the Parthenon, the Erecthæum, and the temple of the Wingless Victory; when we have seen all Greece become covered with monuments of architecture and sculpture, which, without rivalling those of Athens in purity of line or finesse of execution, bear the impress of the same style and the same taste; when we have seen Praxiteles and Scopas succeed to Phidias and Polycletus, will it not cost us a struggle to quit the scene of so many wonders and conclude our voyage? If we leave the Athens of Cimon, of Pericles, and Lycurgus, for the pompous capitals of the heirs of Alexander; if we cross the sea to visit Veii and Clusium, to describe the Etruscan cemeteries with the fantastic magnificence of their decoration; if at last we find ourselves in imperial Rome, among its basilicas, its baths, its amphitheatres, and all the sumptuous evidence of its luxury, we shall now and again turn our eyes with regret to what we have left behind; and, although we shall endeavour to comprehend and to judge with the liberality and largeness of taste and sympathy which is the honour of contemporary criticism, we shall sometimes sigh for that ideal of pure and sovereign beauty which we adored in Greece; and shall feel, now and again, the nostalgia of the exile.

IV.

In this sketch of our plan, we have reserved no place for the art which is called *prehistoric*, the art of the caverns and the lake dwellings. This omission may surprise some of our readers, and we therefore beg to submit for their consideration the reasons which, after grave reflection, have induced us to refrain from retracing the first steps of human industry, from describing the first manifestations of the plastic instinct of mankind.

We are actuated by neither indifference nor disdain. We fully appreciate the importance of such researches, and of the results to which they have led. No sooner had it entered into the mind of man to look for and collect the humble remains upon which so many centuries had looked with indifference, than they were found almost everywhere, thickly dispersed near the surface of the earth, heaped among the bones of deer in the grottoes for which men and animals had once contended, buried in peat marshes and sandy shores, sometimes even sprinkled upon the surface of the fields and country roads. Pieces of flint, bone, or horn, fashioned into instruments of the chase, into fishhooks, and domestic utensils; shells, perforated teeth, amber balls which were once strung upon necklaces and bracelets; fragments of rough tissue and of skin garments; seeds and carbonized fruits; earthen vessels made by hand and dried in the sun or simply in the open air. In some of the cave dwellings, bones and pieces of horn have been found upon which the figures of animals are carved with a truth and spirit which allow their species to be at once and certainly recognized.

But none of these remains bear the slightest trace of a system of signs for the transmission of ideas or recollections; there is nothing which suggests writing; and, more significant still, there is a complete absence of metal. All this is evidence that the remains in question belong to a very remote antiquity, to a period much nearer the primitive barbarism than to the civilization of Egypt and Chaldæa, to say nothing of that of Greece and Rome. The comparative method, which has done so much for natural science, has also taken these remains in hand, has attempted to classify them and to gain from them some notion of the life led by the early human families which manufactured them. These arms, tools, and instruments which have been recovered from the soil of the old and cultivated nations of Europe, have been carefully compared with similar objects still in use by the savage races which people the far corners of the world. These comparisons have enabled us to decide the former use of each of the objects discovered. By collating the observations of the various travellers who have visited the savage races in question, we have been enabled to form for ourselves a probably truthful picture, so far as it goes, of the life and social habits of those primitive Europeans who made use of similar tools and weapons. And that is not all. The general character of those early periods being established, further examination brought to light the local differences which prevailed then as now. Thus the proneness to plastic imitation seems to have been peculiar to a few tribes—although traces of this taste are found elsewhere, it is nowhere so marked as among those primitive cave-dwellers of Perigord whom Christy and Edouard Lartet have so patiently studied.

By dint of careful classification and comparison, we have been enabled to follow the march of progress through those countless centuries whose number will never be known to us, whose total would, perhaps, oppress our imaginations if we knew it; we have been enabled to discover the slow steps by which mankind raised itself from the earliest, almost shapeless, flint axe, found with the bones of the mammoth in the quaternary alluvial deposits, to the rich and varied equipment of "lacustrian civilization," as it has sometimes been called. In this unlimited field, of which one side at least must ever be lost in unfathomable obscurity, the main divisions have been traced; the stone age has been defined and divided into the *palæolithic* and *neolithic* epochs; the age of bronze followed, and then came the iron age. With the appearance of the former metal the tribes of northern and central Europe established a connection with the civilized races which surrounded the Mediterranean, and with iron we are in the full classic period.

We can never be too grateful for the persevering labours of those who have carried on these researches in every corner of Europe; their deserts are all the greater from the fact that they could never count upon those agreeable surprises which come now and then to reward excavators on the sites of ancient and historic cities. Their chances are small of finding those objects of art which, by their beauty and elegance, repay any amount of toil and expense. The remains which they bring to light have little to say to our æsthetic perceptions; they repeat a few types with an extreme monotony;

but, on the other hand, they carry our thoughts back to a point far nearer the cradle of our race than the myths of early history or even the monumental remains of Egypt and Chaldæa. They cast some slight illumination upon those distant ages of which humanity has preserved no recollection. They people with unknown multitudes those remote epochs into which scientific curiosity had, but yesterday, no desire to penetrate. There can be in all this no real question of chronology, but when from the sands of Abbeville or the caverns of Perigord we dig up the first flint implements or those fragments of bone, of ivory, of reindeer horn, which have preserved to us the first attempts made by man to copy the outlines of living beings, it takes us far beyond those days of which our only knowledge comes from vague tradition, and still farther beyond those centuries which saw the first struggling dawn of history.

We have, then, decided not to embark upon these questions of prehistoric art, because, as the title which we have chosen declares, we propose to write a *history*, and the word history, when the human race is in question, implies established relations between certain groups of facts and certain portions of time, measured at least with something approaching to probable truth.

We do not yet possess, probably we shall never possess, any means of estimating even within five or six thousand years, the actual duration of the stone age. From all analogies progress must have been, in the beginning, exceedingly slow; like that of a falling body, the rapidity of industrial progress is continually accelerating. This acceleration is not of course quite regular; the phenomena of social life are too complex, the forces at work are too numerous and sometimes too contrary to allow us to express it by the mathematical formula which may be applied to movement in the physical world; but on the whole this law of constantly accelerated progress holds good, as indeed may be historically proved. So long as man had to do without metals, each generation, in all probability, added but little to the discoveries of that which preceded it; most likely after each happy effort many generations succeeded one another without any further attempt to advance. Ever since they have been under our observation, the savage races of the world have been practically stationary except where European commerce has profoundly modified the conditions of their lives. It is probable, therefore, that more centuries rolled away between the first chipped flints and the well polished weapons which succeeded them than between the latter and the earliest use of bronze. But we cannot prove that it was so, nor satisfy those whom probability and a specious hypothesis will not content. Where neither written evidence nor oral tradition exist there can be little question of historic order. The remains of the stone age are not calculated to dissipate the silence which enshrouds those centuries. In the art of a civilized people we find their successive modes of feeling and thought interpreted by expressive forms; we may even attempt under all reserve to sketch their history with the sole aid of their plastic remains. The chances of error would of course be numerous; but yet if all other materials had, unhappily, failed us, the attempt would have been well worth making. The more ancient portions of our prehistoric collections do not offer the same opportunities; they are too simple and too little varied. The primitive savage who moulded matter to his will with great and painful difficulty, could impress upon it nothing but those gross instincts which are common to man and beast; we can discover nothing from his works, beyond the means which he employed in his struggles with his enemies, and in his never-ending effort to procure food for himself.

The word history cannot then be pronounced in connection with these remote periods, nor can their remains be looked upon in any sense as works of art. Art commences for us with man's first attempts to impress upon matter some form which should be the expression of a sentiment or of an idea. The want of skill shown in these attempts is beside the question; the mere desire on the part of the workman renders him an artist. The most hideous and disgusting of those idols in stone or terra-cotta which are found in the islands of the Greek Archipelago, at Mycenæ and in Bœotia, idols which represent, as we believe, the great goddess mother whose worship the Phœnicians taught to the Greeks, are works of art; but we are unable to give that title to the axes and arrowheads, the harpoons and fish-hooks, the knives, the pins, the needles, the crowds of various utensils which we see in the glass cases of a pre-historic museum; all this, interesting though it be to those who wish to study the history of labour, is nothing but an industry, and a rudimentary industry, which is content with supplying the simplest wants. It is not until we reach the sculptures of the cave-dwellings that we find the first germs of artistic effort, and in truth, man did not cut the figures of animals upon the handles of his tools and upon those objects which have been called, perhaps a little recklessly, batons of command, for any utilitarian purpose; it was to give himself pleasure, it was because he found true æsthetic enjoyment in copying and interpreting living nature. Art was born, we may acknowledge, with those first attempts at the representation of life, and it might fairly be expected that our history should commence with them, were it not that they offer no sequence, no starting point for any continuous movement like that which, beginning in Egypt and Chaldæa, was prosecuted in Greece and led in time to such high developments; even its competent students confess that the art of the cave-men was an isolated episode without fruition or consequence. Specimens of this art are found at but a few points of the vast surface over which the vestiges of primitive man are spread, and neither in the neolithic age, nor even in that of bronze —both far in advance in other ways of that of the cave-dwellings—does it ever seem to have entered into the mind of man to copy the types offered to him by the organic world, still less those of mankind, which, however, had long before been roughly figured in one or two caves in the Dordogne.[30]

Towards the close of the prehistoric age the taste for ornament becomes very marked, but that ornament is always of the kind which we call geometric. Hardly a single decorative motive is taken from the vegetable world. Like the rude efforts of the cave-men, this decoration proves that those by whom it was imagined and who frequently employed it with such happy results, were not contented with bare utility, but, so far as they could, sought after beauty. A secret instinct worked in them and inspired them with the desire to give some appearance of elegance to the objects which they had in daily use. This geometrical style of decoration prevailed all over central Europe until, in the first place, the movements of commerce with Greece and Etruria, and secondly the Roman conquest, introduced the methods of classic art.

From what we have said, it will be seen that we could not have passed over in silence this system of ornamentation; but we shall again find it in our path when we come to treat of that prehistoric Greece which preceded by perhaps two or three centuries the Greece of Homer. By the help of the discoveries which have been lately made in the Troad, at Mycenæ, and in other ancient sites, we shall study the works produced by the ancestors of the Greeks before they went to school to the nations of the East. But even with the discoveries which carry us farthest back, we only reach the end of the period in question, when maritime commerce had already brought to the islands and the mainland of Greece objects of Egyptian, Phœnician or Chaldaic manufacture, but before those objects were sufficiently numerous or the relations with those countries sufficiently intimate to produce any great effect upon the habits of native workmen. Among the deposits to which we have alluded, it is generally possible to distinguish those works which are of foreign origin; and such works excluded, it is easy to form a sufficiently accurate general idea of the art practised by the forefathers of the historic Greeks—by the Pelasgians, to use a conventional term. So long as it was left to its own inspiration, Pelasgic art did not differ, in its general characteristics, from that of the various peoples spread over the continent of Europe, and still practised for centuries after the dawn of Greek civilization in the great plains to the north of the Alps and the Danube. Its guiding spirit and its motives are similar. There is the same richness, or rather the same poverty, the same combinations produced by a small number of never-changing linear elements. One would say that from the shores of the great ocean and the Baltic to those of the Mediterranean, all the workmen laboured for the same masters. Struck by this resemblance, or rather uniformity, one of the most eminent of German archæologists, Herr Conze, has proposed that this kind of ornament shall be called Indo-European; he sees, in the universality of the system, a feature common to all branches of the Aryan race, a special characteristic which may serve to distinguish it from the Semites.

Objections have been brought against this doctrine of which Herr Conze himself has recognized the gravity; by numerous examples taken from the art of nations which do not belong to the Aryan family, it has been shown that, human nature being the same everywhere, all those peoples whose development has been normal, neither interrupted nor accelerated by external causes, have, at some period of their lives, turned to the style in question for the decoration of their weapons, of their earthenware, their furniture, their apparel and their personal ornaments. The less richly endowed among them would have stopped at that point but for the example of their neighbours, who stirred them on to new attempts and further progress; others advanced without impulse from other sources than their own instincts, they reproduced vegetable and animal forms, and finally the human figure in all its beauty and nobility. It was the same with letters. Among the nations which have made a name in history how few there are that possess a true literature, a poetry at once inspired and critical! All however, under one form or another, have a popular poetry which is more or less varied and expressive.

The trace of this earliest spontaneous effort, of this first naïve product of the imagination, never entirely disappears in a literature which is life-like and sincere; it is found even in the most perfect works of its classic period. In the same way the most advanced and refined forms of art draw a part of their motives and effects from geometrical decoration. This style therefore should be studied both for its principle and for the resources of which it disposes, but as we shall have to notice it when we treat of Greece, it seems to us better to adjourn till then any discussion of its merits. Both in Greece and Italy approximate dates can be given to the monuments which it ornaments, they can be placed in their proper historical position, which is by no means the case with the objects gleaned throughout central Europe.

There is another consideration of still greater importance; the artistic remains of Greece form an almost unbroken series, from the humble and timid attempts of nascent sculpture to the brilliant masterpieces of Phidias and Polycletus, and show the steps by which the artist succeeds in passing from one style to another, from curves and interlacing lines, from all mere abstract combinations, to the imitation of nature, to the representation of bodies which breathe, feel, and speak, which move and struggle. Elsewhere force has either been wanting for this development, or evidence of the transition has escaped our researches. Nothing can be much more imperfect or more conventional than the figures which we find upon some of the painted vases from Mycenæ and Cyprus,[31] upon which the workman's hand, accustomed to straight lines and circles, or segments of circles, has succeeded in suggesting by those means the figures of birds and fighting men. Nothing could be farther from the subtlety and variety of the contours presented by living organisms. But in spite of all this, art was born with the awakening of this desire to reproduce the beauty and mobility of living forms. All that had preceded it was but the vague murmuring of a wish which had not yet become self conscious; but, at last the intellect divined the use to which it might be put, and guessed at the part which might be played by the plastic instincts with which it felt itself endowed. All the rest depended upon natural gifts, upon time and circumstance; the march along the road of progress began, and although its rapidity was intermittent, it was certain to arrive, if not always at the production of masterpieces of divine beauty, at least at sufficient competence in painting and modelling to transmit the types of a race and the images of its gods to posterity.

The student of plastic art finds in the remains of prehistoric times rather a tendency to the creation of art, than art itself; by postponing our study of this tendency until we come to investigate the origin of Greek and Italian art, we are enabled to avoid all excursion beyond the limits implied by our title, beyond that which is generally called antiquity. The conventional meaning of this word embraces neither the primitive savages who chipped the first flint, nor the cave-men, but it calls up before our eyes the brilliant cities of northern Africa and hither-Asia, of Greece and Italy, with which our school-days have made us familiar; it reminds us of those nations whose stories we learnt from the sacred and profane authors whose works we read in our youth; and our thoughts revert to their grandiose monuments of architecture and sculpture, to their masterpieces of poetry and eloquence, to those great works of literature in which we took our first lessons in the art of writing and speaking. Behind all these images and associations the intelligence of an educated man tells him—and the discoveries of science every day make the fact more certain—that in the ancient as in the modern world, the nations which figure upon the stage of history were not isolated; they each had neighbours who influenced them, or whom they influenced, by commerce or conquest; each also received something from its predecessors, and in turn transmitted the results of its labour to those which came after it; in a word, the work of civilization was continuous and universal. The nations which, for three or four thousand years, were grouped round the basin of the Mediterranean, belonged to one historical system; to those who take a wide grasp of facts they are but the members and organs of one great body, in which the nervous centres, the sources of life, of movement and of thought, slowly gravitated with the effluxion of time from the east to the west, from Memphis and Babylon to Athens and Rome.

As for the populations which, long before the opening of this period and during the whole of its duration, lived on the north of the Danube, the Alps, and the Pyrenees, they do not belong to the same system; they were attached to it by the Roman conquest, but at a very late period; not long, indeed, before the triumph of Christianity, the invasion of the barbarians, and the fall of the empire, led to the dissolution of the antique system and the substitution for it, after centuries of confusion and violence, of the wider and more comprehensive civilization of modern Europe, a civilization which was destined to cross every sea and to spread itself over the whole surface of the globe. As soon as the victories of the Roman legions, and the construction of the great roads which united Rome with her most distant provinces, had brought them into constant communication with the maritime cities of the Mediterranean, these barbaric nations, who had neither history, nor letters, nor expressive art, received them from their conquerors, whose very language they all, or nearly all, adopted; and for all this they gave practically nothing in return. Elsewhere, the old world had almost finished its task. It had exhausted every form in which those ideas and beliefs could be clothed which it had kept unchanged, or little changed, for millenium after millenium. The old world employed such force and vitality as remained to it in giving birth to the new, to that religion which has led to the foundation of our modern social and political systems. These also were to have their modes of expression, rich and sonorous enough, but dominated by analysis; they were to have arts and literatures, which have given expression to far more complex ideas than those of antiquity. The Celts and Teutons, the Slavs and Scandinavians, all those tribes which the Romans called barbarous, have, in spite of the apparent poverty of their share, made an important contribution to the civilization into which they plunged at so late a period, when they did so much to provide a foundation for those modes of thought and feeling which are only to be found in modern society.

These races do not belong, then, to what we call antiquity. They are separated from it by many things; they have no history, they have neither literary and scientific culture nor anything that deserves the name of art. Hidden behind a thick curtain of mountains and forests, sprinkled over vast regions where no towns existed, they remained in their isolation for thousands of years, furnishing to civilization nothing but a few rough materials which they themselves knew not how to use; they took no part in the work which, throughout those ages, was being prosecuted in the great basin of the Persian Gulf and the Mediterranean, in that accumulation of inventions and creations which, fixed and preserved by writing and realized by art, form the common patrimony of the most civilized portion of the human species. When, at a late hour, these nations entered upon the scene, it was as disturbers and destroyers,—and although they helped to found modern society, they produced none of those elements left to us by antiquity and preserved for us by that Rome in whose hands the heritage of Greece was concentrated.

V.

We have different, but equally valid, reasons for leaving that which is called the far East—India, China, and Japan—outside the limit of our studies. Those rich and populous countries have, doubtless, a civilization which stretches back nearly as far as that of Egypt and Assyria, a civilization which has produced works both of fine and of industrial art which in many respects equalled those of the nations with which we are now occupied. In all those countries there are buildings which impress by their mass and by the marvellous delicacy of their ornamentation, sculptures of a singular freedom and power, and decorative painting which charms by its skilful use of brilliant colour as well as by the facility and inventive fancy of its design. The representation of the human figure has never reached the purity of line or nobility of expression of a Greek statue, but, on the other hand, the science of decoration has never been carried farther than by the wood-carvers, weavers and embroiderers of Hindostan, and the potters of China and Japan.

These styles have their fanatical admirers who see nothing but their brilliant qualities; they have also their detractors, or at least their severe judges, who are chiefly struck by their shortcomings, but no one attempts to deny that each of those nations possesses an art which is always original, and sometimes of great and rare power. Why then, it may be asked, do we refuse to comprehend the more ancient monuments of India and China, those which by their age belong to the centuries with which we are concerned, in this work? Our motives may be easily divined.

We might allege our incompetence for such an extended task, which would be enough to occupy several lives. But we have a still more decisive reason. Neither Aryan India nor Turanian China belongs to the antiquity which we have defined, and as for Indo-China and Japan they are but annexes to those two great nations; religion, written characters, the industrial and plastic arts —all came to them from one or the other of those two great centres of civilization.

So far as China is concerned no doubt or hesitation is possible. Down almost to our own days China and its satellites had no dealings with the western group of nations. It is a human family which has lived in voluntary isolation from the rest of its species. It is separated from western mankind by the largest of the continents, by deserts, by the highest mountains in the world, by seas once impassable, finally, by that contempt and hatred of everything foreign which such conditions of existence are calculated to engender. In the course of her long and laborious existence China has invented many things. She was the first to discover several of those instruments and processes which, in the hands of Europeans, have, in a few centuries, changed the face of the world; not only did she fail to make good use of her inventions, she guarded them so closely that the West had to invent them anew. We may cite printing as an example; nearly two hundred years before our era the Chinese printed with blocks of wood. On the other hand, every useful discovery made in the period and by the group of nations to whom we mean to confine our attention, from the time of Menes and Ourkham, the first historic kings of Egypt and Chaldæa, to the latest of the Roman Emperors, has been turned to the profit of others than its authors, and forms, so to speak, part of the public wealth. A single alphabet, that which the Phœnicians extracted from one of the forms of Egyptian writing, made the tour of the Mediterranean, and served all the nations of the ancient world in turn for preserving their thoughts and the idiom of their language. A system of numerals, of weights and measures, was invented in Babylon and travelled across Western Asia to be adopted by the Greeks, and, through the mediation of the Greek astronomers and geographers, has given us the sexagesimal division which we still employ for the partition of a circumference into degrees, minutes and seconds.

From this point of view, then, there is a profound difference between Egypt or Chaldæa, and China. The most remote epochs in the history of China do not belong to antiquity as we have defined the term. Without knowing it or wishing it, all those nations included in our plan laboured for their neighbours and for their successors. Read as a whole, their history proves to us that they each played a part in the gradual elaboration of civilized life which was absolutely necessary to the total result. But when China is in question our impression is very different, our intellects are quite equal to imagining what the world would have been like had that Empire been absolutely destroyed centuries ago, with all its art, literature, and material wealth. Rightly or wrongly, we should not expect such a catastrophe to have had any great effect upon civilization; we should have been the poorer by a few beautiful plates and vases, and should have had to do without tea, and that would have been the sum of our loss.

The case of India is different. Less remote than China, bathed by an ocean which bore the fleets of Egypt, Chaldæa, Persia, Greece and Rome, she was never beyond the reach of the western nations. The Assyrians, the Persians, and the Greeks carried their arms into the basin of the Indus, some portions of which were annexed for a time to those Empires which had their centre in the valley of the Euphrates and stretched westwards as far as the Mediterranean. There was a continuous coming and going of caravans across the plateau of Iran and the deserts which lie between it and the oases of Bactriana, Aria, and Arachosia, and through the passes which lead down to what is now called the Punjab; between the ports of the Arabian and Persian gulfs and those of the lower Indus and the Malabar coast, a continual commercial movement went on which, though fluctuating with time, was never entirely interrupted. From the latter regions western Asia drew her supplies of aromatic spices, of metals, of precious woods, of jewels, and other treasures, all of which came mainly by the sea route.

All this, however, was but the supply of the raw material for Egyptian, Assyrian, and Phœnician industries. There is no evidence that up to the very last days of antique civilization the inhabitants of Hindostan with all their depths and originality of thought ever exercised such influence upon their neighbours as could have made itself felt as far as Greece. The grand lyric poetry of the Vedas, the epics and dramas of the following epoch, the religious and philosophical speculations, those learned grammatical analyses which are now admired by philologists, all the rich and brilliant intellectual development of a race akin to the Greeks and in many ways no less richly endowed, remained shut up in that basin of the Ganges into which no stranger penetrated until the time of the Mohammedan conquest. Neither Egyptians, Arabs nor Phœnicians reached the true centres of Hindoo civilization; they merely visited those sea-board towns where the mixed population was more occupied with commerce than with intellectual pursuits. The conquerors previous to Alexander did no more than reach the gates of India and reconnoitre its approaches, while Alexander himself failed to penetrate beyond the vestibule.

Let us suppose that the career of the Macedonian hero had not been cut short by the fatigues and terrors of his soldiers. So far as we can judge from what Megasthenes tells us of Palibothra, the capital of Kalaçoka, the most powerful sovereign in the valley of the Ganges in the time of Seleucus Nicator, the Greeks would not, even in that favoured region, have found buildings which they could have studied with any profit, either for their plan, construction, or decoration. Recent researches have proved Megasthenes to be an intelligent observer and an accurate narrator, and he tells us that in the richest parts of the country the Hindoos of his time had nothing better than wooden houses, or huts of pisè or rough concrete. The palace of the sovereign, at Palibothra, impressed the traveller by its situation, its great extent, and the richness of its apartments. It was built upon an artificial, terraced mound, in the midst of a vast garden. It was composed of a series of buildings surrounded by porticos, which contained large reception halls separated from one another by courtyards in which peacocks and tame panthers wandered at will. The columns of the principal saloons were gilt. The general aspect was very imposing. The arrangements seem to have had much in common with those of the Assyrian and Persian palaces. But there was one capital distinction between the two; at Palibothra the residence of the sovereign, like those of his subjects, was built of wood. With its commanding position, and the fine masses of verdure with which it was surrounded, it must have produced a happy and picturesque effect, but, after all, it was little more than a collection of kiosques. Architecture, worthy of the name, began with the employment of those solid and durable materials which defend themselves against destruction by their weight and constructive repose.

The other arts could not have been much more advanced. Ignorant as they were of the working of stone for building, these people can hardly have been sculptors, and as to their painting, we have no information. There is, moreover, no allusion to works of painting or sculpture in their epics and dramas, there are none of those descriptions of pictures and statues which, in the writings of the Greek poets and dramatists, show us that the development of the plastic arts followed closely upon that of poetry. This difference between the two races may perhaps be explained by the opposition between their religions and, consequently, their poetry. In giving to their gods the forms and features of men, the oldest of the Greek singers sketched in advance the figures to be afterwards created by their painters and sculptors. Homer furnished the sketch from which Phidias took his type of the Olympian Jupiter. It was not so with the Vedic hymns. In them the persons of the gods had neither consistence nor tangibility. They are distinguished now by one set of qualities and again by another; each of the immortals who sat down to the banquet on Olympus, had his or her own personal physiognomy, described by poets and interpreted by artists, but it was not so with the Hindoo deities. The Hindoo genius had none of the Greek faculty for clear and well-defined imagery; it betrays a certain vagueness and want of definition which is not to be combined with a complete aptitude for the arts of design. It is the business of these arts to render ideas by forms, and a well marked limit is the essence of form, which is beautiful and expressive in proportion as its contours are clearly and accurately drawn.

Indian art then, for the reasons which we have given, and others which are unknown, was only in its cradle in the time of Alexander, while the artists of Greece were in full possession of all their powers; they had already produced inimitable master-pieces in each of the great divisions of art, and yet their creative force was far from being exhausted. It was the age of

Lysippus and Apelles; of those great architects who, in the temples of Asia Minor, renewed the youth of the Ionic order by their bold and ingenious innovations. Under such conditions, what would the effect have been, had these two forms of civilization entered into close relations with each other? In all probability the result would have been similar to that which ensued when the ancestors of the Greeks began to deal with the more civilized Phœnicians and the people of Asia Minor. But in the case of the Hindoos, as we have said, the disciples had a less, instead of a greater, aptitude for the plastic arts than their teachers, and, moreover, the contact between the two was never complete nor was it of long duration. The only frontier upon which the interchange of idea was frequent and continuous was the northwest, which divided India from that Bactrian kingdom of which we know little more than the mere names of its princes and the date of its fall. But before the end of the second century B.C. this outpost of Hellenism had fallen before the attacks of those barbarians whom we call the Saci. In such an isolated position it could not long hope to maintain itself, especially after the rise of the Parthian monarchy had separated it from the empire of the Seleucidæ. Its existence must always have been precarious, and the mere fact that it did not succumb until the year 136 B.C. is enough to prove that several of its sovereigns must have been remarkable men. Should their annals ever be discovered they would probably form one of the strangest and most interesting episodes in the history of the Greek race.

Through the obscurity in which all the details are enveloped we can clearly perceive that those princes were men of taste. They were, as was natural, attached to the literature and the arts which reminded them of their superior origin and of that distant fatherland with which year after year it became more difficult to communicate. Although they were obliged, in order to defend themselves against so many enemies, to employ those mercenary soldiers, Athenians, Thebans, Spartans and Cretans, which then overran Asia, and to pay them dearly for their services, they also called skilful artists to their court and kept them there at great expense; the beautiful coins which have preserved their images down to our day are evidence of this, the decoration of their cities, of their temples, and of their palaces must have been in keeping with these; everywhere no doubt were Corinthian and Ionic buildings, statues of the Greek gods and heroes mixed with those portraits and historic groups which had been multiplied by the scholars of

Lysippus, wall paintings, and perhaps some of those easel pictures signed by famous masters, for which the heirs of Alexander were such keen competitors. Artisans, who had followed the Greek armies in their march towards the East with the object of supplying the wants of any colonies which might be established in those distant regions, reproduced upon their vases and in their terra-cotta figures the motives of the painting, the sculpture, and the architecture which they left behind; goldsmiths, jewellers and armourers cut, chased, and stamped them in metal. And it was not only the Greek colonists who employed their skill. Like the Scythian tribes among whom the Greek cities of the Euxine were planted, the nations to the north of India were astonished and delighted by the elegance of their ornament and the variety of its forms. They imported from Bactriana these products of an art which was wanting to them, and soon set themselves, with the help perhaps of foreign artists settled among them, to imitate Grecian design in the courts of the Indian rajahs.

That this was so is proved by those coins which bear on their reverse such Hindoo symbols as Siva with his bull, and on their obverse Greek inscriptions, and by the remains of what is now called Græco-Buddhic art, an art which seems to have flourished in the upper valley of the Indus in the third or second century before our era. These remains, formerly much neglected, are now attracting much attention. They have been carefully studied and described by Cunningham[32]; Dr. Curtius has described them and published reproductions of the most curious among them.[33] They are found in the north of the Punjab upon a few ancient sites where excavations have been made. Some of them have been transported to Europe in the collection of Dr. Leitner, while others remain in the museums of Peshawur, Lahore, and Calcutta.[34] In those sacred buildings which have been examined the plan of the Greek temple has not been adopted, but the isolated members of Greek architecture and the most characteristic details of its ornament are everywhere made use of. It is the same with the sculpture; in the selection of types, in the arrangement of drapery, in the design, there is the same mixture of Greek taste with that of India, of elements borrowed from foreign, and those drawn from the national, beliefs. The helmeted Athené and Helios in his quadriga figure by the side of Buddha.

Traces of the same influence are to be found in a less marked degree in other parts of India. Near the mouth of the Indus and upon the Malabar coast, the native sculptors and architects were able to obtain more than one useful suggestion, more than one precious hint as to their technique, from the works of art brought in the ships of maritime traders. It is even possible that Greek workmen may thus have been introduced into seaport towns, and there employed upon the decoration of palaces and temples. However this may be it is incontestable that all the important sacred edifices of that region, whether stone-built or carved in the living rock, date from a period more recent than that of Alexander, and that most of them show details which imply acquaintance with Greek architectural forms and their imitation. We are thus on all hands forced to this conclusion: that, in the domain of the plastic arts, Greece owed nothing to India, with which she made acquaintance very late and at a period when she had no need to take lessons from others. That, moreover, India had little or nothing to give; that her arts were not developed till after her early relations with Greece, and it would even seem that her first stimulus was derived from the models which Greece put within her reach.

From all this it will be seen that we need not go as far as China, or even as the Punjab, in order to explain the origin of Greek art. During the period with which we are concerned, China might as well have been in the planet Saturn for all she had to do with the ancient world, and we need refer to her no more, except now and then perhaps for purposes of illustration. We cannot treat India quite in the same fashion, because there were, as we have said, certain points of contact and reciprocal influences at work between her and the group of nations we are about to treat. But as Greece borrowed nothing from India, at least in the matter of art, the little which we shall have to say of the products of the Hindoos will not be connected with our discussion of the origin of Greek art. A curious though hardly an important episode in history, is seen in the reaction by which the Greek genius, when arrived at maturity, threw itself at the command of Alexander upon that East from which it had received its first lessons.

None of those philosophical discussions to which Ottfried Müller and Stark thought it necessary to give so large a place will be found in our introduction; both of those authors devoted a long chapter to the definition of art and its principal manifestations. Stark went so far as to discuss, with much patience and ingenuity, the definitions of art and of its essential forms which had been given by previous writers. We shall attempt nothing of the kind; we have not undertaken a work of criticism or æsthetic demonstration. We wish to build up the history of ancient civilization through the study, description, and comparison of its plastic remains.

Neither do we feel sure that, in such a question as this, definitions do not lead to confusion rather than to clearness. When short, they are vague and obscure, and only acquire precision through distinctions and developments which have to be discussed at length; and again they generally lead, on one hand or the other, either to objections or reservations. *Omnis definitio in jure periculosa*, says an old maxim, which is certainly true in matters of art. Why should we attempt, unless we are obliged, to define terms which awake sufficiently clear and distinct ideas in all cultivated minds? No satisfactory definition has ever been given of the word *architecture*, and yet, when we use it, every one knows what we mean. Architecture, sculpture, painting, each of these sounds has a precise meaning for those to whom our work is addressed, and we may say the same of certain other expressions, such as *industrial arts, decoration, style, historical painting, genre painting, landscape painting*, which will often be found in our pages. We must refer those who want definitions of these phrases to the *Grammaire des Arts du Dessin* of M. Charles Blanc and kindred works. It will suffice for us that these words should be taken in the ordinary meaning which they bear in the conversation of cultivated men. If our ideas of art and its different branches diverge here and there from those which are commonly received, those divergencies will become evident, and will be discussed and justified to the best of our ability as the work proceeds. But on all occasions we shall do our best to avoid the abstract and pedantic terminology which makes Ottfried Müller's first chapter so difficult to read.

We have now declared the aim of our work and the route which we propose to follow. In order to increase our chances of success, I have sought and obtained the collaboration of M. Charles Chipiez, whose special knowledge is well calculated to neutralise my own deficiencies. To his *Histoire critique des Origines et de la Formation des Ordres grecques*, was awarded, in 1877, one of the highest prizes of the Académie des Inscriptions, and in the Salons of 1878 and 1879 he confirmed his double reputation as a skilful draughtsman and a learned theorist; his *Essais de Restoration d'un Temple grecque hypèthre, et des tours à étages de la Chaldée*, was much noticed and discussed by connoisseurs. It would not be fitting, however, to praise it here. I must confine myself to saying how fortunate I am in having obtained a help which I have found more helpful, more single-minded, more complete, than I had dared to hope for. In all that has to do with architecture, I have not written a line until after consulting M. Chipiez upon all technical points. He has also taken an active part in the revision of the text of certain chapters. As for the plates and illustrations in the text, we have together chosen the objects to be represented, and M. Chipiez, as a professional man and able draughtsman, has personally superintended the execution of the drawings. It remains for me to explain the *rôle* which we have assigned to our illustrations.

VI.

In the single edition of his great work which appeared during his own lifetime, Winckelmann inserted but a small number of illustrations, and those for ornament rather than for instruction. One of his translators, M. Huber, tells us that their execution gave great dissatisfaction to the author. [35] In our days, on the other hand, those who undertake a work of this kind make use of the great progress which has taken place in engraving and typography, to insert numerous figures in their text, to which they offer an indispensable and animated commentary. Without their help many descriptions and observations might remain unnecessarily obscure and doubtful. When forms are to be defined and compared, mere words, in whatever language spoken or written, can never suffice.

With well chosen phrases we may awake the recollections of others, and give renewed life to any impression which they may have received from some striking natural phenomenon or some fine work of art. Their imaginations will call up for a moment some landscape, picture, or statue which has formerly charmed them. But if we wish to explain the complicated plan of some great building, its design and its proportions, the slightest sketch will be of more use than the longest and most minute descriptions. So it will, if we wish to make clear the characteristics which distinguish one style from another, the Assyrian from the Egyptian, the archaic Greek style from that of the Phidian epoch or of the decadence, an Ionic column from the Erechtheum from one of the same order treated by a Roman architect. Between the contour of a figure from a Memphite bas-relief and that of one from Nineveh, what difference is there? A tenth of an inch more or less, a slight difference in the sweep of a line in order to mark more strongly the junction of the thigh and the knee. If we placed three nude torsos side by side, one of the sixth century, another of the fifth century, and the third of the time of Hadrian, a practised eye would at once assign its true date to each, in accordance with the manner in which the skeleton was indicated under the flesh, and the muscles drawn over it and attached to it. Supposing that the same model had served all three artists, it would show in the one case a lively sentiment of form combined with some dryness and rigidity; in another a freer, larger, and more subtle treatment, and in the third a want of vigour and firmness: but it would be difficult to give by words a clear idea of what caused the difference. Between the contour which satisfies us and that which does not there is hardly the difference of a hair; by leaning a little harder with the chisel the aspect of the one surface might have been made identical with the other. By its double astragali, by the fine chiselling of its gorgerin, by the elegant curve which unites the two volutes, and by the general delicacy of its ornament, a capital from the Erechtheum is distinguished above a Roman Ionic capital; it is at once finer in design and richer in ornamentation: by the side of it a capital from the theatre of Marcellus or the Coliseum would look mean and poor.

The whole history of art consists of the succession of subtle changes like these, and it would be impossible to convey them to the reader by the utmost precision of technical language or the most brilliant and life-like descriptions. The best thing that can be done is to make one's remarks in the presence of the statues, pictures and buildings concerned. But it is rarely that we find ourselves in such favourable conditions for teaching and explaining our ideas. But, in default of the objects themselves, we may at least give the most faithful images of them which can be obtained, and that we shall attempt to do throughout the course of this history.

We shall, then, give a large number of figures, in which absolute accuracy and justice of proportion will be aimed at rather than picturesque effects. It is not very long since, in collections of drawings from antique remains, they were all presented under one aspect, so far as the subtleties of style were concerned. The hand of the engraver spread a technical uniformity over them all in which differences of school and date disappeared, just as the delicate carvings and coloured ornament of the middle ages and the renaissance, which gave to each building an individuality of its own, were reduced to dull monotony by the undiscriminating brush of the whitewasher. It seemed to the artist natural enough to clothe the monuments of the past in the style of his own day—and it required much less care than would have been needed for the successful expression of all the diversities of style in his models. We have now, however, grown more exacting. We demand from the draughtsman who pretends to interpret a work of art the same devotion and the same self-sacrifice as from the writer who is charged with the translation of a work of literature from one language into another —we require him to forget himself, so that we may say of him, as the Latin poet says of his *Proteus*:

> "*Omnia transformat sese in miracula rerum.*"

We require him to change his style with every change of subject, to copy the gesture, the accent, and even the faults of his model; to be Chinese in China, Greek in Greece, and Tuscan when he takes us to Siena or Florence. But we have indicated an ideal which is not often reached. Every one of us has his preferences and natural affinities, every artist his own methods and personal modes of thought. One will be conspicuous for his interpretation of the nobility and purity of the antique, another for his treatment of oriental art or of the elegance of our eighteenth century. But the mere enunciation of the principle is of value, for a great effect follows the praise which those who treat their model with scrupulous and intelligent respect are sure to obtain, and the blame to which they who are less conscientious expose themselves.

Fidelity in interpretation is, in fact, the honesty of the draughtsman; it may become, if carried to a great height, his honour, and even his glory. So far as we are concerned, we demand it from all those who are associated with us in this task; and, so far as existing methods will allow, we shall see that we obtain it. Unless our illustrations had that merit they would obscure the text instead of making it more comprehensible. Our readers would search in vain for the features and characteristics to which we might call their attention, and many of our remarks and theories would become difficult to understand. We should be in the same position as an incompetent barrister who has made a bad choice of witnesses; witnesses who, when in the box, prove either to know nothing or to know only facts which tell against the party who has called them.

Our aim in choosing our illustrations will be to place before our readers good reproductions of most of the objects which are discussed in our text. We shall, of course, be unable to figure everything that is of interest, but we can at least ensure that those figures which we give shall each be interesting in some particular or another. So far as possible, we shall select for illustration such objects as have not previously been reproduced, or have been ill reproduced, or have been figured in works which are difficult of access. We shall sometimes, of course, find it necessary to reproduce some famous statue or some building which is familiar to most people; but even then we shall endeavour to give renewed interest to their beauties by displaying them under some fresh aspect and by increased care in the delineation of their forms. Views in perspective, of which we shall make frequent use, give the general aspect of buildings with much greater truth and completeness than a mere plan, or a picturesque sketch of ruinous remains, or even than an elevation.

Most of the more important perspectives and restorations due to the learned pencil of M. Chipiez will be given in plates separate from the text, as well as the most curious or significant of the works in sculpture or painting to which we shall have to refer. Some of these plates will be coloured. But the majority of our illustrations will consist of engravings upon zinc and wood, which will not, we hope, fall short of their more elaborate companions in honesty and fidelity.

From the earliest Egyptian dynasties and from fabled Chaldæa to imperial Rome, from the Pyramids and the Tower of Babel to the Coliseum, from the Statue of Chephren and the bas-reliefs of Shalmaneser III, to the busts of the Cæsars, from the painted decorations of the tomb of Ti, and the enamelled bricks of Nineveh to the wall-paintings of Pompeii, we shall review in due succession all the forms which the great nations of antiquity made use of to express their beliefs, to give shape to their ideas, to satisfy their instincts for luxury and their taste for beauty, to lodge their gods and their kings, and to transmit their own likenesses to posterity.

We propose to trace and explain the origin of, and to describe, without æsthetic dissertations or excessive use of technical terms, those processes which imply the practice of art; the creation and descent of forms; the continual changes, sometimes slight and sometimes great, which they underwent in passing from one people to another, until, among the Greeks, they arrived at the most happy and complete perfection which the world has seen. We hope, too, by the judicious choice and careful execution of our figures, to give a fair idea of this course of development even to those artists who have neither time nor patience to follow our criticisms and descriptions.

I conceived the plan of this history, of which the first instalment is now submitted to the public, at the time when M. Wallon, who is secretary to the *Académie des Inscriptions et Belles-Lettres*, entrusted me with the inauguration, at the Sorbonne, of the teaching of classic archæology. But before it could be realized two conditions had to be fulfilled. I had to find an associate in the work, a companion who would help me in the necessary labour and study, and I found him among my auditors in those first lectures at the Sorbonne. I had also to find a publisher who would understand the wants of the public and of the critics in such a matter. In this, too, I have succeeded, and I am free to undertake a work which is, I hope, destined to carry far beyond the narrow limits of a Parisian lecture room, the methods and principal results of a science, which, having made good its claims to the gratitude of mankind, is progressing with a step which becomes daily more assured. The task is an arduous one, and the continual discoveries which are reported from nearly every quarter of the ancient world, make it heavier every day. As for my colleague and myself, we have resigned ourselves in advance to seeing omissions and defects pointed out even by the most benevolent critics, but we are convinced that in spite of such imperfections as it may contain, our work will do good service, and will cause one of the aspects of ancient civilization to be better understood. This conviction will sustain us through the labours which, perhaps with some temerity, we have taken upon us. How far shall we be allowed to conduct our history? That we cannot tell, but we may venture to promise that it shall be the chief occupation and the dearest study of all that remains to us of life and strength.

GEORGES PERROT.

TO THE READER.

We have been in some doubt as to whether we should append a special bibliography to each section of this work, but after mature reflection we have decided against it. We shall, of course, consider the art of each of the races of antiquity in less detail than if we had undertaken a monograph upon Egyptian, upon Assyrian, or upon Phœnician art; but yet it is our ambition to neglect no source of information which is likely to be really valuable. From many of the books and papers which we shall have to consult we may reproduce nothing but their titles, but we hope that no important work will escape us altogether, and in every case we shall give references which may be easily verified. Under these circumstances a formal list of works would be a mere repetition of our notes and would only have the effect of giving a useless bulk to our volumes.

Whenever our drawings have not been taken directly from the originals we have been careful to indicate the source from which we obtained them, and we have made a point of borrowing only from authors of undoubted authority. Those illustrations which bear neither an artist's name nor the title of a book have been engraved from photographs. As for the perspectives and restorations supplied by M. Chipiez, they are in every case founded upon the study and comparison of all accessible documents; but it would take too long to indicate in each of these drawings how much has been borrowed from special publications and how much has been founded upon photographic evidence. M. Chipiez has sometimes employed the ordinary perspective, sometimes that which is called axonometric perspective. The difference will be at once perceived.

Egyptologists may, perhaps, find mistakes in the hieroglyphs which occur in our illustrations. These hieroglyphs have been as a rule exactly transcribed, but we do not pretend to offer a collection of texts; we have only reproduced these characters on account of their decorative value, and because without them we could not have the general appearance of this or that monument. It will thus be seen that our object is not affected by a mistake or two in such matters.

We may here express our gratitude to all those who have interested themselves in our enterprise and who have helped us to make our work complete. Our dear and lamented Mariette had promised us his most earnest help. During the winter that we passed in Egypt, while he still enjoyed some remains of strength and voice, we obtained from his conversation and his letters some precious pieces of information. We have cited the works of M. Maspero on almost every page, and yet we have learnt more from his conversation than from his writings. Before his departure for Egypt—whither he went to succeed Mariette—M. Maspero was our perpetual counsellor and referee; whenever we were embarrassed we appealed to his well ordered, accurate, and unbiased knowledge. We are also deeply indebted to M. Pierret, the learned *conservateur* of the Louvre; not only has he done everything to facilitate the work of our draughtsmen in the great museum, he has also helped us frequently with his advice and his accumulated knowledge. M. Arthur Rhôné has lent us a plan of the temple of the Sphinx, and M. Ernest Desjardins a view of the interior of that building.

The artists who have visited Egypt have helped us as cordially as the learned men who have deciphered its inscriptions. M. Gerome opened his portfolios and allowed us to take three of those drawings, which express with such truthful precision the character of Egyptian landscape from them. M. Hector Leroux was as generous as M. Gerome, and if we have taken but one illustration from his sketch-books it is because the arrangements for this volume were complete before we had the chance of looking through them. M. Brune has allowed us to reproduce his plans of Karnak and Medinet-Abou.

We have had occasion, in the work itself, to express our acknowledgments to MM. J. Bourgoin, G. Bénédite, and Saint-Elme Gautier, who have drawn for us the principal monuments of the Boulak and Louvre Museums. For the architecture we must name M. A. Guérin, a pupil of M. Chipiez, who prepared the drawings under the direction of his master, and M. Tomaszkievicz, whose light and skilful point has so well engraved them. If the process of engraving upon zinc has given results which, as we hope, will satisfy our readers, much of the honour belongs to the untiring care of M. Comte, whose process has been employed; all these plates have been reviewed and retouched by him with minute care. The steel engravings are by MM. Ramus, Hibon, Guillaumot père and Sulpis. In order that the polychromatic decoration of the Egyptians should be rendered with truth and precision in its refined tones and complicated line, we begged M. Sulpis to make use of a process which had almost fallen into disuse from its difficulty and want of rapidity; we mean that which is called *aquatint*. Our plates II, XIII, and XIV will perhaps convince our readers that its results are superior to those of chromo-lithography, which is now so widely employed.

A HISTORY OF ART IN ANCIENT EGYPT

CHAPTER I.

THE GENERAL CHARACTER OF EGYPTIAN CIVILIZATION.

§ 1. *Egypt's Place in The History of the World.*

Egypt is the eldest daughter of civilization. In undertaking to group the great nations of antiquity and to present them in their proper order, in attempting to assign to each its due share in the continuous and unremitting labour of progress until the birth of Christianity, we have no alternative but to commence with the country of the Pharaohs.

In studying the past of mankind, we have the choice of several points of view. We may attempt to determine the meaning and value of the religious conceptions which succeeded one another during that period, or we may give our attention rather to the literature, the arts and the sciences, to those inventions which in time have done so much to emancipate mankind from natural trammels and to make him master of his destiny. One writer will confine himself to a description of manners, and social and political institutions; another to the enumeration and explanation of the various changes brought on by internal revolutions, by wars and conquests; to what Bossuet calls "*la suite des empires*." Finally, he who has the highest ambition of all will attempt to unite all these various features into a single picture, so as to show, as a whole, the creative activity of a race and the onward movements of its genius in the continual search for "the best." But in any case the commencement must be made with Egypt. It is Egypt that has preserved the earliest attempts of man towards outward expression; it is in Egypt that those monuments exist which contain the first permanent manifestation of thought by written characters or plastic[36] forms; and it is in Egypt that the historian of antique art will find the earliest materials for study.

But, in the first place, we must give some account of the curious conditions under which the people lived who constructed and ornamented so many imposing monuments. We must begin, then, by describing the circumstances and the race characteristics under which this early civilization was developed.

§ 2. *The Valley of the Nile and its Inhabitants.*

The first traveller in Egypt of which we have any record is Herodotus; he sums up, in an often quoted phrase, the impression which that land of wonders made upon him: "Egypt," he says, "is a present from the Nile."[37] The truth could not be better expressed. "Had the equatorial rains not been compelled to win for themselves a passage to the Mediterranean, a passage upon which they deposited the mud which they had accumulated on their long journey, Egypt would not have existed. Egypt began by being the bed of a torrent; the soil was raised by slow degrees ... man appeared there when, by the slow accumulation of fertile earth, the country at last became equal to his support...."[38]

Other rivers do no more than afford humidity for their immediate borders, or, in very low-lying districts, for a certain narrow stretch of country on each hand. When they overflow their banks it is in a violent and irregular fashion, involving wide-spread ruin and destruction. Great floods are feared as public misfortunes. It is very different with the Nile. Every year, at a date which can be almost exactly foretold, it begins to rise slowly and to spread gently over the land. It rises by degrees until its surface is eight or nine metres above low-water mark;[39] it then begins to fall with the same tranquillity, but not until it has deposited, upon the lands over which it has flowed, a thick layer of fertile mud which can be turned over easily with the lightest plough, and in which every seed will germinate, every plant spring up with extraordinary vigour and rapidity.

FIG. 1.—During the Inundation of the Nile.

Thus nature has greatly facilitated the labour of the Egyptian agriculturist; the river takes upon itself the irrigation of the country for the whole width of its valley, and the preparation of the soil for the autumnal seed-time; it restores the virtue annually taken out of the ground by the crops. Each year it brings with it more fertility than can be exhausted in the twelve months, so that there is a constantly accumulating capital, on both banks of the river, of the richest vegetable earth.

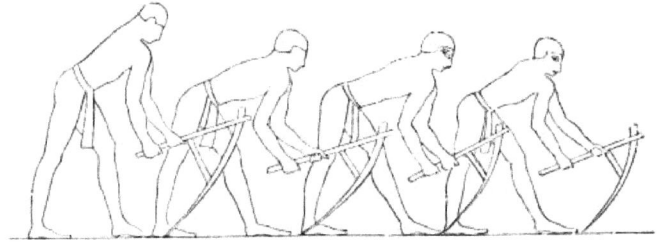

FIG. 2. —Hoeing; Beni-Hassan. (Champollion, pl. 381 *bis*. [40]

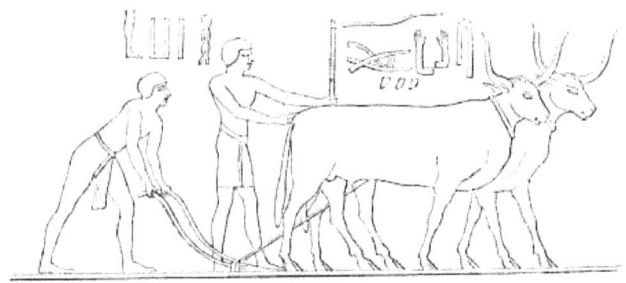

FIG. 3.—Ploughing; from the Necropolis of Memphis.
(*Description de l'Égypte*, ant. V., pl. 17.)

Thus the first tribes established themselves in the country under singularly favourable conditions; thanks to the timely help of the river they found themselves assured of an easy existence.[41] We know how often the lives of those tribes who live by fishing and the chase are oppressed by care; there are some days when game is not to be found, and they die of hunger. Those who live a pastoral life are also exposed to cruel hardships from the destruction of their flocks and herds by those epidemics against which even modern science sometimes struggles in vain. As for agricultural populations, they are everywhere, except in Egypt, at the mercy of the weather; seasons which are either too dry or too wet may reduce them to famine, for in those distant times local famines were far more fatal than in these days, when facility of transport and elaborate commercial connections ensure that where the demand is, thither the supply will be taken. In Egypt the success of the crops varied with the height of the Nile, but they never failed altogether. In bad years the peasant may have had the baton of the tax-collector to fear, but he always had a few onions or a few ears of maize to preserve him from starvation.[42]

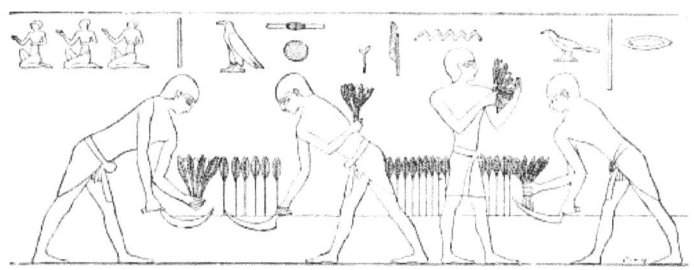

Fig. 4.—Harvest scene; from a tomb at Gizeh. (Champollion, pl. 417.)

The first condition of civilization is a certain measure of security for life. Now, thanks to the beneficent action of the king of rivers, that condition was created sooner in Egypt than elsewhere. In the valley of the Nile man found himself able, for the first time, to calculate upon the forces of nature and to turn them to his certain profit. It is easy then to understand that Egypt saw the birth of the most ancient of those civilizations whose plastic arts we propose to study.

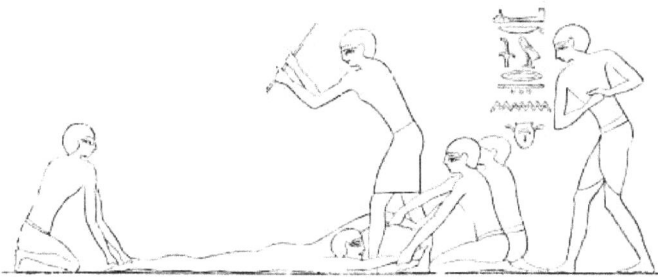

Fig. 5.—The Bastinado; Beni-Hassan. (Champollion, pl. 390.)

Another favourable condition is to be found in the isolation of the country. The tribes who settled there in centuries so remote that they are beyond tradition and even calculation, could live in peace, hidden as it were in a narrow valley and protected on all sides, partly by deserts, partly by an impassable sea. It would perhaps be well to give some idea of the natural features of their country before commencing our study of their art. The terms, *Lower-*, *Middle-*, and *Upper-Egypt*, the *Delta*, and *Ethiopia* will continually recur in these pages, as also will the names of Tanis and Sais, Memphis and Heliopolis, Abydos and Thebes, and of many other cities; it is important therefore that our readers should know exactly what is meant by each of these time-honoured designations; it is necessary that they should at least be able to find upon the map those cities which by their respective periods of supremacy represent the successive epochs of Egyptian history.

"Egypt is that country which, stretching from north to south, occupies the north-east angle of Africa, or Libya as the ancients called it. It is joined to Asia by the isthmus of Suez. It is bounded on the east by that isthmus and the Red Sea; on the south by Nubia, the Ethiopia of the Greeks, which is traversed by the Nile before its entrance into Egypt at the cataracts of Syene; on the west by the desert sprinkled here and there with a few oases, and on the north by the Mediterranean. The desert stretches as far north on the west of the country as the Red Sea does on the east.

"It penetrates moreover far into the interior of Egypt itself. Strictly speaking Egypt consists simply of that part of this corner of Africa over which the waters of the Nile flow during the inundation, to which may be added those districts to which the water is carried by irrigation. All outside this zone is uninhabited, and produces neither corn nor vegetables nor trees nor even grass. No water is to be found there beyond a few wells, all more or less exposed to exhaustion in an ever-parching atmosphere. In Upper Egypt rain is an extremely rare phenomenon. Sand and rock cover the whole country, except the actual valley of the Nile. Up to the point where the river divides into several arms, that is to say for more than three-quarters of the whole length of Egypt, this valley never exceeds an average width of more than four or five leagues. In a few districts it is even narrower than this. For almost its whole length it is shut in between two mountain chains, that on the east called the Arab, that on the west the Libyan chain. These mountains, especially towards the south, sometimes close in and form defiles. On the other hand, in Middle Egypt the Libyan chain falls back and becomes lower, allowing the passage of the canal which carries the fertilizing waters into the Fayoum, the province in which the remains of the famous reservoir which the Greek writers called Lake Mœris exist. Egypt, which was little more than a glen higher up, here widens out to a more imposing size. A little below Cairo, the present capital of Egypt, situated not far from the site of ancient Memphis, the Nile divides into two branches, one of which, the Rosetta branch, turns to the north-west, the other, that of Damietta, to the north and north-east.... The ancients knew five others which, since their time, have either been obliterated or at least have become non-navigable.... All these branches took their names from towns situated near their mouths. A large number of less important watercourses threaded their way through Lower Egypt; but as the earth there is marshy, their channels have shifted greatly from age to age and still go on changing. The Nile forms several lagunes near the sea, shut in by long tongues of earth and sand, and communicating with the Mediterranean by openings here and there. The space comprised between the two most distant branches of the river is called the Delta, on account of its triangular form, which is similar to that of a capital Greek *delta* (Δ)."[43]

At one time the waves of the Mediterranean washed the foot of the sandy plateau which is now crowned by the Great Pyramid; the Nile flowed into the sea at that time slightly to the north of the site upon which Memphis was afterwards built. With the slow passage of time the particles of earth which it brought down from the mountains of Abyssinia were deposited as mud banks upon the coast, and gradually filling up the gulf, created instead wide marshy plains intersected by lakes. Here and there ancient sand ridges indicate the successive watercourses. The never-ceasing industry of its floods had already, at the earliest historic period, carried the mouths of the Nile far beyond the normal line of the neighbouring coasts. The Egyptian priests—whose words have been preserved for us by Herodotus—had a true idea as to how this vast plain had been created, a plain which now comprises twenty-three thousand square kilometres and is continually being added to; but they were strangely deceived when they thought and declared that Menes or Ména, the first of all kings, found almost all Egypt under the waters. The sea, they said, penetrated in those days beyond the site of Memphis, and the remainder of the country, the district of Thebes excepted, was an unhealthy morass.[44] The Delta had, in fact, existed long before the appearance of Menes, and perhaps it may have shown pretty much its present form when the Egyptian race first appeared in the valley of the Nile.[45]

As to the origin of that race, we need not enter at length into a question so purely ethnographical. It is now generally allowed that they were connected with the white races of Europe and Western Asia; the anatomical examination of the bodies recovered from the most ancient tombs, and the study of their statues, bas-reliefs, and pictures, all point to this conclusion. If we take away individual peculiarities these monuments furnish us with the following common type of the race even in the most remote epochs:—

"The average Egyptian was tall, thin, active. He had large and powerful shoulders,[46] a muscular chest, sinewy arms terminating in long and nervous hands, narrow hips, and thin muscular legs. His knees and calves were nervous and muscular, as is generally the case with a pedestrian race; his feet were long, thin, and flattened, by his habit of going barefoot. The head, often too large and powerful for the body, was mild, and even sad in its expression. His forehead was square and perhaps a little low, his nose short and round; his eyes were large and well opened, his cheeks full and round, his lips thick but not turned out like a negro's; his rather large mouth bore an habitually soft and sorrowful expression. These features are to be found in most of the statues of the ancient and middle empires, and in all the later epochs. Even to the present day the peasants, or *fellahs*, have almost everywhere preserved the physiognomy of their ancestors, although the upper classes have lost it by repeated intermarriage with strangers."[47]

When Mariette discovered in the necropolis at Memphis the famous wooden statue of a man standing and holding in his hand the baton of authority, the peasants of Sakkarah recognised at once the feature and attitude of one of themselves, of the rustic dignitary who managed the *corvées* and apportioned the taxation. An astonished fellah cried out: "The Sheikh-el-Beled!" His companions took up the cry, and the statue has been known by that name ever since.[48]

Increased knowledge of the Egyptian language has enabled us to carry our researches much farther than Champollion and his successors. By many of its roots, by its system of pronouns, by its nouns of number, and by some of the arrangements of its conjugations, it seems to have been attached to the

Semitic family of languages. Some of the idioms of these Semitic tongues are found in Egyptian in a rudimentary state. From this it has been concluded that Egyptian and its cognate languages, after having belonged to that group, separated from it at a very early period, while their grammatical system was still in course of formation. Thus, disunited and subjected to diverse influences, the two families made a different use of the elements which they possessed in common.

There would thus seem to have been a community of root between the Egyptians on the one part and the Arabs, Hebrews, and Phœnicians on the other, but the separation took place at such an early period, that the tribes who came to establish themselves in the valley of the Nile had both the time and the opportunity to acquire a very particular and original physiognomy of their own. The Egyptians are therefore said to belong to the proto-Semitic races.

FIG. 6.—Statue from the Ancient Empire in calcareous stone. (Boulak.[49]) Drawn by G. Bénédite.

This opinion has been sustained with more or less plausibility by MM. Lepsius, Benfey, and Bunsen, and accepted by M. Maspero.[50] But other critics of equal authority are more impressed by the differences than by the resemblances, which, however, they neither deny nor explain. M. Renan prefers to rank the Copts, the Tuaregs, and the Berbers in a family which he would call Chamitic, and to which he would refer most of the idioms of Northern Africa.[51] A comparison of the languages is, then, insufficient to decide the question of origin.

FIG. 7.—The *Sheikh-el-Beled*. (Boulak.) Drawn by J. Bourgoin.

The people whose physical characteristics we have described and whose idiom we have defined, came from Asia, to all appearance, by the Isthmus of Suez. Perhaps they found established on the banks of the Nile another race, probably black, and indigenous to the African continent.[52] If this were so the new comers forced the earlier occupants of the country southwards without mixing with them, and set themselves resolutely to the work of improvement. Egypt must then have presented a very different sight from its richness and fertility of to-day. The river when left to itself, was perpetually changing its bed, and even in its highest floods it failed to reach certain parts of the valley, which remained unproductive; in other districts it remained so long that it changed the soil into swamp. The Delta, half of it drowned in the waters of the Nile, the other half under those of the Mediterranean, was simply a huge morass dotted here and there with sandy islands and waving with papyrus, reeds, and lotus, across which the river worked its sluggish and uncertain way; upon both banks the desert swallowed up all the soil left untouched by the yearly inundations. From the crowding vegetation of a tropical marsh to the most absolute aridity was but a step. Little by little the new comers learnt to control the course of the floods, to bank them in and to carry them to the farthest corners of the valley, and Egypt gradually arose out of the waters and became in the hand of man one of the best adapted countries in the world for the development of a great civilization.[53]

How many generations did it require to create the country and the nation? We cannot tell. But we may affirm that a commencement was made by the simultaneous establishment at several different points of small independent states, each of which had its own laws and its own form of worship. These districts remained almost unchanged in number and in their respective boundaries almost up to the end of the ancient world. Their union under one sceptre formed the kingdom of the Pharaohs, the country of Khemi, but their primitive divisions did not therefore disappear; the small independent states became provinces and were the foundation of those local administrative districts which the Greeks called *nomes*.

FIG. 8.—**Hunting in the Marshes; from a bas-relief in the tomb of Ti.**

Besides this division into districts, the Egyptians had one other, and only one—the division into Lower Egypt, or the North Country (*Tomera*, or *Tomeh*), and into Upper Egypt, or the South Country (*To-res*). Lower Egypt consisted of the Delta; Upper Egypt stretched from the southernmost point of the Delta to the first cataract. This division has the advantage of corresponding exactly to the configuration of the country; moreover, it preserves the memory of a period before the time of Menes, during which Egypt was divided into two separate kingdoms—that of the North and that of the South, a division which in later times had often a decisive influence upon the course of events. This state of things was of sufficiently long duration to leave an ineffaceable trace upon the official language of Egypt, and upon that which we may call its blazonry, or heraldic imagery. The sovereigns who united the whole territory under one sceptre are always called, in the royal protocols, the lords of Upper and Lower Egypt; they carry on their heads two crowns, each appropriate to one of the two great divisions of their united kingdom. That of Upper Egypt is known to egyptologists as the White crown, because of the colour which it bears upon painted monuments; that of the North is called the red crown, for a similar reason. Combined with one another they form the complete regal head-dress ordinarily called the pschent. In the hieroglyphics Northern Egypt is indicated by the papyrus; Southern by the lotus.

FIG. 9.—Shadouf; machine for irrigating the land above the level of the canals.

During the Ptolemaic epoch a new administrative division into Upper, Middle, and Lower Egypt was established. The Middle Egypt of the Greek geographers began at the southern point of the Delta, and extended to a little south of Hermopolis. Although this latter division was not established until after the centuries which saw the birth of those monuments with which we shall have to deal, we shall make frequent use of it, as it will facilitate and render more definite our topographical explanations. For the contemporaries of the Pharaohs both Memphis and Thebes belong to Upper Egypt, and if we adopted their method of speech we should be under the continual necessity of stopping the narration to define geographical positions; but with the tri-partite division we may speak of Beni-Hassan as in Middle, and Abydos as in Upper Egypt, and thus give a sufficient idea of their relative positions.

FIG. 10.—The White Crown.   Fig. 11.—The Red Crown.   Fig. 12.—The Pschent.

§ 3. *The Great Divisions of Egyptian History.*

In enumerating and analysing the remains of Egyptian art, we shall classify them chronologically as well as locally. The monuments of the plastic arts will be arranged into groups determined by the periods of their occurrence, as well as by their geographical distribution. We must refer our readers to the works of M. Maspero and others for the lists of kings and dynasties, and for the chief events of each reign, but it will be convenient for us to give here a summary of the principal epochs in Egyptian history. Each of those epochs corresponds to an artistic period with a special character and individuality of its own. The following paragraphs taken from the history of M. Maspero give all the necessary information in a brief form.

"In the last years of the prehistoric period, the sacerdotal class had obtained a supremacy over the other classes of the nation. A man called Menes (Menha or Ména in the Egyptian texts) destroyed this supremacy and founded the Egyptian monarchy.

"This monarchy existed for at least four thousand years, under thirty consecutive dynasties, from the reign of Menes to that of Nectanebo (340 years before our era). This interval of time, the longest of which political history takes note, is usually divided into three parts: the *Ancient Empire*, from the first to the eleventh dynasty; the *Middle Empire*, from the eleventh dynasty to the invasion of the Hyksos or Shepherds; the *New Empire* from the shepherd kings to the Persian conquest. This division is inconvenient in one respect; it takes too little account of the sequence of historical events.

"There were indeed, three great revolutions in the historical development of Egypt. At the beginning of its long succession of human dynasties (the Egyptians, like other peoples, placed a number of dynasties of divine rulers before their first human king) the political centre of the country was at Memphis; Memphis was the capital and the burying-place of the kings; Memphis imposed sovereigns upon the rest of the country and was the chief market for Egyptian commerce and industry. With the commencement of the sixth dynasty, the centre of gravity began to shift southwards. During the ninth and tenth dynasties it rested at Heracleopolis, in Middle Egypt, and in the time of the eleventh dynasty, it fixed itself at Thebes. From that period onwards Thebes was the capital of the country and furnished the sovereign. From the eleventh to the twenty-first all the Egyptian dynasties were Theban with the single exception of the fourteenth Xoite dynasty. At the time of the shepherd invasion, the Thebaïd became the citadel of Egyptian nationality, and its princes, after centuries of war against the intruders, finally succeeded in freeing the whole valley of the Nile for the benefit of the eighteenth dynasty, which opened the era of great foreign wars.

"Under the nineteenth dynasty an inverse movement to that of the first period carried the political centre of the country back towards the north. With the twenty-first Tanite dynasty, Thebes ceased to be the capital, and the cities of the Delta, Tanis, Bubastis, Mendes, Sebennytos, and above all Sais, rose into equal or superior importance. From that time the political life of the country concentrated itself in the maritime districts. The *nomes* of the Thebaïd, ruined by the Ethiopian and Assyrian invasions, lost their influence; and Thebes itself fell into ruin and became nothing more than a *rendezvous* for curious travellers.

"I propose, therefore, to divide Egyptian history into three periods, each corresponding to the political supremacy of one town or province over the whole of Egypt:—

"First Period, Memphite (the first ten dynasties). The supremacy of Memphis and of the sovereigns furnished by her.

"Second Period, Theban (from the eleventh to the twentieth dynasties inclusive). Supremacy of Thebes and the Theban kings. This period is divided into two sub-periods by the Shepherd dynasties.

"*a. The old Theban empire*, from the eleventh to the sixteenth dynasties.

"*b. The new Theban empire*, from the sixteenth to the twentieth dynasties.

"Third Period, Sait (from the twenty-first to the thirtieth dynasties, inclusive). Supremacy of Sais and the other cities of the Delta. This period is divided into two by the Persian invasion:—

"*First Sait period*, from the twenty-first to the twenty-sixth dynasties.

"*Second Sait period*, from the twenty-seventh to the thirtieth dynasties."[54]

Mariette places the accession of Ména or Menes at about the fiftieth century before our era, while Bunsen and other Egyptologists bring forward his date to 3,600 or 3,500 B.C. as they believe some of the dynasties of Manetho to have been contemporary with each other. Neither Mariette nor Maspero deny that Egypt, in the course of its long existence, was often partitioned between princes who reigned in Upper and Lower Egypt respectively; but, guided by circumstances which need not be described here, they incline to believe that Manetho confined himself to enumerating those dynasties which were looked upon as the legitimate ones. The work of elimination which has been attempted by certain modern *savants*, must have been undertaken, to a certain extent, in Egypt itself; and some of the collateral dynasties must have been effaced and passed over in silence, because the monuments still remaining preserve the names of reigning families which are ignored by history.

Whatever may be thought of this initial date, Egypt remains, as has been so well said by M. Renan, "a lighthouse in the profound darkness of remote antiquity." Its period of greatest power was long anterior to the earliest traditions of the Greek race; the reign of Thothmes III., who, according to a contemporary expression, "drew his frontiers where he pleased," is placed by common consent in the seventeenth century, B.C. The Egyptian empire then comprised Abyssinia, the Soudan, Nubia, Syria, Mesopotamia, part of Arabia, Khurdistan, and Armenia. Founded by the kings of the eighteenth dynasty, this greatness was maintained by those of the nineteenth. To this dynasty belonged Rameses II., the Sesostris of the Greeks, who flourished in the fifteenth century. It was the superiority of its civilization, even more than the valour of its princes and soldiers, which made Egypt supreme over Western Asia.

This supremacy declined during the twenty-first and twenty-second dynasties, but, at the same time, Egyptian chronology becomes more certain as opportunities of comparison with the facts of Hebrew history increase. The date of 980, within a year or two, may be given with confidence as that of the accession of Sheshonk I., the contemporary of Solomon and Rehoboam. From that date onwards, the constant struggles between Egypt and its neighbours, especially with Assyria, multiply our opportunities for synchronic comparison. In the seventh century the country was opened to the Greeks, the real creators of history, who brought with them their inquiring spirit and their love for exactitude. After the accession of Psemethek I., the founder of the twenty-sixth dynasty, in 656, our historical materials are abundant. For that we must thank the Greek travellers who penetrated everywhere, taking notes which they afterwards amplified into narratives. It is a singular thing, that even as late as the Ptolemies, when the power of the Macedonian monarchy was fully developed, the Egyptians never seem to have felt the want of what we call an *era*, of some definite point from which they could measure the course of time and the progress of the centuries. "They were satisfied with calculating by the years of the reigning sovereign, and even those calculations had no certain point of departure. Sometimes they counted from the commencement of the year which had witnessed the death of his predecessor, sometimes from the day of his own coronation. The most careful calculations will therefore fail to enable modern science to restore to the Egyptians that which, in fact, they never possessed."[55]

Even thus summarily stated, these historical indications are enough to show how little foundation there is for the opinion which was held by the ancient Greeks, and too long accepted by modern historians. It was, they said, from Ethiopia that Egyptian civilization had come. A colony of Ethiopian priests from the island of Meroë in Upper Nubia, had introduced their religion, their written characters, their art and their civil institutions into the country. The exact opposite of this is the truth. "It was the Egyptians who advanced up the banks of the Nile to found cities, fortresses, and temples in Ethiopia; it was the Egyptians who carried their civilization into the midst of savage negro tribes. The error was caused by the fact that at one epoch in the history of Egypt the Ethiopians played an important part.

"If it were true that Egypt owed its political existence to Ethiopia, we should be able to find in the latter country monuments of a more remote antiquity, and as we descended the Nile, we should find the remains comparatively modern; but, strangely enough, the study of all these monuments incontestably proves that the sequence of towns, holy places, and tombs, constructed by the Egyptians on the banks of their river, follow each other in such chronological order that the oldest remains, the Pyramids, are found in the north, in Lower Egypt, near the southern point of the Delta. The nearer our steps take us to the cataracts of Ethiopia, the less ancient do the monuments become. They show ever increasing signs of the decadence of art, of taste, and of the love for beauty. Finally, the art of Ethiopia, such as its still existing monuments reveal it to us, is entirely wanting in originality. A glance is sufficient to tell us that it represents the degeneracy only of the Egyptian style, that the spirit of Egyptian forms has been weakly grasped, and that their execution is generally mediocre."[56]

We may condense all these views into a simple and easily remembered formula; we may say that *as we mount towards the springs of the Nile, we descend the current of time*. Thebes is younger than Memphis, and Meroë than Thebes. The river which Egypt worshipped, and by which the walls of its cities were bathed, flowed from the centre of Africa, from the south to the north; but the stream of civilization flowed in the other direction, until it was lost in the country of the negro, in the mysterious depths of Ethiopia. The springs of this latter stream must be sought in that district where the waters of the Nile, as if tired by their long journey, divide into several arms before falling into the sea; in that district near the modern capital, over which stretch the long shadows of the Pyramids.

§ 4. *The Constitution of Egyptian Society—Influence of that Constitution upon Monuments of Art.*

During the long sequence of centuries which we have divided into three great periods, the national centre of gravity was more than once displaced. The capital was at one time in Middle Egypt, at another in Upper, and at a third period in Lower Egypt, in accordance with its political necessities. At one period the nation had nothing to fear from external enemies, at others it had to turn a bold front to Asia or Ethiopia. At various times Egypt had to submit to her foreign foes; to the shepherd invaders, to the kings of Assyria and Persia, to the princes of Ethiopia, and finally to Alexander, to whom she lost her independence never again to recover it. And yet it appears that the character and social condition of the race never underwent any great change. At the time of the pyramid-builders, Egypt was the most absolute monarchy that ever existed, and so she remained till her final conquest.

"Successor and descendant of the deities who once reigned over the valley of the Nile, the king was the living manifestation and incarnation of God: child of the sun (*Se Râ*), as he took care to proclaim whenever he wrote his name, the blood of the gods flowed in his veins and assured to him the sovereign power."[57] He was *the priest* above all others. Such a form of worship as that of Egypt, required no doubt a large sacerdotal class, each member of which had his own special function in the complicated and gorgeous ceremonies in which he took part; but the king alone, at least in the principal temples, had the right to enter the sanctuary and to open the door of the kind of chapel in which the symbolical representation of the divinity was kept; he alone saw the god face to face, and spoke to him in the name of his people.[58] The pre-eminent dignity of this priestly office did not, however, prevent the king from taking his proper share in war or political affairs generally. The army of scribes and various functionaries, whose titles may still be read upon the most ancient monuments of the country, depended upon him for their orders from one end of the country to the other, and in war, it was he who led the serried battalions of the Egyptian army. The king was thus a supreme pontif, the immediate chief of all civil and military officers; and, as the people believed that his career was directed by the gods with whom he held converse, he became to them a visible deity and, in the words of an inscription, "the representative of Râ among the living." His divinity, begun on earth, was completed and rendered perpetual in another life. All the dead Pharaohs became gods, so that the Egyptian pantheon obtained a new deity at the death of each sovereign. The deceased Pharaohs thus constituted a series of gods to whom the reigning sovereign would of course address himself when he had anything to ask; hence the monuments upon which we find living Pharaohs offering worship to their predecessors.[59]

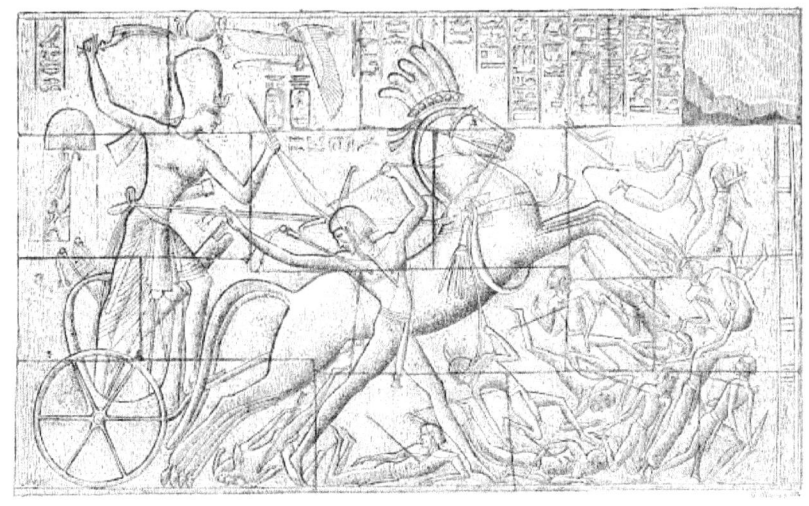

FIG. 13.—Seti I. in his War-Chariot, bas-relief at Thebes. (Champollion, pl. 297.)

FIG. 14.—Rameses II.
in adoration before Seti.
From Abydos (Mariette).

The prestige which such a theory of royalty was calculated to give to the Egyptian kings may easily be imagined. They obtained more than respect; they were the objects of adoration, of idolatry. Brought up from infancy in this religious veneration, to which their hereditary qualities also inclined them, generation succeeded generation among the Egyptians, without any attempt to rebel against the royal authority or even to dispute it. Ancient Egypt, like its modern descendant, was now and then the scene of military revolts. These were generally provoked by the presence of foreign mercenaries, sometimes by their want of discipline and licence, sometimes by the jealousy which they inspired in the native soldiery; but never, from the time of Menes to that of Tewfik-Pacha, has the civil population, whether of the town or of the fields, shown any desire to obtain the slightest guarantee for what we should call their rights and liberties. During all those thousands of years not the faintest trace is to be discovered of that spirit from which sprung the republican constitutions of Greece and ancient Italy, a spirit which, in yet later times, has led to the parliamentary governments of Christian Europe. The Egyptian labourer or artisan never dreamt of calling in question the orders of any one who might be master for the time. Absolute obedience to the will of a single man—such was the constant and instinctive national habit, and by it every movement of the social machine, under foreign and native kings alike, was regulated.

From the construction of the pyramids of Cheops and Chephren, and the cutting of a new canal between the two seas under Nekau, to the Mahmoudieh canal of Mehemet-Ali and that abortive enterprise, the barrage of the Nile, the only method thought of for obtaining the necessary labour was compulsion.[60] An order is received by the governor, who has it proclaimed from one village to another throughout his province; next day the whole male population is driven, like a troop of sheep, to the workshops. Each man carries a bag or basket which holds his provisions for a fortnight or a month, as the case may be; a few dry cakes, onions, garlic, and *Egyptian beans*, as the Greeks called the species of almond which is contained in the fruit of the lotus. Old men and children, all had to obey the summons. The more vigorous and skilful among them dressed and put in place the blocks of granite or limestone; the weakest were useful for the transport of the rubbish to a distance, for carrying clay and water from the Nile to the brickmakers, for arranging the bricks in the sun so that they might be dried and hardened.

FIG. 15.—Homage to Amenophis III. (From Prisse.[61])

Under the stimulus of the rod, this multitude worked well and obediently under the directions of the architect's foreman and of skilled artisans who were permanently employed upon the work; they did all that could be done by men without special education. At the end of a certain period they were relieved by fresh levies from another province, and all who had not succumbed to the hard and continuous work, returned to their own places. Those who died were buried in hasty graves dug in the sands of the desert by the natives of their own village.

The massive grandeur of some of the Egyptian monuments is only to be explained by this levy *en masse* of every available pair of hands. The kings of the ancient empire, at least, were unable to dispose of those prisoners of war captured in myriads, in whole races, by the Assyrian kings, and apparently employed by them in the construction of Nineveh. Now, it is impossible that such works as the Pyramids could have been begun and finished in the course of a single reign by free and remunerated labour, even if it had the help of numerous slaves. Certain arrangements in their design and the marvellously exact execution of the more important details of the masonry, prove that architects of great ability and skilful workmen were, indeed, employed upon those gigantic works; but the great bulk of the task must have required the collective effort of a whole population; of a population devoting themselves night and day to complete the work when once begun, like ants over their subterranean city or bees over their comb.

FIG. 16.—Construction of a Temple at Thebes. (From Prisse.)

Even supposing that history had been silent upon this subject, the architect could easily divine, from these monuments themselves, how they had been constructed. Cast your eyes upon the ruins of the Athenian Acropolis; their dimensions will seem to you small in the extreme if you compare them with the buildings of Egypt and Assyria; on the other hand their workmanship is equally careful throughout; it is as exact and perfect in the concealed parts of the structure as in those which were to be visible, in the structural details as in the ornamental painting and sculpture. By these signs you may recognize at once, that, from its foundation to its completion, the whole work was in the hands of artisans whom long practice had made perfect in their trade, and that each single individual among them had made it a point of honour to acquit himself worthily of the task entrusted to him. In the gangs of docile labourers who succeeded each other in the workshops of Memphis or Thebes, there was, of course, a certain sprinkling of men who had become qualified by experience for the special work upon which they were employed; but the great majority were men suddenly taken from very different occupations, from the oar, the plough, the management of cattle; who therefore could have nothing but their unskilled labour to bestow. To such men as these a great part of the work had perforce to be confided, in order that it might be complete at the required time. In spite of the strictest supervision, the almost religious care in the placing and fixing of masonry, which might be fairly expected from the practised members of a trade guild, could not be ensured. Hence the singular inequalities and inconsistences which have been noticed in most of the great Egyptian buildings; sometimes it is the foundations which are in fault, and, by their sinking, have compromised the safety of the whole building;[62] sometimes it is the built up columns of masonry, which, when deprived by time of their coating of stucco, appear very poor and mean. The infinite foresight and self-respect, the passionate love for perfection for its own sake, which is characteristic of Greek work at its best time, is not here to be found. But this defect was inseparable from the system under which the Egyptian buildings were erected.

FIG. 17.—Columns in the Hypostyle Hall, Karnak.

FIG. 18, 19—Scribes registering the yield of the harvest. From a tomb at Sakkarah. (Boulak, 9-1/2 inches high. Drawn by Bourgoin.)

FIG. 20.—Colossi of Amenophis III. (statues of Memnon) at Thebes.

The absolute and dreaded master whose gesture, whose single word, was sufficient to depopulate a province and to fill quarries and workshops with thousands of men, the sovereign who, in spite of his mortality, was looked up to by his people as one so near akin to the gods as to be hardly distinguishable from them, the high priest and father of his people, the king before whom all heads were bent to the earth; filled with his own glory and majesty the buildings which he caused to spring, as if by magic, from the earth. His effigy was everywhere. Seated in the form of colossal statues in front of the temples, in bas-reliefs upon pylons, upon the walls of porticos and pillared halls, he was represented sometimes offering homage to the gods, sometimes leading his troops to battle or bringing them home victorious. The supreme efforts of architect and sculptor were directed to constructing for their prince a tomb which should excel all others in magnificence and durability, or to immortalizing him by a statue which should raise its head as much above its rivals as the royal power surpassed the power and dignity of ordinary men. The art of Egypt was, in this sense, a monarchical art; and in so being it was the direct expression of the sentiments and ideas of the society which had to create it from its foundations.

FIG. 21.—Scribe registering merchandize. Sakkarah. (9-1/2 inches high. Drawn by Bourgoin.)

After the king came the priests, the soldiers, and the scribes or royal functionaries, each receiving authority directly from the king and superintending the execution of his orders. These three groups formed what we may call the upper class of Egyptian society. The soil was entirely in their hands. They possessed among them the whole valley of the Nile, with the exception of the royal domain. The agriculturists were mere serfs attached to the soil. They cultivated, for a payment in kind, the lands belonging to the privileged classes. They changed masters with the lands upon which they lived, which they were not allowed to quit without the permission of the local authorities.

Their position did not greatly differ from that of the modern fellahs, who cultivate the Egyptian soil for the benefit of the effendis, beys, and pachas or for that of the sovereign, who is still the greatest landowner in the country.

Fig. 22.—Boatmen. Tomb of Ra-ka-pou, 5th dynasty. (Boulak, 16 inches high. Drawn by Bourgoin.)

The shepherds, the fishermen and boatmen of the Nile, the artisans and shopkeepers of the cities were in a similar condition. They lived upon their gains in the same way as the peasant upon the share of the harvest which custom reserved for his use. As a natural consequence of their life in a city and of the character of their occupations, small traders and artisans enjoyed more liberty and independence, more power of coming and going than the agriculturists, although legal rights were the same in both cases. The burden of forced labour must have pressed less heavily upon the latter class, and they must have had better opportunities of escaping from it altogether.

In consequence of a mistaken interpretation of historic evidence, it was long believed that the Egyptians had castes, like the Hindoos. This notion has been dispelled by more careful study of their remains. The vigorous separation of classes according to their social functions, the enforced heredity of professions, and the prohibition of intermarriage between the different groups, never obtained a footing in Egypt. We often find, in Egyptian writings, two members of a single family attached one to the civil service and the other to the army, or the daughter of a general marrying the son of a priest. Nay, it often happens that the offices of soldier and priest, of priest and civil servant, or of civil servant and soldier, are united in the person of a single individual. In families which did not belong to these aristocratic classes there was, in all probability, more heredity of occupation; in the ordinary course the paternal employment fixed that of the children, but yet there was nothing approaching to an absolute rule. The various trades were formed into corporations or guilds, rather than castes in the strict sense of the word. From this it resulted that great natural talents, fortunate circumstances, or the favour of the sovereign could raise a man of the lowest class up to the highest dignities of the state. In the latter days of the monarchy we have an example of this in the case of Amasis, who, born among the dregs of the population, finally raised himself to the throne.[63] Such events were of frequent occurrence in all those oriental monarchies where the will of the sovereign was the supreme and undisputed law. Even in our own days, similar things have taken place in Turkey and Persia to the surprise of none but Europeans. When the master of all is placed so high above his fellow men that his subjects seem mere human dust about his feet, his caprice is quite sufficient to raise the most insignificant of its atoms to a level with the most illustrious.

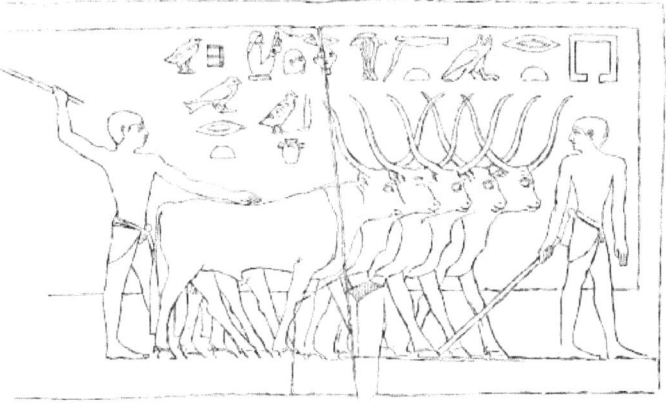

FIG. 23.—Cattle Drovers. From the tomb of Ra-ka-pou, Sakkarah, 5th dynasty. (Boulak. Drawn by Bourgoin.)

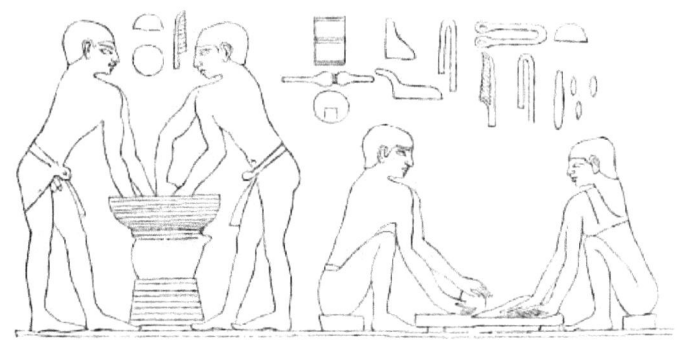

FIG. 24.—Bakers. From a tomb. (Boulak, 9-1/2 inches high. Bourgoin.)

FIG. 25.—Women at a loom. From a tomb at Beni-Hassan. (Champollion, 381 bis)

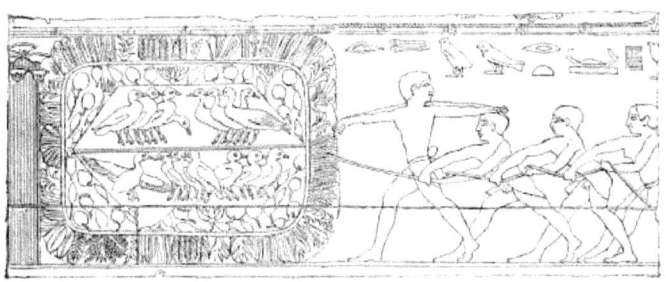

FIG. 26.—Netting birds. From a tomb. (Boulak. Drawn by Bourgoin.)

The priests of the highest rank, the generals and officers of the army and the great civil functionaries, while they made no effort to rival the splendour of the royal creations, consecrated steles, images of the deity, and chapels, at their own expense. It was upon their tombs, however, that most of their care was lavished. These tombs furnish numberless themes of great interest to the historian. The tombs of the Memphite kings have not preserved for us anything that can fairly be called sculpture. All that we know of the style and methods of that art in those early times we owe to the burial-places which the members of the governing classes were in the habit of preparing during their lifetime in the necropolis of Memphis. We may say the same of the early centuries of the Middle Empire. The Egypt of the great kings belonging to the twelfth dynasty has been preserved for us upon the tombs of Ameni and Num-Hotep, the governors of the *nomes* in which they were buried. It is to the burial chambers at Gizeh, at Sakkarah, at Meidoum, and at Beni-Hassan that we must go for complete types of sepulchral architecture at those epochs; to the statues in the recesses of their massive walls and to the bas-reliefs in their narrow chambers, we must turn for those features of early Egyptian civilization which remained for many centuries without material change; by these monuments we are enabled to build up piece by piece a trustworthy representation of the Egyptian people both in their labours and in their pleasures. Finally it is from these tombs of private individuals that the best works of Egyptian artists have been obtained, the works in which they approached most nearly to the ideal which they pursued for so many centuries.

FIG. 27.—Shepherds in the fields. From a tomb at Sakkarah. (Boulak. 8-3/4 inches high. Drawn by Bourgoin.)

FIG. 28.—Winnowing corn. From a tomb at Sakkarah. (Boulak. Drawn by Bourgoin.)

Thanks to these monuments erected at the expense of the great lords and rich burghers of Egypt, thanks also to the climate and to the desert sand which has preserved them without material injury, the art of Egypt appears to us more comprehensive and varied than that of any other nation of which we shall have to treat; than that of Assyria for instance, which represents little but scenes of battle and conquest. A faithful mirror of Egyptian society, it has preserved for us an exhaustive record of the never-ceasing activity which created and preserved the wealth of the country; it has not even neglected the games and various pleasures in which the laborious Egyptian sought for his well earned repose. The king indeed, preserved his first place by the importance of the religious buildings which he raised, by the size of his tomb, and by the number and dimensions of the reproductions of his features; reproductions which show him in the various aspects demanded by the complex nature of the civilization over which he presided. But in the large number of isolated figures, groups, and scenes which have come down to us, we have illustrations of all classes that helped in the work of national development, from the ploughman with his ox, to the scribe crouching, cross-legged, upon his mat, from the shepherd with his flock or the hunter pushing his shallop through the brakes of papyrus, to the directors of the great public works and the princes of the blood who governed conquered provinces or guarded the frontiers of the country at the head of ever faithful armies.

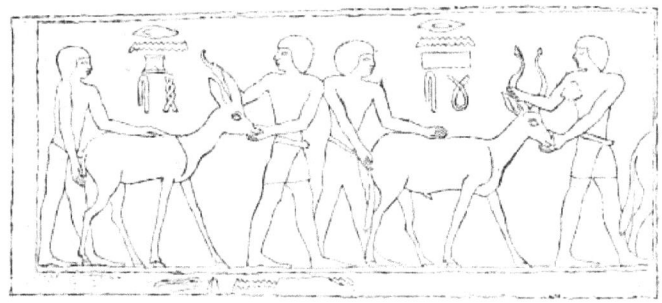

Height 12¾ inches.

Height 6¼ inches.

FIG. 29.—Herdsman. From a tomb at Sakkarah, 5th dynasty. (Boulak.)

The art of Egypt resembled that of Greece in being a complete and catholic art, seeing everything and taking an interest in everything. It was sensitive to military glory, and at the same time it did not scorn to portray the peaceful life of the fields. It set itself with all sincerity to interpret the monarchical sentiment in its most enthusiastic and exaggerated form, but while it placed kings and princes above and almost apart from humanity, it did not forget the "humble and meek," on the contrary, it frankly depicted them in their professional attitudes, with all those ineffaceable characteristics, both of face and figure which the practice of some special trade so certainly imparts. Looked at from this point of view Egyptian art was popular, it might even be called democratic, but that such a phrase would sound curious when used in connection with the most absolute monarchy which the world has ever seen.

This absolute power, however, does not seem, speaking generally, to have been put in force in a hard or oppressive manner either by the king himself or by his agents. M. Maspero and others who, like him, live in intimate communion with the ancient Egyptians, declare that they were by no means unhappy. They tell us that the confidences whispered to them in the pictured tomb-houses of Sakkarah and Memphis complain of no misery, from the time of Mena to that of Psemethek, except during a few violent reigns and a few moments of national crisis. The country suffered only on those comparatively rare occasions when the sceptre passed into the hands of an incapable master or into those of some insatiable warrior who thought only of satisfying his own ambition, and sacrificed to the day the resources of the future. Egypt, with her river, her teeming soil and her splendid climate, found life easy as long as she enjoyed an easy and capable administration. She then gave to her princes almost without an effort all they could desire or demand.

It was one of the fundamental principles of Egyptian morality that those who were powerful should treat the poor and feeble with kindness and consideration. Their sepulchral inscriptions tell us that their kings and princes of the blood, their feudal lords and functionaries of every grade, made it a point of honour to observe this rule. They were not content with strict justice, they practised a bountiful charity which reminds us of that which is the chief beauty of the Christian's morality. The "Book of the Dead"—that passport for Egyptians into the other world which is found upon every mummy—gives us the most simple, and at the same time the most complete description of this virtue. "I have given bread to the hungry, I have given water to the thirsty, I have clothed the naked ... I have not calumniated the slave in the ears of his master." The lengthy panegyrics of which some epitaphs consist, are, in reality no more than amplifications of this theme. "As for me, I have been the staff of the old man, the nurse of the infant, the help of the distressed, a warm shelter for all who were cold in the Thebaïd, the bread and sustenance of the down-trodden, of whom there is no lack in Middle Egypt, and their protector against the barbarians."[64] The prince Entef relates that he has "arrested the arm of the violent, used brute force to those who used brute force, showed hauteur to the haughty, and lowered the shoulders of those who raised them up," that he himself on the other hand, "was a man in a thousand, wise, learned, and of a sound and truthful judgment, knowing the fool from the wise man, paying attention to the skilful and turning his back upon the ignorant, ... the father of the miserable and the mother of the motherless, the terror of the cruel, the protector of the disinherited, the defender of those whose goods were coveted by men stronger than themselves, the husband of the widow, the asylum of the orphan."[65]

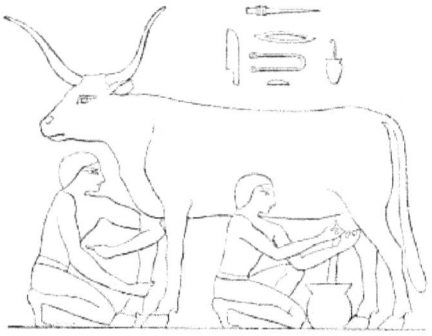

FIG. 30.—From the tomb of Menofre, at Sakkarah. (Champollion, pl. 408.)

Amoni, hereditary prince of the nome of Meh, talks in the same fashion. "I have caused sorrow to no youth under age, I have despoiled no widow, nor have I repelled any labourer, I have imprisoned no shepherd, I have never taken for the labour gangs the serfs of him who had but five, there have been no paupers, nor has any man or woman starved in my time; for, although there have been years of scarcity, I have caused all the tillable land in Meh to be tilled, from the northern frontier to that of the south, and have made such arrangements and such provision for the people that there has been no famine among them; I have given to the widow and to the married woman alike, and I have never made any distinction between the great and the small in my gifts."[66]

Doubtless these laudatory self-descriptions may be exaggerated in some respects; hyperbole has ever been a favourite figure with the composers of epitaphs, and those of Egypt formed no exception to the rule. As M. Maspero remarks in connection with this question, "The man as he is, often differs very greatly from the man as he thinks he is." But we may safely say that the Egyptian realized some portion of the ideal which he set before himself. If only to obtain admiration and esteem, he would practice, to a certain extent, the virtues of which he boasted. Many signs combine to tell us that the Egyptians of all classes possessed a large fund of tenderness and good-will. The master was often both clement and charitable; the peasant, the servant, and the slave, were patient and cheerful, and that in spite of the fatigue of labours which could never enrich them. In a country so favoured by nature, men had so few wants that they had no experience of all that is implied by that doleful word poverty, with us. The pure skies and brilliant sunshine, the deep draughts of Nile water, and the moments of repose under the shadows of the sycamores, the freshness of the evening bath, the starry night with its reinvigorating breezes, were all enjoyments which the poorest could share.

We need feel no surprise therefore at the vivacity with which one of the most learned of the historians of Egypt, Brugsch-Bey, protests against the common misconception of the Egyptians "as a race grave, serious, morose, exclusive, religious, thinking much of the next world, and little of this; living, in a word, like the Trappists of former days. Are we to believe," he cries, "that this majestic river and the fertile soil through which it flows, this azure sky with its unclouded sun, produced a nation of living mummies, a race of solemn philosophers who looked upon life in this world as a burden to be shuffled off as quickly as possible? Travel over Egypt; examine the scenes painted and sculptured upon the walls of sepulchral chambers; read the inscriptions carved upon stone or traced in ink upon the rolls of papyrus, and you will find yourself compelled to modify the false notions you have imbibed as to the Egyptian philosophers. Nothing could be more cheerful, more amusing or more frank, than the social life of this pleasure-loving people. Far from wishing to die, they prayed to the gods for a long life and a happy old age; they prayed that, 'if possible, they might live to the perfect age of one hundred and ten.' They were addicted to all kinds of pleasures. They drank, they sang, they danced, they were fond of excursions into the country, where the sports of hunting and fishing were specially reserved for the upper class. As a natural effect of this desire for enjoyment, gay conversation and pleasantry which was sometimes rather free, jokes and what we should call chaff, were much in vogue: even their tombs were not sacred from their desire for a jest."[67]

The worst government, the sternest oppression, could never extinguish this natural gaiety; it was too intimately connected with the climate and the natural conditions of the country, conditions which had never changed since the days of Menes. Never were the Egyptians more roughly treated than under Mehemet Ali and the late viceroy; their condition was compared, with justice, to that of the negroes in Carolina and Virginia, who, before the American civil war, laboured under the whips of their drivers, and enjoyed no more of the fruits of their own labour than what was barely sufficient to keep life in their bodies. Torn from their homes and kept by force in the public works, the fellahs died in thousands; those who remained in the fields had to pay the taxes one or two years in advance; they were never out of debt, nominally, to the public treasury, and the rattan of the collector extorted from them such savings as they might make during years of plenty, up to the last coin. But still laughter did not cease in Egypt! Look, for instance, at the children in the streets of Cairo who let out mounts to sight-seeing Europeans. Let the tourist trot or gallop as he will, when he stops he finds his donkey-boy by his side, full of spirits and good humour; and yet perhaps while running behind his "fare" he has been making his midday meal upon a few grains of maize tied up in a corner of his shirt.

FIG. 31.—Water Tournament, from a tomb at Khoum-el-Ahmar. (From Prisse.)

In 1862 I returned from Asia Minor in company with M. Edmond Guillaume, the architect, and M. Jules Delbet, the doctor, of our expedition to Ancyra. We took the longest way home, by Syria and Egypt. At Cairo, Mariette, after having shown us the museum at Boulak, wished to introduce us to his own "Serapeum." He took us for a night to his house in the desert, and showed us the galleries of the tomb of Apis by torchlight. We passed the next afternoon in inspecting those excavations in the necropolis of Sakkarah which have led to the recovery of so many wonders of Egyptian art. The works were carried on by the labour of four hundred children and youths, summoned by the *corvée* for fifteen days at a time from some district, I forget which, of Middle Egypt. At sunset these young labourers quitted their work and seated themselves in groups, according to their native villages, upon the still warm sand. Each drew from a little sack, containing his provision for two or three weeks, a dry cake; those whose parents were comfortably off had also, perhaps, a leek or a raw onion. But even for such *gourmands* as those, the repast was not a long one. Supper over, they chattered for a time, and then went to rest; the bigger and stronger among them took possession of some abandoned caves, the others stretched themselves upon the bare earth; but, before going to sleep they sang; they formed themselves into two choirs who alternated and answered one another, and this they kept up to an advanced hour of the night.

FIG. 32.—Mariette's House.

I shall never forget the charm of that night in the desert, nor the weird aspect of the moonlight upon the sea of sand. Were it not that no star was reflected upon its surface, and that no ray scintillated as it does even on the calmest sea, we might have thought ourselves in mid ocean. Sleep came to me reluctantly. While I listened to the alternate rise and fall of the chorus outside, I reflected upon how little those children required; upon the slender wants of their fathers and mothers, who, like them, sink into their nightly sleep with a song upon their lips. I compared this easy happiness with the restless and complicated existence which we should find, at the end of a few days, in the ambitious cities of the West, and I regretted that our year of travel, our twelve months of unrestrained life in the desert or the forest, had come to an end.

§ 5. *The Egyptian Religion and its Influence upon the Plastic Arts.*

We have still to notice the profoundly religious character of Egyptian art. "The first thing that excites our surprise, when we examine the reproductions of Egyptian monuments which have been published in our day, is the extraordinary number of scenes of sacrifice and worship which have come down to us. In the collection of plates which we owe to contemporary archæologists, we can hardly find one which does not contain the figure of some deity, receiving with impassive countenance the prayers or offerings of a prostrate king or priest. One would say that a country with so many sacred pictures and sculptures, must have been inhabited by gods, and by just enough men for the service of their temples.[68] The Egyptians were a devout people. Either by natural tendency or by force of education, they saw God pervading the whole of their universe; they lived in Him and for Him. Their imaginations were full of His greatness, their words of His praise, and their literature was in great part inspired by gratitude for the benefits which He showered upon them. Most of their manuscripts which have come down to us treat of religious matters, and even in those which are ostensibly concerned only with profane subjects, mythological names and allusions occur on every page, almost at every line."[69]

An examination into the primitive religious beliefs of the Egyptians is full of difficulty. In discovering new papyri, in determining the signification of signs which have been puzzling egyptologists, the inquirer will undoubtedly do good work, and will establish facts which are sure not to lack interest and even importance; but even when documents abound and when every separate word they contain is understood, even then it is very difficult to penetrate to the root of their meaning. A glimpse will be caught of it, I admit, by one of those efforts of inductive divination which distinguish modern research; but even then it will remain to explain the primitive and only half-understood notions of five or six thousand years ago in the philosophical vocabularies of to-day. It is here that the most difficult and irksome part of the task begins. We who represent the old age, or, perhaps, the prime, of humanity, think of these matters and speak of them as abstractions, while the Egyptians, who were children compared to us, thought of them under concrete forms. Their very ideals were material, more or less vague and refined perhaps, but still material. Their only conception of a deity was of a figure larger, more vigorous and more beautiful than mortals; the powers and attributes with which it was endowed were all physical. If we attempt to express their conceptions in abstract terms, we falsify their meaning. We cannot avoid altering it to a certain extent, for exact equivalents are not to be found, and, in spite of all precautions, we give to the confused and childish ideas of ancient religion, a precision which is entirely modern.

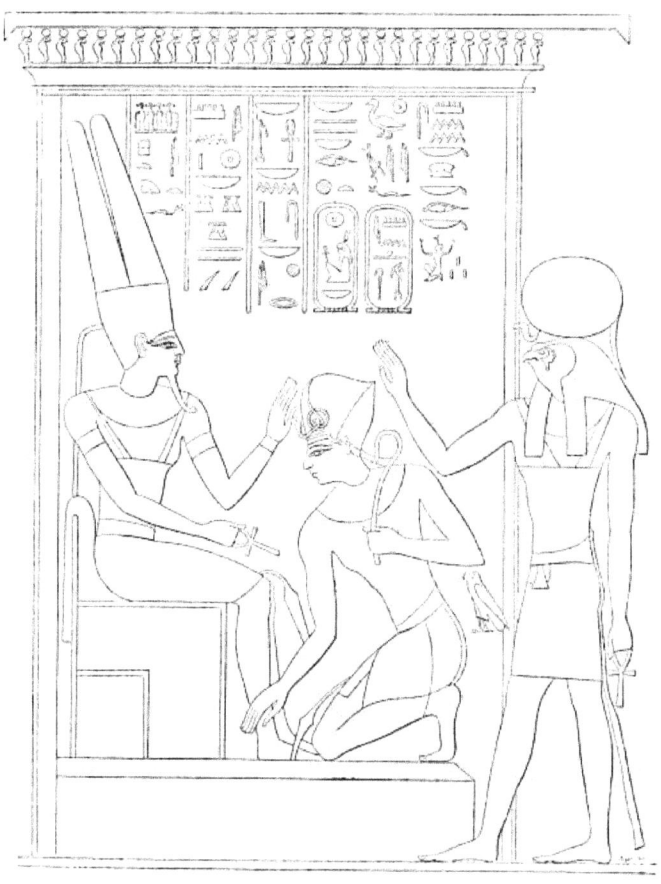

FIG. 33.—Amenhotep or Amenophis III. presented by Phré to Amen-Ra; Thebes. (Champollion, pl. 344.)

If, under these reserves, we study the Egyptian theology in its most learned and refined form—namely, that which it attained during the eighteenth and nineteenth dynasties—we shall dimly perceive that it implies a belief in the unity of the First Cause of all life. But this belief is obscured behind the numerous gods who are, in fact, emanations from its substance and manifestations of its indefatigable activity. It is in the person of these gods that the divine essence takes form. Each of them has his own name, his own figure, and his own special share in the management of the universe; each of them presides over the production of some particular order of phenomena and insures their regularity. These gods are related to each other as fathers, mothers, and sons. They thus form a vast hierarchy of beings, superior to man, and each enjoying a dignity corresponding to his rank in the series. There is, so to speak, most of divinity in those who are nearest to the "one God in heaven or earth who was not begotten." These deities are divided into groups of three, each group constituting a family, like those of earth, consisting of father, mother, and son. Thus from triad to triad, the concealed god develops his sovereign powers to all eternity, or, to use an expression dear to the religious schools of ancient Egypt, "he creates his own members, which are themselves gods."[70]

How should the science of comparative religion class this form of faith? Should it be called polytheism or pantheism? The answer is, perhaps, not of great importance, and this is hardly the place for its discussion. It is certain that, practically, the Egyptians were polytheists. The Egyptian priests, indeed, had, by dint of long reflection, arrived at the comprehension, or at least at the contemplation, of that First Cause which had started the river of life—that inexhaustible stream of which the Nile with its fertilising waves was the concrete image—in its long journey across time and space. But the devotion of the people themselves never succeeded in mounting above the minor divinities, above those intermediaries in whom the divine principle and attributes became personified and put on the tangibility of body necessary to make them intelligible to childish understandings. So, too, was it with artists, and for still more powerful reasons; as by forms only could they express the ideas which they had conceived. Even in those religions which are most clearly and openly monotheistic and spiritual, such as Christianity, art has done something of the same kind. Aided in secret by one of the most powerful instincts of the human soul, it has succeeded, in spite of all resistance and protestation, in giving plastic expression to those parts of our belief which seem least fitted for such treatment; and it has caused those methods of expression to be so accepted by us that we see nothing unnatural in the representation under the features of an old man, of the first Person of the Trinity,—of that Jehovah who, in the Old Testament, proscribed all graven images with such impartial rigour; who, in the Evangel, described Himself as "the Truth and the Life."

In Egypt, both sculptors and painters could multiply their images to infinity without coming into collision with dogma, without provoking the regrets or censures of its most severe interpreters. Doctrine did not condemn these personifications, even when it had been refined and elaborated by the speculative theologians of Thebes and Heliopolis. In the interior of the temples, there was a small class of mystics who took pleasure in contemplating "the 'One' who exists by his own essential power, the only being who substantially exists." Even then men tried, as they have often done since, to define the undefinable, to grasp the incomprehensible, to perceive the supreme "I AM" through the shifting and transparent veil of natural phenomena. But those refined metaphysics never touched and influenced the crowd, and never will. The deity, in order to be perceived by them and to touch their feelings, must have his unity broken; he must, if the expression be admissible, be cut up into morsels for them.

By a process of "abstraction" which is as old as religion itself, the human intelligence is led to consider separately each of the qualities of existence, each of the forces which it perceives to be at work either within man himself or in the exterior world. At first it thinks those forces and qualities are distributed impartially to all creation. It confounds existence with life. Hence the reign of *fetishism*, when man believes, as young children do, that thought, passion, and volition like his own, are to be found in everything he meets. His own image seems to him reflected as in a mirror with a thousand converging facets, and he is unable to distinguish the real condition of things outside it.

Certain celestial and terrestrial bodies make a particularly strong impression upon his mind by their size, their beauty, by their evil or beneficial effects upon himself. They fill him with more than the average gratitude, admiration, or terror. Driven by the illusion which possesses him, he places the origin of those qualities which seem to him the highest and most important, in the bodies which have made so deep an impression upon his senses; to them he attributes the friendly or hostile influences which alternately excite his desire and his fear. According to circumstances a fetish might be a mountain, a rock or a river, a plant or an animal. It might be those heavenly bodies which exercised much more influence over the life of primitive man than they do over us; it might be the moon and stars, which tempered the darkness of the night and diminished its terrors; it might be the cloud, from whose bosom came rain and thunder; above all, it might be the sun which returned every morning to light and warm the world. Differences of climate and race had their modifying effect, but everywhere one common characteristic is to be found. It was always to some material and visible object that the human intellect referred those forces and qualities which it drew from its own consciousness; forces which, when thus united with something tangible, constituted the first types of those divine beings whom mankind have so long adored, to whom they have turned for ages in their hope and fear.

As the years passed away, man advanced beyond his primitive conceptions. He did not entirely renounce them—we may indeed see reminiscences of them all around us—but he superimposed others upon them which were more complex. His powers of observation, still imperfect though they were, began to insinuate into his mind a disbelief in the activity of inanimate matter, and those objects which were nearest to him, which he could touch with his hand, were the first victims of his disenchantment. Thus began a long course of intellectual development, the result of which we know, although the various stages of its progress are difficult to follow at this distance of time. It appears certain, however, that star worship formed the transition between *fetishism* and *polytheism*. Men no longer attributed vital forces and pre-eminent qualities generally to bodies with which they themselves were in immediate contact, to stones and trees; but they found no difficulty in continuing to assign them to those great luminaries whose distance and beauty placed them, so to speak outside the material world. As they gradually deprived inanimate matter of the properties with which they had once gifted it, they sought for new objects to which they might attach those properties. These they found in the stars which shone in the firmament century after century, and knew neither old age nor death; and especially in the most brilliant, the most beneficent, and the most necessary of them all, in that sun whose coming they awaited every morning with an impatience which must once have been mixed with a certain amount of anxiety.

The attributes which awakened intelligence had taken away from the inanimate objects of the world could not be left floating in space. They became gradually and imperceptibly grouped in men's minds around the great luminary of day, and a bond of union was found for the different members of the group by endowing the sun with a personality modelled upon that of man.

This operation was favoured by the constitution of contemporary language, by its idioms made up entirely of those images and metaphors which, by their frank audacity, surprise and charm us in the works of the early poets. It commenced with the first awakening of thought, when man endowed all visible nature with the bounding life which he felt in his own veins. No effort of intelligence was required for its commencement or for its prosecution. The sun became a young hero advancing, full of pride and vigour, upon the path prepared for him by Aurora; a hero who pursued his daily path in spite of all obstacle or hindrance, who, when evening came, went to his rest amid all the glories of an eastern sunset, and amid the confidence of all that after his hours of sleep he would take up his eternal task with renewed vigour. He was an invincible warrior. He was sometimes an angry master, whose glance killed and devoured. He was above all the untiring benefactor of mankind, the nurse and father of all life. Whether as Indra or as Amen-Ra, it was the same cry that went up to him from Egypt and Hindostan; the prayers which we find in the Vedas and in the papyri, breathe the same sentiments and were addressed to the same god.[71]

This solar god and the divinities who resemble him, form the transition from the simple fetish to complete deities, to those gods who played such an important part in the Egyptian religion, and attained to their highest and most complete development in the Hellenic mythology. In some respects, the luminous globe of the sun with its compulsory course, belonged to the same category as the material objects which received the first worship of humanity. But its brilliance, its tranquil and majestic movement, and the distance which conceals its real substance from the eye of man, allowed his imagination to endow it with the purest and noblest characteristics which the finest examples of humanity could show; while the phenomena which depend upon its action are so numerous that there was no hesitation in assigning to it qualities and energies of the most various kinds.

This type when once established was used for the creation of other deities, which were all, so to speak, cast in the same mould. As the intellect became more capable of abstraction and analysis, the personality and moral individuality of these gods gradually threw off its astral or physical characteristics, although it never lost all trace of their existence. It resulted that, both in Egypt and in Greece, there were deities who were mere entities, the simple embodiment of some power, some quality, or some virtue. It requires all the subtle *finesse* of modern criticism to seek out and distinguish the obscure roots which attach these divinities to the naturalistic beliefs of earlier ages. Sometimes absolute certainty is not to be attained, but we may safely say that a race is polytheistic when we find these abstract deities among their gods, such deities as the Ptah, Amen, and Osiris of the Egyptians, and the Apollo and Athenè of the Greeks.[72]

FIG. 34.—Amen or Ammon, from a bronze in the Louvre. Height 22·04 inches.

We may, then, define polytheism as the partition of the highest attributes of life between a limited number of agents. The imagination of man could not give these agents life without at the same time endowing them with essential natural characteristics and with the human form, but, nevertheless, it wished to regard them as stronger, more beautiful and less ephemeral than man. The system had said its last word and was complete, when it had succeeded in embodying in some divine personality each of those forces whose combined energy produces movement in the world or guarantees its duration.

When religious evolution follows its normal course, the work of reflection goes on, and in course of time makes new discoveries. It refers, by efforts of conjecture, all phenomena to a certain number of causes, which it calls gods. It next perceives that these causes, or gods, are of unequal importance, and so it constitutes them into a hierarchy. Still later it begins to comprehend that many of these causes are but different names for one thing, that they form but one force, the application of a single law. Thus by reduction and simplification, by logic and analysis, is it carried on to recognize and proclaim the unity of all cause. And thus monotheism succeeds to polytheism.

FIG. 35.—Ptah,
from a bronze in the Louvre.
Actual size.

In Egypt, religious speculation arrived on the threshold of this doctrine. Its depths were dimly perceived, and it was even taught by the select class of priests who were the philosophers of those days; but the monotheistic conception never penetrated into the minds of the great mass of the people. [73] Moreover, by the very method in which Egyptian mythology described it, it was easily adapted to the national polytheism, or even to fetish worship. The theory of emanations reconciled everything. The different gods were but the different qualities of the eternal substance, the various manifestations of one creative force. These qualities and energies were revealed by being imported into the world of form. They took finite shape and were made comprehensible to the intellect of man by their mysterious birth and generation. It was necessary, if the existence of the gods were to be brought home to mankind, that each of them should have a form and a domicile. Imagination therefore did well in commencing to distinguish and define the gods; artists were piously occupied when they pursued the same course. They gave precision of contour to the forms roughly sketched, and by the established definition which they gave to each divine figure, we might almost say that they created the gods.

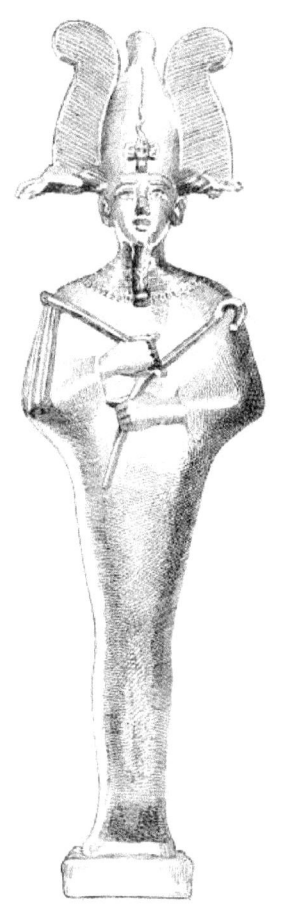

FIG. 36.—Osiris,
from a bronze in the Louvre.
Height 22·8 inches.

Their task was, in one sense, more difficult than that of the Greek artists. When newly born Greek art first began to make representations of Greek deities, the work of intellectual analysis and abstraction had already come to a state of maturity which it never reached in Egypt. The divinities were fewer in number and consequently more fixed and decided in their individual characteristics. The Egyptian polytheism was always more mixed, more strongly tinged with fetishism than that of Greece. Even in those centuries in which the ideas of the Egyptian people were most elevated and refined, the three successive stages, which are always found in the development of religious life, co-existed in the mind of the nation. A few more or less isolated thinkers were already seeking to formulate monotheism. The *élite* of the nation—the king, the priest, and the military class—were adoring Amen and Ptah, Khons or Khonsu, Mouth, Osiris and Horus, Sekhet, Isis, Nephtis and many other divinities; all more or less abstract in their nature, and presiding over special phenomena. As for the lower orders of the people, they knew the names of these deities and associated themselves with the great public honours which were paid to them; but their homage and their faith were more heartily rendered to such concrete and visible gods as the sacred animals, as the bulls Apis and Mnevis, the goat of Mendes, the ibis, the hawk, &c. None of the peculiarities of Egyptian civilization struck Greek travellers with more amazement than this semiworship of animals.[74]

FIG. 37.—The goddess Bast.
(From a bronze in the Louvre.
Actual Size.)

Later theology has succeeded in giving more or less subtle and specious explanations of these forms of worship. Each of these animals has been assigned, as symbol or attribute, to one of the greater deities. As for ourselves we have no doubt that these objects of popular devotion were no more than ancient fetishes. In the long prehistoric centuries, while the Egyptian race was occupied in making good its possession of the Nile valley and bringing it into cultivation, imagination deified these animals, some for the services which they rendered, others for the terror which they inspired; and it was the same with certain vegetables.

We find traces of this phenomenon, which at first seems so inexplicable, among the other races of antiquity, but it is nowhere else so marked as it is in Egypt. When Egypt, after being for three centuries subject to the influence and supremacy of the Greek genius, had lost all but the shadow of its former independence and national life; when all the energy and intellectual activity which remained to it was concentrated at the Greco-Syrian rather than Egyptian Alexandria, the ancient religion of the race lost all its highest branches.[75] The aspirations towards monotheism took a form that was either philosophical and Platonic or Christian; and as for the cultivated spirits who wished to continue the personification of the eternal forces of the world and of the laws which govern them, these laws and forces presented themselves to their minds in the forms which had been figured and described by the sculptors, painters, and writers of Greece. They accepted, without hesitation or dispute, the numbers and physical characteristics of the divine types of Greece. From end to end of the habitable earth, as the Greeks boasted, the gods of the Hellenic pantheon absorbed and assimilated all those of other nationalities; within the boundaries of the Roman Empire, at least, its polytheism became a kind of universal religion for civilized humanity, and was adopted by nations of the most diverse origin and language. The lower classes alone, who read neither Homer nor Hesiod and were unable to admire the statues of the Greek sculptors, were kept free from the powerful and softening influence of poetry and art. They guarded with obstinacy the ancient foundations of their early faith, and in the void left by the disappearance of the national gods, their primitive beliefs seem to have put on a new life and to have enjoyed a restored *prestige*. Thus we may see, in forest clearings, the ancient but still vigorous stumps of great trees which have been felled send out fresh shoots to renew their youth.

This persistence, this apparent recrudescence of fetishism made itself felt in Egypt alone. It amazed and scandalized both pagans and Christians during the early centuries of Christianity. They mocked at a people who "hardly dared to bite a leek or an onion; who adored divinities which grew in their own gardens,"[76] and a god which was nothing but a "beast wallowing on a purple carpet."[77] Guided by a more critical knowledge of the past, we are now better able to understand the origin of these beliefs and the secret of their long duration. We are enabled to account for them by that inexperience which falsifies all the judgments of infancy, in the race as well as in the individual; we see that they are the exaggeration of a natural sentiment, which becomes honourable and worthy of our sympathy when it is addressed to the useful and laborious helpers of man, to domestic animals, for instance, such as the cow and the draught ox.

It would be interesting to know why these beliefs were so curiously tenacious of life in Egypt; perhaps the reason is to be found in the prodigious antiquity of Egyptian civilization. That civilization was the oldest which the world has seen, the least remote from the day of man's first appearance upon the earth. It may therefore be supposed to have received more deeply, and maintained more obstinately, those impressions which characterize the infancy of men as well as of mankind. Add to this, that other races in their efforts to emerge from barbarism, were aided and incited by the example of races which had preceded them on the same road. The inhabitants of the Nile Valley, on the other hand, were alone in the world for many centuries; they had to depend entirely upon their own internal forces for the accomplishment of their emancipation; it is, therefore, hardly surprising that they should have remained longer than their successors in that fetish worship which we have asserted to be the first stage of religious development.[78]

FIG. 38.—**Painted bas-relief.
Boulak. (Drawn by Bourgoin.)**

This stage must never be forgotten, if we wish to understand the part which art played in the figuring of the Egyptian gods. In most of the types which it created it mixed up the physical characteristics of man and beast. Sometimes the head of an animal surmounts the body of a man or woman; sometimes, though more rarely, the opposite arrangement obtains. The Sphinx, and the bird with a human head which symbolizes death, are instances of the latter combination. The usual explanation of these forms is as follows. When men began to embody for the eye of others the ideas which they had formed of the divine powers, they adopted as the foundation for their personifications the noblest living form they knew, that of man. In the next place they required some easy method for distinguishing their imaginary beings one from another. They had to give to each deity some feature which should be peculiar to him or her self, and should allow of his being at once identified and called by his own name. The required result was obtained in a very simple manner, by adding to the constant quantity the human figure, a varying element in the heads of different animals. These the fauna of Egypt itself afforded. In the case of each divinity, the particular animal was selected which had been consecrated to it, which was its symbol or at least its attribute, and the head or body, as the case might be, was detached in order to form part of a complex and imaginary being. The special characteristics of the animal made use of were so frankly insisted upon that no confusion could arise between one deity and another. Even a child could not fail to see the difference between Sekhet, with the head of a cat or a lioness, and Hathor, with that of a cow.

We do not refuse to accept this explanation, but yet we may express our surprise that the Egyptians, who were able, even in the days of the ancient empire, to endow the statues of their kings with so much purity and nobility of form, were not disgusted by the strangeness of such combinations, by their extreme grotesqueness, and by the disagreeable results which they sometimes produced. A certain beauty may be found in such creations as the Sphinx, and a few others, in which the human face is allied to the wings of a bird, and the trunk and posterior members of the most graceful and powerful of quadrupeds. But could any notion be more unhappy than that of crowning the bust of a man or woman with the ugly and ponderous head of a crocodile, or with the slender neck and flat head of a snake?

FIG. 39.—Sekhet. Louvre. (Granite. Height 0·50 metres.)

Every polytheistic nation attacked this problem in turn, and each solved it in its own manner. The Hindoos multiplied the human figure by itself, and painted or carved their gods with three heads and many pairs of arms and legs, of which proceeding traces are to be found among the Western Asiatics, the Greeks, and even the Latins. The Greeks represented all their gods in human form, and yet by the delicacy of their contours and the general coherence of their characterization, they were enabled to avoid all confusion between them. With them, too, costume and attributes helped to mark the difference. But even where these are absent, our minds are never left in doubt. Even a fragment of a torso can be at once recognized at sight as part of a statue of Zeus, of Apollo, or of Bacchus, and a head of Demeter or Hera would never be confounded with one of Artemis or Pallas.

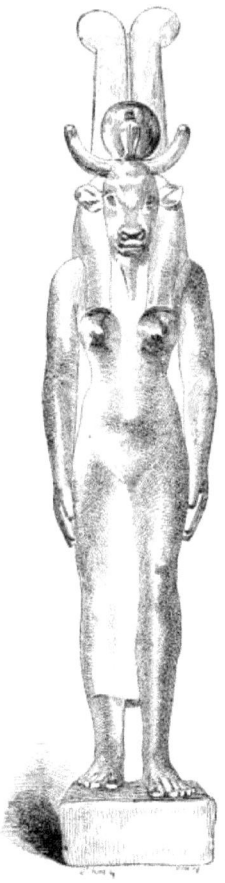

Fig. 40.—Isis-Hathor. Louvre.
(Bronze. Actual size.)

It may be said that the artists of Egypt were lacking in the skill necessary for all this, or that they generalized their forms to such a degree as to leave no scope for such subtle differences. But, in fact, we find in their oldest statues a facility of execution which suggests that, had they chosen, they could have expressed anything which can be expressed by the chisel. That they did not do so, we know. They contented themselves with plastic interpretations so rough and awkward that, perhaps, we should rather seek their explanation in some hereditary predisposition, some habit of thought and action contracted in the infancy of the race and fortified by long transmission.

FIG. 41.—A Sphinx; in rose granite. Thirteenth dynasty. Louvre. Drawn by Saint-Elme Gautier.

We have already spoken of that which we believe to be the cause of the peculiar forms under which the Egyptians figured their deities, namely, the fetish worship, which was the earliest, and for many centuries the only, form of religion which they possessed. That worship had struck its roots so deeply into the souls of the people, that it could not be torn up even when a large part of the nation had gradually educated itself to the comprehension of the highest religious conceptions. Its practices never fell into total neglect, and its influence was so far maintained that during the decadence of the nation it again became the ruling faith, so that foreign observers were led to believe that the Egyptian religion began and ended in the adoration of plants and sacred animals. The eyes and the imagination being thus educated by immemorial custom, it is not surprising that even the most cultivated section of the people should have seen nothing offensive in the representation of their gods sometimes under the complete form of an animal (Horus is often symbolized under the likeness of a hawk), sometimes as composite monsters with human bodies and animal heads.

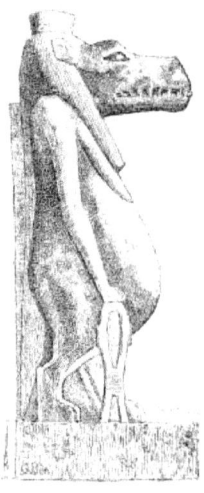

FIG. 42.—Touaris. Boulak.
(Drawn by G. Bénédite.)

Take, for a moment, the bird to which we have just alluded. The hawk, like the vulture, plays an important part in Egyptian art. The vulture symbolizes Maut, the spouse of Amen. It furnishes the sign by which her name is written, and sometimes, as the symbol of maternity, its head appears over the brow of the goddess, its wings forming her head-dress. The goddess Nekheb, who symbolizes the region of the South, is also represented by a vulture.[79] So it is with the ibis. It supplies the character by which the name Thoth is written, and that god is figured with the head of an Ibis. The part played by these birds in the representation of the gods, both in the plastic arts and in writing, is to be explained by the sentiments of gratitude and religious veneration of which they were the objects, sentiments which were the natural outcome of the practical services which they rendered to mankind.

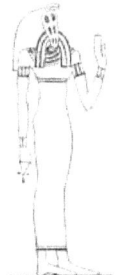

FIG. 43.—Rannu
(from Wilkinson).

When the early fathers of the nation first established themselves upon the banks of the Nile, they found invaluable allies in those energetic birds of prey, and the alliance has been continued to their latest descendants. After the annual inundation the damp earth was overrun by toads and frogs, by snakes and lizards and all kinds of creeping things. Fishes, left by the retreating flood in pools which were soon dried up by the blazing sun, perished, and, decomposing, rendered the air noisome and malarious. In addition to this there were the corpses of wild and domestic animals, and the offal of every kind which accumulated round the dwellings of the peasantry and rapidly became putrid under the sun of Egypt. If left to decompose they would soon have bred a pestilence, and in those days human effort was not to be reckoned upon in the work of sanitation. To birds of prey, then, was assigned the indispensable work of elimination and transformation, an office which they yet fill satisfactorily in the towns and villages of Africa. Thanks to their appetite and to the powerful wings which carried them in a twinkling to wherever their presence was required, the multiplication of the inferior animals was kept within due limits, and decomposing matter was recalled into the service of organic life. Had these unpaid scavengers but struck work for a day, the plague, as Michelet puts it, would soon have become the only inhabitant of the country.[80]

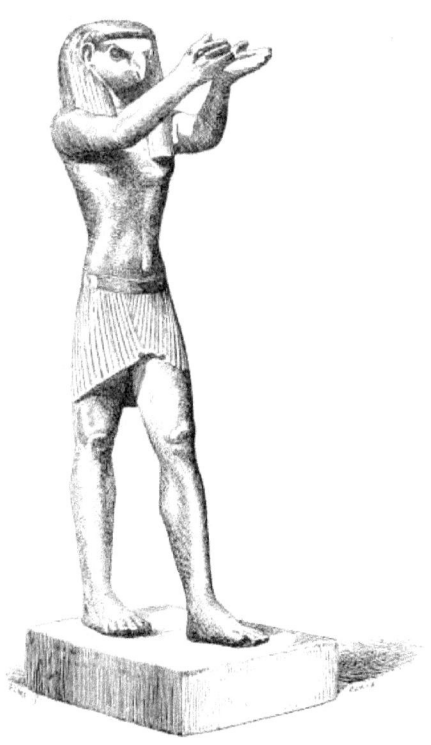

FIG. 44.—Horus; from a bronze in the Posno collection. (Height 38 inches.)

The worship of the hawk, the vulture, and the ibis, had, then, preceded by many centuries that of the gods who correspond to the personages of the Hellenic pantheon. Rooted by long custom in the minds of the people, it did not excite the ire of the wise men of Heliopolis or Thebes. The doctrine of emanation and of successive incarnations of the deity, permitted their theology to explain and to accept anything, even those things which at a later epoch seemed nothing more than the grossest creations of popular superstition. These objects of veneration were therefore enabled to maintain their places by the side of the superior gods, to represent them in written characters and in plastic creations, and, in the latter case, to be blended with the forms of man himself. To us, accustomed as we are to the types created by Greek anthropomorphism, these figures are surprising; but to the Egyptians they seemed perfectly natural, for they offered the characteristic features of the animals which they had loved, respected, and adored ever since the birth of their civilization.

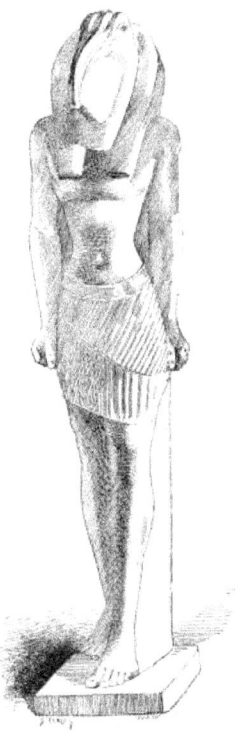

FIG. 45.—Thoth. Louvre.
Enamelled clay.
Actual size.

It is difficult for us to see things with the same eyes as the contemporaries of Cheops or even of Rameses; to enter into their ideas and sentiments so as to feel with them and to think with their brains. Let us attempt to do so for a moment; let us make one of those intellectual efforts which are demanded from the historian, and we shall then understand how it was, that the Egyptians were not offended by a combination of two classes of forms which, to us, seem so differently constituted and so unequal in dignity. The deity took the form of an animal and revealed himself in it, just as he took that of a man, or of a statue which he was supposed to animate, and to which he was attached. In one of his most curious and most penetrating essays, M. Maspero explains that the sacred animal was—like the king, the son of Amen; like the statue fashioned by the hands of a sculptor—the manifestation of the deity, the strength and support of his life, his *double*, to use an expression dear to the Egyptians. At Memphis, Apis repeated and constantly renewed the life of Ptah; he was, in a word, his living statue.[81]

Egyptian art was, then, the faithful and skilful interpretation of the ideas of the people. What the Egyptians wished to say, that they did say with great clearness and a rare happiness of plastic expression. To accuse them, as they have been sometimes accused, of a want of taste, would be to form a very narrow conception of art, to sin against both the method and the spirit of modern criticism. This latter seeks for originality and admires it, and all art which is at once powerful and sincere arouses its interest. We do not, however, wish to deny that their conception of divinity is less favourable to the plastic arts than the anthropomorphism of the Greeks. No more simple method of distinguishing one god from another could well be imagined than that of giving to each, as his exclusive property, the head of some well-known animal; the employment of such an unmistakable sign rendered the task of the artist too easy, in giving him assurance that his meaning would be understood at a glance without any particular effort on his part.

FIG. 46.—Sacrifice to Apis,
from Mariette.

The value of an artistic result is in proportion to the difficulty of its achievement. The Greek sculptor had nothing beyond the bodily form and the features of man with which to give a distinct individuality to each god and goddess of his mythology; he was therefore obliged to make use of the most delicate and subtle distinctions of feature and contour. This necessity was a great incentive to perfection; it drove him to study the human form with a continuous energy which, unhappily for himself, was not required of the Egyptian sculptor or painter. Art and religion have ever been so closely allied that it was necessary that we should give some account of the original characteristics of the Egyptian beliefs, but we shall make no attempt to describe, or even to enumerate, the chief divinities of the Egyptian pantheon; such an attempt would be foreign to the purposes which we have in view. We have, however, already mentioned most of the chief deities of Egypt, and we shall have occasion to draw the attention of our readers to others, in speaking of the tombs and temples, the statues and bas-reliefs, of the country. Now, each of these gods began by being no more than the local divinity of some particular nome or city. As a city grew in importance, so did its peculiar god, and sometimes it came about that both a dynasty of kings and a divinity were imposed upon Egypt by the power of what we may call their native city. In the course of time a number of successive deities thus held the supreme place, each of whom preserved, even after his fall, some of the dignity which he had acquired during his period of supremacy.

The two first dynasties, the authors of Egyptian unity, had their capital in the nome of Abydos, the nome which contained the tomb of Osiris; and it was in their reign that, from one end to the other of the Nile valley, spread the worship of that god; of that Osiris who, with Isis, seemed to Herodotus to be the only deity whom all the Egyptians combined to adore.[82] Under the following dynasties, whose capital was Memphis, Ptah rose into the first place; but, as if by a kind of compromise, his dignity is combined with that of the great god of Abydos under the names of Ptah-Osiris and Ptah-Sokar-Osiris. Toum, the chief deity of Heliopolis, never rose above the second rank because Heliopolis itself was neither a royal city nor even the birthplace of any powerful dynasty. During all this period we hear nothing of Amen, the local deity of Thebes; his name is hardly to be found upon any monument earlier than the eleventh dynasty, but, with the rise of the Theban empire he began to be a conspicuous figure in Egypt. During the domination of the Hyksos, their national deity, Soutekh or Set, overshadowed the ancient divinities of the soil; but the final victory of Thebes under Ahmes I. installed Amen as the national god, and we shall see hereafter what magnificent temples were raised in his honour by the kings of the brilliant Theban dynasties. His successor would no doubt have been Aten, the solar disc, had Tell-el-Amarna, the new capital of Amenophis IV., and the worship which was there inaugurated, enjoyed a less ephemeral existence; but Thebes and Amen soon regained their supremacy. Again, when the Egyptian centre of gravity was transported to the Delta, the local deities of the district, and especially Neith, conquered the first place in the religious sentiments of the people. Under the Persians they returned to Amen, as to the protector who could give back to the nation its former independence and power. Under the Ptolemies, Horus and Hathor were in the ascendant, and later still, under the Roman emperors, the worship of the Isis of Philæ became popular and was prolonged in that island sanctuary until the sixth century of our era.

The movement of religious thought in Egypt was very different from what we shall find in Greece. We find no god, like that of the Hellenes, whose pre-eminence dates back to the remote origin of the Aryan race, a pre-eminence which was never menaced or questioned;[83] we find no Zeus, no Jupiter, whose godhead was conceived from century to century in an ever larger and more purified spirit, until at last it was defined in the famous hymn of Cleanthe as that "which governed all things according to law." We have pointed out how greatly the Greek artists profited by their efforts to endow the piety of their countrymen with an image of this great and good being, which should be worthy of the popular faith in him as the father of gods and men. The Egyptian artist could find no such inspiration in a long succession of gods, no one of whom succeeded in concentrating supreme power in his hands. No such ideal existed for them as that which the popular conscience and the genius of the national poets created in the lord of Olympus. Neither Thebes nor Sais could give birth to a Phidias; to an artist who should feel himself spurred on by the work of all previous generations to produce a masterpiece in which the highest religious conception, to which the intelligence of the race had mounted by slow degrees, should be realized in visible form.

§ 6. *That Egyptian Art did not escape the Law of Change, and that its History may therefore be written.*

It may be well, before embarking upon the study of Egyptian architecture, sculpture, and painting, to dispel a prejudice which in spite of recent discoveries still exists in some minds; we mean, the belief in the immobility of Egyptian art. This mistake is a very ancient one. The Greeks were the first to make it, and they transmitted their error to us. In regard to this we must cite the famous passage of Plato[84]:—"Long ago they appear to have recognized the very principle of which we are now speaking—that their young citizens must be habituated to forms and strains of virtue. These they fixed, and exhibited patterns of them in their temples; and no painter or artist is allowed to innovate upon them, or to leave the traditional forms and invent new ones. To this day no alteration is allowed, either in these arts or in music, at all. And you will find that their works of art are painted or moulded in the same forms that they had ten thousand years ago—(this is literally true and no exaggeration)—their ancient paintings and sculptures are not a whit better or worse than the work of to-day, but are made with just the same skill."

This strange assertion was long accepted without question even in modern times. We need not go back to the archæologists of the last century, whose credulity is to be accounted for by their lack of materials for the formation of a better judgment. In 1828 in his first lecture at the Bibliothèque Royale, Raoul-Rochette turned his attention to Egypt. He had before his eyes, in the Parisian museums and in the *Description de l'Égypte*, works which dated from the finest periods of the Theban dynasties, although the still more ancient monuments which now form the glory of the Boulak Museum were not yet discovered; he might have perceived and pointed out the difference between the statues of Ousourtesen, Thothmes, and Rameses on the one hand, and those of the Sait epoch; still more should he have remarked upon the characteristics which distinguish the monuments of independent Egypt from those which were erected under the Ptolemies and the Roman emperors. What he did say, however, and say with consummate confidence was: "From the first of the Pharaohs to the last of the Ptolemies, the art of Egypt never varied."[85]

Such crude notions as this can no longer be upheld. M. Marriette protests in the following almost indignant terms against certain utterances of M. Renan which seemed to him to imply the same doctrine. "M. Renan loves[86] to represent ancient Egypt as a sort of China, walled in and fortified against the exterior world, immovable, old even in its infancy, and arrived by a single spring at a degree of civilization which it never surpassed. He looks upon the country as a great plain, green indeed and fertile, but without accidents of contour to break the monotony of the landscape. And yet Egypt had periods of grandeur and decadence more marked than those of other countries. Her civilization went through all the different phases; it went through many complete transformations, it had its sudden moments of brilliancy and its epochs of eclipse. Its art was not so stationary as to prevent us from writing its history. The influence of Egypt was felt from Mesopotamia to the equator. Thothmes, in a word, was no Chinaman. Egypt perished because in attacking foreign nations she provoked a reaction which was fatal to her."[87]

Now that we are enabled to contrast the statues of the Ptolemaic period with those of the pyramid builders, we find nothing surprising in Mariette's language; but even before these means of study were open to us, criticism should have cast more than doubt upon the assertions of Plato; it should have appealed from a theory which was at variance with all historical analogies to the monuments themselves to tell the truth, to those monuments which were best known and understood. Was it likely, was it possible, that such a people as that which created these monuments, should remain for more than forty centuries unaffected by the law of continual, even if almost insensible, change? What right have we thus to place Egypt and China apart from the rest of humanity? There are, it is true, some peoples who are more attached than others to traditional customs and ancient institutions; they are more conservative, to use the modern phrase. But, although their evolution is a slower process, it is there; our eyes cannot perceive any movement in the small hand of a watch, but yet it does move exactly in the same fashion as that which marks the seconds. Upon the banks of the Peiho as upon those of the Nile, upon the whole surface of our planet, man *is* not; he *becomes*, to borrow one of the favourite expressions of German philosophy. History can admit no exception to this law either for China or Egypt. In the cases of both those countries there is a certain illusion, which is to be explained by our ignorance. We are not well enough acquainted with them to grasp the different periods of their political and social, their artistic and literary development. For one who is too far off or very short-sighted the details of the most varied landscape become obliterated or confused; waste land and smiling fields are blended together; hollows and hillocks lose the vigour of their contours.

China, as we have said, does not enter into our purview; and as for Egypt, the deeper we penetrate into her history the more are we convinced that her long career was troubled by moments of crisis similar to those which have come to other human societies. The narratives of the Greek historians give us reason to suspect that it was so, and the monuments which have been discovered insist upon the same truth, and compel us to accept it. For certain epochs these are very abundant, beautiful, and varied. Afterwards they become rare and clumsy, or altogether wanting; and again they reappear in great numbers and in their full nobility, but with a different general character. These contrasts and temporary eclipses occur again and again. How, then, can we doubt that here, as elsewhere, there were alternations of grandeur and poverty, of periods of conquest and expansion and epochs of civil war or of defeat by foreign invaders? May we not believe that through the clouds which obscure the causes of such changes we may catch glimpses of those periods of decadence and renascence which, following one upon the other, exhausted in the end the genius of the race?

Let us take a single example—the most striking of all. "After the sixth dynasty all documents cease; they are absolutely wanting until the eleventh, the first of the Middle Empire. This is one of those sudden interruptions in the history of Egypt which may be compared to the temporary disappearance of those curious rivers which run partly underground."[88]

FIG. 47.—**Statue from the Ancient Empire, in limestone. Boulak. Drawn by Bourgoin.**

When historians, living as long after our nineteenth century as we do after the epochs of Memphite and Theban supremacy in Egypt, come to treat the history of the past, they will perhaps look upon the ages which rolled away between the fall of Græco-Roman civilization and the revival of learning in the fifteenth and sixteenth centuries as no longer than that which divided the ancient from the middle empire of Egypt, or the latter from the dynasties of Thebes. In the distant future men will know, in a vague fashion, that between the fall of Rome and the discovery of printing, or that of America, there were great movements among the nations, and an apparent recoil of civilization; but memory and imagination will leap without effort over the gap, over that period which we call the Middle Ages. The Roman empire will seem to touch our modern civilization, and many of the differences which strike us so strongly will be imperceptible. They will perceive that we had a new religion and new inventions, but they will take more account of the resemblances than of the differences. Our languages, manners, laws, and forms of government will seem to them continuations of those of Greece and Rome. In that which we call antiquity, and in Christian Europe, they will find similar literary habits and standards of criticism, the same judicial nomenclature, the same terms for monarchy, empire, and republic, the same titles for kings and Cæsars. These different civilizations are like star clusters. To us who are among them they seem distinct enough, but to generations which are divided from them by a vast space of time they will seem to form but one nebulous body.

FIG. 48.—**Woman kneading dough. Statuette from the Ancient Empire, in limestone.**
Drawn by Bourgoin.

FIG. 49.—**The Scribe Chaphré.**
Fifth dynasty. Boulak. Limestone.

Egypt, then, had her great convulsions like the rest of the world. She met with disasters, and underwent periods of confusion like those which overtook the nations of the West between the reigns of Trajan and Charlemagne. Wars and invasions, the action and reaction of civilization, had upon her the same influence as upon them, and, in transforming her sentiments and ideas, caused their plastic expression to pass through a series of changes in taste and style. The Theban tomb of the time of Rameses is very different from that of Memphis and the ancient empire; the new empire constructed no buildings like the greater pyramids, but its temples were larger and more magnificent than any of their predecessors. It was the same with sculpture. A cultivated eye has no need to run to inscriptions to enable it to distinguish between works of the ancient and of the middle empire; nor will it confound works created in either of those periods with those of the Sait epoch. The differences are almost as well marked as those which enable archæologists to distinguish a torso of the time of Phidias from one of the school of Praxiteles or Lysippus. These differences it will be our duty to describe hereafter, but our readers may perhaps discover them for themselves if they examine the illustrations to this chapter, which are arranged in chronological order.

Variety is universal in Egypt, local variety as well as that of different periods. Language had its dialects as well as art. The pronunciation of Upper and that of Lower Egypt was quite dissimilar, except in the case of a few letters. In the same way different cities had distinct schools of sculpture and painting, which were distinguished from one another by their traditional methods of conception and execution. Neither under Ousourtesen nor under Rameses, had art the same character in the cities of the Delta, in Memphis, and in Thebes. Among the works in sculpture executed for Rameses II., those of Abydos were more elegant and refined than those of Thebes.

FIG. 50.—The Lady Naï. Wooden statue from the 19th or 20th dynasty. Louvre.

How, then, are we to explain the error committed by Plato, and by him transmitted to posterity? The explanation is easy. The Greeks visited Egypt too late in its history to form a true judgment. In Plato's time the Egyptians were still trying, by violent but spasmodic efforts, to reconquer the independence which had been destroyed by the successor of Cyrus. But the moment was at hand when even these intermittent struggles were to be abandoned, and they were to finally succumb to sovereigns of foreign blood.

Their still brilliant civilization might deceive a passing stranger, but the decadence had commenced—a decadence slow indeed, but none the more remediable.

Some years after the visit of Plato, the two Nectanebos, more especially the second, devoted themselves with energetic ardour to the restoration of the ancient buildings of the country and to the construction of new ones, such as the temple at Philæ. Buildings signed with their name are to be found all over Egypt; but these simultaneous undertakings seem to betray a sense of vanishing power, an uncertainty of the morrow, a feverish activity seeking to deceive itself and to hide its own weakness. Nothing could be more precarious than the political conditions under which this activity was displayed. The independence of the country was maintained by the dearly bought services of Spartan and Athenian mercenaries. Twice already had Persia crushed Egyptian revolts, and she was, perhaps, but watching her opportunity to cast the hordes of Asia upon the unhappy country for a third time. Ill obeyed as he was, the "Great King" could always find troops to take part in the spoiling of a country whose riches had proved so inexhaustible. And if, by any remote chance, the Persians should fail in their enterprise, another and a graver danger would menace the Egyptian monarchy from the rapid growth of the Greek power in the Mediterranean. Since the period of the Persian wars, the language, the literature, the arts, the mythology of Greece, had spread with great rapidity; and the moment might be foreseen when a supremacy founded upon intellectual worth would be confirmed by military triumph and the creation of a vast Hellenic empire. The conquest of Egypt was begun by the Ionian soldiers and merchants who were introduced into the Nile valley by Psemethek; it was bloodlessly completed by the arms of Alexander. For three centuries the Egyptians had been accustomed to see the Greeks freely coming and going among them as merchants, as mercenary officers, as travellers eager for instruction. The latter posed as disciples before the priests of Memphis and Heliopolis, and freely expressed a warmth of admiration which could not fail to flatter the national vanity. The Greeks would be better masters than their rivals from Persia. From them the Egyptians would, at least, obtain good administration and complete freedom in the exercise of their religion in return for their taxes. The Greeks were clear-sighted enough to understand their own interests; they were too philosophical and large minded for any fanatical persecution of, or even hindrance to, the national religion; they were too much of connoisseurs to fail in respect to a form of civilization whose prodigious antiquity they divined, and before which the most eminent among them were ever inclined to bow, like youths before an old man, or a parvenu before the descendant of a long line of kings.

Thus Egypt gradually fell into the hands of strangers after the commencement of the fourth century before Christ. Ethiopians, Assyrians and Persians had by turns overrun the country. Great numbers of the Phœnicians had established themselves in it, and, after the fall of Jerusalem and Samaria, many Jews followed their example. Finally, the Greeks came in by thousands through the breaches which their predecessors had made, penetrating into all parts, and making everywhere felt the superiority of a people who had, by appropriating the useful results obtained in a long succession of centuries by more ancient races, become wealthier, stronger, and better instructed than any of their forerunners.

Thus Egypt lost her power of national rejuvenation, her power of rising again after calamity. She existed on through the centuries by mere force of habit, but she lived no more. Her population was so homogeneous, and her institutions were so solid, that the social conditions of the country could not be changed in a day or even in a century. The teachings of her religion had been established by so long a course of development, and the hands of her artists were so well practised, that the monumental types which had been created in more fertile periods of her history were reproduced until a late date, in a machine-like and instinctive fashion. Imagination was dead, and the best that could be hoped for was the faithful repetition of those forms which the genius of the race had conceived in its last moments of original thought.

Under the Sait princes, under the Psemetheks and Nekau, under Apries and Amasis, Egypt was delivered from her enemies and again became mistress of Syria and of the Island of Cyprus. She thus recovered confidence in herself and in her future, and a period ensued which had an art of its own with distinctive features which we shall endeavour to trace. In the intervals of precarious repose which characterized the Persian domination, the Egyptians had leisure neither to invent nor to improve. They copied, as well as they could, the monuments of the twenty-sixth dynasty. Art became a mere collection of technical precepts, kept together and transmitted in the intercourse of the studio, by instruction and practice; it became a mere matter of routine implying, perhaps, great technical skill, but displaying no sincere and personal feeling. Nature was no longer studied or cared for. Artists knew that the human figure should be divided into so many parts. They knew that in the representation of this or that god a certain attitude or attribute was necessary; and they carved the statues required of them after the traditional recipes. Thus Egyptian art became conventional, and so it remained to the end. So it was in the time of Diodorus. The sculptors whom that historian saw at work in Memphis and Thebes, during the reign of Augustus, carved a statue as a modern mechanic would make the different parts of a machine; they worked with a rapidity and an easy decision more characteristic of the precise workman than of the artist.[89] Thought was no longer necessary to them. The due proportions and measurements had been ascertained and fixed many centuries before their time.

FIG. 51.—Ouah-ab-ra, 26th dynasty. Louvre. Grey granite, height 37 inches.

But research must still precede discovery. We admit that a day arrived when convention was supreme in Egyptian art, but it could not have begun with convention any more than the arts of other nations. We must here define the terms which we shall have occasion to employ. Every work of art is an interpretation of nature. Let us take the example of the human figure. In the works of a single period and of a single people, it is always full of striking similarity; and yet two original artists never look at it with the same eyes. One will look at it in certain aspects and will bring out certain qualities, which another, although his contemporary and fellow-countryman, will leave in the obscurity of shadows. One will devote himself to the beauty of form, another to the accidents of colour or the expression of passion and thought. The original remains the same, although its interpretations are so various. And these varieties become still more marked when we compare the arts of different races or of different periods—the art of Egypt with that of Assyria or Greece, antique art with that of modern times.

On the other hand, the great resemblance which the arts of a single time and country bear to each other, is accounted for by the fact that their creators look upon the external facts of life through a glass, if we may put it so, tinted with the colours of the national genius. They bring to their study of an eternal model the same transient prejudices, the same preoccupations, the same desires. And yet among those highly gifted races where art holds or has held a lofty place, groups of artists are formed, either successively or simultaneously, which we call schools. Each of these groups professes to make a fresh reference to nature, to interpret her works more faithfully than its predecessors, and to draw from them typical forms which shall be more expressive of the real desires and sentiments of the public for which it caters. Between the works of these different schools, there are, however, many similarities, which are to be explained by the identity of race and belief. There are also diversities which are caused either by different conditions or by the influence of some master spirit. Wherever these schools spring up, art lives, moves, and progresses. But sooner or later comes a time when this ardour comes to an end, and exhaustion takes its place. The civilization to which it belongs becomes old and languid, and its creative power ceases like the imperceptible sinking of a flood. Now, it often happens that just before this period of lassitude, in the last days of reproductive strength and healthy maturity, a rich and brilliant school springs up, which interprets the characteristic sentiments of the civilization to which it belongs, with the greatest vigour and by admirably selected means. If such an interpretation be found satisfactory at all points, why should a better be sought for at the risk of choosing a worse? This question is but a confession of impotence on the part of those who ask it. From that moment convention will be supreme, and convention in the sense of an artificial set of rules which will release the artist from his obligation of continual reference to nature.

FIG. 52.—Sculptor at work upon an arm, Thebes. (Champollion, pl. 180.)

Such a revolution is not the work of a day. Art requires time thus to inclose itself in mere mechanical dexterity. As a nation grows old, its art, like its literature, continually becomes more and more conventional. Every great period or school leaves to the generations that come after it types which have made a vivid impression upon taste and imagination. As time goes on these types become more numerous and more brilliant, and their prestige increases until it becomes little less than tyranny. Society can only escape from its thrall at the expense of some great religious or philosophical revolution, or by the infusion of new blood from without. And these changes western civilization had to undergo in the early centuries of our era, in the establishment of Christianity, the invasion of the barbarians, and the fall of the Roman Empire.

Thanks to the peculiar circumstances of the country, Egyptian society was enabled to maintain the originality of its genius and the vitality of its institutions with unusual success. After each period of internal commotion or foreign invasion, the Egyptians set themselves to renew the chain of their national traditions. In spite of the foreign elements which had been received among them, the great mass of the people remained the same down to the latest days of antiquity. Heterogeneous constituents were absorbed by the nation without leaving any apparent trace. The ideas which the people had formed for themselves of the ultimate destiny of humanity were developed, indeed, and in successive ages varied slightly in general colour, but in none of their variations did they give rise to a new religion, as Brahmanism gave birth to Buddhism.

As often as a new dynasty of kings succeeded in driving out the foreign conqueror and in re-establishing the unity of the kingdom, so often was there a complete restoration. The aim which they had in view was ever to restore, in all its parts, a *régime* which was founded upon national pride. Enjoying a civilization which for ages had been alone in the world, it was in its full and glorious past that Egyptian society found the ideal to which it clung in spite of all obstacles and misfortunes. Its gaze was turned backwards towards those early sovereigns who seemed transfigured by distance, but whose presence in the memory kept alive the perpetual worship which had been vowed to them.

FIG. 53.—Sculptor carving a statue, Thebes. (Champollion, pl. 180.)

Every restoration is inspired by a more or less blind and superstitious reverence for the past. This has often been asserted in connection with politics and religion, and the assertion is equally true in respect to art. Each of those dynasties to which Egypt owed its political restoration, set themselves to repair the temples which had been destroyed, and to replace upon their pedestals the statues of gods or ancestors which had been overthrown. When new temples and new statues were to be erected, the first idea of the artists employed was to study the ancient monuments and to try to equal them. As long as Egypt preserved her vitality, the wants of the present and external influences no doubt had their effect in introducing certain changes, both in the arrangement of her buildings, and in the modelling, movement, and expression of the statues which adorned them. Ancient types were not servilely copied, but the temptation to borrow from them a point of departure, at least, for new attempts at progression, was too strong to be resisted. It was necessary that all buildings and statues should be in harmony with the remains which subsisted from previous ages, and from this it resulted that each new creative effort began by imitating what had gone before. The 'school' in process of foundation accepted on trust the architectural disposition left by its predecessor, as well as its methods of looking at nature. And this is equivalent to saying that, from its first moment, it must have been conventional in a certain degree.

This conventionality must have increased at every fresh renascence, because each new development had its own processes to transmit to posterity as well as those of its ancestors. After each recoil or pause in the progress of art, the weight of the past must have seemed heavier to those who attempted to revive the onward movement. On the one hand, the more ancient of the traditional elements had acquired, by their constant and often repeated transmission, a prestige and authority which placed them above discussion; on the other, the legacy of admitted principles and processes was continually increasing, until it became a source of embarrassment to the artist, and of destruction to his liberty. When at last the decadence of the race had advanced so far that all initiative power and independence of thought had disappeared, the time arrived when convention was everything, like one of those elaborate rituals which regulate every word, and even gesture of the officiating priest. When Plato visited Egypt, the schools of sculpture were nothing more than institutions for teaching pupils, who were remarkable for docility and for dexterity of hand, to transmit to their successors an assemblage of precepts and receipts which provided for every contingency and left no room for the exercise of fancy or discretion.

At that very time Greek art was progressing with a power and rapidity which has never been rivalled. To the school of Phidias, a school established in that Athens which yet possessed so many works of the archaic period, had succeeded those of Praxiteles and Scopas. The Greeks found means to improve, or at least to innovate, upon perfection itself. Plato did not, and could not, perceive, in his hasty journey through the Egyptian cities, that they too had seen their periods of change, their different schools and developments of style, less marked, perhaps, than those of Greece, and certainly less rapid, but yet quite perceptible to the practised observer. We are now in a better position to estimate these differences. Monuments have been brought before our eyes such as Plato never saw; namely, the statues of the ancient empire which were hidden for so many ages in the thickness of walls or in the depths of sepulchral pits. Even now these statues have not reached the age of ten thousand years so persistently attributed by the Greek philosopher to the early works which he did see, works which seemed to him exactly the same as those which were being made in his presence. But although the statues of the early empire were then no more than some thirty centuries old, Plato could not have helped seeing, if he had seen them at all, that they were quite distinct from the works which the sculptors of Nectanebo had in progress, always supposing that he looked at them with reasonable attention. The art of the pyramid builders, an art which possesses in a very high degree certain qualities for which the Egyptians have been too commonly refused credit, is known to us chiefly through the excavations of Mariette and the contents of the Boulak museum. But even before Cheops, Chefren, and their subjects had risen from their tombs, the historian might have divined by analogy, and described by no very bold conjecture, the essential characteristics of Egyptian art during its first centuries. Whether we speak of an individual, of a school, or of a people, every artistic career which follows its natural course and is not rudely broken through, ends sooner or later in conventionality, in that which is technically called *mannerism*. But mannerism is never the beginning of art. Art always begins by humble and sincere attempts to render what it sees. Its awkwardness is at first extreme and its power of imitation very imperfect. But it is not discouraged; it tries different processes; it takes account now of one, now of another aspect of life; it consults nature incessantly and humbly, taking note of her answers and modifying its work in obedience to their teaching. This teaching is not always rightly understood, but it is ever received with docility and good faith.

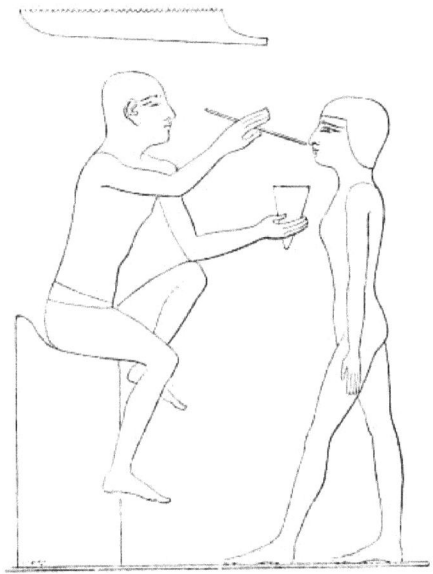

FIG. 54.—Artist painting a statue, Thebes. (Champollion, pl. 180.)

Every work which bears the marks of frank and loyal effort is interesting; but the moment in an artistic career which gives birth to real *chefs d'œuvre* is towards the end of that period, when the eye has become sure, and the hand sufficiently well practised, for the faithful interpretation of any model whose beauty or original expression may have caught the fancy. Success is then achieved, always provided that the model is never lost sight of or studied with anything short of passionate devotion. But the time comes when this devotion is relaxed. The artist thinks that such constant reference to nature is no longer required when he has made his final choice between the different methods which his art employs. In devoting himself to the reproduction of certain features for which he has a marked preference, he has himself produced types which he thenceforward takes pleasure in repeating, as if they were in themselves an epitome of nature's infinite diversity.

In the case of Egypt, even those discoveries which carry us back farthest do not enable us to grasp, as we can in the case of Greece, the first attempts at plastic expression, the first rude efforts of the modeller or painter; but they carry us to the end of that period which, in the case of other countries, we call archaic; and above all they transport us into the centre of the epoch which was to Egypt what the fifth century was to Greece, namely, the age of perfection. The Egyptian people had already lived so long and worked so hard that they could not free their work from certain common and irrepressible characteristics. In the plastic arts and in poetry they had their own style, and that style was both individual and original in an extraordinary degree. This style was already formed, but it was not yet robbed of its vitality by indolent content or petrified by mannerism; it had neither renounced its freedom nor said its last word.

FIG. 55.—Isis nursing Horus. Ptolemaic bronze; in the Louvre. Height, 19 inches.

§ 7. *Of the place held in this work by the monuments of the Memphite period, and of the limits of our inquiry.*

It will be found that a very large space in the present work, some may say too large a space, is devoted to the pre-conventional art of the ancient empire. We had reasons for taking such a course, and reasons that may be easily divined.

This early art is much less known than that of the later epochs. While the great museums of Europe are filled with statues and reliefs from Thebes, or, at least, contemporary with the Theban and Sait dynasties, monuments from the Memphite period are still rare out of Egypt. Thanks to Mariette and Lepsius, Paris and Berlin are not without remarkable examples of the art in question, but it is in Egypt itself, at the Boulak museum, that any detailed study must be made. It is there that the masterpieces of an art whose very existence was unsuspected by Champollion, are to be found; the Chephren, the two statues from Meidoum, the bas-reliefs from the tomb of Ti, and many others of similar style and value. These figures have been drawn for our readers by two skilful artists, MM. Bourgoin and Bénédite. They have rendered with fidelity and sincerity more than one object which had never before been reproduced, either by photography or otherwise. A few specimens of these treasures, selected by him who had been the means of bringing them to light and whom we now mourn, were seen at the Universal Exhibitions of 1867 and 1878, but they soon returned to Cairo, and western archæologists had but slight opportunity to become acquainted with their characteristics.

The art of the early dynasties has thus been practically ignored by those who have never visited Egypt. The lifelike and enthusiastic descriptions of M. Eugene Melchior de Vogüé and others have done something to arouse the attention of connoisseurs; but in such a matter the slightest sketch, provided it be correct so far as it goes, is of more value, as a definition of style, than the most picturesque or eloquent writing.

These reflections would by themselves justify our efforts to incorporate in our pages, reproductions of all the more important objects with which the necropolis at Memphis has enriched the museum at Boulak; but we were impelled by other motives also. The extant monuments of the ancient empire are less numerous than those of the Theban and Sait dynasties; they are of comparatively modest dimensions, and, with rare exceptions they all belong to one category, that of works relating to death and burial. They also have a special interest of their own. They enable us to protest, and to give tangible justification for our protestations, against a prejudice which dates back to a remote antiquity; even if all evidence had perished the critic would have no great difficulty in casting doubt upon assertions which were in themselves extremely improbable, but his task is rendered much easier when he is able to point to existing monuments in support of his contention, and his pleasure is great in seeing the certainty of his critical methods borne out, and Egyptian art replacing itself, as if of its own motion, under the normal conditions of historic development.

FIG. 56.—Chephren.
Sketched by Bourgoin.
See also Fig. 460.

This volume, then, will treat of the remains of early Egyptian art at a length which would seem at first sight out of due proportion to their number, but later ages will also be represented by a series of monuments, which will bring us down to the Persian conquest. This limit will hardly be over-passed in our choice of examples for study, and that for two reasons.

The first is, that at the latter period the evolution of Egyptian art was complete, it had created all that it could and had become a slave to its own past. Disposing under the Ptolemies of all the resources of a great empire, it indeed introduced certain architectural changes which do not seem to have been borrowed from previous buildings, but those changes were of no very great importance and were mostly in matters of detail. In sculpture and painting we can easily see that it abandoned itself to mere copying, to the repetition of a lesson learnt by rote. Whatever had to be done, was done in accordance with fixed tradition, and one monument only differed from another in the amount of care and manual dexterity bestowed upon it.

Our second reason is this, that Egypt was opened to the Greeks in the time of the Sait princes. From the year 650 B.C. onwards, there was constant communication between Ionia and the cities of the Delta. If at any time Greek art borrowed directly from that of Egypt, it was during the second half of the seventh century and the first half of the sixth. By the end of the sixth century, it had become so original and so skilful in the management of its selected methods of expression that it could not have been very receptive to foreign influences. After the Persian wars such influences would be still more powerless. In the Ptolemaic era the state of things was reversed; Greece imposed her language, her literature, her religious conceptions and their visible symbols upon the whole eastern world. Even then the art of Egypt could defend, and even perpetuate itself, by the power of custom and of a tradition which had been handed down through so many centuries, but the day was past when it could provoke imitation.

FIG. 57.—Ti, with his wife and son.

As for the indirect borrowings of forms and motives which Greece received from Egypt through the Phœnicians, their transmission had come to an end before the Persian conquest, even before the time of Psemethek. Egypt was represented, either immediately or through the imitative powers of the Syrian manufacturers, in the first textiles, jewels, and vases of clay or metal, carried by the Sidonian merchants to the savage ancestors of the Greeks. In this roundabout manner she had probably more influence over Greece than in their periods of more direct communication. The rays kindled upon her hearth, the earliest of civilization, fell upon the Hellenic isles as refracted rays, after passing through the varied media of Chaldæa, Assyria or Phœnicia.

Thus if we wish thoroughly to understand Greece, we must start from Memphis and go through Babylon and Nineveh, Tyre and Sidon. But Greece will be the aim of our voyage, and Egypt will interest us less on her own account than on account of that unique and unrivalled people who inherited her inventions and discoveries, and made them the foundation for a productiveness in which are summarized all the useful labours of antiquity. Egyptian art will be followed by us down to the moment in which it lost its creative force and with it its prestige. We shall rarely have occasion to speak of the Ptolemaic remains of Egyptian art. Now and then we shall go to them for examples when any particular detail which we desire to mention has not been preserved for us by earlier monuments, but even then we shall require to have good reasons for believing that such detail did in fact originate in the creative periods of the national history.

The Egypt of the Pharaohs has not even yet been entirely explored. Are we to believe that the splendid edifices reared in the cities of the Delta, and especially at Sais, by the twenty-sixth dynasty, have perished to the last stone? We are loth to think that it is so, but no remains have yet been discovered. Some day, perhaps, well directed excavations may bring to light the temples which Herodotus so greatly admired; and who knows but that we may find in them more than one of those motives and arrangements which at present are only known to exist in the buildings of the Ptolemies and of the Roman emperors?

CHAPTER II.

PRINCIPLES AND GENERAL CHARACTERISTICS OF EGYPTIAN ARCHITECTURE.

§ 1. *Method to be Employed by us in our Study of this Architecture.*

In the enterprise which we have undertaken the study of oriental art is but an introduction to that of Greece. Without an attentive examination of its remains we should be unable to distinguish the original elements in the work of the Greek genius from those which it borrowed from other nations. We must pass in review the whole artistic production of several great nations who occupied a vast surface of the globe, and whose fertility was prolonged through a long course of centuries, but we shall not attempt to describe singly the great buildings of Egypt and Assyria, of Persia and Phœnicia, as such an attempt would perhaps cause us to lose sight of the main object of our work.

Our task is no easy one. While limiting our study in the fashion which has been described, we must not fail to extend our purview to every fact which may help to justify the comparison which we propose to institute between the arts of Greece and those of the nations by whose teachings she profited. There is but one road to success in this double task. We must devote the greatest possible care to our study of the details in question, and then give the general results of that study; we must make ourselves thoroughly acquainted with all the phenomena, but must confine our exposition to the general laws which governed them, such as our minute inquiries have presented them to us. No circumstantial description need, therefore, be looked for in these pages even in the case of the most important and famous buildings of Egypt. No monograph upon any tomb or temple will be found, but we shall ourselves have examined many tombs and temples; we shall, to speak figuratively, have taken them to pieces, and by means of the knowledge acquired we shall endeavour to make our readers acquainted with the notions of the Egyptians upon sepulchral and religious architecture, and with the changes which those conceptions underwent in the course of centuries.

Thus, for example, we have explored the pages of Lepsius[90] and Prisse d'Avennes[91] for information relating to the sepulchres of the first six dynasties, and further researches have been made on the spot expressly for the present work, but we shall not give any descriptions or illustrations of those works individually; we shall merely use them for an ideal restoration of the characteristic tombhouse of the ancient empire. We may, perhaps, for this purpose, make a more particular reference to one or two sepulchres which are in unusually good preservation, but only for the sake of giving firm definition to the type and to its main variations.

By this analytical method of treatment we shall be enabled to give an account, which shall be at once accurate and not too long, of the constructive processes employed by the Egyptians, of the general aspect of their buildings, and of the modifications enforced by the decorative forms of which they made use. We shall be enabled to see how far those forms were decided by natural conditions, by ancient tradition, or by special wants. We shall thus include in a single chapter all that relates to principal or accessory openings, to doors and their construction, to those loftily placed windows which were calculated to give so little light. In another chapter we shall discuss the column and its capital; we shall describe the variations produced by time and materials upon its proportions and its entasis. Each assertion will be justified by reference to characteristic examples. In this matter our only difficulty will be an *embarras de richesse*, a difficulty of choice among the vast number of remains still existing of ancient Egypt from the time of Menes to that of the Persian conquest.

In order to avoid repetition and to put before the reader ideas which he will have no difficulty in assimilating, we shall push our work of analysis and generalization farther still. Before we embark upon the study of any special class of buildings we shall endeavour to define the general and unchanging characteristics of Egyptian architecture as a whole; characteristics which were fixed by the idiosyncracy of the race, by its beliefs and social customs, by the nature of the climate, and of the materials of which the architect could dispose. We shall do the same for Assyria and Chaldæa, for Persia and Phœnicia, for each, indeed, of the nationalities which are to be considered in our history.

These theoretical chapters will be illustrated in the same fashion as the others, except that the illustrations will partake of the generalized and abstract character of the text which they accompany. In most cases they will be simple diagrams composed for the express purpose of illustrating the definitions or descriptions to which they belong. They will each refer to some essential element in the national architecture, to some element which is not peculiar to any one edifice more than another, but is to be found in all those which have similar aims and are constructed of the same materials. Such elements are above and outside such accidental variations as may be found in details of plan or ornament; they form part of the substantial inner constitution of the arts of Egypt and Chaldæa, and make their originality indisputable.

§ 2. *General Principles of Form.*

The external forms of Egyptian edifices are *pyramidoid*; in other words, the outward surfaces of their walls affect the form of a *trapezium*. Thus if we prolong these surfaces vertically we find that they unite at last in a point, in the case of square buildings (Fig. 58), and in a ridge in those which are oblong in plan (Fig. 59).[92] A square building will sometimes end in a ridge, or *arête*, when the principal *façade* and the corresponding one in its rear are vertical, the other two being inclined.

Horizontal lines predominate over inclined or vertical lines, and buildings, therefore, tend to develop in length and depth rather than in height. To this general rule, however, the pylons afford exceptions.

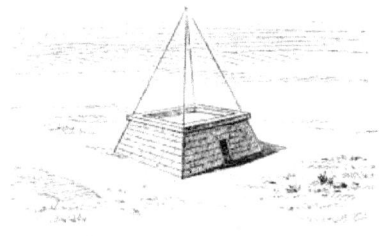

FIG. 58.—Square building.

The terminations of their edifices were also horizontal. There was no necessity for sloping roofs, as, away from the immediate proximity of the sea, it hardly ever rains in Egypt. Moreover, the natural conformation of the country had its influence upon the creations of its inhabitants. The unforeseen and sudden variations, the contrasts of hill and plain, which we find in a mountainous country like Greece, are here unknown. Lower Egypt is a verdant plain, intersected by canals, and stretching from the sea to the desert; in Upper and Middle Egypt the lazy river is accompanied throughout its journey from south to north by two long chains of hills, the Arab chain and the Libyan, whose summits form an almost unbroken line. Between these aspects of nature and the works of man which they enframe, there is a striking general sympathy.[93]

FIG. 59.—Rectangular and oblong building.

The peculiar character of Egyptian architecture is owing to its lateral extension, and to those wide-spreading bases and foundations which suggest the inclination of the superincumbent walls. In looking at one of these buildings, we feel that it is capable of infinite extension horizontally, and that but one of its dimensions, that of height, is limited by its essential forms. These characteristics give a look of sturdy power to Egyptian architecture which is peculiar to itself, and suggests an idea of unbounded durability.[94]

FIG. 60.—The Libyan chain, above the necropolis of Thebes.

An appearance of incomparable gravity, of solemnity, is also stamped upon it by the small number of openings for the admission of light of which it makes use, and also by their arrangement. Compared to our modern architecture, in which windows play such an important part, that of Egypt is prison-like in its gloom; but, in consequence of its rare openings and their small size, it presents more imposing walls than any other style.

One of the essential arrangements of Egyptian architecture is shared by many other countries, that of the *portico*, by which we mean an alternation of voids and solids in certain well defined proportions, either for ornamenting the exterior and providing a covered way, or for dividing the halls of the interior and supporting their roofs.

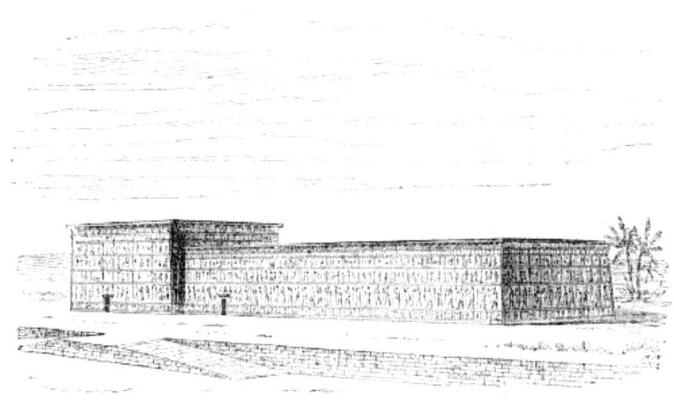

FIG. 61.—General appearance of an Egyptian Temple.[95]

The relation between voids and solids in any style of architecture is one of the most vital characteristics.

In the case of Egypt this relation gives rise to the following remarks:

1. Supports of the same kind and of the same diameter may have very different heights in one and the same building (Fig. 62).

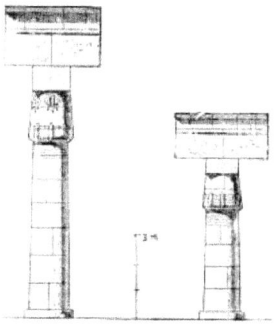

FIG. 62.—Temple of Khons, at Thebes.
(*Description de l'Égypte*, t. iii., pl. 55.)

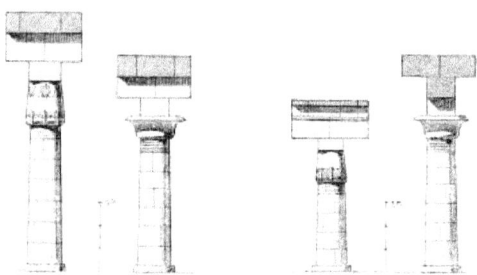

FIG. 63.—Temple of Khons, Thebes. (*Descr. de l'Égypte*, t. iii., pl. 55.)
FIG. 64.—Temple of Khons, Thebes. (*Descr. de l'Égypte*, t. iii., pl. 55.)

In a single edifice supports of different kinds but of the same diameter, have no fixed proportions, one to the other. A column with a *lotus* capital may be higher than one with a bell-shaped termination, and *vice versâ* (Figs. 63 and 64), while, again in a single building, we may find these two differently shaped columns equal to each other both in average diameter and in height (Fig. 65).

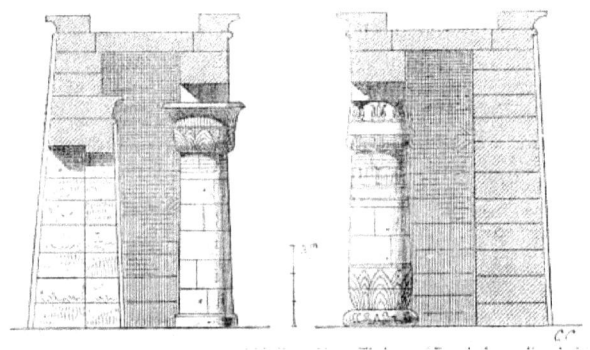

FIG. 65.—From the second court of Medinet-Abou, Thebes.
(*Description*, t. ii., pl. 6.)

2. The spaces, or voids, between columns of one size and similar design, may vary considerably (Fig. 66), and the entablatures which they support may differ greatly in height (Fig. 66).

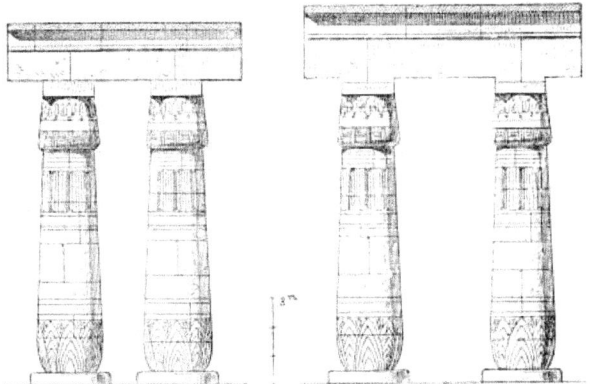

FIG. 66.—Ramesseum, Thebes.
(*Description de l'Égypte*, t. ii., pl. 28.)

The proportional combinations of these elements are such that they cannot be methodically classified, and in this the architecture of Egypt is distinguished from that which we call classic. In Greek art there is a *modulus* which determines the quantitative relation of forms to each other, and fixes a mutual and invariable interdependence. This *modulus* is found in the diameter of the column, and the standard of proportion which is based upon it is called a *canon*. In Egypt, as in other countries, there must have been a certain connection between the diameter of a column and its height, but there was no approach to that rigid and immutable law which had its effect upon every detail of a Greek temple. The *modulus*, in Egyptian art, was used with such freedom, and gave rise to such varied proportions, that we may say that no *canon* existed. The elementary forms of an Egyptian edifice had so little dependence upon the *modulus* that we need not take it into consideration, and, in this sense, the art of Egypt was not mathematical, like that of Greece.

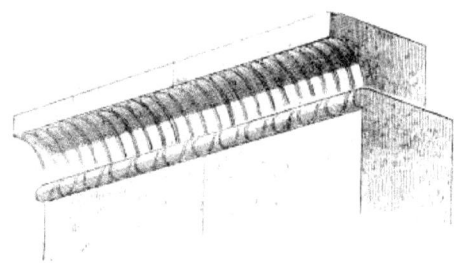

FIG. 67.—The Egyptian Gorge or Cornice.

Finally, all Egyptian buildings are crowned by the same entablature, an architrave and the moulding which is called the Egyptian *gorge* (Fig. 67).[96] An architectural member, the plain quadrangular architrave, is invariably inserted between this termination and the upper extremity of the voids and points of support.

THE ARAB CHAIN FROM NEAR KENEH

THE PYRAMIDS FROM OLD CAIRO

§ 3. *General Principles of Construction.—Materials.*

In studying a natural architecture and in attempting to assign reasons for its particular characteristics, many circumstances have to be taken into consideration. The innate genius of the race, the physical and moral conditions of its development, the perfection of its civilization, the spirit of its religion, and the ardour of its faith; none of these must be forgotten, but some of them act in such a complex fashion that they are extremely difficult to follow. In its aspirations towards the infinite and the eternal, the Egyptian religion raised from the surface of the earth many buildings which varied as greatly in form and aspect as they did in date and situation. The climatic conditions of the world have changed but little since the beginning of the historic period, and every nation has to take them into the first consideration in deciding upon its own architectural forms and principles. We have here a problem whose data do not vary, and yet its solutions have not always been the same even in a single country. Without ever being absolutely incorrect, they attached themselves now to one principle, now to another, and so gave much variety to the appearance of successive buildings under one sky and destined for similar uses.

As for the materials employed, we cannot go so far as to say that their different properties absolutely determined the characteristics of Egyptian building in advance. Stone, the chief of all materials, can lend itself to forms of great variety in principle; and so, too, can brick and wood. But although no material can narrowly confine a skilful architect, there are, nevertheless, certain systems and constructions which are only possible with those which possess certain properties.

To give but a single example, neither the hypo-style halls of Egypt and Persepolis, nor the Greek temples, with their architraves resting upon widely spaced columns, with the coffered roofs of their porticos, and their decorative and expressive sculpture, could have been carried out in brick. In stone, or rather in marble, alone, could the typical temple, such as the Parthenon, have been realised; without such a material the Greeks could never have created that incomparable ensemble whose different parts are so intimately allied one with another, in which the richest decoration is in complete unity with the constructive forms which it accentuates and embellishes. Brick could never have led to the invention or employment of these forms. Those who try to imitate them in any such material have to make up for its deficiencies by various ingenious devices. The joints between the bricks have to be hidden under stucco, the mouldings and carved ornaments of stone have to be replaced, as in the temple of the Deus Rediculus, by moulded terra cotta (Fig. 68). The result is sometimes pleasing enough, especially by the surprise which it causes. Santa Maria delle Grazie, at Milan, is a masterpiece of its kind, thanks to the skill and tact displayed by Bramante in the management of the burnt clay which was the only material afforded him by the plains of Lombardy; but where Bramante succeeded, less skilful artists have failed. They have demanded effects from brick which it was unable to give, with a profound discord between form and matter as a result.

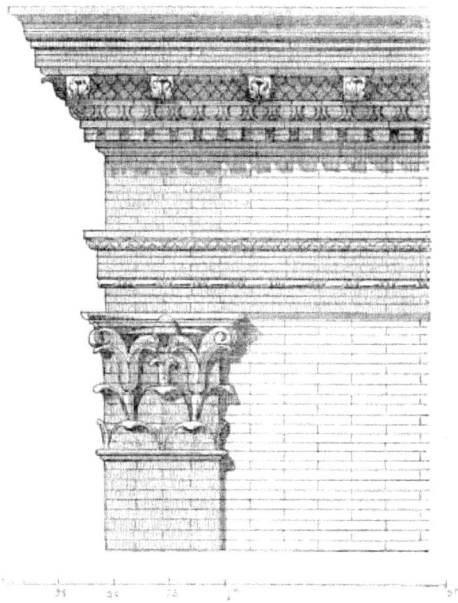

Fig. 68.—Capital and entablature of the temple of the Deus Rediculus at Rome.[97]

Of all the causes which modify the forms of architecture and determine its character, the most important is the nature, the genius, if we may say so, of the materials used. So, before we can arrive at a correct judgment of the rules and principles of any style, we must begin by appreciating and describing the materials of which it disposes. We never forget this in the case of sculpture, still less should we do so in the case of architecture, where the material is still more despotic.

The materials made use of by the Egyptians were granite,[98] sandstone,[99] and limestone.[100] A softer stone, namely alabaster, was often employed for lining.[101]

Sandstone and limestone, especially the latter, are used nearly everywhere; granite is of less frequent occurrence and suggests an important observation.

Granite is not a sedimentary, stratified rock like limestone; it is a material compacted in great masses, to a depth or, to speak more accurately, in a volume which is practically unlimited; the dimensions of the stones which may be cut from these masses are therefore infinite to all intents and purposes.[102]

The Egyptians also made use of both burnt and unburnt brick.

The employment of these different materials gave birth to what we may call "dressed construction," that is, construction the elements of which are squared upon each face and put into close juxtaposition one with another.

Concrete or pisé, compressed, as in the pylons, between moulds or caissons of woodwork, was also made use of by the Egyptians. This material gave rise to what we may call compact construction.

Again, although trees, except the palm, were rare enough in the valley of the Nile, the Egyptians built also in wood, by which a third kind of construction, called construction by assemblage, in which the elementary units were held together by being introduced one into another, was obtained.

In a few buildings of the latter class metal seems to have been employed, sometimes in the construction, sometimes for lining, and sometimes for outward decoration.

§ 4. *Dressed Construction.*

The constructive elements which enter into the composition of this first class of buildings are stone and brick.

In the first place, these elements are horizontal or vertical.

The horizontal elements constitute the planes, as they cover the voids by horizontal superposition.

They consist of courses and architraves.

The courses form the walls. They are arranged in horizontal bands, with vertical and sometimes sloping joints. The separate stones are often bound together upon their horizontal surfaces by dovetails or tenons of wood. The blocks made use of in this form of construction are usually of large dimensions, but the Egyptians also made use of small stones or rubble, lined on the exterior by large flat ones which concealed the meanness of the material behind them.[103] (Fig. 70.)

Various peculiarities of construction which are comparatively seldom met with will be noticed when we come to describe the monuments in which they are to be found.

Architraves were stone beams used to bridge over the voids and to support the covering of the building, which latter was composed of long and heavy slabs.

The vertical elements support the architraves and combine them one with another. These vertical supports vary greatly in size. Those of small or medium dimensions are monoliths; others are composed of many courses of stone one upon another, courses which in this case take the name of *drums*.

FIG. 69.—The Egyptian "bond."

Upon exterior surfaces, supports take various forms of development which may all be referred to the type which we have defined, namely, the portico. In the interiors the form of support is a logical consequence of the material employed. Whenever the stones which form the roof are too small to bridge over the whole of the space comprised within two walls, they must be made to rest upon intermediate supports; and this necessity springs up in every building of any importance. This very elementary combination fulfils all the requirements of circulation. The number of supports depends upon the number of rows of the flat stones which form the roof. They are sometimes multiplied to such an extent that they remind us of that planting arrangement in our gardens which we call a quincunx.

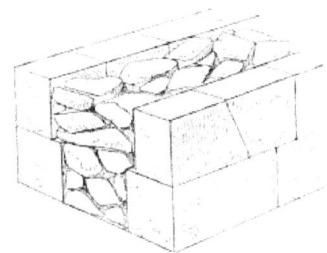

FIG. 70.—Double-faced wall.

We cannot, however, affirm that the number of supports is invariably decided by the length of the architraves, or of the roofing stones. Some very long monoliths are supported at regular intervals, lest they should break with their own weight or with that put upon them. The walls, architraves, and vertical supports are always far stronger than the mere weight of the roof would require.

FIGS. 71, 72.—Elements of the portico.

The following woodcut shows the arrangement of supports, architraves and roof. These simple arrangements constitute a complete system of construction which, belonging exclusively to Egypt, has had results upon which we cannot too strongly insist. Both roof and architraves being horizontal, all the pressure upon the walls is vertical. There is no force tending to thrust the walls outwards nor to affect the immobility of the supports.

FIG. 73.—Egyptian construction, epitomized by Ch. Chipiez.

Consequently, if the proportions of the vertical and horizontal elements of a building, that is to say, its sections, have been skilfully determined, there is in the building itself no latent cause of disruption; its equilibrium is perfect, and can only be destroyed by external physical causes, by long exposure to the weather, by earthquakes, or by the hand of man.[104]

We see then that the first impression caused by the external lines of the architectural monuments of Egypt is confirmed and explained by further study. They are built, as said the Pharaohs themselves, "for eternity." Stability, in a word, in its highest and most simple form is the distinguishing characteristic, the true originality, of Egyptian architecture.

This character is most strongly marked in stone buildings, but it is by no means absent from those built of materials created by human industry. Works in brick form the transition between the construction that we have described and that which we call compact. A stone roof is not often found, and the termination is generally a terrace in which wood is the chief element. In some cases the secondary parts of such edifices, and sometimes the whole of them, are covered in by brick vaults, and maintained by walls of a sufficient thickness.

Although the use of monoliths for roofing purposes was general in Egypt, it must not be thought that the architects of that country were ignorant of the art of covering voids with materials of small size, that is to say, of building vaults. There are numerous examples of Egyptian vaults, some of them of great antiquity, and, moreover, the Egyptian builders constructed their vaults after a method of their own. In spite of the facilities which they afforded, they played, however, but a secondary *rôle* in the development of art. They were never used in the buildings to which greater importance was attached; they are introduced chiefly in out-of-the-way corners of the building, and in the substructures of great monumental combinations. This method of construction, being confined within such narrow limits, never resulted in Egypt in an architectural system;[105] neither did it give birth to any of those accessory forms which spring from its use.

Egyptian vaults may be divided into two great categories, according to the method of their construction.

1. *Off-set vaults.* These vaults are composed of courses off-set one from another, and with their faces hollowed to the segment of a circle. (Fig. 74.)

FIG. 74.—Element of an off-set arch.

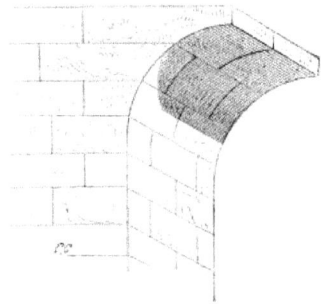

FIG. 75.—Arrangement of the courses in an off-set arch.

If the face of those stones which, in the form of inverted steps, are turned to the void which has to be covered, be cut into the line of a continuous curve, the superficial appearance of a segmental arch or barrel vault will be obtained; but this appearance will be no more than superficial, the vault will be in fact a false one, because, in such a construction, all the stones which enframe the void and offer to the eye the form of a vault, are really laid horizontally one upon another, and their lateral joints are vertical. (Fig. 76.) When the units of such vaults are properly proportioned they are stable in themselves, and they have no lateral thrust.

FIG. 76.—Off-set semicircular arch.

2. *Centred vaults.* These are true vaults. They are composed of voussoirs, whose lateral joints are oblique, and radiate towards one centre or more. (Figs. 77, 78, and 79.)

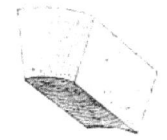

FIG. 77.—Voussoir.

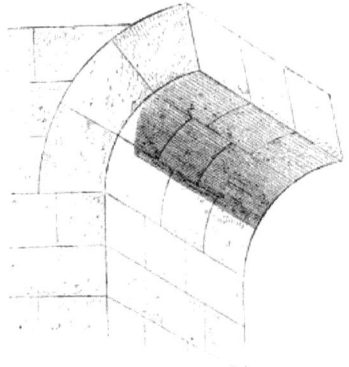

FIG. 78.—Arrangement of voussoirs.

This method of construction is very convenient because it enables the builder to utilize constructive units of very small dimensions, such as bricks. But this advantage has a corresponding drawback. These voussoirs thrust one against another and tend towards disintegration. They are not stable in themselves, and in order to give them stability they must be kept in place by surrounding them with opposing forces which will effectually prevent their setting up any movement in the structure of which they form a part. This function is fulfilled by the wall in Egyptian architecture, which is consequently very thick, but the radiating arch never arrived at such a development in Egypt as to lead to the adoption of any contrivance specially charged with the maintenance of vaults in a state of proper rigidity. The Egyptians not only employed the semicircular arch; they made use, in a few instances, of the pointed form, and many of their underground buildings have roofs cut out of the rock in the form of a segmental vault. The fact that these sepulchral chambers affected the aspect of vaulted halls, can only be explained by the supposition that a similar construction was common in the dwellings of the living.[106]

Fig. 79.—Semicircular vault.

§ 5. *Compact Construction.*

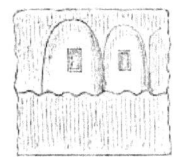

Fig. 80.—Granaries,
from a bas-relief.

The methods employed in what we may call *compact construction* permit the use, in considerable quantities, of moulded clay mixed with chopped straw. This material was used in buildings which were homogeneous; it was poured into a mould formed by planks, which was raised as the work progressed and the mixture dried. But the material had little strength, and was far inferior to those modern concretes which have the density and durability of the hardest stone. The Egyptians do not seem to have been acquainted with concrete proper, and unburnt bricks did not differ essentially from pisé. Such bricks, when placed one upon another after being imperfectly dried, combined, under the influence of the weather and their own weight, into one homogeneous mass so that the separate courses became undistinguishable. This latter fact has been frequently noticed in Assyria, by those who had to cut through the thickness of walls in the process of excavation.

FIG. 81.—Modern pigeon house, Thebes.

If voids have to be covered in pisé, one of those self-supporting curves which we have described under the name of vaults, must be made use of, and the vault must be constructed over a centring of wood. But we have no evidence that the Egyptians could carry the art of construction to this point in pisé. On the contrary, we have good reason to believe that they generally made use of this material for the quiescent body of the edifice alone, and that voids were mostly covered with stone or wood. In a word, the Egyptians did not carry the use of artificial material far enough to form a complete system based upon it. They made great use of it, but only in a strictly limited fashion. It is only found in certain well-defined parts of buildings, which were never of any very great interest from an artistic point of view (Fig. 80). It deserved to be mentioned, if only for the frequency of its use in Egypt, in the private architecture of both ancient and modern times (Fig. 81), but it need not detain us longer.

§ 6. *Construction by Assemblage.*

Carpentry, or construction by assemblage, played a considerable part in ancient Egypt, but, as may easily be understood, few traces of it are to be found in our day. Those edifices which were constructed of wood have, of course, all perished; but, in spite of their disappearance, we can form a very good idea of their aspect and of the principles of their construction. In the most ancient epoch of Egyptian art, the people took pleasure in copying, in their stone buildings, the arrangements which had characterised their work in wood; besides which, their paintings and reliefs often represent buildings of the less durable material. The constructive principles which we have next to notice, have thus left traces behind them which will enable us to describe them with almost as much accuracy as if the carpenters of Cheops and Rameses were working before our eyes.

We need not insist upon the characteristics which distinguish assembled construction from masonry or brickwork. The different parts of the former are, of course, much more intimately allied than in buildings constructed of large stones. Supports of dressed stone truly fixed with the plumb line are perfectly stable of themselves.

In both Egypt and Greece we often come upon a few columns still standing upright amid their desolate surroundings, and announcing to the traveller the site of some city or famous temple which has been long destroyed. But wooden supports have little thickness in comparison with their height, and the material of which they are formed, being far less dense than stone, cannot maintain itself in place by its own weight. It is the same with wooden architraves. The heaviest beams of wood will not keep their places when simply laid one upon another, and are in that matter far inferior to those well dressed stones which, in so many ancient walls, have resisted change with neither tenons nor cement to help them.

As a general principle, when wood has to be employed to the best advantage, and endowed with all the solidity and resisting power of which it is capable, the separate pieces must be introduced one into another (Fig. 82). But even when thus combined and held in place by mechanical contrivances, such as bolts and nails, they will never form a homogeneous and impenetrable mass like brick or stone. By such methods an open structure is obtained, the voids of which have afterwards to be filled up by successive additions, and these additions often take the form of what we call panels.

We may look upon the different faces of a wooden building as separate pieces of construction which should be put together upon the ground before being combined with each other. This process, though not always made use of in practice, is at least the most logical method for those who wish to make the best use of their materials. But even when thus put together, one of these single faces has not much more stability than each of its constituent elements. In order to form a rigid and stable whole, the several faces must be allied by reciprocal interpenetration at the angles.

It was necessary to call attention once for all to these general characteristics of wooden construction, because we shall hereafter have occasion to examine the forms and motives which stone architecture borrowed from wood in the case of other people besides the Egyptians. We must now determine the particular characteristics offered by the material in Egypt, as they may be learnt in the representations to which we have already referred.

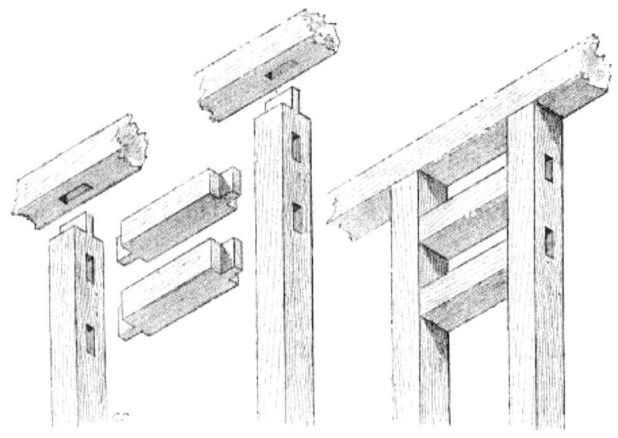

FIG. 82.—**Elements of wooden construction.**

When a wall has to be built of wood so as neither to warp nor give way, it is necessary to make use of a certain number of oblique members. This is one of the elementary rules of the carpenter's art, and to form an idea how it was applied in our own country it is enough to cast an eye over any of the wooden buildings of the middle ages or of the renaissance. The Egyptians were not ignorant of the advantages conferred by the use of these oblique members because they employed them frequently in their furniture; but they seem never to have introduced them into the construction of their buildings. All joints are there made at a right angle. They were probably led to reject oblique lines by their unwillingness to break in upon the simple harmony of vertical and horizontal lines which is the distinguishing principle of all their architecture. Thus self-deprived of a valuable resource, they were driven to the discovery of some other means of giving the required cohesion and stability to their walls. This requirement they thought they had fulfilled in exaggerating the points of connection between the vertical and horizontal members, which were thus brought into more intimate relation than would in these days be thought necessary.[107] The consequence of this was that their wooden buildings presented much the same closed appearance (Fig. 83) as we have already noticed in their stone constructions; and, moreover, as every joint was made at right angles, the pyramidal form was entirely absent.

FIG. 83.—Wooden building (first system), composed by Charles Chipiez.
[108]

But the Egyptians also made use of wood for buildings very different from those to which we have hitherto alluded. Those were closed; but we have now to speak of another system, of one which, by contrast, might be called an open system of construction. The edifices upon which it was employed were generally of small size, and in this respect resembled those which we have described, but they were distinguished by a different system of carpentering. We know them only by the figured representations which have come down to us, for they were little calculated to outlast the centuries (Fig. 84). This second system lends itself as little as the first to pyramidal and kindred forms; horizontal lines, also, were in it of but secondary importance. Composed of a few vertical members bound together at the top, such a building was allied to the portico type which has already been described. This method of carpentry seems to have been used only for subordinate buildings; but yet it should not be passed by in silence. It was frequently used for the construction of light decorative pavilions, and it had a set of principles which are as susceptible of definition as those of the most ambitious architecture.

FIG. 84.—Wooden building (second system), composed by Charles Chipiez.

Metal must have entered into the construction of these pavilions. It may have furnished either the horizontal or the vertical members, and it is certain that it was partly used for the roofs.

In all wooden structures the roof must also be of wood, because the light walls which are proper to the material could not support the great weight of a flat stone covering, still less could they stand up against the combined weight and thrust of a stone or brick vault, which would destroy them in very summary fashion.

§ 7. *Decoration.*

We have hitherto described Egyptian architecture according to the general character of its forms and principles of construction; we must now attempt to give a true idea of its method of decoration. This may be described in a very few words. For the decoration of the vast surfaces, either plain or curved, which their style of architecture placed at their disposal, the Egyptians made use of paint. They overlaid with a rich system of colour the whole inside and outside of their buildings, and that with no desire to accentuate, by a carefully balanced set of tones, the great constructive lines, contours and mouldings, nor with any wish to produce merely a complicated, polychromatic ornamentation. Groups of figures borrowed from the animal and vegetable kingdoms form its chief constituents. In these picture decorations, man is seen in every attitude or vocation, side by side with birds, fishes and quadrupeds, and with those composite forms which have been created by himself to represent his gods.

Intaglio and bas-relief often lend their help to the ornament. Images and explanatory inscriptions are sometimes cut in the stone, sometimes modelled in slight relief; but in either case all figures are distinguished by their proper colour as well as by the carved or modelled outlines.

It will thus be seen that Egyptian decoration is distinguished by the intimate and constant alliance of two elements which are often separated in that of other races. The first is the employment of colour to give variety to surfaces and to distinguish different members of the architecture by the opposition of tones. The second is the employment of colour for the representation of life, for which purpose every surface is seized upon, whether the face of a wall, or the round shaft of a column. The decorator is not satisfied to use colour to give force to the lines of a building and to increase its general effect; he also makes use of it to interpret, to multiply, and to immortalize the ideas which float through his own brain. A building thus ornamented presents us with a series of pictures embodied in its own constitution. From cornice to foundation, upon wall and column, it is covered with an unending series of wall paintings, which, like a gorgeous tapestry, envelop and embellish it without hiding any of the details of its construction.

The polychromatic decoration of the Egyptians is to be explained, like that of the Assyrians, of the Greeks, of the Italians, and of all other southern nations, by the quality and quantity of their daylight and the way in which it affected their visual organs. The more intense the light, the more pleasure does the eye receive from strength and variety of colour. The science of optics gives us an explanation of this fact, but at present we are concerned only with the fact itself, which is a matter of daily experience. It is notorious that the colours of birds and butterflies, and of the petals of flowers, become brighter and gayer in exact proportion as we near the equator and leave the pole;[109] the same rule holds good with the habitations of mankind, with his clothes and furniture, which become more brilliant in colour, and more audaciously abrupt in their transitions from one hue to another. Delicate shades of difference are imperceptible by an eye blinded with the southern sun; it sees nothing but the simplest, strongest, and frankest colour notes to the exclusion of all half-tint.[110]

Under a burning and never clouded sun, objects of a neutral colour do not stand out against their background, and their shadows lose a part of their value, "*comme dévorées par la diffusion et la réverbération d'une incomparable lumière.*"[111] In Egypt, a column, a minaret, a dome, hardly seem to be modelled as they stand against the depths of the sky. All three seem almost flat. The warm and varied hues with which polychromatic decoration endows buildings help us to distinguish them in such situations from the ground upon which they stand, and to accentuate their different planes. They also compensate, in some degree, for the absence of those strong shadows which elsewhere help to make contours visible. Attention is drawn to the dominant and bounding lines of an architectural composition by contrasts of tint which also serve to give force to wall paintings and bas-reliefs.

Polychromy is thus a help to our eyes in those countries where a blinding light would otherwise prevent us from appreciating the structural beauties of their architecture. It is by no means peculiar to Egypt, but that country was the first to employ it upon rich and vast undertakings, she employed it more constantly and more universally than any other people, and she carried it to its logical conclusion with a boldness which was quite unique.

The Egyptian habit of sprinkling figures over every surface without regard to its shape, its functions, or those of the mass to which it belonged, was also peculiar to themselves. Upon the round shaft of the column, upon the bare expanse of the wall, these figures were multiplied and developed to an extent which was limited only by the length of the wall or the height of the column. They were generally painted in bands of equal height, separated one from another by a narrow fillet which indicated the plane upon which the groups of figures had a footing. There is no visible connection between the bands of figures and the structures which they ornament; right and left, above and below, they spread over every surface and pay no attention to the joints and other structural accidents by which they are seamed (Fig. 85 and Pl. III.).

It may be said that these joints were invisible until the passage of centuries had laid them bare by destroying the stucco which, especially where sandstone or limestone was used, once veiled the surface of the bare walls. [112] Doubtless this is true; but even in a climate such as that of Egypt, the architect could not believe that a thin coat of plaster would endure as long as the massive walls upon which he laid it. We have here a great contrast in principle between the decoration and the architecture of Egypt. In the latter the chief, if not the only aim, seems to have been to make sure of absolute stability, of indefinite duration; and yet these eternal walls are lined with a rich decoration which is spoiled by the fall of a piece of plaster, which is injured by the unavoidable settlings of the masonry and destroyed by the slightest earthquake! Of this we need give but one conclusive instance. Our third plate reproduces that admirable portrait of Seti I., which is the wonder of the temple at Abydos. This beautiful work in relief is sculptured upon the internal faces of four unequal stones in the wall of one of the rooms. The joints may be distinguished, but as yet they have not opened sufficiently to do much damage to the artistic beauty of the work; but it cannot be denied that the preservation of the royal effigy would have been much more certainly assured if the sculptor had chosen a single stone to work upon, instead of a built-up wall which so many causes would help to destroy.

When Egyptian buildings were new and their colour fresh, this method of decoration must have given them a most fascinating brilliancy. Whether the pencil alone were employed to trace the designs upon the smooth walls, or whether its powers were supplemented by the work of the chisel, these figures, which succeeded each other in thousands upon every wall and pillar, mingled with inscriptions which were in themselves pictures, and dressed in the most vivid colours, must have at once amused the eye and stirred the brain by the variety of their tints and of the scenes which they represented. But in spite of its breadth and vivacity the system had two grave defects.

The first was the fragility of the plaster surface upon which it was displayed. This surface may be compared to a tapestry stretched over the whole interior of the building, and, to continue the comparison, when once any portion of the plaster coat became detached from the wall, there was nothing left but the ground or reverse of the stuff.[113] The design and colour may still be distinguished or divined, but there is a great difference between painted ornament which is subject to such damage and a woven hanging at any time before the threads of the woof have been discoloured and entirely worn out. The other defect in the system, is its uniformity. It is monotonous and confused in spite of all its richness. It suffers from the absence of that learned balance between plain and decorated surface which the Greeks understood so thoroughly. In the Greek temples, sculptured figures had the more importance in that the eye of the spectator was drawn forcibly to them by the very limitation of the space reserved for them. They were cut from separate blocks of marble, which, though carefully and skilfully allied with the architecture which they were meant to adorn, did not form an integral part of it. Such figures ran no risk of being cut in two by the opening of the joints between the stones. Although marvellously well adapted to the places for which they were intended, and closely allied to the architecture by their subject as well as their material shape, they yet preserved a life and individuality of their own. To take decorative art as a whole, the Greeks did not make use of so many figures as the Egyptians, but they knew better how to economize the sources of effect, and to preserve their works against the destructive action of time.

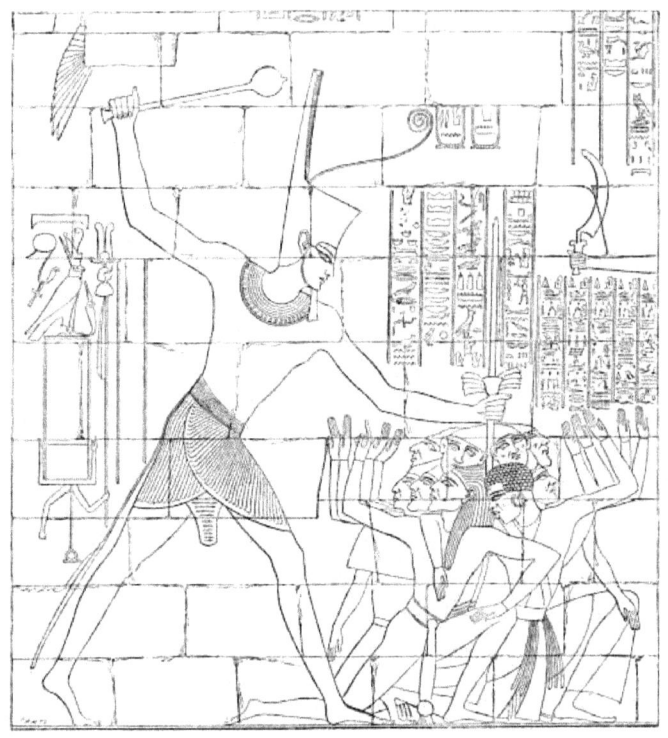

FIG. 85.—Seti I. striking prisoners of war with his mace. Karnak, Thebes. (Champollion, Pl. 294.)

J. Sulpis del.
KARNAK
BAS-RELIEFS IN THE GRANITE CHAMBERS

To Egypt, then, belongs the credit of having been the first to discover the obligation imposed upon the architect by the sunlight of the south—to accentuate the main lines of his edifice by means of colour. She thoroughly understood how to make different tones distinguish between the various parts of a structure and defend its contours against the effect of a dazzling light. On the other hand, she went too far when she covered every surface, without choice or stint, with her endless figure processions. Such a decoration was only rendered possible by the use of a material which compromised its durability; and that is not her only shortcoming. She failed to understand the value of repose and the absolute necessity of contrast; she failed to perceive that by multiplying figures to infinity, she lessened their effect and made them a fatigue to the eye and the intellect.

CHAPTER III.

Sepulchral Architecture.

§ 1. *The Egyptian Belief as to a Future Life and its Influence upon their Sepulchral Architecture.*

The most ancient monuments which have yet been discovered in Egypt are the tombs; they have therefore a right to the first place in our sketch of Egyptian architecture.

In every country the forms and characteristics of the sepulchre are determined by the ideas of the natives as to the fate of their bodies and souls after life is over. In order to understand the Egyptian arrangements, we must begin then by inquiring into their notions upon death and its consequences; we must ask whether they believed in another life, and in what kind of life. We shall find a complete answer to our question in the collation of written texts with figured monuments.

In the first period of his intellectual development, man is unable to comprehend any life but that which he experiences in his own person. He is as yet unable to observe, to analyse or to generalize. He does not perceive the characteristics which distinguish him from things about him, and he sees nothing in nature but a repetition of himself. He is therefore incapable of distinguishing between life such as he leads it and mere existence. He dreams of no other way of being than his own. As such is the tendency of his intellect, nothing could be more natural or more logical than the conception to which it leads him in presence of the problem offered to him every time that a corpse descends into the grave. M. Maspero has so thoroughly understood the originality of the solution adopted by the Egyptians that we cannot do better, in attempting to explain the hypothesis, at once gross and subtle, to which they had recourse for consolation, than borrow his rendering of the texts which throw light upon this subject, together with some of the reflections which those texts suggested to him.[114]

J. Sulpis del. et sc.
SETI I

BAS-RELIEF AT ABYDOS

Were we to affirm that during thousands of years no change took place in the ideas of the Egyptians upon a future life, we should not be believed, and, as a fact, those ideas underwent a continual process of refinement. Under the eighteenth and nineteenth dynasties, during those centuries when the limits of Egyptian empire and Egyptian thought were carried farthest afield, we find traces of doctrines which offer notable variations, and even, when closely examined, actual contradictions. These are successive answers made during a long course of time to the eternal and never-changing enigma. As they became more capable of philosophic speculation the Egyptians modified their definition of the soul, and, by a necessary consequence, of the manner in which its persistence after death must be understood, and as always happens in such a case, these successive conceptions are super-imposed one upon another; the last comer did not dethrone its predecessor but became inextricably blended with it in the popular imagination.

We refer all those who wish to follow minutely this curious development of the Egyptian intellect to the subtle analysis of M. Maspero. That historian has applied himself to the apprehension of every delicate shade of meaning in a system of thought which has to be grasped through the veil thrown around it by extreme difficulties of language and written character, but at the same time he has never attempted to endow it with a precision or logical completeness to which it had no claim. By well chosen comparisons and illustrations he enables us to understand how the Egyptian contented himself with vague notions, and how he managed to harmonize ideas which seem to us inconsistent.

We shall not enter into those details. We shall not seek to determine the sense which the Egyptians attached, after a certain period, to the word *bâi*,[115] which has been translated *soul*, nor the distinction between it and *khou*, luminousness, which the soul seems to have enveloped like a garment. We shall not follow the soul and its internal light in its subterranean journey across *Ament*, the Egyptian Hades, to which it entered by a cleft, *Pega*, to the west of Abydos, which was the only portal to the kingdom of the shades; nor shall we accompany them in the successive transformations which made them acquainted with every corner of the earth and sky in the infinite series of their *becomes* (to use the Egyptian expression); what we have to do is to trace out the most ancient of their religious conceptions, the conception which, like the first teachings of infancy, was so deeply engraved upon the soul and intellect of the race as to exercise a much stronger influence than the later more abstract and more philosophical theories, which were superimposed upon it. In this primitive conception we ought to find the determining cause of the Egyptian form of tomb. Its constitution was already settled in the time of the ancient Empire, and, from the Memphite dynasties until the end, it remained unchanged in principle. In this constitution we shall find embodied the essential idea adopted by the Egyptians when they first attempted to find some eternal element in man, or, at least, some element which should resist the annihilation of death for a period much longer than the few days which make up our mortal life.

The Egyptians called that which does not perish as the dying man draws his last sigh, the *ka*, a term which M. Maspero has rendered as the *double*. "This *double* was a duplicate of the body in a matter less dense than that of the body, a projection, coloured but aërial, of the individual, reproducing him feature for feature, a child if coming from a child, a woman if from a woman, and a man if from a man."[116]

This *double* had to be installed in a lodging suitable to its existence, had to be surrounded by objects which it had used in its former state, had to be supplied with the food which was necessary for the sustenance of its life. And all these things it obtained from the piety of its relations, who, on fixed days, brought them to the threshold of the *good dwelling* or the *eternal dwelling*, which were the phrases used by the Egyptians.[117] By these offerings alone could the hungry and thirsty phantom which had replaced the living man be kept alive. The first duty of the survivors was to take care that this dependent existence should not be extinguished by their neglect, to provide food and drink for the support, if we may use such a phrase, of the precarious life of the dead, who would otherwise be irritated against them and use the almost godlike power attributed to his mysterious condition for the punishment of his ungrateful posterity.[118]

This conception is not peculiar to Egypt. The *double* of the Egyptian sepulchral records corresponds exactly to the εἴδωλον[119] of the Greeks and the *umbra* of the Latins. Both Greeks and Latins believed that when the funeral rites had been duly accomplished, this image or shadow entered upon the possession of a subterranean dwelling and began a life which was no more than the continuation of that in the light.[120] The dead thus remained in close relation with the living, on the one hand by the nourishment which they received, on the other by the protection which they afforded; even in the funeral repast they took their parts, in the strictest sense of the word, in the eating and drinking.[121] They looked impatiently forward to these supplies because, for a moment, they awoke their dormant thoughts and feelings and gave them glimpses of the true life, the life above ground and in the sunshine. [122] If they were kept waiting too long they became angry and revenged themselves upon those who had caused their sufferings. Woe to the family or city which was not careful to interest the dead in its stability and thus to associate them with its prosperity![123]

These beliefs seem to have been common to all ancient peoples during that period of their existence which is lost in the shadow of prehistoric times. From India to Italy all the primitive forms of public and private rights betray their presence. For this fact and its consequences we may refer our readers to the fine work of M. Fustel de Coulange, *La Cité antique*.[124]

FIG. 86.—Stele of the 11th dynasty. Boulak. Drawn by Bourgoin.

With the progress of centuries and the development of religious thought, more elevated ideas prevailed. The growth of the scientific spirit tended to make the notion of a being suspended between life and death ever more strange and inadmissible. Experience accumulated its results and it became daily more evident that death not only put an end to the activity of the organs, but that, immediately upon its occurrence, it began to dissolve and decompose their tissues. As time rolled on men must have found it very difficult to believe in a shadow thus placed outside the normal conditions of life, in a something which was not a spirit and yet survived the destruction of its organs.

It would seem then that observation and logical reflection should soon have led to the abandonment of a theory which now appears so puerile; but, even in these scientific times, those whose intellects demand well defined ideas are few indeed.[125] At a period when the diffusion of intellectual culture and the perfection of scientific methods add daily to our accumulations of positive knowledge, most men allow their souls to be stirred and their actions to be prompted by the vaguest words and notions; how much greater then must the influence of those confused beliefs and baseless images have been in antiquity when but a few rare minds, and those ill provided with means of research and analysis, attempted to think with originality, clearness and freedom.

The prestige of this illusion was increased and perpetuated by its intimate connection with several of those sentiments which are most honourable to human nature. Such a worship of the dead surprises and even scandalizes us by its frank materialism, but if we seek for the source of its inspiration and its primitive meaning, we find them in the remembrance of lost objects of affection, in feelings broken by the supreme separation, in the gratitude of children to the parents who gave them birth and nourished their infancy, in the recognition by the living of the blessings which they enjoy through the long and laborious efforts of their ancestors. There was no doubt a perishable element in the funerary ideas of Egypt, an element which the progress of reason was sure to destroy, and we may be tempted to smile when we think of the Greek or Egyptian giving himself the trouble to feed his departed ancestors with blood, milk, or honey, but with all their simplicity, both one and the other were alive to a truth which the revolutionary spirit of our days, with its childish and brutal contempt for the past, is often unable to grasp. They realized the complete solidarity of one human generation with another. Guided by their hearts alone they anticipated the results at which modern thought has arrived by close and attentive study of history. From a reasoned out conviction of this truth and its consequences, philosophy now draws the principles of a high morality! but long before our days this idea and the tender, grateful, sentiments which it provoked had been a powerful instrument in the moral improvement of the first-born of civilization and a bond of union for their civil and domestic life.

We have thought it right to dwell upon this worship of the dead and to describe its character at some length, because the beliefs upon which it was based are not to be found so clearly set forth in the art of any other people. Their most complete, clear, and eloquent expression, in a plastic form, is to be seen in the tombs which border the Nile. And why is this so? It is because the Egyptian industries were already in full possession of their resources at the period when those beliefs had their strongest hold over the minds and feelings of the people. In the case of Greece, art did not arrive at its full development until the worship of the dead had lost its high place in the national conscience. When the Greek genius had arrived, after much striving, at its complete power of plastic expression, the gods of Olympus had been created for several centuries, and art was called upon to interpret the brilliant polytheism of Homer and Hesiod, to give outward image to those gods, and to construct worthy dwellings for their habitation. Sculptors, painters, and architects still worked indeed, at the decoration of the tomb. They strove to give it beauty of shape and arrangement, and to adorn its walls with bas-reliefs and pictures; they designed for it those vases and terra cottas which, in our own day, have been found in thousands in the cemeteries of Greece and Italy, but all this was only a subordinate use of their talent. Their ambition was to build temples, to model statues of Zeus, Pallas, and Apollo. On the other hand, those distant ages in which primitive and childish ideas of religion prevailed, had no art in which to manifest their beliefs with clearness and precision.

It was otherwise in the valley of the Nile. A well provided industry and an experienced art laid themselves out to interpret the popular beliefs and to defend the dead against final dissolution, or the agonies of hunger and thirst. Egypt did not differ from other nations in its opinions upon the mystery of death. In the infancy of every race the same notions on this matter are to be found, and in this respect the only difference between the Egyptians and the rest of the world is very much to the credit of the former; they rapidly attained to a degree of civilization which was only reached by other races after their religious development was comparatively mature. Thanks to this advantage, they were enabled to push their ideas to consequences which were not to be attained by tribes which were little less than barbarous, and they had no difficulty in expressing them with sufficient force and precision.

It remains for us to show the use which the Egyptians made of their superiority in doing more honour to their dead, in guarding them more safely against the chances which might shorten the duration or destroy the happiness of their life in the tomb. The fulfilment of this duty was, as the Greek travellers rightly affirmed, their chief pre-occupation. Their sepulchral architecture was, of all their creations, the most original and the most characteristic of their genius, especially in the forms which we find in the cemeteries of the Ancient Empire. In the time of the New Empire, at Thebes, it is less complete and homogeneous. In the latter the arrangement and decoration do not spring, as a whole, from a unique conception; we find traces in it of new hypotheses and novel forms of belief. These do not supersede the primitive ideas; they are added to them, and they bear witness to the restless efforts made by human thought to solve the problem of human destiny. These apparent contradictions and hesitations are of great interest to the student of the Egyptian religion, but from the art point of view the Memphite tombs are more curious and important than those of later date. They have the great merit of being complete in their unity both of artistic form and of intellectual conception. They are the offspring of a single growth, and are perfect in their clear logical expression. And again, they are the type of all the later tombs, of those at Abydos, at Beni-Hassan, and at Thebes. Certain details, indeed, are modified, but the general disposition remains the same to the end. We shall, therefore, find the ruling principle of Egyptian sepulchral architecture most clearly laid down in the cemeteries of Gizeh and Sakkarah.

The first and most obvious necessity for the obscure form of life which was supposed to commence as soon as the tomb had received its inmate, was the body. No pains, therefore, were spared which could retard its dissolution and preserve the organs to which the *double* and the soul might one day return. [126] Embalming, practised as it was by the Egyptians, rendered a mummy almost indestructible, so long, at least, as it remained in the dry soil of Egypt. On the warm sands of Sakkarah and close to the excavations from which the fellahs of the *corvée* were returning at the end of their day's labour, we—my travelling companions and myself—stripped a great lady of the time of Ramses of the linen cloths and bandages in which she was closely enveloped, and found her body much in the same condition as it must have been when it left the workshop of the Memphite embalmer! Her black hair was plaited into fine tresses; all her teeth were in place between the slightly contracted lips; the almond-shaped nails of her feet and hands were stained with henna. The limbs were flexible and the graceful shapes but little altered under the still firm and smooth skin, which, moreover, seemed to be still supported by flesh in some parts. Had it not been for its colour of tarred linen or scorched paper, and the smell of naphtha which arose from the body and from the numberless bandages which were strewn about, we might have shared the sentiment attributed to Lord Evandale in Theophile Gautier's brilliant *Roman de la Momie*; with an effort of good-will we could almost sympathise with those emotions of tenderness and admiration which were excited in the breast of the young Englishman at the sight of the unveiled charms of that daughter of Egypt whose perfect beauty had once troubled the heart of the proudest of the Pharaohs.[127]

In order that all the expense of embalming should not be thrown away, the mummy had to be so placed that it could not be reached by the highest inundations of the river. The cemeteries were therefore established either upon a plateau surrounded by the desert, as in the case of Memphis and Abydos, or in the sides of the mountain ranges and in the ravines by which they were pierced, as at Thebes and Beni-Hassan. In the whole valley of the Nile, no ancient tomb has been discovered which was within reach of the inundation at its highest.[128]

Fig. 87.—Mummy case from the 18th dynasty. Boulak.

The corpse was thus preserved from destruction, first by careful and scientific embalming, secondly by placing its dwelling above the highest "Nile." Besides this we shall see that the Egyptian architects made use of many curious artifices of construction in order to conceal the entrance to the tomb, and to prevent the intrusion of any one coming with evil intentions. All kinds of obstacles and pitfalls are accumulated in the path of the unbidden visitor, with a fertility and patient ingenuity of invention which has often carried despair into the minds of modern explorers, especially in the case of the pyramids. Mariette was fond of saying that there are mummies in Egypt which will never, in the strictest sense of the word, be brought to light.

But in spite of all this pious and subtle foresight, it sometimes happened that private hate or, more often, the greed of gain, upset every calculation.

Enemies might succeed in penetrating to the sepulchres of the dead, in destroying their bodies, and thus inflicting a second death worse than the first; or a thief might drag the corpse from its resting place, and leave it naked and dishonoured upon the sands, that he might, with the greater ease, possess himself of the gold and jewels with which it had been adorned.

The liability of the mummy to accident had to be provided against. The idea of the unhappy condition in which the *double* would find itself when its mummy had been destroyed, led to the provision of an artificial support for it in the shape of a statue. Art was sufficiently advanced not only to reproduce the costume and ordinary attitude of the defunct and to mark his age and sex, but even to render the individual characteristics of his physiognomy. It aspired to portraiture; and the development of writing allowed the name and qualities of the deceased to be inscribed upon his statue. Thus identified by its resemblance and its inscriptions it served to perpetuate the life of the *double*, which was in continual danger of dissolution or evaporation in the absence of a material support.

The statues were more solid than the mummy, and nothing stood in the way of their multiplication. The body gave but one chance of duration to the *double*; twenty statues represented twenty chances more. Hence the astonishing number of statues which are sometimes found in a single tomb. The images of the dead were multiplied by the piety of surviving relations, and consequently the *double* was assured a duration which practically amounted to immortality.[129]

FIG. 88.—Man and his wife in the style of the 5th dynasty. Calcareous stone. From the Louvre.

We shall see that a special recess was prepared in the thickness of the built up portion of the tomb for the reception of wooden or stone statues, so that they might be kept out of sight and safe from all indiscreet curiosity. Other effigies were placed in the chambers of the tomb or the courts in front of it. Finally, we know that persons of consideration obtained from the king permission to erect statues in the temples, where they were protected by the sanctity of the place and the vigilance of the priests.[130]

FIG. 89.—Sekhem-ka, his wife Ata, and his son Khnem,
in the style of the 5th dynasty.
Limestone. From the Louvre.

From the point of view of the ancient Egyptians such precautions were by no means futile. Many of these effigies have come down to us safely through fifty or sixty centuries and have found an asylum in our museums where they have nothing to fear but the slow effects of climate and time. Those which remain intact may therefore count upon immortality. If the *double* required nothing to preserve it from annihilation but the continued existence of the image, that of Chephren, the builder of the second great pyramid, would be still alive, preserved by the magnificent statue of diorite which is the glory of

Boulak, and thanks to the durability of its material, it would have every chance of lasting as long as the world itself. But, unhappily for the shade of Pharaoh, this posthumous existence which is so difficult of comprehension to us, was only to be prolonged by attention to conditions most of which could not long continue to be observed.

FIG. 90.—Stele of Nefer-oun. Boulak.

It was entirely a material life. The dead-alive had need of food and drink, which he obtained from supplies placed beside him in the tomb,[131] and afterwards, when these were consumed, by the repasts which took place periodically in the tomb, of which he had his share. The first of these feasts was given upon the conclusion of the funeral ceremonies,[132] and they were repeated from year to year on days fixed by tradition and sometimes by the expressed wish of the deceased.[133] An open and public chamber was contrived in the tomb for the celebration of these anniversaries. It was a kind of chapel, or, perhaps, to speak more accurately, a saloon in which all the relations and friends of the deceased could find room. At the foot of the stele upon which the dead man was represented sacrificing to Osiris, the god of the dead, was placed a table for offerings, upon which the share intended for the *double* was deposited and the libations poured. A conduit was reserved in the thickness of the wall by which the odour of the roast meats and perfumed fruits and the smoke of the incense might reach the concealed statues.[134]

FIG. 91.—**Preparation of the victims and arrival of funeral gifts, 5th dynasty.
Height of each band, 13-1/2 inches. Boulak. Drawn by Bourgoin.**

The Egyptians did not trust only to the piety of their descendants to preserve them from a final death by inanition in their neglected tombs. At the end of a few generations that piety might grow cold and relax its care; besides, a family might become extinct. All those who could afford it provided against such contingencies as these by giving their tombs what we now call a perpetual foundation. They devoted to the purpose the revenues of some part of their property, which was also charged with the maintenance of the priest or priests who had to perform the ceremonial rites which we have described. [135] We find that, even under the Ptolemies, special ministers were attached to the sepulchral chapel of Cheops, the builder of the great pyramid.[136] It may seem difficult to believe that a "foundation" of the ancient empire should have survived so many changes of *régime*, but the honours paid to the early kings had become one of the national institutions of Egypt. Each restoring sovereign made it a point of duty to give renewed life to the worship of those remote princes who represented the first glories of the national history.

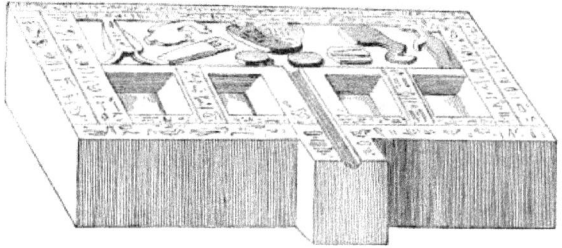

F<small>IG</small>. 92.—Table for offerings. Louvre.

Besides which there were priests attached to each necropolis, who, for certain fees, officiated at each tomb in turn. They were identified by Mariette upon some of the bas-reliefs at Sakkarah. Their services were retained much in the same way as masses are bought in our days.[137]

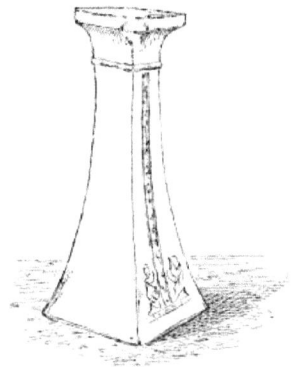

FIG. 93.—Another form of the table for offerings. Boulak.

The same sentiment led to the burial with the dead of all arms, clothes, jewels, and other objects of which they might have need in the next life. We know what treasures of this kind have been obtained from the Egyptian tombs and how they fill the cases of our museums. But neither was this habit peculiar to Egypt. It was common to all ancient people whether civilized or barbarous. Traces are to be found even in the early traditions of the Hellenic race of a time when, like those Scythians described by Herodotus,[138] the Greeks sacrificed, at the death of a chief, his wives and servants that they might accompany him to the next world. When she began to reveal herself in the arts Egypt was already too far civilized for such practices as these; thanks to the simultaneous development of science, art and religion, she found means to give the same advantages to her dead without permitting Scythian cruelties. Those personal attendants and domestic officers whose services would be so necessary in another life, were secured to them at a small expense; instead of slaying them at the door of the tomb, they were represented upon its walls in all the variety of their occupations and in the actual moment of labour. So too with all objects of luxury or necessity which the *double* would wish to have at hand, as for instance his food and drink.[139]

A custom which would seem to have established itself a little later may be referred to the same desire; we mean the habit of placing in the tomb those statuettes which we meet with in such vast numbers after the commencement of the second Theban Empire.[140] Mariette obtained some from tombs of the twelfth dynasty, and the sixth chapter of the *Book of the Dead*, which is engraved upon them, seems to be one of the most ancient. Egyptologists are now inclined to believe that the essential parts of this ritual date back as far as the Memphite period.

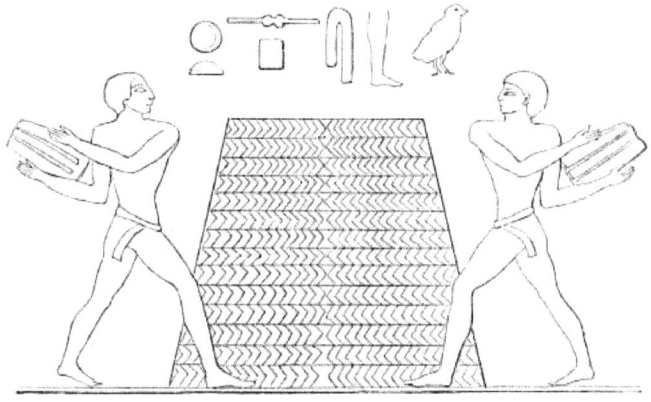

FIG. 94.—Labourers heaping up ears of corn, from a tomb at Gizeh. (*Description de l'Égypte.*)

These statuettes are of different sizes and materials. As a rule they do not exceed from eight to twelve inches, but there are a few which are three feet or more in height. Some are in wood, some in limestone, and some in granite, but as a rule they are made of that kind of terra cotta which, when covered with green or blue enamel, has been called Egyptian porcelain. They are like a mummy in appearance; their hands are crossed upon the breast and hold instruments of agriculture such as hoes and picks, and a sack meant for grain hangs from their shoulders. The meaning of all this is to be sought in the Egyptian notions of a future life; it is also explained by the picture in chapter XC. of the *Ritual*, which shows us the dead tilling, sowing and harvesting in the fields of the other world. The texts of the Ritual and of certain inscriptions call these little figures *oushebti* or *answerers* from the verb *ousheb*, to answer. It is therefore easy to divine the part attributed to them by the popular imagination. They answered to the name traced upon the tomb and acted as substitute for its tenant in the cultivation of the subterranean regions.[141] With the help of the attendants painted and sculptured upon the walls they saved him from fatigue and from the chance of want. This is another branch of the same old idea. In his desire to take every precaution against the misery and final annihilation which would result from abandonment, the Egyptian thought he could never go too far in furnishing, provisioning and peopling his tomb.

FIGS. 95, 96.—Sepulchral statuettes, from the Louvre.

The ingenuity of their contrivances is extraordinary. Food in its natural state would not keep, and various accidents, might, as we have shown, lead to the death of the *double* by inanition. It was the same with furniture and clothes; the narrow dimensions of the tomb, moreover, would forbid the accumulation there of everything which its sombre tenant might desire. On the other hand the funerary statuettes were made of the most indestructible materials and the bas-reliefs and paintings were one with the thick walls of stone or living rock. These have survived practically unaltered until our day. We visited the tomb of Ti a short time after its chambers had been opened and cleared. It was marvellous to see how form and colour had been preserved intact and fresh under the sand, and this work which was four or five thousand years old seemed to be but lately finished. By the brightness of their colours and the sharp precision of their contours these charming reliefs had the effect of a newly struck medal. Such scenes from the daily life of the people continued to be figured upon Egyptian tombs from the old empire to the new. When their study and comparison were first begun different explanations were put forward. Some believed that they were an illustrated biography of the deceased, a representation of his achievements or of those over which he had presided during the course of his mortal life; others saw in them an illustration of his future life, a setting forth of the joys and pleasures of the Egyptian Elysium.

Both these interpretations have had to give way before the critical examination of the pictures themselves and the decipherment of their accompanying inscriptions. It was soon perceived, through comparisons easily made, that these scenes were not anecdotic. On a few very rare occasions they seem to be connected with circumstances peculiar to the inhabitant of the tomb. There are a few steles and tombs upon which the dead man seems to have caused his services to be described, with the object, no doubt, of continuing in the next world his career of honour and success in this. Such an inscription is so far biographical, and a similar spirit may extend to the decorations of the stele and walls of the tomb. As an example of such narrative epigraphs we may cite the long inscription of Ouna, which gives us the life of a sort of grand-vizier to the two first Kings of the sixth dynasty;[142] also the inscriptions upon the tombs of those feudal princes who were buried at Beni-Hassan. In the latter there are historical representations as commentaries upon the text. Among these is the often reproduced painting of a band of Asiatic emigrants bringing presents to the prince and demanding, perhaps, a supply of wheat in return, like the Hebrews in the time of Jacob.

FIG. 97.—Vignette from a Ritual upon papyrus, in the Louvre. Chap. XC., 20th dynasty.

But all this is exceptional. As a rule the same subjects occur upon the tombs again and again, in the persistent fashion which characterizes traditional themes. The figures by which the flocks and herds and other possessions of the deceased were numbered are too great for literal truth.[143] On the other hand the pictured tradesmen and artificers, from the labourer, the baker, and the butcher up to the sculptor, seem to apply themselves to their work with an energy which excludes the notion of ideal felicity. They, one and all, labour conscientiously, and we feel that they are carrying out a task which has been imposed upon them as a duty.

For whose benefit do they take all this trouble? If we attempt to enter into the minds of the people who traced these images and compare the pictured representations with the texts which accompany them, we shall be enabled to answer that question. Let us take by chance any one of the inscriptions which accompany the scenes figured upon the famous tomb of Ti, and here is what we find. "To see the picking and pressing of the grape and all the labours of the country." Again, "To see the picking of the flax, the reaping of the corn, the transport upon donkeys, the stacking of the crops of the tomb." Again, "Ti sees the stalls of the oxen and of the small animals, the gutters and water-channels of the tomb."

It is for the dead that the vintage takes place, that the flax is picked, that the wheat is threshed, that oxen are driven into the fields, that the soil is ploughed and irrigated. It is for the supply of his wants that all these sturdy arms are employed.

We shall leave M. Maspero to sum up the ideas which presided at the construction of the Egyptian tomb, but first we must draw our readers' notice to the fact that he, more than once, alludes to a conception of the future life which differs somewhat from the early Egyptian notions, and belongs rather to the Second Theban Empire and its successors.

FIG. 98.—Arrival in Egypt of a company of Asiatic emigrants
(Champollion, pls. 362, 393).

FIG. 98, *Continued*.—Arrival in Egypt of a company of Asiatic emigrants (Champollion, pls. 362, 393).

"The scenes chosen for the decoration of tomb walls had a magic intention; whether drawn from civil life in the world or from that of Hades, they were meant to preserve the dead from danger and to insure him a happy existence beyond the tomb.... Their reproduction upon the walls of the sepulchre guaranteed the performance of the acts represented. The *double* shut up in his σύριγξ[144] saw himself going to the chase upon the surrounding walls and he went to the chase; eating and drinking with his wife, and he ate and drank with her; crossing in safety the terrible gulfs of the lower world in the barque of the gods, and he crossed them in safety. The tilling, reaping, and housing on his walls were for him real tilling, reaping, and housing. So, too, the statuettes placed in his tomb carried out for him under magic influence all the work of the fields, and, like the sorcerer's pestle in Goethe's ballad, drew water for him and carried grain. The workmen painted in his papyri made shoes for him and cooked his food; they carried him to hunt in the deserts or to fish in the marshes. And, after all, the world of vassals upon the sides of the sepulchre was as real as the *double* for which they laboured; the picture of a slave might well satisfy the shadow of a master. The Egyptian thought that by filling his tomb with pictures he insured the reality of all the objects, people, and scenes represented in another world, and he was thus encouraged to construct his tomb while he was yet alive. Relations, too, thought that they were doing a service to the deceased when they carried out all the mysterious ceremonies which accompanied his burial. The certainty that they had been the cause of some benefit to him consoled and supported them on their return from the cemetery where they had left their regretted dead in possession of his imaginary domain."[145]

Such a belief is astonishing to us; it demands an effort of the imagination to which we moderns are in no way equal. We have great difficulty in realising a state of mind so different from what ours has become after centuries of progress and thought. Those early races had neither a long enough experience of things, nor a sufficiently capable power of reflection to enable them to distinguish the possible from the impossible. They did not appreciate the difference between living things and those which we call inanimate. They endowed all things about them with souls like their own. They found no more difficulty in giving life to their carved and painted domestics, than to the mummy or statue of the deceased, or to the phantom which they called the double. Is it not natural to the child to take revenge upon the table against which he hurts himself, or to speak tenderly to the doll which he holds in his arms?

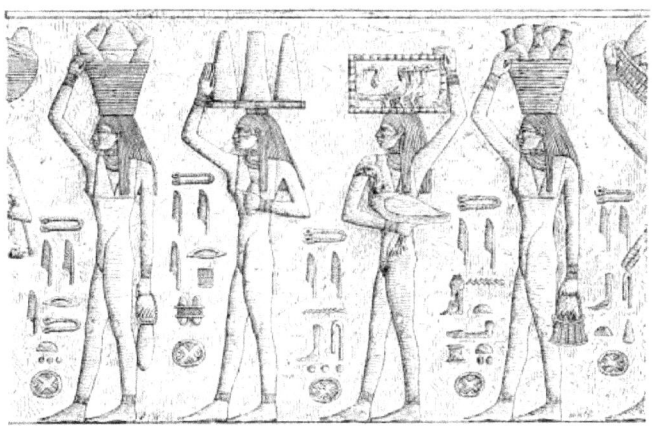

FIG. 99.—The tomb of Ti;
women, representing the lands of the deceased,
carrying the funeral gifts.

This power to endow all things with life and personality is now reserved for the poet and the infant, but in the primitive days of civilization it belonged to all people alike. Imagination had then a power over a whole race which in our days is the gift of great poets alone. In the efforts which they made to forestall the wants of the helpless dead, they were not content with providing the food and furniture which we find upon the walls. They had a secret impression that these might be insufficient for wants renewed through eternity, and they made another step upon the way upon which they had embarked. By a still more curious and still bolder fiction than those which had gone before, they attributed to prayer the power of multiplying, by the use of a few magic sentences, all objects of the first necessity to the inhabitants of the tomb.

Every sepulchre has a *stele*, that is to say, an upright stone tablet which varied in form and place in different epochs, but always served the same purpose and had the same general character. Most of these steles were adorned with painting and sculpture; all of them had more or less complicated inscriptions. [146] In the semicircle which forms the upper part of most of these inscribed slabs, the dead person, accompanied by his family, presents offerings to a god, who is usually Osiris. Under this an inscription is carved after an unchanging formula: "Offering to Osiris (or to some other deity, as the case may be) in order that he may give provision of bread, liquid, beef, geese, milk, wine, beer, clothes, perfumes, and all good and pure things upon which the god subsists, to the ka of N..., son of M...." Below this the defunct is often shown in the act of himself receiving the offerings of his family. In both divisions the objects figured are looked upon as real, as in the wall decorations. In the lower division they are offered directly to him who is to profit by them; in the upper, the god is charged to see that they are delivered to the right address. The provisions which the god is asked to pass on to the defunct are first presented to him; by the intervention of Osiris the *doubles* of bread, meat and drink pass into the other world to nourish the double of man. But it was not essential for the gift to be effective that it should be real, or even *quasi*-real; that its image should even be given in paint or stone. The first-comer could procure all things necessary for the deceased by their enumeration in the proper form. We find therefore that many Egyptians caused the following invocation to passing strangers, to be engraved upon their tombs:

"Oh you who still exist upon the earth, whether you be private individuals, priests, scribes, or ministers entering into this tomb, if you love life and do not know death, if you wish to be in favour with the gods of your cities and to avoid the terrors of the other world, if you wish to be entombed in your own sepulchres and to transmit your dignities to your children, you must if you be scribes, recite the words inscribed upon this stone, or, if not, you must listen to their recital: say, offering to Amen, master of Karnak, that he may give thousands of loaves of bread, thousands of jars of drink, thousands of oxen, thousands of geese, thousands of garments, thousands of all good and pure things to the *ka*, or *double*, of the prince Entef."[147]

Thanks to all these subtle precautions, and to the goodwill with which the Egyptian intellect lent itself to their bold fictions, the tomb deserved the name it received, the *house of the double*. The *double*, when thus installed in a dwelling furnished for his use, received the visits and offerings of his friends and relations; "he had priests retained and paid to offer sacrifices to him; he had slaves, beasts of burden, and estates charged with his support. He was like a great lord sojourning in a strange country and having his wants attended to by intermediary officials assigned to his service."[148]

This analogy between the house and the tomb is so complete that it embraces details which do not seem very congruous. Like the house of the living, the tomb was strictly oriented, but after a mystic principle of its own.

As soon as the Egyptian began to think he perceived the most obvious of the similarities between the sun's career and that of man. Man has his dawn and his setting. Man grows from the early glimmerings of infancy to the apogee of his wisdom and strength; he then begins to decline and, like the magnified evening sun, ends by disappearing after his death into the depths of the soil.

In Egypt the sun sets every evening behind the Libyan chain; thence he penetrates into those subterranean regions of Ament across which he has to make his way before the dawn of the next day. The Egyptian cemeteries were therefore placed on the left bank of the Nile, that is, in the west of the country. All the known pyramids were built in the west, and there we find all the more important "cities of the dead," the necropolis of Memphis and those of Abydos and Thebes. A few unimportant groups of tombs have indeed been found upon the eastern bank; but these exceptions to a general rule are doubtless to be explained by a question of distance. For any city placed near the eastern border of the wider parts of the Nile valley, a burying-place in the Libyan chain would be very inconvenient both for the transport of the dead, and for the sepulchral duties of the survivors.[149]

Each morning sees the sun rise as youthful and ardent as the morning before. Why then should not man, after completing his subterranean journey and triumphing over the terrors of Ament, cast off the darkness of the tomb and again see the light of day? This undying hope was revivified at each dawn as by a new promise, and the Egyptians followed out the analogy by the way in which they disposed their sepulchres. They were placed in the west of their country, towards the setting sun, but their doors, the openings through which their inmates would one day regain the light, were turned to the east. In the necropolis of Memphis, the door of nearly every tomb is turned to the east,[150] and there is not a single stele which does not face in that direction.[151] In the necropolis of Abydos, both door and stele are more often turned towards the south, that is towards the sun at its zenith.[152] But neither at Memphis, at Abydos, nor at Thebes is there a tomb which is lighted from the west or presents its inscription to the setting sun.[153] Thus, from the shadowy depths where they dwell, the dead have their eyes turned to that quarter of the heavens where the life-giving flame is each day rekindled, and seem to be waiting for the ray which is to destroy their night and to rouse them from their long repose.[154]

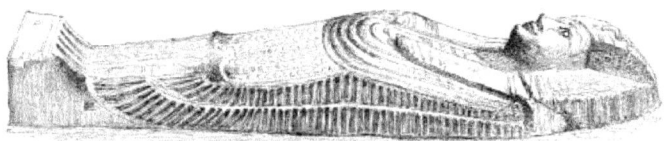

FIG. 100.—Lid of the coffin of Entef, 11th dynasty. Louvre.

The ideas and beliefs which we have described were common to all Egyptians, irrespective of class. When he felt his last hour approaching, the humble peasant or boatman on the Nile was as anxious as Pharaoh himself to insure the survival of his double and to guard against the terrors of annihilation:

> . . . . Mais, jusqu'en son trépas,
> Le riche a des honneurs que le pauvre n'a pas.

Those who, when alive, had to be content with a hut of earth or of reeds, could not, when dead, expect to have a tomb of stone or brick, a habitation for eternity; they could not look for joys in the other world which they had been unable to procure in this. So that such tombs as those which most fully embodied the ideas we have described must always have remained the exclusive privilege more or less of the governing classes. These consisted of the king, the princes and nobles, the priests, the military chiefs, and functionaries of every kind down to the humblest of the scribes attached to the administration. As for those Egyptians who did not belong to this aristocracy, they had to be content with less expensive arrangements. The less poor among them at least took measures to be embalmed and to be placed in a coffin of wood or *papier-mâché*, accompanied by scarabs and other charms to protect them against malignant spirits. The painted figures upon the coffin also helped to keep off evil influences. If they could afford it they purchased places in a common tomb, where the mummies were heaped one upon the other and confided to the care of priests who performed the funerary rites for a whole chamber at once.[155] It was the frequent custom to put with the dead those pillows of wood or alabaster which the Egyptians seem to have used from the most ancient times for the support of their heads in sleep. This contrivance, which does away with the necessity for continually rearranging their complicated head-dress, is still used by the Nubians and Abyssinians.

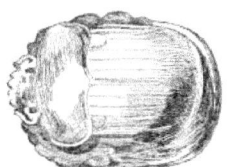 

FIGS. 101, 102.—Scarabs. Louvre.

FIGS. 103, 104.—Funerary amulets. *Oudja* and *ta*. Louvre.

But those who could procure even these slight advantages were still among the favourites of fortune. Many were unable to obtain even this minimum of funeral honours. On the confines of all the great cemeteries, at Thebes as well as at Memphis, corpses are found deposited in the loose sand two or three feet from the surface. Some of these are packed in the leaves of the palm, others are roughly enveloped in a few morsels of linen. They have been hastily dipped in a bath of natron, which has dirtied rather than embalmed them.[156] Sometimes even these slender precautions have been omitted. Bodies have been found in the earth without vestige of either coffin or linen swathes. The sand seems to have been intrusted with the work of drying them, and they have been found in our days in the condition of skeletons.

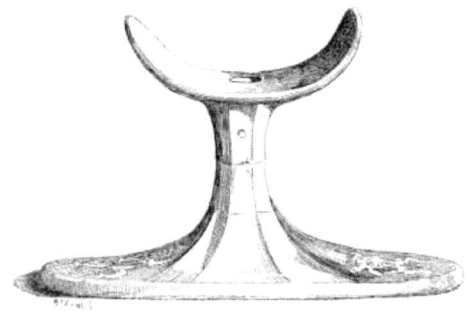

FIG. 105.—Pillow, Louvre.

On the other hand, the fortunate ones of the world, those who were so easy in their circumstances in this life that they could place themselves in the same happy condition in the next, spared no expense in anything connected with their burial. They never allowed themselves to be surprised by death, as we so often do. Whether kings or private individuals, they made their preparations while they were still alive, and caused their tombs to be constructed under their own eyes.[157] Their forethought when living and the piety of relations spared nothing that could add to the beauty and convenience of dwellings which were to be the eternal resting places of their inmates. The palaces of the princes and rich men of Egypt were so lightly built that they have left no traces upon the soil; but many of their tombs have subsisted uninjured to our day, and it is from them that we have obtained our treasures of Egyptian art. All the other nations of the ancient world followed the good example thus set, or rather, to speak more accurately, being all penetrated with similar ideas, they took similar courses without borrowing one from the other. Whenever we moderns have opened any of those ancient tombs which have happily remained intact, we have been met by the same discoveries. Whether it be in Egypt or Phœnicia, in Asia Minor, Cyprus or Greece, in Etruria or Campania, the same astonishing sight meets our eyes. The tombs are filled with precious objects and *chefs d'œuvres* of art which their depositors had intended never again to see the light of day.

In modern times, when piety or pride stimulates to the decoration of a tomb, all the care of the architect, the sculptor and the painter is given to the outside, to the edifice which surmounts the actual grave. The grave or other receptacle for the coffin is as plain and simple in the most sumptuous monuments of our cemeteries as in the most humble. Our funerary architecture is based upon our belief that the tomb is empty; that the vital part of the deposit confided to it has escaped to rejoin the current of eternal life. Under such conditions the tomb becomes above all things a commemorative structure, a more or less sincere manifestation of the grief of a family or of society at large for the loss of one of its members. As for the narrow pit into which the "mortal coil" is lowered, all that we demand of it is that it should be deep enough and properly closed. Art makes no attempt to illumine its darkness. She leaves to workmen the task of excavation and of building its walls and confines herself to the visible parts of the tomb. The dead within furnishes the pretext for her activity, but it is the admiration of the living that is her real incentive.

The ideas of the ancients on this matter were, as we have seen, very different. They looked upon the tomb as an inhabited house; as a house in which the dead was to lead some kind of existence. Rich men wished their tombs to look well outside, even to the distant spectator, but it was to the inside that their chief attention was turned. They wished to find there all the necessaries, the comforts, the luxuries, to which they had been accustomed during life. So we find that the Egyptians, the Greeks or the Etruscans, were willing enough, when they built their own tombs or those of their relations, to throw a *tumulus* of earth above it, or, later, a constructed building which was conspicuous at a distance. In those sepulchres which were cut out of the side of a mountain, the fronts were carved with frieze, pediment and columns into the shape of a regularly constructed portico; but the chief object of solicitude to the proud possessor of such a tomb, was its internal furnishing and disposition. For him there was no removal should he be discontented with his lodging. When a man is condemned by illness or accident to keep his room, he takes care to surround himself with everything that he may want. He gathers immediately about him all the comforts and luxuries which he can afford; and death is an illness from which there is no recovery.

Impelled by such ideas as these, the ancients filled their tombs with precious objects and decorated them with sumptuous art, all the more that they seemed well guarded against intrusion for the sake of gain. Thus the Achæans of Mycenæ (if that be the proper name of those mysterious people) buried, in the sepulchres discovered by Dr. Schliemann, the innumerable objects of gold and silver which now fill the museum of Athens; thus the tombs of Bœotia were filled with those marvels of grace and delicate workmanship, the terra cottas of Tanagra; and those of Etruria and Campania with the most beautiful painted vases ever produced by Greek taste.

Identity of religious conception thus led, from end to end of the antique world, to funerary arrangements which bore a curious resemblance one to another, so that sepulchral architecture among the ancients had, as a whole, a very different character from that of the moderns. This character is more strongly marked in Egypt than anywhere else, and therefore we have studied it in detail. The general observations to which it has given rise have been made once for all, and we shall not have to repeat them when we describe the funeral customs of other ancient peoples. We shall then confine ourselves to pointing out the slight differences which naturally spring up in the several interpretations of a common belief.

We have still to show how the varying circumstances of time and place caused the Egyptian tomb to pass through certain modifications of form and decoration, which, however, were never of so radical a nature as to affect its general appearance and arrangement. Until Egypt became a mere geographical expression and her venerable civilization lost its independence and originality, these latter remained practically unchanged.

§ 2. *The Tomb under the Ancient Empire.*

Among the tombs which date from the time of the ancient empire, the most interesting to the traveller are, of course, the Pyramids. Long before his arrival at Cairo he sees the summits of those artificial mountains rising into the air above the vapours raised by the sun, and above the dust thrown up by the teeming population of the city. At that distance their peaks seem light and slender from their height above the horizon (Plate I. 2).

The tourist's first visit is paid to the Pyramids, and many an European leaves Egypt without seeing any other ancient building. He thinks that he has qualified himself to discourse upon Egyptian architecture because a few shouting Arabs have landed him, exhausted, upon the topmost stone of the pyramid of Cheops, and have painfully dragged and thrust him along those passages of the interior which will ever be among his most disagreeable recollections. During all this his eyes and thoughts are entirely given to the preservation of his own equilibrium, and he sees nothing of the real constitution of the structure he has come to visit.

In spite of the wonderful panorama which repays the fatigues of the ascent, and of the overpowering impression made upon the mind by their colossal mass, the Pyramids, as we see them to-day are far from being the most complete and interesting of the sepulchral monuments left to us by the early dynasties. The largest and best preserved are not so old as some of the tombs in the necropolis of Memphis, and, royal burying-places as they are, their arrangement and ornamentation are less rich and expressive than those of many sepulchres built by private individuals. Many of the latter, in their comparatively restricted dimensions, answer better to the definition of a tomb suggested to us by our study of the national beliefs.

We shall, therefore, reserve the Pyramids for future treatment, and in our review of the successive forms taken by sepulchral architecture, we shall assign the first place to those private tombs, dating from the Ancient Empire, which are to be found in the necropolis of Memphis. Notwithstanding a few differences, to which we shall refer hereafter, these tombs, as a whole, can be traced to a single type, of which Lepsius was the first to perceive the interest. [158] This type, which was first clearly brought to light by the many and deep excavations carried out by Mariette, has been known for some years past by the Arab term *mastaba*,[159] which means literally a *bench*, a bench of stone or wood. This name was given by the labourers employed upon the excavations, and seemed well adapted to their long and low shapes, which bear some resemblance to those divans, or ottomans, which are found in every room of an oriental dwelling. Mariette was struck by the fitness of the expression, and used it ever after to designate that particular kind of tomb.

Mariette will be our constant guide in this part of our study. After having opened many hundreds of these monuments, he published in the *Revue archéologique*, what we may call a *theory of the mastaba*.[160] In all essential matters we shall allow his words to speak for themselves; when he enters into more detail than is necessary for our purpose, we shall content ourselves with epitomizing his descriptions.

THE MASTABAS OF THE NECROPOLIS OF MEMPHIS.

The space over which the monuments which we propose to describe are spread, is on the left bank of the Nile, and extends from *Abou-Roash* to

Dashour; it is thus, in all probability, the largest cemetery in the world, being more than fifteen miles in length, and of an average width of from two to two and a half miles.[161] It was, in a word, the burial-place for Memphis and its suburbs, and Memphis seems to have been the largest city of Egypt, and to have boasted an antiquity which only Thinis could rival. Excavations have failed, apparently, to confirm the assertion of Strabo, who describes the early capital of Egypt as reaching to the foot of the Libyan chain. On the contrary, it seems to have been confined between the canal which is called the *Bahr Yussef* and the Nile. It would thus have formed a very long and rather narrow city, close upon the river, of which the site may still be traced by the more or less barren hillocks strewn with blocks of granite and fragments of walls, which crop up from the plain between Gizeh and Chinbab. For forty centuries there was a continual procession of corpses from Memphis itself, and probably from towns on the other side of the Nile, such as Heliopolis, to the plateau which lies along the foot of the Libyan chain. The formation of this plateau makes it peculiarly well adapted for the purpose to which it was put. It consists of a thick bed of soft limestone, covered by a layer of sand which varies in depth from many yards to a few feet according to the inequalities of the ground beneath it.

It was easy, therefore, either to lay bare the rock and to construct the tomb upon it, or to dig the mummy pits in its substance, and the winds might be trusted to quickly cover the grave with sand which would protect it when made. The same sand covered the coffinless corpse of the pauper with its kindly particles. Age after age the dead were interred by millions in this great haven of rest. At first there was plenty of room, and the corpses were strewn somewhat thinly in the sand,[162] but with time economy of space had to be practised, until at last bodies were squeezed into the narrowest spaces between older inhabitants. Sometimes these new comers even intruded into the tombs of those who had gone before them, and that without always troubling themselves to conceal their usurpation by effacing the name of the rightful owner.[163]

The number of tombs was increased to a prodigious extent by the non-employment of those family tombs which, as we shall see, were made use of by the Phœnicians, the Greeks, and the Etruscans. The Egyptian sepulchre was a personal appanage. The husband and father of a family admitted into it only his wife and such of their children as died young. The son, when he in turn became the head of a family, built a tomb for himself. Each generation, each human couple marked their passage through the world by the erection of a new tomb.

All the *mastabas* belong to the period of the Memphite empire. Those who built them were able to give free play to their fancies, and to develop the structure, both above and below ground, both in arrangement and in decoration, to any extent they pleased. We may therefore look upon them as the freest, the most spontaneous, and the most complete expression of the ideas formed by the men of that remote age concerning death and the life beyond the grave.

The mastabas of Sakkarah will receive most of our attention, and in describing them we shall often have occasion to quote the words of Mariette. [164] Those which are to be found in the more northern part of the necropolis, in the neighbourhood of the Great Pyramid, differ only in unimportant details from those at Sakkarah. The general appearance now presented by these monuments may be guessed from the sketch which M. Bourgoin has sent us of the tomb of Sabou (Fig. 106). The other mastabas figured by us have all been more or less restored.

"The *mastaba* is a massive structure, rectangular on plan, with four faces of plain walling, each being inclined at a stated angle towards their common centre. This inclination has led some people to assert that it is nothing more than an unfinished pyramid. Such an idea is refuted, however, by the fact that the divergence from the perpendicular is in some cases so slight that, were the walls prolonged upwards, their ridges, or *arêtes*, would not meet for some eight or nine hundred yards. The mastaba might be more justly compared to the space comprised between two horizontal sections of an obelisk, supposing the obelisk to have an oblong base.

**Fig. 106.—Actual condition of a mastaba.
The tomb of Sabou. Drawn by Bourgoin.**

"The major axis of the rectangle upon which these structures are planned, always runs due north and south, and at the pyramids of Gizeh, the necropolis of the west, they are arranged upon a symmetrical plan so as to resemble a chess board on which all the squares are strictly oriented.[165] The more carefully built mastabas are oriented according to the true astronomical north. All the others show the same intention, and, in those instances where an error of a few degrees is to be discovered, it is to be clearly attributed to carelessness on the part of the builder, a common fault in these tombs, and not to a difference of intention. We often find that the northern face is not strictly parallel to the southern, nor that on the west to that on the east.

FIG. 107.—Three mastabas at Gizeh.
Perspective view, after the plan of Lepsius.
(*Denkmæler*, vol. i. pl. 24.)

"Although not varying much from true orientation, the mastabas of Sakkarah are not arranged with the symmetry which distinguishes those on the south and west of the Great Pyramid.[166] They are sprinkled about in a rather haphazard fashion. Here we find them well interspaced and there actually placed one upon another. It follows that the chess-board arrangement which is so conspicuous at Gizeh is not here to be noticed. Even at Sakkarah there were streets between the rows of tombs, but they are so irregularly placed, and they are often so narrow, many of them being nothing more than blind alleys, that the inexperienced visitor may well fancy himself in a maze.

"The Sakkarah mastabas are built either of stone or brick.

"The mastabas of stone are of two kinds: those of a very hard blue siliceous limestone and those of a softer chalky limestone which is found upon the spot. This latter stone was used for the Stepped Pyramid. The tombs upon which it was used seem to be much the oldest in the necropolis; they are also the least rich and important.

FIG. 108.—Restoration of part of the Necropolis of Gizeh.

"Our general notion of Egyptian architecture would lead us to look for the use of huge stones in these mastabas, and, in fact, certain important monuments, such as the *Mastabat-el-Faraoun*, and parts of important monuments, such as the Temple of the Sphinx and the passages and chambers of the greater pyramids, were constructed of very large blocks. But the Sakkarah architects were more modest. Apart from the ceilings, architraves and other places where big stones were necessary, the blocks are of an average height of about half a yard, with a proportionate length and thickness.

"The brick-built sepulchres are of two kinds also. The more elaborate are of black brick, while a yellowish brick is used for the others. The yellow bricks are a mixture of sand and pebbles with a little clay; the black bricks are of earth and straw. The former are always small (8·8 in. x 4·4 in. x 2·8 in.); the latter are comparatively large (15·2 in. x 7·2 in. x 5·6 in.). Both kinds are dried simply in the sun. The yellow bricks seem to be the more ancient. Their employment begins and ends with the Ancient Empire. The black bricks, on the other hand, appear for the first time about midway through the fourth dynasty. At first they were rarely employed, but under the eighteenth dynasty and those which followed it, they came to be exclusively used."

FIG. 109.—The Mastabat-el-Faraoun.

All these mastabas, whether of brick or stone, betray an amount of negligence in their construction which is astonishing. Considering the ideas which the Egyptians had formed of a future life, the chief preoccupation of their architects should have been to give a stability to their sepulchres which would have insured their perpetuity, and, with it, that of the deposit committed to their charge. The whole of our description will be pervaded by accounts of the minute precautions devised to that end. "Now these mastabas are constructed with care on their outsides alone. The core of their walls is composed of sand, of rubbish, of blocks of stone mingled with the flakes struck off by the masons, and all this in most cases without any cement to give it coherence. The mastabas of Sakkarah are not homogeneous constructions of masonry and cement, like the pyramids and most of the mastabas of Gizeh. They are confused heaps of ill assorted materials, which would collapse but for the retaining strength of their covering of solid stone.

"At Sakkarah the outward faces of the mastaba are not smooth. Each successive course is slightly set back from the one below it. At Gizeh the walls form a smooth plane gently inclined from the perpendicular.

"There are mastabas of all sizes. That of Sabou measures 172 feet by 84; that of Ha-ar, 149 by 74; that of Ra-en-ma 169 by 81, and that of Hapi no more than 25 ft. 6 in. by 19 ft. 6 in. In height they vary less. The highest are not more than from 26 to 30 ft. high, the smallest about 12."

FIG. 110.—Entrance to a Mastaba at Sakkarah. Mariette.

The roof of the mastaba is a plain surface without irregularity of any kind; but the soil above it is sprinkled with vases buried at a slight depth. These vases are pretty evenly distributed, but they are rather more numerous in that part of the soil which covers the ceilings of the chambers, a circumstance of which Mariette often made use to guide him in his excavations. Like all the vases of this epoch, those which are found upon the roof of the mastabas are roughly made, pointed at the bottom and without handles. They each contain a thin film of yellow clay deposited by the water with which they were filled. They were placed in their curious position under the notion that the water which they contained would quench the thirst of the dead man below. The mouths of the jars were covered with flat stones, and the water would last long enough to satisfy at least the immediate necessities of the inhabitant of the tomb.

"The principal face of the mastaba is turned to the east. In four cases out of five the entrance to its chambers, when there is one, is found upon this face. The general arrangement is, almost always, as follows: 1. At a few metres distance from the *north-eastern* angle we come upon a quadrangular niche or recess, very high and very narrow, in the depths of which those long vertical grooves which distinguish the steles of this epoch are carved upon the actual masonry of the tomb. For this recess an unimportant stele, with or without inscription, is occasionally substituted, or (2) we find, at a few metres distance from the *south-eastern* angle, either a deeper, larger, and more carefully built recess, in the depths of which a monolithic stele of white limestone covered with hieroglyphs is placed; or a regular architectural façade in miniature with a door in the centre. When the recess is found near the southern angle of the eastern face, the tomb begins and ends there. It has no internal chamber, or rather, the recess acts as substitute for one. But when, instead of the niche or recess, we meet with a door, we then know that we have come upon a regularly completed tomb. The name of its proprietor is often carved upon the lintel. Several of these lintels, of a peculiar shape, are to be seen in the Louvre.

FIG. 111.—Lintel of the tomb of Teta, 6th dynasty. Louvre.

"Next after the eastern face, in relative importance, comes that which is turned to the north. When the entrance is in the northern wall the door is invariably at the back of a kind of vestibule, in front of which are two monolithic columns, without base or capital, supporting the architrave which, in turn, supports the roof.

"Still more seldom than in the northern face, the entrance is occasionally found upon that which is turned to the south. This exceptional arrangement is, in most instances, caused by some local circumstance which may readily be perceived. When the entrance is on the south its arrangement is sometimes the one, sometimes the other, of the two which we have described.

"As for the western face, we have no evidence that it ever played any more ambitious *rôle* than that of completing the inclosure. It is always destitute of both openings and ornaments."

We have thus explored, with Mariette, the outside of the mastaba. We have described its form and general aspect, we have noticed the materials of which it was constructed, the principles upon which it was oriented, and its average size. We have explained, too, how this single type of sepulchre was repeated many thousands of times with but slight variations, until, upon the plateau between Memphis and the desert there gradually arose a metropolis of the dead more populous than that of the living. It remains to describe the contents of those huge blocks of masonry. We shall begin by visiting the chambers planned by the architect in the building itself; we shall afterwards penetrate, by the paths which modern curiosity has established through the *débris* of ages and the depths of the soil, to those recesses of the tomb which were meant to be for ever inaccessible.

The interior of a mastaba is composed of three parts—the chamber, the *serdab*, and the well. The last-named of the three is the only part which is never wanting. Many of the mastabas are, in fact, solid. In them the chamber is in a very rudimentary condition, being represented merely by one of those external niches which Mariette has described. This arrangement was the earliest, and, as long as the mastaba continued to be built, the less ambitious tenants of the necropolis were contented to reproduce it. But in these pages, as in a natural history, it is important to study the species when fully developed and provided with all its organs. When we have clearly established a general type nothing is more easy than to recognise and point out its variations. It suffices to say here that some tombs are wanting in one, some in another of those constituent parts whose meaning and uses we shall attempt to determine, and that, in a few, they are of an unaccustomed importance.

It is natural that we should first turn our attention to the chamber. This was a kind of neutral ground upon which the quick and the dead could meet, the former to present, the latter to receive the funeral offerings.

"The interior of a mastaba may be divided into several 'chambers' (there are three in the tomb of Ti), but generally there is only one. It is entered by the door in the middle of the *façade*.

"These chambers have, as a rule, to depend upon the door for light, but there are a few instances in which they are lighted from openings in the roof. A remarkable example of the latter arrangement is to be seen in the tomb of Ti, where the innermost chamber, which otherwise would be in complete darkness, is lighted from the roof.

"The chamber is sometimes quite bare, sometimes covered with sculptures and paintings such as those whose character and meaning we have already pointed out. At its further end, and always facing eastwards, stands the inscribed tablet or stele. There are some chambers in which the walls are bare and the stele engraved, but there are none where the walls are carved and the stele plain."

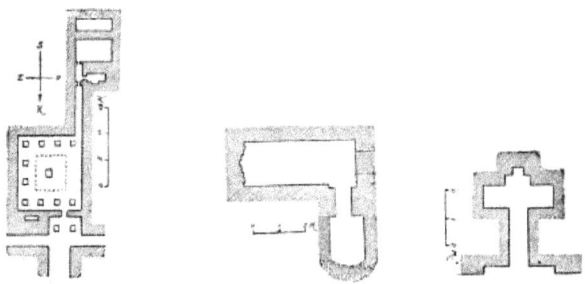

FIG. 112.—**Plan of the tomb of Ti.**
FIGS. 113, 114.—**Mastaba at Sakkarah, from Prisse.**

In the tomb of Ptah-Hotep, of which we reproduce the principal side, the stele proper is on the left, but the figures and the funerary inscriptions cover all the central part of the richly decorated wall (Fig. 115).

We see, then, that the stele is the one indispensable part of this complicated whole. It was, in fact, upon the formula with which it was inscribed, that the Egyptians depended for those magical agencies by which Osiris became the active medium of transmission between the living and the dead.

"At the foot of the stele there was often a table for offerings, in granite, alabaster, or limestone. This was laid flat upon the ground (Fig. 92).

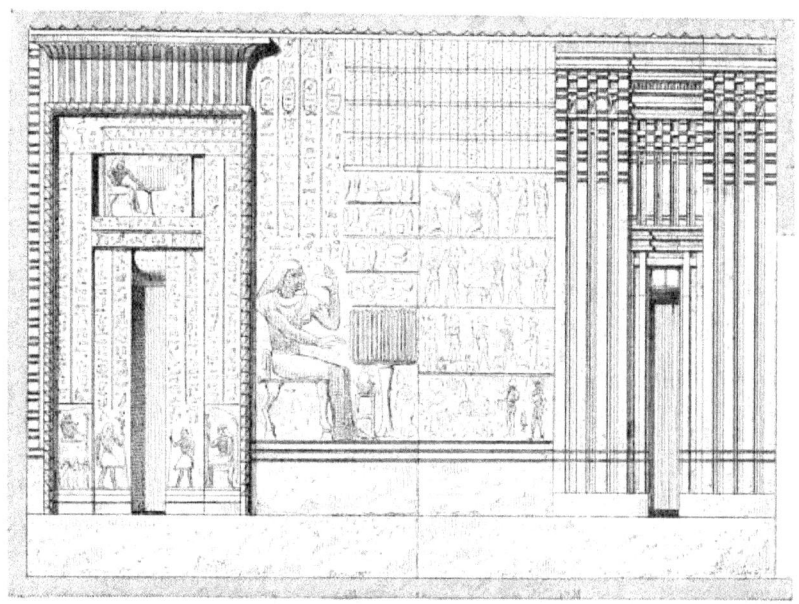

FIG. 115.—**Western wall in the chamber of the tomb of Ptah-Hotep, 5th dynasty. Drawn by Bourgoin.**

"As a rule this was the only piece of furniture in the chamber; but occasionally we find, on each side of the stele and always placed upon the ground, either two small limestone obelisks, or two objects in that material resembling table legs hollowed out at the top for the reception of offerings."

This chamber was left open to every comer. The entrance was in fact left without a door. To this rule Mariette found but two exceptions in the many hundreds of tombs which he examined.[167]

"Not far from the chamber, oftener on the south than the north, and oftener on the north than the west, a passage in the masonry, high, narrow, and built of very large stones, is found. The workmen employed upon the excavations christened it the *serdab*, or corridor, and their name has been generally adopted."[168] In Figs. 116-119 we give the plan and three sections of a mastaba at Gizeh which has four serdabs.

"Sometimes the serdab has no communication with the other parts of the mastaba, it is entirely walled in, but in other instances there is a narrow quadrangular opening, a sort of pipe or conduit, which unites the serdab with the chamber. It is so small that the hand can only be introduced into it with difficulty.[169]

"The use of the serdab is revealed by the objects which have been found in it; it was to hold one or more statues of the deceased. The Egyptians believed these statues to be the most certain guarantees, always with the exception of the mummy itself, of a future life for the dead. Hidden from sight in their dark prison, they were protected from all violence, while they were separated only by a few stones from the chamber where the friends and relations met together, and the conduit by which the intervening wall was often pierced, allowed the smell of fruit and incense and the smoke of burnt fat to come to their nostrils.[170]

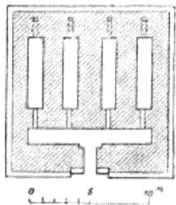

FIG. 116.—**Plan of a mastaba with four Serdabs. (Lepsius, i., pl. 24.)**

FIG. 117.—Longitudinal section of the same mastaba.

"No inscriptions have been found in a serdab except those upon the statues. And no objects other than statues have ever been found in a serdab." So that the function of the serdab was to afford a safe and final asylum to the statues. These were, no doubt, to be found in other situations also, because, not to mention the numerous bas-reliefs upon which the figure of the deceased appeared in the chamber or in the niche which sometimes took its place, he was sometimes portrayed in high relief, and of full life size, in the public hall of the tomb.[171] Sometimes, also, we find a statue in one of those front courts which, especially at the time of the fourth dynasty, seem to have been in great favour. But this court, as well as the chamber, was open to every chance passer by, and the statues which they both contained were in continual danger from careless or malicious hands. It was to guard against such chances as these that the inventive architects of Egypt contrived a safe retreat in the heart of the massive structure which should provide a reserve of statues against every contingency. When all those which were exposed to accident should have perished, these would still survive and would furnish to the *double* the material support, the tangible body, to which that phantom was obliged to attach himself unless he wished to perish entirely.

FIG. 118.—Transverse section through the chamber.

These precautions were not ill conceived. The serdab kept efficient guard over its deposit; the museum of Boulak contains at least a hundred statues from the ancient empire which were found at Sakkarah, and nine-tenths of them were found in the serdabs.

FIG. 119.—Transverse section through the serdabs.

We have now described all those parts of the tomb which were above ground. We have not been content with visiting the chamber only, which was freely left open, we have penetrated into the farthest recesses, and have discovered those secrets of the massive walls which their constructor thought to hide for ever from the eye of man. But even yet we have not arrived at the actual place of burial; we shall reach it, however, through our third internal division, the well or pit.

"The well is an artificial excavation, square or rectangular in plan, never round, at the bottom of which is the chamber in which the mummy is deposited.

"To arrive at the opening of the well, we must mount to the platform, or roof, of the mastaba (Fig. 122). As there was never any staircase to a mastaba either within or without, it will be seen that the well must have been a very inaccessible part of the tomb." In one single instance, namely, in the tomb of Ti, the well is sunk from the floor of the largest of the internal chambers, but whether it opened upon the roof or upon the floor of the chamber, it was always closed with the utmost care by means of a large flat stone.

FIG. 120.—**Figures in high relief, from a mastaba at Gizeh, 5th dynasty (from Lepsius).**

"The well is generally situated upon the major axis of the mastaba, and, as a rule, nearer to the north than to the south. Its depth varies, but, on an average, it is about forty feet. Now and then, however, it has a depth of sixty-five or even eighty feet. As the well begins at the platform and ends in the rock-carved mummy chamber, it follows that it passes vertically first through the mastaba, secondly through the rock upon which the mastaba is founded. The built part of the well is carefully constructed of large and perfect stones, and in this we find one of the distinguishing characteristics of the tombs of the ancient empire." In the tomb of Ti the well takes the form of an inclined plain like a passage in the pyramids. In the common form of well the mummy pit could only be reached by means of ropes.

"When the bottom of the well is reached a gaping passage is seen in the rock which forms its southern wall. This passage, which is not high enough to allow one to walk upright, does not run quite parallel to the axis of the mastaba. It is directed obliquely towards the south-east, like the chamber above. Suddenly it becomes enlarged into a small cavern, which is the mortuary chamber properly speaking, that is to say, the room with a view to which the whole structure has been planned and to which all its other parts are but accessories.

"This mortuary chamber is vertically under the public hall above, so that the survivors who came together in the latter for the funeral ceremonies had the corpse of the deceased under their feet, at a distance which varied according to the depth of the well."

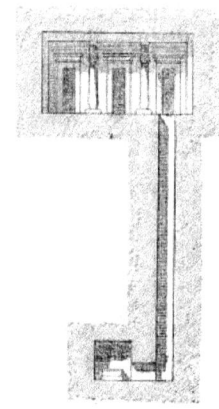

FIG. 121.—The upper chamber, well, and mummy chamber.[172]

The mortuary chambers are large and carefully built, but generally without ornament or inscription. Of all those explored by him Mariette found but one which had its walls ornamented; in the middle of its decorations, which he does not describe, he contrived to make out a few phrases which seemed to belong to the *Ritual of the Dead*.

The sarcophagus was placed in one corner of the chamber. It was generally of fine limestone, sometimes of red granite, and on a few occasions of opaque black basalt. It was rectangular on plan with a round-topped lid squared at the angles.

Mariette found none at Sakkarah with inscriptions. On the other hand we find them upon the sarcophagus at Khoo-foo-Ankh, which was discovered at Gizeh and belongs to the fourth dynasty (Figs. 123, 124).

"The Egyptians did not always trust to the mere size and weight of the lid for the secure closing of the sarcophagus. The under-side of the cover is made with a rebate at its edge which fits into a corresponding groove on the upper edge of the sarcophagus, and the two edges were bound still more tightly together by a very hard cement. Finally, as if all these precautions were not enough, wooden bolts were affixed to the under-side of the lid which fitted into slots in the sarcophagus and helped to render the two inseparable."

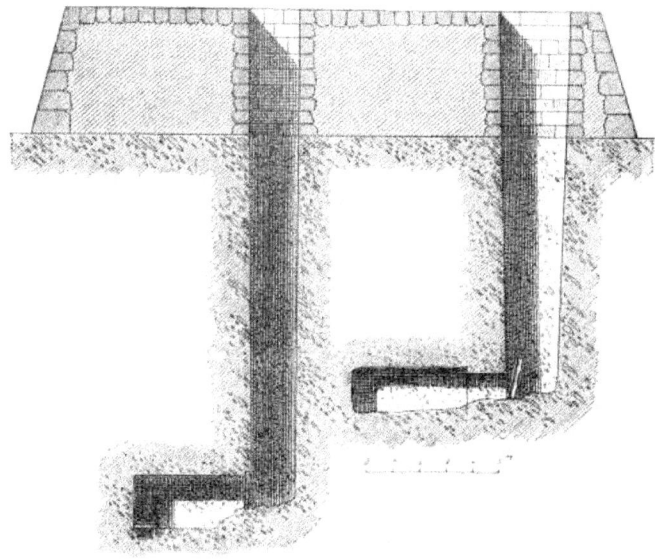

FIG. 122.—Double mastaba at Gizeh, transverse section (from Lepsius, t. i., pl. 22).

So far as we can judge from the few human remains which have been gathered from these ancient tombs, the process of embalmment was then carried on in simple and elementary fashion, and it was this imperfection that the Egyptians attempted to neutralize, by the innumerable and complicated precautions which they took to insure that the corpse should not be disturbed in its envelope of stone. In later times, when the preparation of the mummy was better understood, they were not so careful to seal up the sarcophagus from the outer air.

"The furniture of the mummy chamber comprised neither statues, nor funerary statuettes, nor amulets of any kind. Sometimes a few ox bones bestrew the ground. Two or three large and pointed red vases, containing nothing but a thin deposit of clay, rest against the walls. Within the sarcophagus we find the same sobriety of sepulchral furniture. Beyond a wooden or alabaster pillow (Fig. 105) and half a dozen little drinking cups of alabaster, nothing has been found there but the mummy itself."

FIG. 123.—Sarcophagus of Khoo-foo-Ankh. Perspective after Bourgoin. Red granite. Height 1·33 metres. Boulak.

These beef bones must be the remains of the quarters of meat which were placed in the tomb for the nourishment of the dead. No scene is more frequently represented upon the walls of the public chamber of the mastaba than the killing and flaying of victims for the funeral ceremonies (Fig. 125).

Like those which are found upon the roof, the vases must have held water for the double. The pillow was placed under the head of the mummy, it was the one he had used during his life. As for the drinking cups, their use has not yet been determined, so far as we know.

"As soon as the mummy was in the sarcophagus, the sarcophagus sealed, and the various objects which we have described in place, the opening at the bottom of the well was walled up; the well itself was filled with stones, earth, and sand, and the dead was left to his eternal sleep."[173] These precautions make it no easy thing to reach the mummy chamber. To find the entrance to the well is the first difficulty, and when it is found, many hands and no little time are required to remove the rubbish with which it is filled. The only mechanical helps which the Egyptians have ever used in such work are those which we ourselves have seen in the hands of Mariette's labourers, namely, the wooden shovel and the little rush basket which is filled with a few handfuls of sand and pebbles, and then carried on the head to be emptied at a convenient distance. It may be guessed how many journeys to and fro have to be made before a few cubic yards of *débris* are cleared by such means as this!

FIG. 124.—Details of the Sarcophagus of Khoo-foo-Ankh.

We have so far followed Mariette, and have frequently had to make use of his *ipsissima verba*. To his pages and to the plates of the great work of Lepsius, we must refer those readers who are not contented with being told general rules but wish to know the exceptions also. We shall not go into all the changes which variety of taste and the progress of art introduced into the arrangement and decoration of Egyptian buildings; they do not affect the general statements which we have made. We shall not re-state the evidence which enabled Mariette to apportion the 142 painted and sculptured mastabas explored by him in 1869, to the first six dynasties. It is certain that those monuments form a chronological series extending over a space of from twelve to fifteen centuries, and that during the whole of that long period, the general character of Egyptian sepulchral architecture remained unchanged.

FIG. 125.—Bas-relief from Sakkarah. Boulak.

We should here, perhaps, in order to make our description complete, attempt to convey a true idea of the reliefs which cover the sides of the chamber, and of the statues which fill the serdab. We should, perhaps, by a judicious choice of examples, endeavour to estimate their style and composition; but we shall postpone all such examination until we come to treat of sculpture, and of the way in which the earliest Egyptian artists treated the human form. A didactic and analytic method is so far despotic that it compels us, in order to marshal our facts and to make them easily understood, to separate phenomena which are intimately connected, and to destroy the unity of natural groups. We have thus been driven to separate the figured decorations of the tomb from the architectural arrangements which enframe and support them; with the latter, alone, are we now concerned.

We may sum up the foregoing details by the following general description of the Egyptian tomb as it was established in the early ages of the national life, in those years when the national civilization put on the form and colour which it retained until the last days of antiquity.

This tomb, when complete, included (1) a built up part which, being raised well above the surface of the soil, was a conspicuous object in the landscape; and (2) a subterranean part cut in the living rock which was never more than a few feet below the surface of the sand. The constructed part inclosed a chamber which was sometimes internal and sometimes external, a chamber in which the relations of the deceased deposited the funeral offerings, and in which the priests officiated before the stele, to which the most conspicuous place was always given. Sometimes this chamber is nothing more than a recess in the *façade*, a mere frame for the stele. The structure also contains a retreat in its thickness where the statues of the deceased were walled up. The subterranean part is composed of the well and the mummy chamber. The well is sunk from different parts of the building; usually traversing its whole depth; it leads to the mummy chamber which is found at varying depths in the bowels of the earth.

Such are the constituent elements of the *mastaba*, that is to say, of those private tombs which were contemporary with the Pyramids. All over Egypt, in every one of the cemeteries, no matter where they are situated or what their date, the same elements are to be found, modified in certain particulars by the rank of the deceased, by the nature of the soil, by the size of the tomb, and by the changes of fashion, but always to be easily recognized. Of all these elements there is but one which does not persistently reappear in monuments other than the mastaba, and that is the *serdab*. This retreat for statues has not, as yet, been found in any of the royal tombs of the first six dynasties, neither has it been met with in the tombs of the two Theban empires, or of later epochs. And yet it was connected with one of the most vital hopes of the Egyptian religion. It fulfilled in the happiest manner, one of the conditions imposed upon the Egyptian architect by the strange conceptions of a future life which we have described. Why then do we, as a rule, find the serdab only in the mastabas of the Memphite necropolis? Its absence under the Theban princes is, perhaps to be explained by the progress made in the science of embalming. The heads of more than one mummy have now been exhibited in the cases of European museums for many years, and, in spite of the dampness of our climates, they still preserve their skin, their teeth and their hair (Fig. 126). When they had learnt the secret of preserving the body from corruption, so that after a long series of centuries it should be pretty much in the same condition as on the day after death, they did not indeed, cease to make those images which were supposed to guard the *double* from annihilation, but they attached less importance to their safety, and took less trouble to hide them. They considered that they had done enough for their preservation by putting them in the precincts of their tombs and temples, and so under the guardianship of their venerated religion.

As for the other parts of the tomb, a little attention will always suffice for their identification even in those sepulchres which differ most from the mastaba. In some instances we shall find the mummy chamber contrived in the upper structure, in others the whole tomb is cut in the living rock. Sometimes we find the chapel, as we may call the public chamber in which the miraculous nourishment of the *double* took place, more or less distantly separated from the mummy chamber; sometimes the well almost disappears, sometimes it ceases to be vertical and becomes a long corridor with but a gentle slope. As a rule all these variations are easily explained, and may be connected without difficulty with that primitive type which we have attempted to define by its most wide-spread and constant features.

FIG. 126.—**Head of a Mummy. Louvre.**

Another method of sepulture was made use of in the Ancient Empire, a method which afterwards came into general use in Egypt, we mean the *hypogeum*, or subterranean tomb. The Egyptian Commission has described several rock-cut tombs in the neighbourhood of the Pyramids, especially some which face the western slope of the Second Pyramid. Similar tombs are to be found near the pyramid of Mycerinus. Some of these sepulchral grottos declare their extreme antiquity by their imitations of wooden architecture; [174] others by their inscriptions dating from the fourth and fifth dynasties. We shall not dwell long upon these rock-cut tombs. They are generally composed of one or two small sculptured chambers, upon one of which the well opens which leads to the mummy chamber. We shall postpone their study to a later chapter, as the time of the Middle Empire affords us richer and more complete examples of them than the earlier period; but, indeed, the New Empire has left us the most important examples of this kind of sepulchre. We shall here content ourselves with pointing out that the architects of Memphis did not ignore the facilities offered by the easily cut limestone rocks, not only for construction of well and mummy chamber, but also for those open parts of the tomb where the funeral rites and the ceremonies of the Ritual of the Dead were performed. In the whole course of her long vitality Egypt did little more, either in art or religion, than develop, with variations, the themes presented to her by the generations which were ruled by her first six dynasties.

THE PYRAMIDS.

The *mastaba* was the private tomb of the great lord or rich citizen of primitive Egypt; the *pyramid* was the royal tomb for the same epoch, the tomb of that son of the gods, almost a god himself, before whom all foreheads were bowed into the dust. As his head towered over those of his prostrate subjects during life, so, after death, should his sepulchre rise high above the comparatively humble tombs of his proudest servants. The most imposing mastabas, before the sand had buried them to the summit, must have looked small enough beside those prodigious masses. They were ant-hills at the foot of a palace.

It may seem that in considering the mastaba before the pyramid we have reversed the natural order. We were led to do so by the fact that the enormous mass of the pyramids and their peculiarities of construction compelled their architects to separate elements which are found closely allied in the mastaba. In consequence of this separation the elements in question have not all had the same fate. In the case of the mastaba all survived or perished together, but, in the pyramids, some are in a marvellous state of preservation, while others have disappeared and left hardly a trace behind. We are therefore obliged to make use of the private tomb in our restoration of that which was peculiar to the king.

Philologists have attempted to trace back the etymology of the word πυραμίς to the ancient language of Egypt. The term was first employed by the Greeks, and from their language it has been adopted into that of every civilized nation, with a meaning which is scientifically exact. Its origin has been sought for in the coptic term *pi-rama*, height, and in the term *pir-aa*, which occurs continually in Exodus, and was used by Moses to signify the reigning Pharaoh. But egyptologists now seem to be unanimous in rejecting both these derivations. They are, we are told, refuted by the fact that the terms which are supposed to have meant a pyramid are never used in that sense in any of the texts. 'The words which mean a royal tomb or a tomb of any kind, have not the remotest likeness,' says Herr Brugsch,[175] 'to the term πυραμίς. Each royal pyramid had its own name, a composite epithet which was peculiar to itself.' Thus the largest of them all was called "the brilliant dwelling of Choufou;" the second, "the great;" the third, "that which is on high." The word *pyramid* appears therefore to be a purely Greek term, derived from πῦρ, fire, and suggested by the similarity between its shape and that of a tongue of flame.

We shall not waste our time in noticing and refuting those fantastic explanations of the pyramids which have been given in modern times. We shall not trouble ourselves to prove that they were not observatories. Those sloping tunnels, at the bottom of which some modern writers would set unlucky astronomers to watch the passage of stars across the meridian, were hermetically sealed, and minute precautions were taken with the sole object of obstructing and concealing their entrance. The four slopes of the pyramid faced to the cardinal points, simply because the orientation of the tomb was habitual with the Egyptians; we have already explained its meaning. Still less need we occupy ourselves with the theory, which made, however, some stir in its time, that the pyramids were bulwarks by which the ancient Egyptians attempted to keep back the sand from the fertile valley of the Nile. The science of M. de Persigny was well worthy of his policy. There was in both, the same turn for fantastic invention, the same want of reflection and common sense. If such a costly barrier had been either useful or necessary it should at least have been prolonged from one end of Egypt to the other, and all the pyramids would not have been found assembled, with but few exceptions, in the neighbourhood of Memphis.[176]

No one in our day thinks of either starting or discussing such theories as these. There are, of course, several obscure points in the history of the pyramids, several details of their construction, which stimulate to fresh research and lend themselves to many different explanations; but there can be no doubt as to their general character. Their exploration and the interpretations of the Egyptian texts have confirmed the assertions of those Greek writers who were most familiar with Egypt, such as Herodotus,[177] Diodorus Siculus,[178] and Strabo.[179] The Pyramids are sepulchres. "They are massive, simply conceived, carefully sealed up tombs. All entrance is forbidden even to their most carefully built corridors. They are tombs without windows, without doors, without exterior openings of any kind. They are the gigantic and impregnable dwellings of the mummy; ... their colossal dimensions have been invoked to bear out the arguments of those who would attribute to them some other destination, but they are in fact to be found of all sizes, some being no more than twenty feet high. Besides this, it must be remembered that in all Egypt no pyramid, or rather group of pyramids, is to be found, which is not the centre of a necropolis, a fact which is enough by itself to indicate their funerary character."[180] It is proved still more definitely, if that be possible, by the sarcophagi which have been found in the internal chambers, empty in most cases, because those chambers had been entered and despoiled, either in the days of antiquity or in those of the middle ages, but sometimes intact, as in the pyramid of Mycerinus. The pyramids were hermetically sealed. Even without direct evidence we might assert that it was so, knowing as we do the precautions which the Egyptians took elsewhere to guard their tombs against intrusion; but direct proof of the fact is not wanting. When in the ninth century the Kaliph Al-Mamoun wished to penetrate into the Great Pyramid he was only enabled to do so by breaking into it violently, near the centre of its northern face, and thus stumbling accidentally upon the descending passage at some distance from its mouth. That he was reduced to employ this method at the risk of meeting with nothing but the solid masonry shows that no external indication had been left of the opening through which the mummy had been carried in. The casing seems to have been then complete and consequently the four sides of the Pyramid must have been free from *débris* and generally uniform. That the Arabs should have chosen the right side for their attack was perhaps owing to the survival of some ancient tradition indicating the northern side to be that of the entrance, which, as a fact, it has been found to be in all the pyramids as yet explored. Perhaps too the Arabs may have been guided by the traces of previous attempts made either in the time of the Persians or in that of the Romans.[181] However this may be it is very certain that had they perceived any signs of an original doorway, they would have directed their attentions to it. Those who seek for treasure do not, like archæologists, strike out lines of exploration in all directions for the satisfaction of their curiosity, they go straight to their point.

The pyramid includes two of those four parts into which we have divided the typical Egyptian tomb; it contains the well and the mummy chamber. As for the funerary chapel, there were obvious difficulties in the way of including it in the thickness of the monument itself. It would have been difficult to preserve it from being crushed by the immense weight above it, and as it would have had to be lighted from the door alone, it must always have been of the most restricted dimensions. A different arrangement had therefore to be devised from that adopted in the case of the mastaba. The open part of the monument was separated from that which was destined to be sealed up from the outer world. The chapel or temple, in which the successors of the prince buried in the pyramid and the priests told off for its service performed the prescribed rites, was erected at some distance from the eastern face. The remains of such buildings have been found to the east of both the second and third pyramids. That of Cheops has not been discovered, but we may assert with confidence that it has either been destroyed by the hand of man, or that it still lies under the veil of sand. Were there any *serdabs* concealed in the thickness of the temple walls? That question cannot be answered. The remains of those buildings are in such a condition that all traces of such an arrangement would have vanished had there been any. The walls have disappeared. The lower courses of masonry are still in place, and allow us to follow the very simple plan upon which these chapels were erected; and that is all. It is possible, however, that the Egyptians depended solely upon the profound respect which was felt for the royal person, combined with the sacredness of the spot and the vigilance of the established priesthood of the necropolis, to preserve the august images of the sovereign from insult or destruction. The seven or eight statues of Chephren which were found at the bottom of a pit in what is called the *Temple of the Sphinx*, were all more or less mutilated, proving that this want of precaution was sometimes disastrous. In the course of so many centuries, during which the Hyksos, the Ethiopians, the Assyrians, and the Persians overran the country by turns, such statues as were not sheltered in some well dissembled retreat must more than once have been struck off their pedestals and broken, or, like those of the unlucky Chephren, thrown head-foremost into the depths of the earth.

FIG. 127.—**Plans of the temples belonging to the second and third pyramids; from Perring.**

As such vast importance was attached to the preservation of the portrait statues upon which the prolongation of life after death was made so largely to depend, is it not probable that the idea of hiding some of them in the innermost recesses of the pyramids themselves may have occurred to those who caused those monuments to be built? It is obvious that no hiding-place could be more secure. No such retreats have yet been discovered in any of the galleries which have been explored by modern curiosity, but it does not follow that they do not exist in some corner which has not yet been reached, which will perhaps never be reached by the most persevering explorer. Quite lately M. Maspero believed that he recognized a serdab in a subterranean chamber with three niches which he found near the mummy chamber in the Pyramid of Ounas, the last king of the fifth dynasty.[182] Before we could say that such an arrangement does not exist elsewhere, we should have to take some pyramid to pieces from the first stone to the last. It might, however, be asserted that the images of the deceased would, if hidden in the pyramid, be too far removed from that public hall to which his relations brought their offerings and their pious homage. At such a distance they would not have heard the friendly voices or the magic chants; nor would the scent of the incense have reached their nostrils. In a word, they would have been ill placed for the fulfilment of the office assigned to them by the Egyptian faith.

We have hitherto spoken only of the social purposes of the pyramid, of its office as the sepulchre of the ancient kings of Egypt, or rather as the part of that sepulchre that corresponded to the least interesting parts of private tombs. In the plants of our gardens and orchards, we see cultivation develop certain organs at the expense of others. We find stamens changed into petals, giving us double flowers, and the envelope of the seeds thickened and made to shed perfume. We see the same process of development in the tombs of the early Egyptian monarchs. Under the influence of their pride of station, and as a consequence of the effort which they made to perpetuate their rank even after death, the stone hiding-place which protected the mummy took a size which is oppressive to the imagination, while the funerary chapel remained of modest dimensions. This disproportion is to be easily explained. The simple method of construction which distinguishes the pyramid permitted almost indefinite extension, while architecture, properly speaking, was not yet sufficiently advanced to make use of those grandiose orders which distinguish the porticos and hypostyle temples of the Theban period.

We have now to consider the pyramids from another point of view, from that of their probable origin, of their variety of form, and of the materials of which they are composed. Descriptions of these monuments, such as those contained in the great works of Vyse[183] and Perring[184], works which gave to the world the accumulated results of long and costly explorations, must not be looked for in these volumes. We do not think it necessary that we should give even a succinct account of the more important pyramids, such as that given by Bædeker or Isambert. Such a proceeding would be a mere duplication of those excellent manuals, and would moreover, be foreign to the purpose which we have before us. We take the pyramids as known. The two books just mentioned are within the reach of all. Thanks to the precise information and the numerous figures which they contain, we may content ourselves with making a few general observations. Some of these observations will refer to the pyramids as a whole, some to the peculiarities of construction which distinguish a few, peculiarities which do not affect that general type which seems to be as old as the Egyptian monarchy itself.

As soon as a society had sprung up on the banks of the Nile which attempted to organize itself under the directing lead of chiefs or headmen, the latter seem to have been stung by the desire to make known their final resting-place by some conspicuous sign. The most simple way of arriving at the desired result was to heap up the earth over the corpse, so as to form an artificial hillock which should be visible from a distance over the level plain. This was the origin of that funerary mound which modern archæologists call a *tumulus*. The tumulus is to be found in most districts of the ancient as well as of the modern world. But to confine ourselves to our own province, it is to be found in pre-Christian times among the Scythians of Herodotus and our ancestors the Gauls, as well as among the Greeks of the heroic age. We all know the frequent expression of Homer, σῆμα χεύειν, which is literally to *display a signal*, that is to say, to accumulate over the corpse of a warrior a sufficient number of spadefuls of earth to *signalize* it, for the worship and admiration of posterity. Tradition ascribes those tumuli which are yet to be seen on the plain of Troy to the observance of this custom.

The funerary architecture of Egypt commenced in the same fashion, in those distant ages which were called by the Egyptians themselves the times of *Hor-schesou* or slaves of Horus. We cannot doubt that the pyramid sprang from the mound. Its birth must have taken place after Menes had, by uniting the various tribes under his own sceptre, caused the whole race to take a distinct step onwards in civilization. The pyramid is but a built mound. It is a tumulus in which brick and stone take the place of earth. This substitution adds very greatly to its chances of duration, and makes it a much safer place of deposit and a much more lasting monument for the body committed to its charge. The Nile mud, when moulded and dried in the sun, gave bricks which still remain good; their manufacture and their constructive use seem to have been understood by the Egyptians as soon as they emerged from primitive barbarism. Thanks to the facilities thus afforded, they were enabled to build monuments upon the graves of their rulers which could offer a better resistance to injuries of time and human enemies than a few handfuls of earth and grass. They began, perhaps, by placing a few blocks of stone upon their mounds, so as to fix them more securely, or by covering them with a thin coat of brickwork. But, after a few experiments in that direction, they found it better to construct the whole body of the tumulus in the harder material. Its size increased with the constructive skill and material appliances of its builders, until it became first a hillock and finally a mountain of stone, with the impenetrable rock for its base and flanks of solid masonry.

The built-up tumulus of masonry took a form very different, in its definite lines, from the rounded slopes of the mound. The squared forms of brick or cut stone infallibly give to the edifice upon which they are employed one of those more or less rigid forms which are defined by geometry. When they leave the hands of the builder they are either cubes or parallelopipeds, pyramids or prisms, cylinders or cones. They present the general appearance, they possess the essential properties, of one of those forms. We may say that architecture was born on the day when man began to use the unyielding materials by which definite geometrical forms can alone be given. As soon as this early development was reached he set to work to combine those elementary forms in different proportions and to add to their effect by elegance and richness of decoration, and so in the end to form national architectures.

When the first pyramid was built upon the borders of the desert man was on the threshold of the movement to which we have referred. The form adopted for the royal tomb was one of the most simple which could be chosen for a building. The most simple of all would have been the *tetrahedron*, or pyramid built upon a triangular base. But not a single pyramid of that kind has been discovered in Egypt. The whole of the pyramids, large or small, are built upon a right-angled base, and in most instances upon one with sides practically equal.[185] Mystic reasons for this shape have been given. It has been said that each face was dedicated to one of the four powers of Amen, which corresponded to the cardinal points of heaven.[186] We are not yet sufficiently well acquainted with the genesis of the Egyptian religion to be able to decide how far into the past the four powers of Amen may be traced: but it is quite possible that they were derived from the four faces of the strictly oriented pyramids. Were we inclined to enter into this discussion we should rather, perhaps, attribute the shape of the pyramid to the prevailing Egyptian desire to turn one face of their tombs towards the west, the abode of the dead, and another to the east, whence the hoped-for resurrection was to come. The three-sided pyramid would not have lent itself to such an arrangement.

There is also something unpleasant to the eye in the sharp angles which form the three *arêtes* of the tetrahedron; it looks as if there had been a lack of material, and as if the structure would suffer in consequence. The four-sided pyramid has more dignity and more amplitude; its four faces, placed back to back in pairs, seem to counterpoise and sustain each other in a fashion which is impossible in the case of the tetrahedron.

FIG. 128.—Plan of the Pyramid of Cheops.

The one characteristic possessed in common by those relics of the Ancient Empire which we call pyramids, is their four-sidedness. To an attentive observer these buildings offer more diversities than would at first sight be believed. From Meidoum in the south to Abou-Roash in the north is a distance of 43-1/2 miles as the crow flies. Between these two points, which may be called the northern and southern boundaries of the pyramid field, about one hundred have been discovered, sixty-seven of which have been examined by Lepsius. Now, in this whole number there are not two which resemble each other in all particulars, or which seem to be copies of one model. We do not refer only to their height, which differs in an extreme degree. The three large pyramids at Gizeh are 482, 454, and 218 feet high respectively, while at their feet are several little pyramids which hardly exceed from 50 to 70 feet of vertical height. Between these two extremes many of intermediate sizes may be inserted. The Stepped Pyramid, near Sakkarah, is about 190 feet high; the largest of those at Abousir is about 165; one of those at Dashour is not quite 100 feet. These differences in height are easily explained by one of those national habits to which we have already alluded. Every Egyptian, as soon as he arrived at years of discretion, set about building his own tomb. He dug the well and the mummy chamber, he caused the sarcophagus to be carved and the funerary chapel to be built. It often happened that those who had ordered such works died long before they were finished, and it would seem that their heirs were content with doing no more than was strictly necessary. They placed the mummy in its grave with the prescribed ceremonies, they filled up the well and sealed the private parts of the tomb; but being occupied with the preparations for their own funeral, they did not continue the decoration of the chapel, which thenceforward remained *in statu quo*. Thus only can we explain the state in which several important tombs have been discovered both at Memphis and at Thebes. On one wall we find paintings and sculptures carried out with the greatest care and finish, while on another nothing is to be seen but the first rough outline, in red paint, by the artist charged with the undertaking. The completion of the work must have been suddenly arrested by the death of the destined inhabitant of the tomb.

FIG. 129.—The great pyramid and the small pyramids at its foot; from Perring.

It was the same with the sepulchres of the kings. Each sovereign began the construction of his pyramid as soon as he found himself upon the throne. But, in case his life and his reign should be cut short, he began with those constituents of the tomb which were absolutely necessary. He pressed on the work until he had raised a pyramid of moderate size with its mummy chamber. When this point had been reached, his immediate anxiety came to an end; but that was no reason for interrupting the course of the work. The higher and wider his pyramid, the more efficient a guardian of his body would it be, and the more impressive would be the message carried down by it to posterity as to the power of its builder. Year after year, therefore, he employed crowds of impressed workmen to clothe it in layer after layer of dressed stone or brick, so that the edifice raised in comparative haste at the beginning of his reign, became in time nothing but the nucleus or kernel of one many times its size.[187] The construction was thus begun in the centre and was developed outwards, like the timber of a tree in successive years. As the pyramid grew in extent and height, each successive coat, so to speak, required more hands and more time. We have no reason to believe that each coat had to be finished within a certain period, and so it would be futile to attempt to found any calculation as to the duration of the different reigns upon the number of these concentric layers; but we may assert in a general way that the highest pyramids correspond to the longest reigns. We know, by the witness of ancient authors, that the kings who built the three great pyramids at Gizeh, namely, Cheops, Chephren, and Mycerinus, each reigned about sixty years. History thus confirms the truth of the induction which arises from the study of those monuments and from a comparison of the constructive processes made use of by the architects of the pyramids. [188]

The author of Bædeker's *Guide* has not been content with believing, like Perring, Lepsius, and Mariette, that the pyramid grew by the application of successive envelopes of stone round the central mass, either in horizontal courses or in courses sloping towards the axis of the building. He has brought forward an elaborate theory of construction, which, though very ingenious, encounters several grave objections. We shall point out those objections while we endeavour to explain the system itself by the help of special illustrations drawn for us by the author of the *Guide* in question.[189]

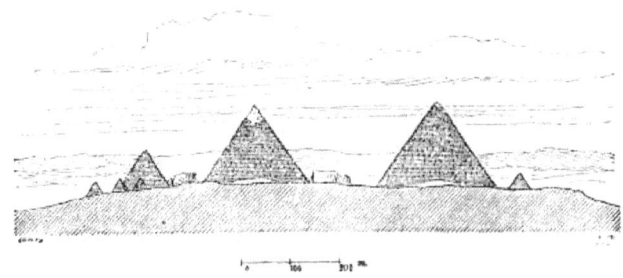

FIG. 130.—The three great pyramids; from the south.

When Cheops first began to think about building his tomb, he could not have counted upon giving it the colossal dimensions which it presents even in its actual injured condition. The area of the great pyramid is more than double that of Saint Peter's at Rome. If we deduct from its total volume the core of rock which it incloses[190] and the openings which it contains, the masonry in its primitive integrity must have amounted to a total of 3,479,600 cubic yards. Even now, when so much of its substances has been detached and carried away, there still remains the enormous mass of 3,246,600 cubic yards. Supposing that, two or three years after the commencement of a work upon this colossal scale, death had carried off its projector, can we believe that any successor, even a son who was sincerely devoted to the memory of his father, would have burthened himself with the continuation and completion of such an enterprise? The new sovereign would have enough to do in commencing and carrying on the erection of his own tomb, and, moreover, would be irresistibly tempted to make use, for its construction, of the accumulated material and collected labour of his predecessor.

Even four or five thousand years before our era, men were too sagacious to reckon upon the piety or gratitude of an heir. For the closing and final sealing up of the pyramid, its builder and destined inhabitant was obliged to depend upon his survivors, he could not do it himself. Moreover, the external completion, which, in the case of the greater monuments, must have been a long and costly matter, had to be entrusted to the same hands. The reigning king, so long as he was not too sternly reminded of the end by disease or the infirmities of age, must have felt great reluctance to order the cessation of the work which had gone on under his own eye for so many years, or to arrest that course of development which, after being a continual source of pride and pleasure to himself, might end in giving him a monument surpassing those of his famous predecessors. He was, therefore, very likely to be surprised by death with his tomb still unfinished, with the final cope-stone still upon the ground, or, even when that had been put in place so as to show the total height, with the casing of polished stone which was destined to hide the inner courses of the masonry and the entrances, still incomplete. Upon two-thirds or three-quarters of each face, his pyramid would still present the aspect which necessarily belonged to it during the period of its construction; an aspect which has again distinguished the great pyramid since it was despoiled of its casing. As each course was set back from that upon which it was placed, the final *ensemble* looked like an enormous staircase with steps gradually diminishing in length as they neared the summit.

There were many of the Egyptian princes who from want of patience or zeal, or from some other motive, failed to carry on the enterprise of their predecessors to its destined conclusion. We are ignorant as to the condition of the three great pyramids of Gizeh at the death of their projectors. But they appear to have been finished in most of their details with a care which would seem to indicate that Cheops, Chephren, and Mycerinus, must have been there to overlook the smallest details of their execution. Other pyramids, on the other hand, seem to have been left in a comparatively imperfect state.

These observations furnish us with an initial objection to the theory to which we have referred. Some may refuse to believe that Cheops intended from the beginning that his pyramid should have the dimensions and the internal arrangements which we now see. But why should he not have done so? If he had died at the end of a few years, his pyramid would, perhaps, have presented to us a shape like that of some other edifices of the same kind, a large base which had never received either its cope-stone or its casing. So too with those of Mycerinus and Chephren. Have not absolute monarchs existed at all times, whose infinite power seems to have made them forget the eternal limits of time and space? Sometimes Fortune has been cruel to them: but often she seems to have placed herself entirely at their disposal.

Among the causes which combine to make the royal tombs of the first six dynasties so unequal in height and appearance, the very unequal length of the reigns is the most important. If we were better acquainted with the condition of Egypt in those remote epochs, we should, no doubt, be enabled to give other reasons for their want of uniformity. The chances of completion and even of preservation in its complete state enjoyed by a pyramid must have greatly depended upon the descent of the crown. When king succeeded king in one family those chances were much better than when dynasty succeeded dynasty, whether the break were due to internal revolution or to the failure of the legitimate line. It is even possible that some of those pyramids which are now to outward appearance mere heaps of *débris* never received the mummy for whose reception they were designed and built.

The pyramids differ also in the materials employed. The great pyramids at Gizeh are built of fine limestone from Mokattam and Toura; the chief one at Sakkarah of a bad clayish limestone from the neighbouring rocks; at Dashour and Abou-Roash there are pyramids of unburnt brick. Finally there are pyramids built chiefly of stone which is kept in place by a carefully constructed skeleton, so to speak, of brick. This construction is to be found in the pyramid of Illahoun, at the entrance to the Fayoum (Fig. 131).

There is the same variety in the position of the mummy chamber. Sometimes this is within the sides of the pyramid itself, as in that of Cheops; sometimes, after the example of the mastaba, it is cut out of the living rock upon which the pyramid stands. This arrangement is to be found, for instance, in the pyramid of Mycerinus, where the roof of the mummy chamber is about 33 feet below the lowest course of the pyramid itself. So too in the Stepped Pyramid, where the whole complicated system of corridors and cells, which distinguishes that edifice, is cut in the rock, so that the building itself is absolutely solid. Most of the pyramids have no more than one or two entrances, giving access to narrow galleries, sometimes ascending, sometimes descending, which lead to one or two chambers of very small dimensions when compared to the enormous mass which rises above and around them (Fig. 132). In the subterranean part of the Stepped Pyramid the proportion of voids to solids is far less insignificant. This pyramid, which is not nearly so carefully oriented as the others, has four entrances and a series of internal passages, horizontal galleries, staircases and cells, which make it little else than a subterranean labyrinth. It is singular also in having, upon its central axis and at the point upon which, at various heights, all its galleries converge, a sort of large well, a chamber about twenty feet square and eighty feet high, in the pavement of which a huge block of granite cut into the shape of a cork or plug was so placed as to open at will[191] and leave a free passage for the descent into a second chamber, the purpose of which is more than obscure, as it is too small even to have contained a sarcophagus.[192] The end of the long passage which leads to the thirty chambers which have been counted beneath this pyramid has been found in the neighbouring sands (Fig. 134).

Fig. 131.—The pyramid of Illahoun, horizontal section in perspective; from the plan of Perring.

Another point of difference: most of the pyramids are built round a core of living rock, which is embraced by the lower courses of their masonry. But the pyramid of Mycerinus is just the reverse of this. It is built over a hollow in the rock which is filled up with masonry. The inequalities of the surface were usually taken advantage of so as to economize material, and make a greater show with less labour. Mycerinus, however, did not fear to increase his task by rearing his pyramid over a depression in the plateau.

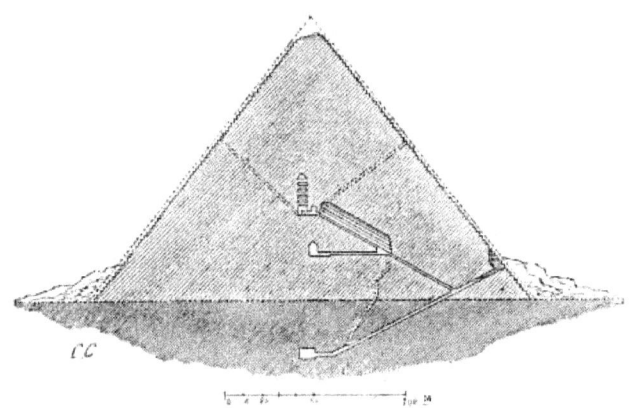

FIG. 132.—Section of the pyramid of Cheops; from Perring.

There is no less diversity in the external aspects of the pyramids. We are most familiar with the shapes of the great pyramids at Gizeh (Fig. 130 and Pl. 1, 2); their images have been multiplied to infinity by engraving and photography, but we make a great mistake when we imagine all the royal tombs at Memphis to be built upon this one model. They do not all present the same simplicity of form, the same regular slope from summit to base, or the smooth and polished casing which distinguished those great monuments when they were in complete preservation. The southern pyramid of Dashour offers us one of the most curious variations upon the original theme (Fig. 133). Its angle-ridges are not unbroken straight lines from base to summit. The slope of its faces becomes less steep at about half their height. The lower part of its sides make angles of 54° 41' with the horizon, while above they suddenly fall back to an angle of 42° 59'. This latter slope does not greatly differ from the 43° 36' of the other pyramid in the same neighbourhood. No indication has yet been discovered as to the builder of this pyramid.

A second variation, still more unlike the Gizeh type, is to be found in the great pyramid of Sakkarah, the Stepped Pyramid, which was considered by Mariette as the oldest of them all. Taking a passage from Manetho as his authority, he thought himself justified in attributing it to the fourth king of the first dynasty, Ouenephes or Ata, and he was inclined to see in it the Serapeum, or Apis tomb, of the Ancient Empire. Its present elevation is about 190 feet. Each of its sides is divided horizontally into six large steps with inclined faces. The height of these steps decreases progressively, from the base to the summit, from 38 feet 2 inches to 29 feet 6 inches. The width of each step is nearly 7 feet. It will be seen, therefore, that this building rather tends to the pyramidal form than achieves it; it is a rough sketch for a pyramid.

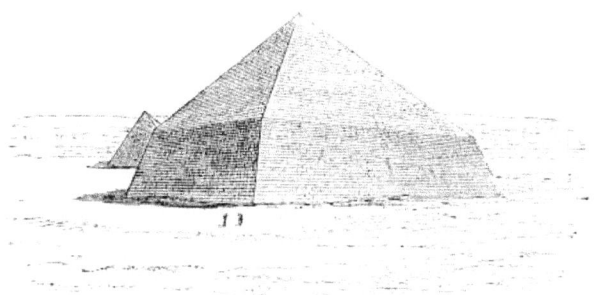

FIG. 133.—The southern pyramid of Dashour; from the measurements of Perring.

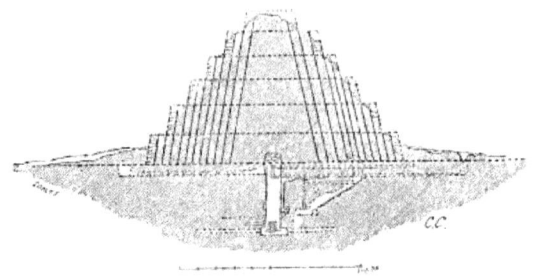

FIG. 134.—Section of the Stepped Pyramid; from Perring.

Does this want of completion result from accidental causes, or must it be referred to ignorance of the full beauties of the pyramidal form on the part of its builders? If the conjecture of Mariette is well founded, the Stepped Pyramid is not only the most ancient building in Egypt but in the whole world; and in the remote century which witnessed its construction men may not yet have learnt to fill up the angles left in their masonry, they may have been quite satisfied to leave their work in a condition which to us seems imperfect.

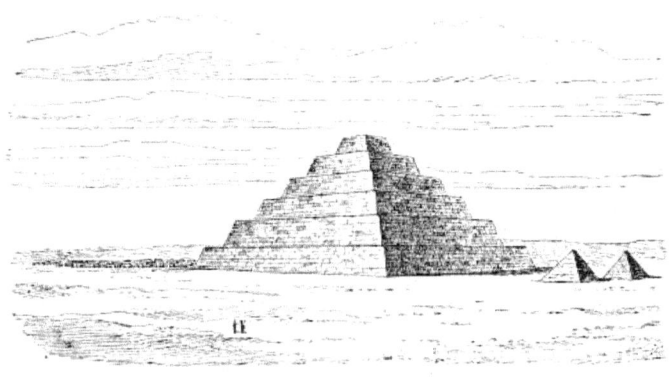

FIG. 135.—The Stepped Pyramid; restored from the measurements of Perring.

The Germans have evolved a complicated system of construction from notes made by Lepsius upon the details of the masonry in different pyramids. In order that this system may be more easily understood, we give, on the opposite page, a series of representations of such a pyramid in different stages of completion (Figs. 136 to 142). A commencement was made by erecting a very narrow and perpendicular pyramid crowned by a pyramidion, like a stumpy obelisk (Fig. 136). This finished, sloping masses were erected against it so as to form, with the pyramidion of the first mass, a second pyramid. The apex of this pyramid, a pyramidion of a single stone, might be put in place and the work considered finished (Fig. 137); or, if the builder were sanguine as to time, he might seek to push on still farther. Then, at the line where the slopes of the pyramid left the earth, four perpendicular walls were erected to the height of the pyramidion. The space between the sides of the pyramid and the inner faces of these walls was filled in, and thus a kind of terrace, or huge rectangular block, was obtained (Fig. 138), which served as the core for a new pyramid (Fig. 139). This again disappeared under a pyramid of larger section and gentler slope (Fig. 140), whose sides reached the ground far beyond the foundations of the terrace. In the case of a long reign this operation might be repeated over and over again (Figs. 140 and 142). A large pyramid would thus be composed of a series of pyramidal envelopes placed one upon another. The mummy-chamber was either cut in the rock before the laying of the first course of stone, or it was contrived in the thickness of the masonry itself; as the casing of stone went on increasing in thickness, galleries were left for ventilation and for the introduction of the sarcophagus and the mummy. The mummy-chamber is always found either upon the axis of the pyramid, or in its immediate neighbourhood, and always nearer the base than the summit.

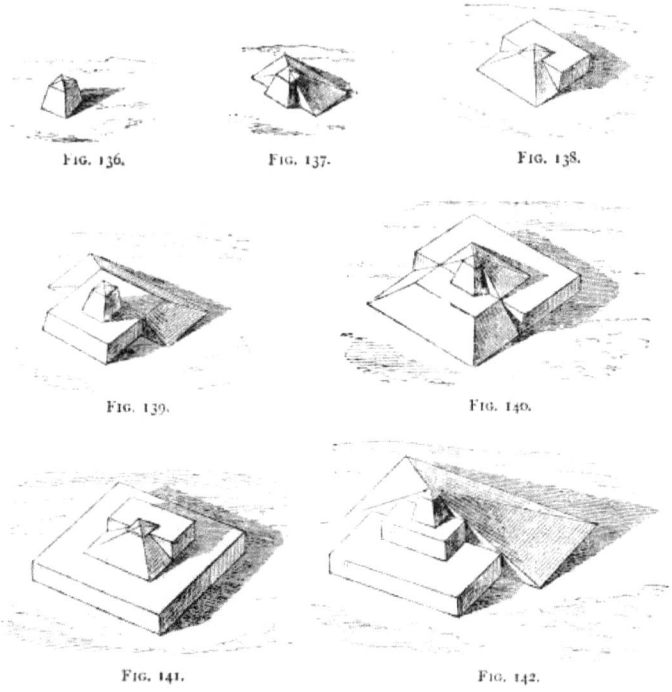

FIGS. 136-142.—Successive states of a pyramid, according to the system advocated in Bædeker's *Guide*.

We are told that the system of construction here set forth is rendered almost certain by the fact that "the deeper we penetrate into the pyramid the more careful do we find the construction, which becomes more and more careless as the exterior is approached. In fact, as each new envelope was commenced, the chances of its being completed became less." The mass of stone to be worked and placed was greater, while the king, upon whose life the whole operation depended, was older and nearer his death. The builders became less sure of the morrow; they pressed on so as to increase, at all hazards, the size of the monument, and trusted to the final casing to conceal all defects of workmanship.

This system of pyramid building would explain the curious shapes which we have noticed in the Stepped Pyramid and the southern pyramid of Dashour.[193] Both of those erections would thus be unfinished pyramids. At Sakkarah, the angles left by the successive stages would be waiting for their filling in; at Dashour, the upper part of a pyramid of gentle slope would have been constructed upon the nucleus which was first erected, but the continuation of the slope to the ground would have been prevented by the stoppage of the works at the point of intersection of the upper pyramid and its provisional substructure. Hence the broken slope which has such a strange effect, an effect which could not have entered into the original calculations of the architect.

But although this theory seems satisfactorily to explain some puzzling appearances, it also, when tested by facts, encounters some very grave objections. The explorers of the pyramids have more than once, in their search for lost galleries and hidden chambers, cut for themselves a passage through the masonry, but neither in these breaches made by violence, nor in the ancient and carefully constructed passages to which they were the means of giving access, have any signs been, discovered, or at least, reported, of the junctions of different surfaces and slopes which must have existed according to the theory which we are noticing. We should expect, at least, to find the nearly upright sides of the cubic mass with which the pyramid began, contrasting with the comparatively gentle slopes which were built against it. These different parts of the pyramid, we are told, were built and finished separately, a proceeding which, if the later parts were to be properly fitted to the earlier and the final stability of the monument assured, would have demanded a minute and scrupulous care which was not common with Egyptian workmen. How, without numerous through bonding-stones, could those slides and settlements be prevented to which the want of homogeneity in the structure would otherwise be sure to lead? But we are not told that any such junctions of old and new work are to be found even in those points where they would be most conspicuous, namely, in the galleries leading to the internal chambers, where a practised eye could hardly fail to note the transition. We do not say that there are no such transitions, but we think the advocates of the new theory should have begun by pointing them out if they exist.

There is another difficulty in their way. How is their system to explain the position of the mummy-chamber in certain pyramids? Let us take that of Cheops as an example. If its internal arrangements had been fixed from the beginning, if the intention had been from the first to place the mummy-chamber where we now find it, at about one-third of the whole height, why should the builders have complicated their task by imposing upon themselves these ever difficult junctions? Would it not have been far better to build the pyramid at once to the required height, leaving in its thickness the necessary galleries? The same observation applies to the discharging chambers above the mummy-chamber. The whole of these arrangements, the high vestibule with its wonderful masonry, the chambers and the structural voids above them, appear to have been conceived and carried out at one time, and by the same brains and hands. Not a sign is to be found of those more or less well-veiled transitions which are never absent when the work of one time and one set of hands has to be united with that of another. Or are we to believe that they commenced by building a hill of stone composed of those different pyramids one within another, and that they afterwards carved the necessary chambers and corridors out of its mass? One of the heroes of Hoffmann, the fantastic Crespel, made use indeed of some such method in giving doors and windows to his newly-built house, but we may be sure that no architect, either in Egypt or elsewhere, ever thought of employing it. The disintegration to which it would lead may easily be imagined.

We may here call attention to a circumstance which justifies all our reserves. There is but one pyramid which seems to have been built upon a system which, though much less complicated, resembled that which we are noticing in some degree, we mean the Stepped Pyramid of Sakkarah. Now we find that the whole of the complicated net-work of chambers and passages in that pyramid is cut out of the living rock beneath its base, and that they are approached from without by subterranean passages. The difficulty of deciding upon the position of the chambers in advance, and of constructing the galleries through the various slopes of the concentric masses which were to form the pyramid, was thus avoided, and the builder was able to devote all his attention to increasing the size of the monument, by multiplying those parallel wedges disposed around a central core of which it is composed.

The observations made by Lepsius in the Stepped Pyramid and in one at Abousir seem to prove that some pyramids were constructed in this manner. In both of those buildings all necessary precautions were taken to guard against the weaknesses of such a system. It is difficult to understand how separate slices of masonry, placed one upon the other in the fashion shown by the section which we have borrowed from Perring's work (Fig. 134), could have had sufficient adherence one to another. Lepsius made a breach in the southern face of this pyramid, and the examination which he was thus enabled to institute led him to suggest a rather more probable system of construction. Upon the external sloping face of each step he found two casing-walls, but these did not extend from the ground to the apex of the monument, they reached no higher than the single step, so that they found a true resisting base in the flat mass (see Fig. 143) upon which they rested. Moreover, the architect provided for the lateral tying of the different sections of his work, as Lepsius proves to us by a partial section of the pyramid of Abousir. Two walls of fine limestone blocks inclose a filling in of rubble, to which they are bound by perpend stones which penetrate its substance. This method of construction has its faults, but it is so rapid that its employment is not to be wondered at.

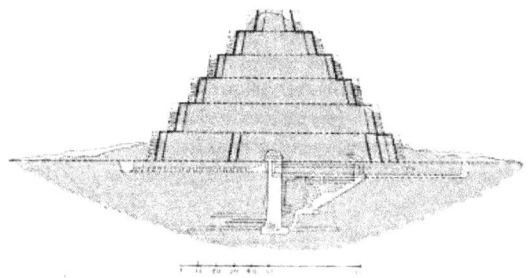

FIG. 143.—Section of the Stepped Pyramid at Sakkarah; from Lepsius.

FIG. 144.—Construction of the Pyramid of Abousir in parallel layers; transverse section in perspective from the geometrical section of Lepsius.[195]

Do these parallel walls reach from top to bottom? A detail discovered by Minutoli would seem to indicate that a base was first constructed of sufficient extent for the whole monument. In the lower part of the Stepped Pyramid Minutoli[196] shows concave courses of stone laid out to the segment of a circle. These courses formed a kind of inverted vault, abutting, at its edges, upon the rock. This curious arrangement should be studied upon the spot by some competent observer. As we do not know whether these curves exist upon each face or not, or whether they meet each other and penetrate deeply into the structure or not, we cannot say what their purpose may have been. But however this may be, they afford another argument against the notion that all the great pyramids were built round such a pyramidoid core as that represented by our Fig. 136. We fear that this system must be regarded merely as an intellectual plaything. The views of Lepsius as to the enlargement of the pyramid by the addition of parallel slices are worthy of more respect, and their truth seems to be demonstrated in the case of some pyramids. But these all belong to that category of monuments which have subterranean chambers only. We have yet to learn that they were ever made use of in those pyramids which inclose the mummy-chamber and its avenues in their own substance. Variety is universal in that Egypt which has so often been described as the land of uniformity and immobility—no two of the pyramids resemble each other exactly.

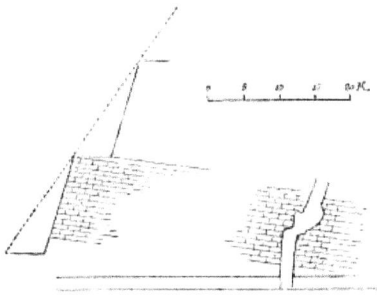

FIG. 145.—Partial section of the Stepped Pyramid; from Minutoli.

We have yet to speak of two ancient monuments in which some would recognize unfinished pyramids, namely, the Pyramid of Meidoum and the Mastabat-el-Faraoun. We do not agree with this opinion, which has, however, been lately put forward, so far, at least, as the former monument is concerned.[197] These two sepulchres seem to us to represent a different type of funerary architecture, a type created by the ancient empire, and meriting special notice at our hands.

The monument which rises so conspicuously from the plain near the village of Meidoum on the road to the Fayoum, is called by Arabs the Haram-el-Kabbab, or "the false pyramid." It is, in fact, not so much a pyramid, strictly speaking, as a mass formed of three square towers with slightly inclined sides superimposed one upon the other, the second being less in area than the first, and the third than the second. The remains of a fourth story may be distinguished on the summit of the third; some see in them the remains of a small pyramid; others those of a cone. Judging from the names found in the neighbouring mastabas, which were opened and examined by Mariette, this is the tomb of Snefrou I., one of the greatest kings of the third dynasty.[198]

FIG. 146.—The Pyramid of Meidoum; from Perring.

The Mastabat-el-Faraoun or "Seat of Pharaoh," as the Arabs call it, is a huge rectangular mass with sloping sides; it is about 66 feet high, 340 long, and 240 deep. It is oriented like the pyramids. It is a royal tomb with internal arrangements which resemble those in the pyramid of Mycerinus; the same sloping galleries, the same chambers, the same great lateral niches. Upon a block lying at the foot of the structure of which it had once formed a part, Mariette found a quarry-mark traced in red ochre which seemed to him to form part of the name of Ounas, one of the last kings of the fifth dynasty (Figs. 109 and 147).

FIG. 147.—The Mastabat-el-Faraoun; from Lepsius.

Upon the platform of the Mastabat-el-Faraoun certain blocks are to be found which, from their position, must have been bonding-stones. They seem to hint, therefore, either that the structure was never finished, or that it has lost its former crown. The latter hypothesis is the more probable. Among the titles of people buried in the necropolis at Sakkarah, we often come upon those of priests attached to the service of some monument with a form similar to that represented by our Fig. 148. Who can say asks Mariette, that it is not the Mastabat-el-Faraoun itself?[199]

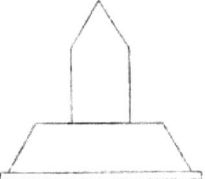

Fig. 148.—Funerary monument represented in the inscriptions.

M. Mariette cites, in support of this conjecture, certain other structures of a similar character, such as the large tomb situated near the south-eastern angle of the second pyramid at Gizeh, and the little monument which is called the Pyramid of Righa. From these he concludes that the principles of the mastaba and the pyramid were sometimes combined under the ancient empire. The royal tombs in the Memphite region were not always pyramids, they were sometimes composed of a mastaba and of one or more high square tower-like erections upon it, the whole ending in one of those small pyramids which we call pyramidions. This type allowed of numerous combinations, many of which are to be discovered in the monuments of a later period.

The pyramid was employed as a terminal form throughout the whole of Egyptian history. Both Thebes and Abydos offer us many examples of its use, either in those sepulchral edifices which are still extant, or in the representations of them upon bas-reliefs. But the pyramid properly speaking was confined to the Memphite period. The princes of the twelfth dynasty seem to have constructed some in the Fayoum. The pyramids of Hawara and Illahoon correspond to those which, we are told, were built in connection with the labyrinth and upon the islands of Lake Mœris respectively. These, so far as we can judge, were the last of the pyramids. There are, indeed, in the necropolis of Thebes, upon the rocks of Drah-abou'l-neggah, a few pyramids of crude brick, some of which seem to belong to Entefs of the eleventh dynasty; but they are small and carelessly constructed.[200] When the art of Egypt had arrived at its full development, such purely geometrical forms would seem unworthy of its powers, as they did not allow of those varied beauties of construction and decoration which its architects had gradually mastered.

The pyramids have never failed to impress the imaginations of those foreign travellers who have visited Egypt. Their venerable antiquity; the memories, partly fable, partly history, which were attached to them by popular tradition; their colossal mass and the vast space of ground which they covered, at the very gates of the capital and upon the boundary between the desert and the cultivated land, all combined to heighten their effect. Those nations who came under the living influence of Egypt could hardly, then, escape from the desire to imitate her pyramids in their own manner. We shall find the pyramidal form employed to crown buildings in Phœnicia, Judæa, and elsewhere. But the kingdom of Ethiopia, the southern annexe of Egypt and the copyist of her civilization, was the chief reproducer of the Egyptian pyramid as it was created by the kings of the ancient empire. Napata, Meroe, and other places have pyramids which may be counted by dozens. Like those in Egypt, they are the tombs of the native monarchs.

We shall not attempt any study of these remains. Like all the other products of Ethiopian art, they are neither original nor interesting. The people who inhabited the region which we now call by the names of Nubia and the Soudan, had, indeed, reconquered their political independence a thousand years before our era, but they were not gifted by nature with power to assimilate the lessons of their former masters. Even during the short period when the Ethiopian monarchs reigned over a divided and weakened Egypt, Ethiopia remained the clumsy pupil and imitator of the northern people. She never learnt to give to her royal pyramids the air of grandeur which distinguishes the great structures of Memphis. The Ethiopian pyramids were generally so narrow and steep in slope that their whole character was different from those of Egypt. In Egypt the base line was always greater than the vertical height, upon the Upper Nile the proportions were reversed. [201] The latter edifices thus lost some of that appearance of indestructible solidity which is their natural expression. They remind one at once of the obelisk and the pyramid. Add to this that an unintelligent taste overspread them with ill-devised decoration. Thus the upper part of their eastern faces, for they are oriented, generally bears a false window surmounted by a cornice, about as incongruous an ornament as could well be conceived, and one which expresses nothing either to the eye or the mind.

We shall, therefore, take no further notice of these more or less ill-designed variations upon the type which was created by the Egyptians in the early days of their civilization and fully understood by themselves alone.

We must return, however, to that type for a moment, in order to show, in as few words as possible, how far the art of working and fixing stone had advanced even at the time of the first dynasties.

The Great Pyramid affords us a curious example of the elaborate precautions taken against the violation of the royal tomb (Fig. 132). At the point where the ascending gallery branched off from that descending corridor which was the only entrance to the pyramid, the mouth of the former was closed by a block of granite which exactly fitted it. This block was so heavy and so well adjusted, that entrance could only be obtained by cutting a passage through the surrounding masonry, which, being of limestone, did not offer such an unyielding resistance to the tools brought against it. Formerly the mouth of a gallery, which seemed to be the continuation of the entrance corridor, remained open, and, when followed to the end, led to an unfinished chamber cut in the rock at about the level of the Nile. If this had been finished the waters would perhaps have invaded it by infiltration. This seems to have been intended by the constructor, because Herodotus, who no doubt thought the work had been completed, tells us of a subterranean conduit which admitted the waters of the Nile.[202] The violaters of the tomb would believe the corpse to be in this unsuspected reservoir, and would search no farther, or if they guessed the deception and persevered till they found the entrance to the ascending gallery, they would find another obstacle to their success which would be likely to arrest them longer than the first. The upper extremity of the great gallery, at which we suppose them arrived, opens upon a small vestibule which would still separate them from the sarcophagus-chamber itself. Four flat blocks of granite, sliding in grooves, masked the entrance to the latter; Figs. 150 and 151 show the arrangement of these portcullis stones. The narrow passage leading to the discharging chambers above the mummy-chamber, would be likely to lead our supposed robbers into the upper part of the pyramid. The entrance to this passage is high up in the end wall of the grand gallery; it was left open. The unbidden visitors would thus have explored the interior of the pyramid high and low without result, and even supposing that they expended considerable time and trouble in the search, they might easily have failed to penetrate into the mummy-chamber itself.[203]

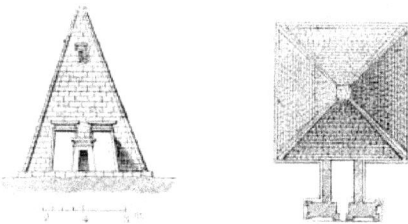

FIG. 149.—Plan and elevation of a pyramid at Meroe: from Prisse.

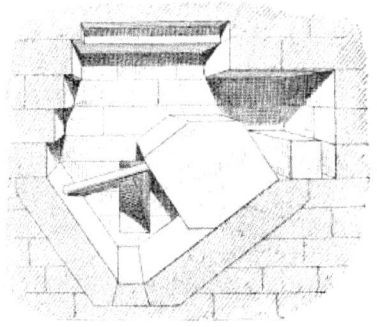

FIG. 150.—Method of closing a gallery by a stone portcullis;
from the southern pyramid of Dashour.
Drawn in perspective from the plans and elevations of Perring.

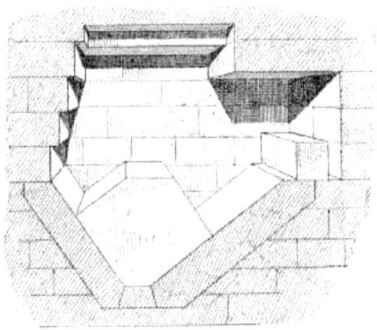

FIG. 151.—**Portcullis closed.**

Another ingenious arrangement which demands our notice is that of those discharging chambers to which we have already alluded. These chambers were explored, not without trouble, by Colonel Howard Vyse and J. L. Perring, who at once comprehended their use. The roof of the sarcophagus-chamber consists of nine slabs of fine red granite, like those which form the walls of the same chamber. They are 18 feet 9 inches long and their ends rest upon the side walls of the chamber. In spite of their thickness and of the hard nature of the rock of which they are composed, it was feared that they might give way under the enormous weight of the masonry above, for the floor of the chamber is still nearly 340 feet below the actual apex of the pyramid. This danger was met in the fashion figured above.

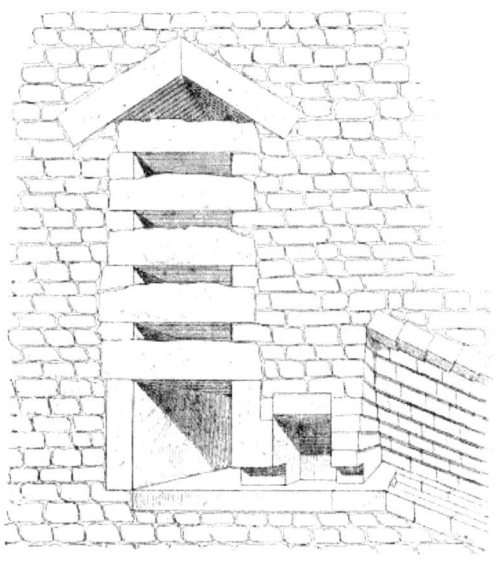

FIG. 152.—Transverse section, in perspective,
through the sarcophagus-chamber and the discharging chambers;
from the elevation of Perring.

As the structure grew above the roof of the mummy-chamber, five small chambers were left, one above the other, to a total height of 56 feet, which would relieve the flat ceiling of the mummy-chamber of the weight to be placed above it. The first four of these chambers were of similar shape and had flat roofs, but the roof of the fifth was formed of sloping slabs, meeting in a ridge, and giving the chamber a triangular section (see Fig. 152). Thanks to this succession of voids immediately over the main chamber, and to the pointed arch which surmounts them, the vertical pressure of the superstructure is discharged from the chamber itself and distributed over the lateral parts of the pyramid. These precautions have been quite effectual. Not a stone has been stirred either by the inward thrust or by the crushing of their substance; not a block is out of place but those which have been disturbed by the violence of man; and, moreover, the whole structure is so well bonded and so well balanced that even his violent attacks have led neither to disruption nor settlement in the apartment of Cheops or in the galleries which lead to it.[204]

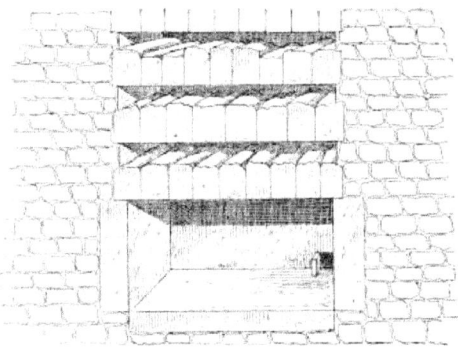

FIG. 153.—Longitudinal section through the lower chambers; perspective after Perring.

The glory of the workmen who built the Great Pyramid is the masonry of the Grand Gallery, the gallery which opens immediately into the vestibule of the King's Chamber. As this corridor is 28 feet high and 7 feet wide, the visitor can breathe more freely than in the low and narrow passages which lead to it, and can examine at his ease the beautiful blocks of limestone from Mokattam of which its polished walls are composed. The faces of these blocks have been dressed with a care which is not to be surpassed even by the most perfect examples of Hellenic architecture on the Acropolis at Athens. The internal faces must have been worked with equal care. No cement has been employed in the fixing, and the adherence is so perfect that, in the words of Abd-ul-Latif "not a needle, not even a hair, can be introduced into the joints."[205] These joints are not even to be distinguished without careful examination. The roof of this gallery is built with no less care.[206] Each of the upper courses is slightly set off from the one below it, so that in time they come so near together that the opening may be closed by a single stone, or rather, row of stones. These, being held between the two upper courses of a quasi vault, play the part of key stones. This method of vaulting has been employed in other parts of the pyramid, especially in what is called the *Queen's Chamber*, which is almost directly beneath the king's, or sarcophagus-chamber. The same care is conspicuous in those linings of red granite which form the walls of the two chambers. Even the fine limestone used for the walls of the Grand Gallery was not considered rich and solid enough for the walls of the apartment in which the prince in whose honour the whole of the colossal edifice was reared would repose; and it was determined to use the richest and most costly material of which the Egyptian architect could dispose.[207] The plain sarcophagus, without either inscription or ornament, which is still in the King's Chamber, is also of red granite.

The external casing of the pyramid has entirely disappeared, as we have already said. On account of their moderate size the stones of which it was composed would seem to be especially well fitted for use in building those great cities which, after the collapse of the ancient civilization, succeeded each other, under different names, in the neighbourhood of the Memphite necropolis. This casing seems to have been made of more than one kind of stone, if we may believe an ancient text which has been interpreted by Letronne with the skill and sagacity of which he has given so many proofs.[208]

The author, named Philo, of a treatise upon the Seven Wonders of the World, tells us that the Egyptians employed upon this work "the most brilliant and varied stones, which were carefully fixed." He mentions as contributing to the splendid result white marble, basalt, porphyry, and a green breccia from Arabia, which must have been what is called *verde antique*. And as for his white marble, it must have been the white limestone from Mokattam, which, in its best strata, is almost as white and fine in grain as marble. Marble, properly speaking, was only introduced into Egypt by the Greeks, and that in very small quantities, for the use of sculptors. Philo says nothing of granite, but its use was so general that it must have found a place in the scheme of decoration.[209]

The various kinds of stone must have been so placed as to form zones, and perhaps patterns, of different colours, white, red, black, rose, green, and so on. To form an idea of the effect we must think of Giotto's campanile at Florence and various other Italian buildings of the same kind.

It has been questioned whether the testimony of this Philo is to be depended upon, as few of those who have busied themselves with the pyramids seem to have laid much stress upon it. It seems to us to be worthy of great respect. We do not know when Philo lived, but we know that the casing of the pyramid was still in place, at least in part, during the Middle Ages, because in the time of Abd-ul-Latif it had almost its original height, and its ascent was still very difficult.[210] On the other hand we have proofs that, although the author of the Seven Wonders of the World may have written more in the tone of a rhetorician than of an eyewitness of the wonders which he describes, he took some of his information from excellent sources. In fact with the exception of Pliny, he is the only ancient writer who gives us an approximately true statement of the length of the base line of Cheops' Pyramid. While the measurements of other writers are very far from accurate, the figure given by Philo is only 16 feet 6 inches in excess of the truth. The idea of decorating such an expanse of surface with varied colour was quite in accordance with Egyptian taste. They loved polychromatic ornaments; they covered every available surface with the gayest hues; they delighted in the juxtaposition of the most brilliant tones. They could hardly think of covering such an immense surface with paint, and as it was necessary, in any case, to cover it with a smooth casing, it would be no more difficult to employ many kinds of stone than one. They would thus obtain a kind of gigantic mosaic which may perhaps have been heightened in effect by the use of gold. We know that the pyramidion of an obelisk was frequently gilded, and it is probable enough that similar means were sometimes taken, in the case of the more magnificent and carefully finished pyramids, to draw the eye to their topmost stone and thus to add to the impression made by their height. No more fitting adornment could be imagined for the sharp peak of a pyramid rising nearly five hundred feet into the pure blue of an Egyptian sky.

But this is a conjecture which can never be verified. Even if the topmost stone were still in place upon any of the pyramids it would, after all these ages, have lost all traces of gilding; but the whole of those edifices have their apex more or less truncated. Even before our era, Diodorus[211] found the Great Pyramid crowned by a plateau six cubits square.

It has sometimes been supposed that the pyramids, when complete, were terminated by such a plateau as that described by Diodorus, and that it bore a statue of the king whose mummy rested below. This hypothesis is founded upon the passage of Herodotus which treats of the Lake Mœris. "There are," he says, "in the middle of the lake, two pyramids, each fifty fathoms high (309 feet) ... each of them is surmounted by a colossal stone statue seated upon a throne."[212] Herodotus insists so often upon having seen the Labyrinth and Lake Mœris with his own eyes, that we cannot affect to doubt his assertions; we shall therefore confine ourselves to a few observations upon them.

In the descriptions which he gives of the three great pyramids, and among his comments upon the methods employed in their construction, Herodotus does not say a word which can be construed into the most distant allusion to statues upon their summits. If he had seen colossi perched upon those lofty pedestals, or if he had heard from his dragomans—whose exaggerations he has elsewhere so naïvely reproduced—that they had formerly existed, would he not have made some allusion to them in that passage, at least, where he explains how they raised such huge stones to so great a height, and describes the successive stages in the construction of a pyramid?[213] Would he not have found room, in the elaborate antithetical passage in which he contrasts the virtues of Mycerinus with the imaginary wickedness of Cheops and Chephren, for moral and critical reflections called up by the sight of their statues upon their respective pyramids; still more if one of them had happened to be missing? Would he not have attempted, through some popular tradition, to have accounted for the presence of one statue and the absence of another? It is evident, therefore, that Herodotus neither saw any statues upon the Pyramids of Memphis nor had he any reason to suppose those structures had ever been crowned in such a fashion. He lays stress upon the seated statues of the pyramids in Lake Mœris because they were new to him, because he had seen nothing of the same kind in the neighbourhood of the ancient capital.

Unless we are very much mistaken, this superposition of a colossus upon a pyramid was a novelty devised by the architects of the middle empire, when, under the Ousourtesens and Amenemhats, it was proposed to revive the pyramidal form of tomb with which the early Pharaohs had obtained such imposing results. Although most conservative on the whole, the art of

Egypt attempted, at each period of renascence, to introduce new combinations into the details, at least, of the ancient forms, and this was one of the number.

Another innovation of the same kind is to be found in the decoration which covered, again according to Herodotus,[214] another pyramid constructed at about the same time, namely, that which formed one side of the Labyrinth. "It had," says the historian, "forty fathoms, and it was sculptured with animals of large size. The entrance was by a subterranean passage." From the Greek word used (ἐγγέγλυπται) we see that Herodotus means that the faces, or perhaps only the principal face, of this pyramid about two hundred and fifty feet high, were covered with bas-reliefs. There is in Egypt no other example of a pyramid so decorated. The architectural works of this period have almost entirely vanished, but we may, perhaps, look upon it as one of their characteristics that the bareness which they had inherited from the early creators of Egyptian art, was relieved and adorned by the intervention of the sculptor.

It was the desire for such ornament that made them convert their pyramids into gigantic pedestals for statues. According to all the analogies afforded by later ages, these statues must have been those of the princes who built the pyramids in question. We have no reason to suppose that any of the kings of the first six dynasties erected any colossal figures like those which were set up in such numbers by the Theban dynasties; with the single exception of the Sphinx, none of the statues left to us by the ancient empire greatly exceed the natural size. But it is evident that such figures as would be fit to crown the pyramids of Cheops and Chephren would have to be of extravagant size even if no more than their general outlines were to be visible from below. Seen from a point nearly 500 feet below, and in consequence of the inclination of the pyramid faces, at some considerable distance laterally, even a statue fifty feet high, like the two colossi of Amenophis III. on the plain of Thebes, would appear small enough to a spectator. Its artistic results would be very slender, and yet its erection would require prodigious mechanical efforts. It would have required all the multitudes of labourers, the patience, and the time, which the Egyptians alone dared to expend upon their monuments. But perhaps it may be said that these colossi were statues built-up of comparatively small stones. To this we must answer that every colossus as yet discovered in Egypt is a monolith. A statue, of whatever size, made in different pieces would form an exception to the whole practice of Egyptian sculpture as we know it. Until such works are proved to exist we decline to believe in them.

The problem was a much simpler one in the cases of the pyramids in Lake Mœris. They were not nearly so lofty. According to Herodotus they were about 309 feet high, doubtless including their statues. Situated as they were in the middle of the lake, Herodotus could not himself have measured them, and his statement that they sank as far below the level of the water as they rose above it is an obvious exaggeration. When the bed of the lake was formed, two masses of rock were no doubt reserved, as in the cases of the other pyramids, to form the core of the projected edifices, and therefore it is likely enough that the lowest courses of the constructions themselves dipped but little below the surface of the lake.[215] In his amazement at the scale upon which the Egyptian buildings were conceived, Herodotus has too often attributed excessive dimensions to them; thus he says that the height of the Great Pyramid was eight plethra, or about 820 feet, nearly 340 feet in excess of the truth. It is therefore probable that the figures which he gives for the lake pyramids are also exaggerated. These pyramids were, on account of their comparatively modest dimensions, much better adapted to the ideas of the Ousourtesens and Amenemhats than the gigantic piles of Cheops, Chephren, and Mycerinus.

Finally there is not a text to be found, outside the pages of Herodotus, which mentions pyramids surmounted by statues, and upon none of those monuments which in one way or another bear representations of the pyramids are they shown in any other way than with pointed summits. Thus do we find them in the papyri, upon those steles of the Memphite necropolis which commemorate the priests devoted to their service, and in those tombs at Memphis, Abydos, and Thebes where the pyramid, placed upon rectangular figures of various heights, is used as a terminal element. Neither in the small number of pyramids which have come down to us comparatively intact, nor in those which are represented in reliefs, is there the smallest sign of a truncated summit or of any platform which could by any possibility have borne a statue.

FIG. 154.—Pyramidion: Louvre.

We may say the same of those small pyramidions which have been found in such great numbers in tombs and which fill our museums. It is well known that these are votive offerings in connection with the worship of the sun. "The principal figure," says M. de Rougé, "is generally shown in a posture of adoration, with his face turned to the sun. On his left hand is the invocation to the rising, and on his right that to the setting sun. These arrangements are modified in various ways, but they are always upon the same genera lines as the orientation of the tombs themselves."[216] These minute pyramids also end in a point whether they be of basalt, granite, or calcareous stone, and it is natural that we should look upon them as the faithful reproductions upon a small scale of those great funerary monuments which furnished a type, consecrated by the most venerable of the national traditions, of that structure facing the four cardinal points which we may call the normal Egyptian tomb.

We may believe, then, that the pyramid of the ancient empire terminated in a pyramidion. This apex once fixed in place, the workmen charged with the final completion of the edifice worked downwards from one course to another, covering the immense steps which each face displayed five or six thousand years ago and now displays again, with the final casing which protected them for so many centuries. Even Herodotus saw that this must have been the method of completion.[217] Any other way of proceeding would have been too dangerous after the slope of the sides had been made smooth and continuous by the completion of the casing of polished granite. Workmen could only have kept their footing upon such a surface, with its 51 or 52 degrees of elevation, by means of a complicated arrangement of ropes and ladders. And again, points of resistance could not have been obtained for the elevation of the materials to ever increasing heights without cutting or leaving holes in the casing, which would afterwards have to be filled up. These difficulties would have unnecessarily complicated an operation which was a simple matter when begun from the top. The masons could then make use of the steps for their own locomotion, and when the stones were too large to be lifted from hand to hand, nothing could be easier than to fix windlasses by which the largest blocks could be raised with facility.

Dummy Footnote Text Greek: Exepoiêthê d'ôn ta aiôtata autês prôta, meta de ta hepomena toutôn exepoieun ... (ii. 125).

As the workmen approached the base they left above them an ever increasing extent of polished surface, sloping at such an angle that no foot could rest upon it, and forming the only safeguard against the degradation of the pyramid by removing its copestone or its violation by breaking into the passages which led to the mummy-chamber. The casing gave to the pyramid those continuous lines which were necessary to make its beauty complete, and, if the materials employed were varied in the way suggested, it furnished colour effects which had their beauty also. But, above all, it was a protection, a defensive armour. So long as the pyramid preserved its cuirass intact, it was difficult for those who meditated violence to know where to begin their attack. But this obstacle once pierced it was comparatively easy to learn all the secrets of the building. The inner mass was much less carefully built than the casing; the joints were comparatively open, and the stones were soft and easily cut. Hence we see that some pyramids, especially those which were built of bricks, have been reduced by the action of time into heaps of *débris*, in which the pyramidal form is hardly to be recognised.

Philo, who seems to be so well informed, tells us with what extreme care the casing was put in place. "The whole work," he says, "is so well adjusted, and so thoroughly polished, that the whole envelope seems but one block of stone."[218] The pyramid of Cheops has been entirely despoiled of its outer covering, and it is to that of Mycerinus that we must now turn if we wish to have some idea of the care with which the work was done. The lower part of this pyramid is still covered with long blocks of the finest granite, fixed and polished in the most perfect manner. At the foot of the Great Pyramid several blocks have been found which seem to have formed part of the casing of that edifice.[219] They are trapezoidal in form, and they show, as Letronne[220] long ago remarked, that the casing stones were placed one upon another, and adjusted by their external faces. They were not, as was at first supposed, sunk into the upper face of the course below by mortices which would correspond to the trench in the living rock in which the first course was fixed. As to whether the external faces of these blocks were dressed to the required angle before they left the quarry, or whether the work were done after they were in place we cannot say with any certainty, but it is most likely that the methods of proceeding changed with the progress of time and the succession of architects. In such a matter we should find, if we entered into details, diversity similar to that which we have already shown to have characterized the forms of the pyramids, their internal arrangements, and the materials of which they were composed.

Thus some triangular prisms of granite have been found at the foot of the pyramid of Chephren, which seem to have formed part of its lower casing.[221] Such a section seems, upon paper, the simplest that could be adopted for the filling in of the angle between two of the steps, but it is far inferior in solidity to the trapezoidal section. The prisms had no alliance one with another; they had to depend for their security entirely upon their adherence to the faces of the graded core, so that they could easily be carried off, or become dislocated from natural causes. This system, unlike the first described, did not give a homogeneous envelope with a thickness of its own, and partly independent of the monument which it protected.[222]

FIG. 155.—The casing of the pyramids; drawn in perspective from the elevation of Perring.

The casing of the Second Pyramid, moreover, does not seem to have been carried out on the same principle from top to bottom. The upper part, which still remains in place, is composed of a hard cement formed of chalk, gypsum, and pieces of burnt brick. They may have wished to obtain the parti-coloured effect of which Philo speaks, by making simultaneous use of granite and concrete, and it is quite possible that yet other materials entered into the composition of the casing.[223]

In other pyramids we find different combinations again. In the double-sloped erection at Dashour, the courses of casing stones are vertical instead of horizontal,[224] while a brick pyramid—the most northern—in the same locality, was covered with slabs of limestone, fixed, no doubt, with mortar.

Sometimes we find the revetment in a state of semi-completion; the blocks in place, and cut to the proper angle, but without their final polish. Such is the case with the Second Pyramid, upon which blocks of granite are to be found which are still rough in face. It would seem that the patience required for the minute completion of such a terribly long and tedious piece of work was not forthcoming. But we ought in fact to be surprised, not so much at the unfinished state of a pyramid here and there, but rather that they should ever have been completed.

The variety which is so conspicuous in the architectural construction of the pyramids is also to be found in their epigraphy. The first explorers of the

Pyramids of Gizeh were surprised at the absence of all inscriptions beyond the masons' marks; the silence of those enormous structures seemed amazing; but soon Colonel Vyse discovered in the pyramid of Mycerinus the sarcophagus of that king, and the mummy case, now in the British Museum, which bears an inscription of some length. Recent discoveries, too, of which full details are yet wanting, prove that some of the pyramids contained long texts, which contain the names of kings and other information which is of great importance to the historian of the Egyptian religion. In 1879 and 1880, Mariette caused three pyramids at Sakkarah to be opened, which until then had remained unexplored. One of them was silent and empty, but in the others the inscriptions and sarcophagi of two kings of the sixth dynasty, Papi and his son Merenzi, were found. Fragments of a Ritual of the Dead were recognized among them. Pleasure at this discovery, the last which he was destined to make in the soil of Egypt, brightened the last days of Mariette.[225]

In March 1881, M. Maspero, the successor of M. Mariette as director of the excavations, opened a pyramid belonging to a different group, which turned out to be the tomb of Ounas, the last Pharaoh of the fifth dynasty. In this pyramid, portcullis stones similar to those which have already been figured were found. When these obstacles were passed "the continuation of the passage was found, the first part of polished granite, the second of the close-grained limestone of Tourah. The side walls are covered with fine hieroglyphs painted green, the roof sprinkled with stars of the same hue. The passage finally opens into a chamber half filled with débris, upon the walls of which the inscription is continued.... The mummy-chamber, like that which precedes it, is covered with hieroglyphs, with the exception of the wall opposite to the entrance. This wall is of the finest alabaster, and is effectively decorated with painted ornaments. The sarcophagus is of black basalt, without inscription.... The text of the inscription which covers the walls is almost identical with that in the tomb of Papi, but it has the advantage of being complete. M. Maspero, whom Mariette had previously entrusted with taking squeezes from the inscription in the tomb of Papi, recognised certain formulæ and phrases which had already struck him in another place.... These texts make up a composition analogous to one which covers the walls of certain little known Theban tombs. Without presenting any very considerable difficulties, they demand careful examination from those who would comprehend their meaning.

"M. Maspero, encouraged by this first success, ordered a second pyramid to be opened. He wished to verify, upon the spot, a theory which he had long upheld in spite of the adverse opinions of the majority of egyptologists. It is well known that between the sixth and the tenth dynasties a great gap exists, so far as monumental remains are concerned. M. Maspero has always believed that there is no such gap. He has observed that the pyramids are, so to speak, grouped chronologically from north to south; those of the fourth dynasty at Gizeh, those of the fifth at Abooseer, those of the twelfth in the Fayoum. The excavations of Mariette as well as his own showed the tombs of the fifth and sixth dynasties to have been at Sakkarah. Hence M. Maspero thinks that the pyramids erected by the sovereigns of the seventh, eighth, ninth, and tenth dynasties are those between Sakkarah and the Fayoum. The future will show whether he is right or wrong. In any case science will profit by the new excavations which he is about to undertake."
[226]

When cross-examined by such questioners as M. Maspero the pyramids will tell us much. Hitherto they have attracted but little of that examination which discovers the most curious secrets, but their size and the beauty of their masonry will ever make the three great pyramids of Gizeh the most striking objects to the traveller and to the historian of art.

Considering their age, these three pyramids are wonderfully well preserved. In their presence, even in their actual state of partial ruin, the oriental hyperbolism of Abd-ul-Latif, an Arab writer of the thirteenth century, seems no more than natural. "All things fear Time," he cries, "but Time fears the Pyramids!" And yet time has done its work during the last few hundreds of years. The summits of the great structures have been slightly lowered; the gaping breaches in their flanks have been gradually widened; and although in spite of their stripped flanks and open wounds they still rear their heads proudly into the Egyptian sky, all those accessory structures which surrounded them, and fulfilled their own well-defined offices in the general monumental *ensemble*, have either been destroyed by the violence of man or engulfed by the encroaching sand. Where, for example, are those wide and substantial causeways, whose large and carefully adjusted blocks excited the wonder of Herodotus.[227] After having afforded an unyielding roadway for the transport of so many heavy materials, they formed truly regal avenues by which the funeral processions of the Egyptians reached the centre of the necropolis as long as their civilization lasted. In the plain they were above the level of the highest inundations, and their gentle slope gave easy access to the western plateau. The great Sphinx, the image of Harmachis, or the Rising Sun, was placed at the threshold of the plateau. Immovable among the dead of the vast cemetery, he personified the idea of the resurrection, of that eternal life which, like the morning sun, is ever destined to triumph over darkness and death. His head alone now rises above the sand, but in the days of Herodotus his vast bulk, cut from a rock nearly 70 feet high, was well calculated to prepare the eye of the traveller for the still more colossal masses of the pyramids. His features have now been disfigured by all kinds of outrage, but in the thirteenth century, although even then he had been mutilated, Abd-ul-Latif was able to admire his serene smile, his head enframed in a richly carved wig which added to its size and dignity. His body was never more than roughly blocked out, but a painted decoration, of which traces may still be found, compensated in some degree for the deficiencies in the modelling.

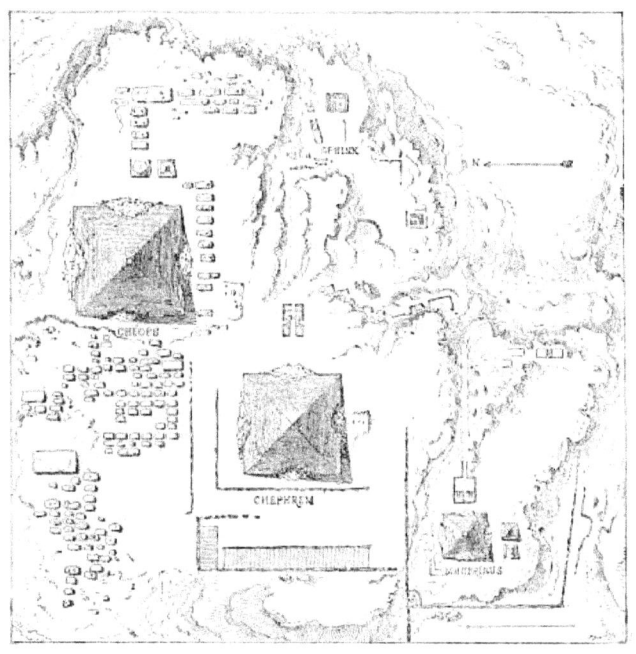

FIG. 156.—**Plan of the Pyramids of Gizeh and of that part of the necropolis which immediately surrounds them.**

The soil around each pyramid was carefully levelled and paved with dressed limestone slabs. Upon this pavement rested the foundations of the stylobate surrounding the pyramid. Both stylobate and pavement are now in almost every case concealed by sand and *débris*, but at the pyramid of Chephren, which is less banked up than the others, traces of them have been proved to exist. They added somewhat to the imposing effect of those monuments upon the eye, and gave additional definition to their bases.[228] The area thus paved was inclosed with a wall, which had an opening towards the east, in front of which the temple, or funerary chapel of the pyramid, was raised. The latter, no doubt, was magnificently decorated. At the foot of the mountains of stone under which reposed the ashes of the

Pharaohs themselves, smaller pyramids were raised for their wives and children. Of these some half dozen still exist upon the plateau of Gizeh. One of them has been recognized as the tomb of that daughter of Cheops, about whom Herodotus tells one of those absurd stories invented by the Egyptians of the decadence, with which his dragomans took such delight in imposing upon his simple faith.[229] Around the space which was thus consecrated to the adoration of the dead monarch, the long rows of mastabas stretched away for miles through the vast necropolis.

FIG. 157.—The Sphinx.

The great ones of Egypt, all those who had been near the Pharaoh and had received some of his reflected glory, grouped their tombs as closely as possible about his. Distributed thus by reigns, the private tombs were erected in close juxtaposition one with another, each being provided with a stele, or sepulchral tablet upon which the name of the deceased was inscribed, most of them being adorned with painted bas-reliefs, and a few with statues placed upon their façades. Upon the causeways which connected Memphis with the necropolis, upon the esplanades erected by the Pharaohs to the memory and for the adoration of their ancestors, in the countless streets, lanes, and blind alleys which gave access to the private tombs, advanced endless processions of mourners, driving before them the bleating and lowing victims for the funeral rites. Priests in white linen, friends and relations of the dead with their hands full of fruit and flowers, flitted hither and thither. On the days appointed for the commemoration of the dead, all this must have afforded a curiously animated scene. The city of the dead had its peculiar life, we might almost say its festivals, like that of the living. But amid the coming and going, amid all the bustle of the Egyptian *jour des morts*, it was the giant forms of the pyramids, with their polished slopes[230] and their long shadows turning with the sun, that gave the scene a peculiar solemnity and a character of its own. Morning and evening this shadow passed over hundreds of tombs, and thus, in a fashion, symbolized the royal dignity and the almost superhuman majesty of the kingly office.

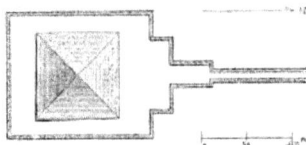

FIG. 158.—**Pyramid with its inclosure, Abousir; from Perring.**

Of all this harmonious conception but a few fragments remain. The necropolis is almost as empty and deserted as the desert which it adjoins. The silence is only broken by the cry of the jackal, by the footsteps of a few casual visitors hurrying along its deserted avenues, and by the harsh voices of the Bedouins who have taken possession of the Pyramid of Cheops, and, in their own fashion, do its honours to the curious visitor. But despoiled though they be of their ornaments and of their proper surroundings, the pyramids are yet among those monuments of the world which are sure to impress all who possess sensibility or powers of reflection. In a remarkable passage in the *Description générale de Memphis et des Pyramides*, Jomard has well defined the effect which they produce upon the traveller and the impressions which they leave behind: "The general effect produced by the pyramids is very curious. Their summits, when seen from a distance, look like those of high mountains standing out against the sky. As we approach them this effect diminishes; but when we arrive within a very short distance of their sides a totally different impression succeeds; we begin to be amazed, to be oppressed, almost to be stupefied by their size. When quite close to them their summits and angles can no longer be seen. The wonder which they cause is not like that caused by a great work of art. It is the sense of their simple grandeur of form and of the disproportion between the individual power and stature of man and these colossal creations of his hands. The eye can hardly embrace them, nor the imagination grasp their mass. We then begin to form some idea of the prodigious quantity of dressed stone which goes to make up their height. We see hundreds of stones each containing two hundred cubic feet and weighing some thirty tons, and thousands of others which are but little less. We touch them with our hands and endeavour to realize the power which must have been required to quarry, dress, carry, and fix such a number of colossal blocks, how many men must have been employed on the work, what machines they used, and how many years it must have taken; and the less we are able to understand all these things, the greater is our admiration for the patience and power which overcame such obstacles."[231]

§ 3. *The Tomb under the Middle Empire.*

We have shown how the mastaba, that is to say, the most ancient form of tomb in the necropolis of Memphis, was an expression, both in arrangement and in decoration, of the ideas of the Egyptians as to a future life. In literature and in art the works created by a people in its infancy, or at least in its youth, are the most interesting to the historian, because they are the results of the sincere and unfettered expansion of vital forces; this is especially the case when there is no possibility of a desire to imitate foreign models. The mastaba deserved therefore to be very carefully studied. No other race has given birth in its funerary architecture, to a type so pure, a type which may be explained in every detail by a master-idea at once original and well defined. We therefore dwelt upon it at some length and described it with the care which it demanded. We found it again in the pyramids, the royal tombs of the Ancient Empire, which though sensibly modified by the great change in proportion, by the colossal dimensions which the pride of the Pharaohs gave to one part of their tomb, are yet penetrated by the same spirit. We have yet to follow the development of the same idea through the later years of Egyptian civilization, and in localities more or less removed from that in which she gave her first tokens of power. In one place we shall find it modified by the nature of the soil to which the corpse had to be committed, in another by the inevitable progress of ideas, by the development of art, and by the caprices of fashion, which was no more stationary in Egypt than elsewhere.

The most important necropolis of the First Theban Empire was that of Abydos in Upper Egypt, upon the left bank of the river. The great number of sepultures which took place in it, from the first years of the monarchy until the end of the ancient civilization, is to be explained by the peculiarly sacred character of the city of Abydos, and by the great popularity, from one end of the Nile valley to the other, of the myths which centred in it. According to the Egyptian belief, the opening through which the setting sun sank into the bowels of the earth for its nightly transit, was situated to the west of Abydos. We know how the Egyptian intellect had established an analogy between the career of the sun and that of man; we may therefore conclude that in choosing a final resting-place as near as possible to the spot where the great luminary seemed to make its nightly plunge, they believed they were making more completely sure of triumphing, like him, over darkness and death.

The sun is not extinguished, he is but hidden for a moment from the eyes of man. This sun of the infernal regions is Osiris, who, of all the Egyptian gods, was most universally adored. Although many Egyptian towns could show tombs in which the members of Osiris, which had been dispersed by Set, were re-united by Isis and Nephthys, none of them were so famous, or the object of such deep devotion, as that at Abydos. It was, if we may be permitted to use such a phrase, the *Holy Sepulchre of Egypt*. As, in the early centuries of Christianity, the faithful laid great stress upon burial in the neighbourhood of some holy martyr, "The richest and most influential Egyptians," says a well informed Greek writer, "were ambitious of a common tomb with Osiris."[232]

Under such conditions it may readily be understood why Mariette should have concentrated so much of his attention upon Abydos. In spite of all his researches he did not succeed in discovering the tomb of Osiris itself, but yet his digging campaigns afforded results which are most interesting and important from every point of view.[233]

FIG. 159.—The river transport of the Mummy. (Champollion, pl. 173.)

One district of this necropolis is made up by a vast number of tombs dating from the time of the ancient empire, and particularly from the sixth dynasty. Arrangements similar to those of the mastabas at Sakkarah are found, but on a smaller scale—the same funerary chambers, the same wells, sometimes vertical, sometimes horizontal as in the tomb of Ti and the pyramids, the same materials. The situation of this tomb-district, which Mariette calls the central cemetery, has allowed arrangements to be adopted similar to those on the plateau of Memphis, where the sand is the only covering to a stratum of living rock in which it was easy to cut the well and the mummy-chamber.

In the remainder of the space occupied by the tombs the subsoil is of a very different nature. "The hard and impenetrable rock is there covered with a sandstone in course of formation; this is friable at some points, at others so soft that but few mummies have been entrusted to it."[234] This formation extends over nearly the whole of the ground upon which the tombs of the eleventh, twelfth, and especially of the thirteenth, dynasties, are packed closely together. This Mariette calls the northern cemetery. The tombs of Abydos have no subterranean story, properly speaking. Well, mummy-chamber, and funerary chapel are all constructed, not dug. In the few instances in which the ground has been excavated down to the friable sandstone which over-lies the hard rock, the opening has been lined with rubble.

Fig. 160.—Tomb at Abydos;
drawn in perspective from the elevation of Mariette.

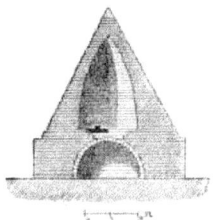

Fig. 161.—Section of the above tomb.

"Hence the peculiar aspect which the necropolis of Abydos must have presented when intact. Imagine a multitude of small pyramids five or six metres high, carelessly oriented or not at all, and uniformly built of crude brick. These pyramids always stand upon a plinth, they are hollow, and within they are formed into a clumsy cupola by means of roughly built off-sets. The pyramid stands directly over a chamber in its foundations which shelters the mummy. As soon as the latter was in place, the door of its chamber was closed by masonry."[235] An exterior chamber was often built in front of the pyramid, and being always left open, served for the performance of the sepulchral rites; but sometimes this chamber was absent and then those rites were carried through in the open air, before the stele of the deceased.

This latter was sometimes erected upon the plinth, sometimes let into its face. A little cube of masonry is sometimes found at the foot of the stele, destined, no doubt, for funeral offerings. Sometimes the tomb had a surrounding wall of the same height as its plinth; this served to mark out the ground which belonged to it, and when the friends of the deceased met to do him honour, the entrance could be closed, and comparative privacy assured even in the absence of a funerary chapel.

FIG. 162.—Tomb at Abydos;
drawn in perspective from the elevation of Mariette.

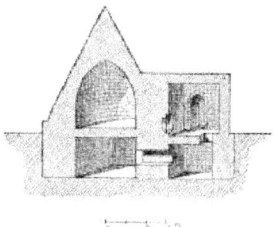

FIG. 163.—Section of the above tomb.

These tombs, which were generally constructed with no great care, were for the most part without casing. The pyramidal form was given by setting each course of bricks slightly back from the one below it. When this part of the work was finished, each face was covered, as a rule, with a coat of rough concrete, which, in its turn, was hidden under a layer of white stucco. This multitude of little monuments, all of the same shape and of much the same size, must, when complete, have looked like the tents of an encamped army.

FIG. 164.—Stele of the eleventh dynasty, Abydos.
Drawn by Bourgoin. (Boulak.)

As these tombs were all upon the surface of the ground they have suffered more than any others from the attacks of man. Those which are reproduced among these lines of text were only recovered by Mariette by dint of patient excavation. And although these ill constructed edifices, so far as their materials are concerned, are still standing, they will soon follow the many thousands which once stood in serried ranks round the sepulchre of Osiris. The only remains of this necropolis which are likely to be preserved are the numberless steles which Mariette rescued from its *débris*. They form about four-fifths of the total number of those monuments now preserved in the museum at Boulak.[236] We figure two of them, one belonging to the Middle, the other to the New Empire (Figs. 164 and 165).

FIG. 165.—Stele of Pinahsi, priest of Ma: Abydos. New Empire. Drawn by Bourgoin. (Boulak.)

Whenever religious motives did not affect their choice, the Egyptians preferred, during the period we are now considering, to cut their tombs horizontally out of some rocky eminence. Such a tomb was called a σπέος by the Greeks. The most interesting examples of these constructions are offered by the tombs of the twelfth dynasty at Beni-Hassan and at Siout, both situated between Memphis and Abydos.

Champollion was the first to appreciate the importance of the grottos of Beni-Hassan. Ever since his time they have received, for various reasons, much of the attention of egyptologists. We have already referred to their inscriptions, which are as interesting to the historian of ideas as to the student of political and social organizations. We have alluded above to the varied scenes which cover the walls of their chambers, the most important of which have been reproduced by Champollion, Lepsius, and Prisse d'Avennes; we have finally to speak of those famous protodoric columns, as they are called, in which some have thought they saw the original model of the oldest and most beautiful of the Grecian orders. We are at present concerned, however, with the arrangement of the tombs themselves. These are the same, with but slight variations, for the smallest and most simple tombs as for those which are largest and most elaborately decorated.

These façades are cut into the cliff-like sides of the hills of the Arab Chain, about half-way up their total height. They are, therefore, high above the surface of the river. When the cutting was made, two or three columns were left to form a portico, the deep shadows of which stand out strongly against the whiteness of the rock. This portico leads to a chamber which is lighted only from the door. Its ceiling is often cut into the form of a vault. A deep square niche is cut, sometimes opposite to the door, sometimes in one of the angles. It once contained the statue of the deceased. Most of the tombs have but one chamber, but a few have two or three. In a corner either of the only chamber or of that which is farthest from the door, the opening of a square well is found; this leads to the mummy-chamber, which is excavated at a lower level.

FIG. 166.—Façade of a tomb at Beni-Hassan.

The chamber upon which the portico opens is the funerary chapel, the place of reunion for the friends and relations of the dead. As Mariette very truly remarks, from the first step which the traveller makes in the tomb of Numhotep at Beni-Hassan, he perceives that, in spite of all differences of situation, the traditions of the Ancient Empire are still full of vitality. "The spirit which governed the decorators of the tomb of Ti at Sakkarah still inspired the painters who covered the walls of the tomb of Numhotep at Beni-Hassan. The defunct is at home among his own possessions; he fishes and hunts, his cattle defile before him, his people build boats, cut down trees, cultivate the vine and gather the grapes, till the earth, or give themselves up to gymnastics or to games of skill and chance, and among them the figure of the dead is carried hither and thither in a palanquin. We have already found pictures like these in the mastabas of the Ancient Empire, and here we find them again. But at Beni-Hassan this painted decoration becomes more personal to the occupant of the tomb, the inscriptions enter into precise and copious biographical details, which are never found elsewhere."[237]

FIG. 167.—Façade of a tomb at Beni-Hassan, showing some of the adjoining tombs.

The necropolis of Siout, in the Libyan chain, offers the same general characteristics. The tomb of Hapi-Tefa, a feudal prince of the twelfth dynasty, and consequently a contemporary of those princes of the nome of Meh who are buried at Beni-Hassan, is the most remarkable. It is composed of three large chambers communicating one with another, and with the external air by a wide portico. The mummy-pit is reached from the innermost of these chambers.

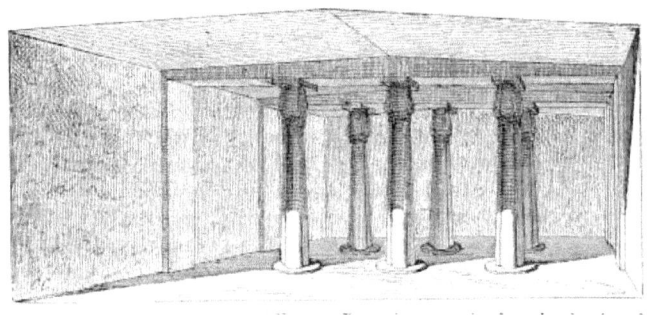

FIG. 168.—Interior of a tomb at Beni-Hassan.
Drawn in perspective from the elevation of Lepsius (i. pl. 60).

Neither statues, mummies, nor any other movable objects have been found in these grottos. When their accessible situation and their conspicuous appearance is remembered, this should not cause surprise. Many centuries ago the acacia doors, which are mentioned in one of the texts at Beni-Hassan, disappeared, and, in spite of the accumulation of sand, the mouths of the wells could be found so easily, and could so readily be cleared, that all objects of value and interest must have been abstracted from the mummy-chambers in very remote times, perhaps before the fall of the antique civilization. The inscriptions and the painted walls alone remained practically intact down to the commencement of the present century. The dryness of the climate, and the difficulty of detaching them from the wall contributed to their preservation, which was nowhere more complete than at Beni-Hassan. But since travelling in Egypt became the fashion their sufferings have begun. The mania for carving names upon every surface, and for preserving souvenirs of all places of interest, has destroyed the whole of one wall. The smoke of torches has also done its work in reducing the brilliant tones and blunting the delicate contours. Happily, the more interesting examples are all reproduced in those great works to which we have already had such frequent occasion to refer.

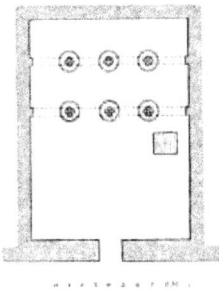

FIG. 169.—Plan of the above tomb.

The rich necropolis of Thebes has not preserved any monuments from this period in such good condition as those of Abydos, Beni-Hassan, or Siout. M. Maspero has discovered, however, in the district known as the *Drah-Aboul-Neggah*, some remains of the royal tombs of the eleventh dynasty. Several of these tombs resemble in their general arrangements those of the feudal princes of Meh and Siout. Thus the sepulchre of the King *Ra-Anoub-Khoper-Entef* is what the Greeks called a *hemi-speos*, that is, it was partly built and partly hollowed out of the living rock. Before the façade thus built against the mountain, two obelisks were reared. The tombs of the other princes belonging to the family of Entef were built upon the open plain. They were structures in masonry, and seem at one time to have been crowned by pyramids. Some idea of their shape may be obtained from our illustrations of the tombs at Abydos.[238]

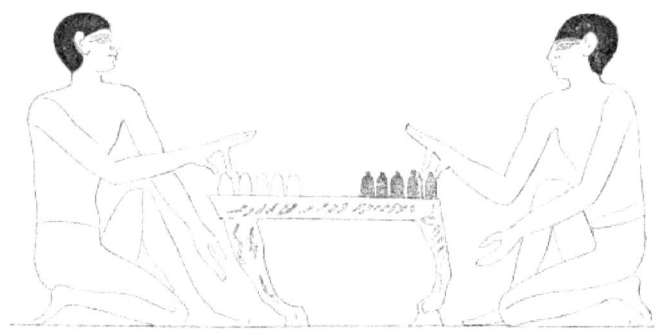

FIG. 170.—Chess players, Beni-Hassan. (Champollion, pl. 369.)

To complete our observations upon the tombs of the first Theban Empire, it will be sufficient to recall what we have already said about the pyramids in the Fayoum, which were the work of the thirteenth dynasty. It is difficult to form an accurate idea of the appearance of those monuments when complete. Time has treated them with great severity, and in their present state it is impossible to verify the assertions of Herodotus as to the peculiarities of their casing and crowning ornaments. But it is quite certain that the Middle Empire made no original inventions in the matter of sepulchral architecture. It appears to have discontinued some of the ancient arrangements, but in those which it preserved its efforts were confined to putting old elements together in a new fashion and with new proportions. It made frequent use of one mode of sepulture which had previously been quite exceptional. No mastaba is known which dates from this epoch, but the kings had not ceased to confide their mummies and the perpetuation of their glory to pyramids, but these were no longer of such colossal dimensions as under the Ancient Empire, while their character was complicated, to some extent, by the colossi with which they are said to have been surmounted, and the figured decoration of their walls. Finally, they were often employed, not as self-contained monuments in themselves, but merely as the culminating points in a more complex *ensemble*. They were built upon a rectangular platform or tower with walls slightly inclined from the perpendicular.

It would seem that the idea of this arrangement had occurred to the primitive Egyptians. So, too, had that of the *speos* or rock-cut tomb; but the Memphite architects have left nothing which at all resembles the grottos in the mountain sides of Beni-Hassan and Siout. Neither in the neighbourhood of the pyramids nor in any other district where the tombs of the early epoch are found, has any sepulchre been discovered which shows the monumental façades, the large internal development, and the simple and dignified lines of the artificial chambers in the Arab and Libyan chains.

§ 4. *The Tomb under the New Empire.*

The subterranean tombs for which the first Theban Empire had shown so marked a preference, became firmly seated in public favour during the succeeding centuries. We do not know what the funeral customs may have been during those centuries when the Hyksos, or shepherd kings, were masters of Egypt; but, after their expulsion, the great Theban dynasties, the eighteenth, the nineteenth, and the twentieth, by whom the glory of Egyptian arms and culture was spread so widely, hardly made use of any sepulchre but the chamber hollowed laboriously in the rocky sides of that part of the Libyan chain which lies to the west of Thebes. Every traveller visits the royal tombs which lie in the gloomy ravine called the *Bab-el-Molouk*, or the Gate of the Kings. The valley is about three miles in length and has a mean width of about eleven hundred yards; its sides are riddled with galleries penetrating more or less deeply into the mountains, and starting sometimes from the slopes, sometimes from the base of the cliffs, which here and there attain a height of 400 feet. The word speos seeming to the Greeks to give an inadequate idea of the depth of these excavations and of their narrow proportions, they called them συρίγγες or pipes; and modern archæologists have often employed the same picturesque term in speaking of the Theban tombs. Five-and-twenty of these tombs are royal; the rest belong to wealthy subjects, priests, warriors, and high officers of state. In extent and richness of ornament some of the latter are in no way inferior to the tombs of the sovereigns.

Our studies must first, however, be directed to the royal tombs, because in them we find the most original types, the most important variations upon those which have gone before. In them the art of the New Empire gives a clearer indication of all the changes which the progress of ideas had brought about in the Egyptian conception of a future life. In them, too, the Egyptian taste for ample dimensions and luxuriant decoration is more freely indulged. The architects of Seti and Rameses had resources at command far beyond those of which their early rivals could dispose. They were, therefore, enabled to indulge their employers' tastes for magnificence, and to give to certain parts of the tomb a splendour which had been previously unknown. And such parts were never those upon which the pyramid builders had lavished most of their attention.

Nothing could be more simple than the course of proceeding of the earlier architects, whose services and high social position are indicated for us by more than one stele from the Ancient Empire. They had to distinguish the royal from the private tomb, and no means to such an end could be more obvious than to make use of a form of construction which allowed the height and extent to be added to *ad infinitum* without compromising the stability of the monument. Their one idea, therefore, was to push the apex of the pyramid as far up into the sky as they could. The height grew as the flanks swelled, so that it became, by one process of accretion, ever more imposing and better fitted to safeguard the precious deposit hidden within it. In such a system the important point was this envelope of the mummy-chamber, an envelope composed of thousands of the most carefully dressed and fixed blocks of stone, which, in their turn, were covered with a cuirass of still harder and more durable materials. In order that all access to the sarcophagus might be more safely guarded against, the funerary chapel was separated from the mountain of hewn stone which inclosed the mummy-chamber. Supposing the latter to be decorated with all the taste and richness which we find in the tomb of Ti, it would still be comparatively small and unimportant beside the colossal mass which overshadowed it, and to which it belonged. The disproportion is easily explained. When the pyramids were built, the workman, the actual mason, had little more to learn. He was a thorough master of the dressing and fixing of stone and other materials; but, on the other hand, the art of architecture was yet in its infancy. It had no suspicion of those rich and varied effects which the later Egyptians were to obtain by the majesty of their orders and the variety of their capitals. It was not till much later that it learnt to raise the pylon before the sacred inclosures, to throw solemn colonnades about their courts, and to greet the visitor to the temples with long naves clothed in all the glory of colour.

Two periods of national renascence, in the thirteenth and eighteenth dynasties, had to intervene before these marvels could be realized. The earlier of these two periods is only known to us by a few works of sculpture in our museums. We are forced to guess at its architecture, as we have nothing but descriptions, which are at once incomplete and exaggerated, to guide our imaginations.

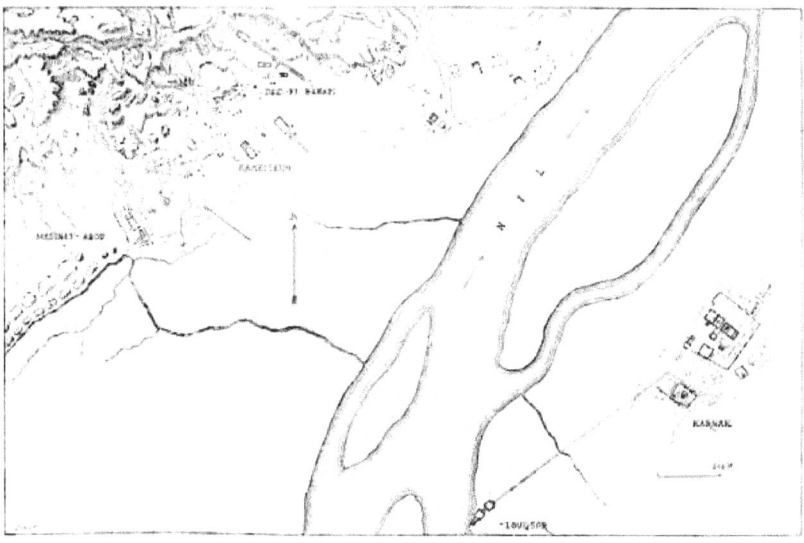

FIG. 171.—General plan of Thebes.

The second Theban Empire may be studied under very different conditions. The architects of that epoch excelled all their predecessors in the skill with which they used their materials, and the artistic ability with which they laid their plans. In a word, they realized the ideal towards which Egyptian builders had been tending for many centuries, and their genius is still to be seen in buildings which, even in their ruin, charm by the grandeur of their conception and the finish of their execution.

In the century which saw the construction of the great temples of Abydos, of Karnak, and of Luxor, the architect who was charged with the building of the royal tombs could dispose of all the resources of an empire which stretched from the southern boundaries of Ethiopia to Damascus and Nineveh. He would have fulfilled the wishes of neither prince nor people had he not found means to give an amplitude and a beauty to those tombs which should stand a comparison with the sumptuous edifices which the same kings had erected, in another part of the city, in honour of the great deities of the country.

The simple and massive forms of the pyramid did not lend themselves to success in such an enterprise. They afforded no opportunity for the happy combinations of horizontal and vertical lines, for the contrasts of light and shadow and splendour of decoration which distinguished the epoch. The experience of the Middle Empire proved that it was better to make a fresh departure than to attempt to foist upon the pyramid a class of ornament which was destructive to the simplicity in which so much of its grandeur consisted. The highest expression of the new form of art was in the temple, the development of which was rather in a horizontal than in a vertical direction; in the long avenues of sphinxes, in the pylons and colossal statues of the kings, in porticoes and forests of columns. The problem, therefore, was to embody some of these elements in the design of the tomb. For this purpose it was necessary to give increased dimensions and greater importance to a part of the royal sepulchre which had been hitherto comparatively neglected. The funerary chapel had to be expanded into a temple in miniature, into a temple where the king, who had rejoined the deities from whom he was descended, could receive the homage and worship of his people.

The exploits of these princes, which were greater than anything of which Egypt had to boast in the whole of its glorious past, must have helped to suggest the temple form of their tombs. To this form the general movement of the national art also pointed, and to give it effect nothing more was required than the separation of the chapel from the tomb proper, to which previous tradition had so closely allied it. The situation of the sepulchre, after Thebes had become a populous city and the real capital of Egypt, was no longer a matter of question. It was in the rocky flanks of the Libyan chain that all its inhabitants sought that asylum for their dead which the inhabitants of

Memphis found upon the eastern edge of the desert. The Libyan chain to the west of Thebes offers no platform like that of the necropolis of Memphis. Its cliffs and intersecting ravines offer no sites for constructed works; hence the ordinary form of Theban tomb is the *speos*, or the *pipe*, which is but an exaggerated form of the *speos*.

Like the chief men among his subjects, the sovereign loved to take his last repose in the immediate neighbourhood of the city in which he had dwelt during his life, in which the streets had so often resounded to the cries of triumph which greeted his return from some successful campaign, or had seen him pass in some of those long processions which are figured upon the walls of Medinet-Abou (Fig. 172).[239] His tomb was a cavern like that of his subjects. Fashion and the physical conditions of the country governed him as well as his inferiors in rank. From the reign of Seti I. onwards, the kings chose for their place of sepulture the wild and deserted valley in which Belzoni found the tomb of that conqueror. In the time of the Ptolemies it contained the bones of no less than forty Egyptian monarchs. It would be difficult to imagine any site better calculated for the isolation and concealment of the mummy than this valley, where the rocks split and crumble under the sun, and the sand blown hither and thither by the winds from the desert fills up every crevice in the cliffs.

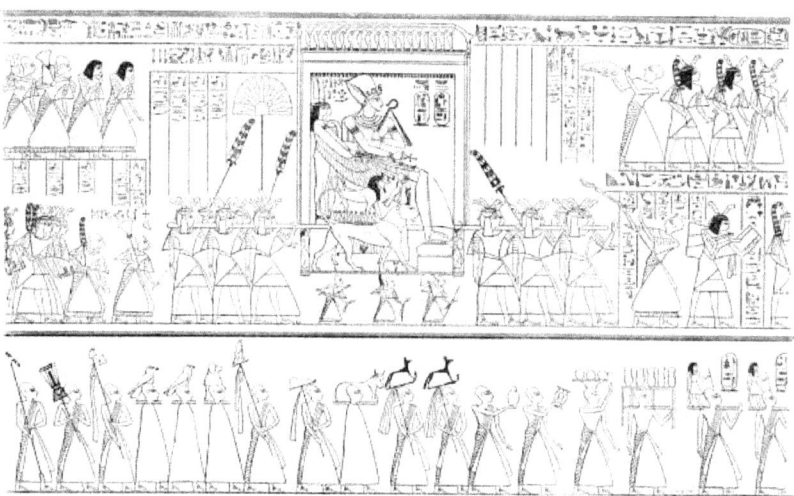

FIG. 172.—Rameses III. conducting a religious procession, at Medinet-Abou. (Wilkinson, iii., pl. 50.)

Nothing could be easier than to mask the entrance in such a place, but, on the other hand, no constructed building of any importance was possible except at a great expenditure of time and labour.[240]

But the plain at the foot of the range offered all that the architect could wish. It was still within the district consecrated to the dead, and yet its level surface presented no obstacles to an unlimited extension of any buildings which might be placed upon it.

We have here then the facts which determined the course of the Egyptian architects.

In the space inclosed between the left bank of the river and the first slopes of the Libyan chain, certain edifices were raised which are still, in great part, extant. Their funerary signification was never completely understood, in spite of the confused hints to that effect given by the Greek writers, until within the last few years. To Mariette belongs the credit of having at last removed all doubt on the subject. It is probable enough that the number of these buildings was formerly much greater than it is at present, but those which have come down to us are still in sufficiently good preservation to enable us to discern and define their true character, a character which was doubtless common to all the temples on the left bank of the Nile.

They were certainly temples. Their general arrangements do not differ from those of other religious edifices, both in Thebes itself, and elsewhere in Egypt. There is, however, a difference which was not perceived until the texts which contained the history of each temple and of the prince who claimed the credit of its erection were deciphered. The famous buildings at Luxor and Karnak may be taken as typical examples of the temple, properly speaking, in its richest and most complete development. The translation of the inscriptions and royal ovals which cover their walls has sufficed to show that they were national monuments, public sanctuaries consecrated by the king, as the representative of the people, to the worship of those great deities who were at once the principles of life and the faithful protectors of the Egyptian race. Century after century they never ceased to found such temples, to increase and to embellish them. From the princes of the twelfth dynasty down to the Ptolemies, and even to the Roman emperors, every successive family which occupied the throne held it a point of honour to add to the creations of its predecessors. One prince built a hypostyle hall, or a court surrounded by a colonnade; another added to the long rows of human or ram-headed sphinxes which lined the approaches; a third added a pylon, and a fourth a laboriously chiselled obelisk. Some kings, who reigned in periods of recuperation after civil war or barbaric invasion, set themselves to repair the damage caused by time and the violence of man. They strengthened foundations, they lifted fallen columns, they restored the faded colours of the painted decorations. The foreign conquerors themselves, whether Ethiopians, Persians, or Greeks, as soon as they believed themselves to have a firm hold upon the country, set themselves with zeal to obliterate the traces of their own violence. Each of these sovereigns, whether his contribution to any work had been great or small, took care to inscribe his own name upon it, and thus to call upon both posterity and his own contemporaries to bear witness to his piety.

The temple as we see it at Karnak and Luxor is the collective and successive work of many generations. Such, too, was the character of the great buildings at Memphis which were consecrated to Ptah and Neith.

But on the left bank of the Nile, and in the neighbourhood of the Theban necropolis, we find a group of temples whose physiognomy is peculiar to themselves. Nothing exactly like them is to be found elsewhere;[241] and they all belong to one period, that of the three great Theban dynasties, the eighteenth, nineteenth, and twentieth.[242] "These temples are monuments raised by the kings themselves to their own glory. They are not, like the temples at Karnak and Luxor, the accumulated results of several generations. Each temple was begun and finished by the king who planned it, so far at least as construction was concerned. In those cases where the decoration was left incomplete at the death of the royal builder, his successor finished it in his name. In these decorations the founder of the temple was represented either worshipping the gods, or in the eventful moments of his military career, or in his great hunts; and thus, while yet alive, he laid the foundations of an edifice destined to carry the memory of his glory and piety down to the latest posterity."[243]

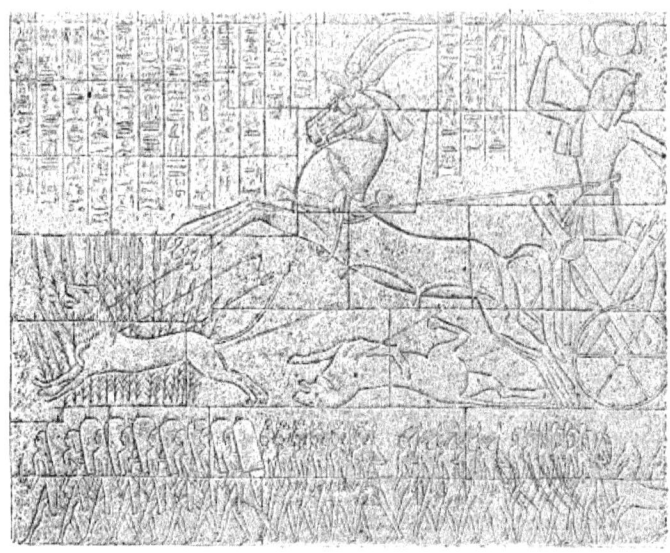

FIG. 173.—Rameses III. hunting; from Medinet-Abou.

Surrounded on all sides by tombs and packed into a comparatively narrow space, these temples are separated from the Bab-el-Molouk only by the slopes of the surrounding El-Assassif. The oldest of them is that at Dayr-el-Bahari. It was built by the regent Hatasu, of whose career we know enough to strongly excite, but too little to satisfy, our curiosity. We know that Hatasu, the wife and sister of Thothmes II., governed Egypt with skill and energy for seventeen years, in trust for her brother, Thothmes III. Where does her mummy repose? Is it in that ravine on the south-west of the Bab-el-Molouk which is called the *Valley of the Queens*, because the tombs of many Theban princesses have been found in it? Or is it in the slopes of the mountain behind the temple itself? Numerous sepulchral excavations have been found there, and many mummies have been drawn from their recesses. The artists to whom the decoration of the temple was committed, were charged to represent the chief actions of Hatasu as regent, and, although their works do not give us a detailed history of her eminently successful administration, they deal at length with the enterprise of which the regent herself seems to have been most proud, namely, the maritime expedition against *Punt*, a distant region which must have been either southern Arabia, the country of the Somalis, or the eastern coast of Africa.

Next in point of age to the building of Queen Hatasu is that which is called the *Ramesseum*; this is no other, as the members of the *Institut d'Égypte* have clearly proved, than the so-called *Tomb of Osymandias* which is described at such length by Diodorus.[244] Erroneous though it be, this latter designation is by no means without interest, as it proves that, at the time of Diodorus, persistent tradition ascribed a funerary origin to the edifice. The whole temple, inside and out, recalled Rameses II.; the great conqueror seemed to live and breathe on every stone; here majestic and calm, like force in repose, there menacing and terrible, with his threatening hand raised over the heads of his conquered enemies. His seated statue, fifty-six feet in height, was raised in the courtyard; to-day it lies broken upon the ground. Battle scenes are to be distinguished upon the remains of the walls. An episode of the war against the Khetas may be recognized, which seems to have made a great impression upon the king and his comrades in arms. It deals with that battle fought upon the bank of the Orontes, in which Rameses, when surrounded by the enemy, won safety for himself by his own personal valour and presence of mind. His prowess was celebrated by Pentaour, a contemporary poet, in an epic canto which has survived to our day. Rameses is there made to ascribe his safety and all the honour of his victory to his father Amen, who heard his appeal for help and, precipitating himself into the *mêlée*, snatched him from the very hands of his enemies.

Medinet-Abou, which might be called *The Second Ramesseum*, is to Rameses III. what the pretended tomb of Osymandias is to Rameses II. His presence pervades both the temple itself and its adjoining pavilion. Its bas-reliefs represent one of the greatest events in Egyptian, we might almost say, in ancient, history, namely, the victory won by Rameses over a confederation of the nations of the north and west, of those who were called the maritime races. This victory was mainly instrumental in driving westwards certain peoples who were destined, in more recent times, to play a great part in the politics of the Mediterranean.

Each of the buildings which we have just noticed had but a single proprietor. They were each dedicated to the memory of some one individual; but there was nothing to prevent the association in a single temple of two sovereigns who might happen to be united by strong ties of blood, and this course was taken in the temple of Gournah, situated in the same district of Thebes. It was commenced by Rameses I., the founder of the nineteenth dynasty, continued by his son, Seti I., and finished by his grandson, Rameses II. The first Rameses and Seti figure in it with the attributes of Osiris. The inscriptions enumerate the sources of revenue set aside by the king, in each nome, for the service of the annual sacrificial celebrations; and thus the building reveals itself as a temple to the perpetual honour of the two first princes of a race which did so much to add to the greatness and prosperity of Egypt.

The famous colossi of Amenophis III., known to the ancients as the *Statues of Memnon*, no doubt formed part of a similar building (fig. 18 and pl. vi). The temple built by this prince near the site of the Ramesseum has almost entirely disappeared, but the slight traces which still exist cover a vast space, and suggest that the building must have been one of rare magnificence.[245]

Only one of those Theban temples which rise upon the left bank of the river is free from all trace of a funerary or commemorative purpose, namely, the temple at Medinet-Abou which bears the ovals of Thothmes II. and Thothmes III. It shows signs, moreover, of having been frequently enlarged and added to, some of the additions having been made as recently as in the time of the Roman Emperors. In this respect it resembles, in spite of its comparatively small size, the great temples upon the right bank of the river. Like them, its creation was a gradual and impersonal matter. Every century added its stone, and each successive king engraved his name upon its walls. How to account for its exceptional situation we do not know. It is possible that those funerary temples of which we have spoken were an original invention of the successors of Thothmes; perhaps that constructed by Hatasu at Dayr-el-Bahari was the first of the series.

However this may have been, the new type became a success as soon as it was invented; all the other temples in the district may be more or less immediately referred to it. The great deities of Egypt, and more particularly those of Thebes, are never forgotten in them. They contain numerous representations of the princes in whose honour they were erected performing acts of worship before Amen-Ra, the Theban god *par excellence*, who is often accompanied by Mout and Khons, the other two members of the Theban triad. These temples were therefore consecrated, like almost all the other sacred buildings of Thebes, to those local deities which, after the establishment of that city as the capital of the whole country, became the supreme national gods. Those gods were as much at home in the temples of which we are speaking as in their own peculiar sanctuaries on the right bank of the river. In both places they received the same homage and sacrifices, but in the funerary temples of the left bank they found themselves associated, *paredral* as the Greeks would say, with the princes to whose memory the temples were raised. These princes were represented with the attributes of Osiris, both in the statues which were placed against the piers in the courtyard and in the bas-reliefs upon the long flat surfaces of the walls. By these attributes they became more closely allied with the great deity who was the common protector of the dead and the guarantor of their future resurrection. In this capacity the deceased prince was worshipped as a god by his own family. Thus, in the temple of Gournah, we find Rameses I. seated in a *naos* and receiving the homage of his grandson, Rameses II.; and, again, the latter worshipping Amen-Ra, Khons, and Rameses I. at one and the same time. This presentation of offerings to the deified king, as represented in the chambers of these temples, recalls the scene which is carved upon almost all the steles, and with greater variety and more detail, in the bas-reliefs on the internal walls of the mastabas.

The analogy which we are endeavouring to establish between the western temples at Thebes and the funerary chambers of the private tombs, is completed by the biographical nature of the pictures which form almost the sole decoration of those temples. The images presented to our gaze by the chamber walls of the mastaba are not, indeed, so personal and anecdotical as those of the temples, but they contain an epitomized representation of the every-day life, of the pleasures and the more serious occupations of a rich Egyptian. It is easy to understand how, with the progress of civilization, the more historic incidents in the life of an individual, and especially when that individual was a king, came to be figured in preference to those which were more general in their application. To embellish the tomb of a conqueror with pictures of his battles and victories was to surround him after death with the images, at least, of those things which made his happiness or his honour while alive. Pictures of some famous feat of arms would give joy to the *double* of him who had performed them, and would help to relieve the *ennui* of the monotonous life after death. Hence the tendency which is so marked in the bas-reliefs of the first Theban Empire, especially in those at Beni-Hassan. The constant and universal themes which sufficed for the early centuries of the Egyptian monarchy were not abandoned; scenes similar to those of the mastabas, are, indeed, frequently met with in the Theban tombs; but it is evident that in many cases scenes were sought out for reproduction which would have a more particular application; there is an evident desire to hand down to future generations concrete presentments of any political or other events which might appear worthy of remembrance. History and biography thus came in time to play an important part in sepulchral decoration, especially when kings or other royal personages were concerned.

Similar pictures are to be met with here and there in temples proper, as may be seen by a glance at the bas-relief figured upon the opposite page (Fig. 174), but in such cases they are invariably on the outer walls. At Luxor, for instance, the campaigns of Rameses II. against the peoples of Syria are thus displayed; and at Karnak it is upon the external walls of the hypostyle hall that the victories of Seti I. and Rameses II. are sculptured. In the interiors of all these courts and halls we hardly find any subjects treated but those which are purely religious; such as female deities assisting at the birth of a king, or taking him upon their knees and nourishing him from their breasts, a theme which is also found in royal tombs (Fig. 175); or one god presenting the king to another (Fig. 33); or the king paying homage to sometimes one, sometimes another, of his divine protectors (Figs. 14 and 176). We find such religious motives as these continually repeated, upon wall and column alike, from the first Theban kings to the epoch of the Ptolemies. On the right bank of the river pictures of a mystically religious character are universal; on the left bank those with an historical aim are more frequent.

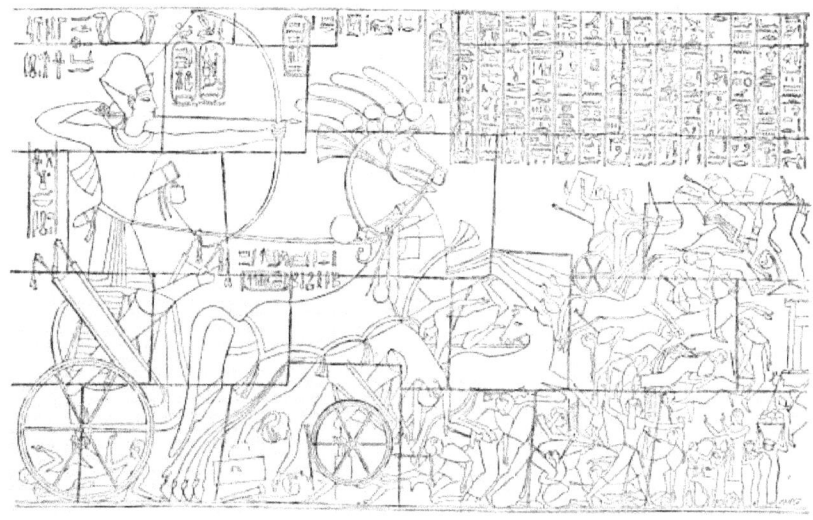

FIG. 174.—Rameses II. in battle; Luxor. (Champollion, pl. 331.)

It will be seen that the difference between the two kinds of temple, between that of the necropolis and that of the city, is not so striking and conspicuous as to be readily perceived by the first comer who crosses from the one bank of the river to the other; but the variations are quite sufficiently marked to justify the distinction propounded by Mariette. According to him the temples in the necropolis are funerary chapels which owe their increased size and the richness of their decoration to the general magnificence and highly developed taste of the century in which they were built. But it is enough for our present purpose to have indicated the places which they occupied in the vast architectural compositions which formed the tombs of a Seti or a Rameses. They had each a double function to fulfil. They were foundations made to the perpetual honour of a deceased king, chapels in which his fête-day could be kept and the memory of his achievements renewed; but they were at the same time temples in which the national gods were worshipped by himself and his descendants, in which those gods were perpetually adored for the services which they had done him while alive and for those which they might still do him when dead. In their latter capacity these buildings have a right to be considered temples, and we shall defer the consideration of their architectural arrangements, which differ only in details from those of the purely religious buildings, until we come to speak of the religious architecture of Egypt.

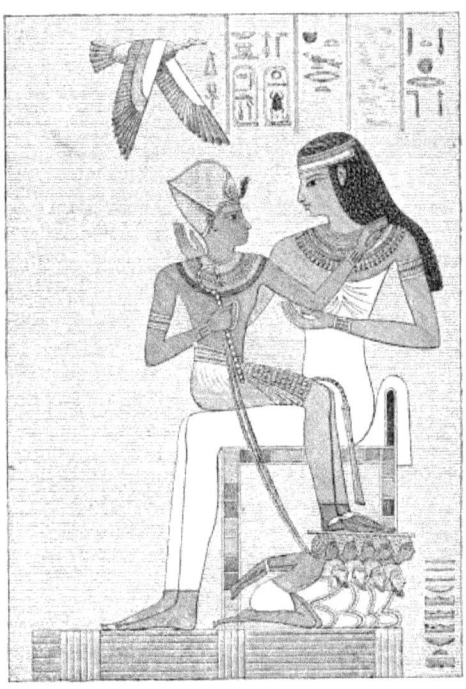

FIG. 175.—**Painting in a royal tomb at Gournah. Amenophis II. upon the lap of a goddess. (Champollion, pl. 160.)**

We shall here content ourselves with remarking that the separation of the tomb and the funerary chapel by some mile or mile and a half was a novelty in Egypt. The different parts of the royal tomb were closely connected under the Memphite Empire, and the change in arrangement must have been a consequence of some modification in the Egyptian notions as to a second life.

FIG. 176.—Amenophis III.
presenting an offering to Amen.
Decoration of a pier at Thebes;
from Prisse.

In the mastaba the *double* had everything within reach of his hand. Without trouble to himself he could make use of all of the matters which had been provided for the support of his precarious existence: the corpse in the mummy pit, the statues in the *serdab*, the portraits in bas-relief upon the walls of the public chamber. Through the chinks between the pieces of stone by which the well was filled up, and through the conduits contrived in the thickness of the walls, the magic formulæ of the funerary prayers, the grateful scent of the incense, and of the burnt fat of the victims (Fig. 177), reached his attentive senses. Brought thus into juxtaposition one with another, the elements of the tomb were mutually helpful. They lent themselves to that intermittent act of condensation, so to speak, which from time to time gave renewed substance and consistency to the phantom upon which the future life of the deceased depended. This concentration of all the acts and objects, which had for their aim the preservation of the deceased for a second term of life, was obviously destroyed as soon as the division of the tomb into two parts took place. The mummy, hidden away in the depths of those horizontal wells in the flank of the Western Range of which we have spoken, would seem to be in danger of losing the benefit of the services held in its honour upon the Theban plain. At such a distance it would neither hear the prayers nor catch the scent of the offerings. And the *double*? Is it to be supposed that he oscillated between the colossi in the temple where the funerary sites were celebrated, and the chamber in which the corpse reposed?

FIG. 177.—**Flaying the funerary victim. From a tomb of the 5th dynasty at Sakkarah. (Boulak.)**

Before they could have accepted this division of the tomb into two parts the Egyptians must have arrived at some less childish conception of the future life than that of their early civilization. That primitive conception was not entirely banished from their minds; evidence of its persistency is, indeed plentiful, but a more intelligent and less material notion gradually superimposed itself upon the ancient belief. The indescribable being which was the representative of the deceased after death became gradually less material and more spiritual; in time it escaped from its enforced sojourn in the tomb and approached more nearly to that which we call the soul. This soul, like the nocturnal sun, passed a period of probation and purgation in the under world, and, thanks to the protection of Osiris and the other deities of the shades, was at last enabled to return to earth and rejoin the body which it had formerly inhabited. The problem of death and a future life was resolved in much the same way by the Greeks and by all other races who drew much of their inspiration from the Egyptians. They all looked upon the corpse as still alive when they expressed their hopes that the earth upon which they poured out wine and milk would like lie lightly upon it. After a time they added Tartarus and the Elysian Fields to their beliefs, they introduced the heroic fathers of their race into the councils of the gods, and they described and figured the joys which awaited the just upon the Happy Islands.

These various hypotheses are contradictory enough from a logical point of view; they exclude and destroy one another. But when it is a question of notions which are essentially incapable of being strictly defined, the human intelligence is singularly content to rest in vague generalities. Contradictions do not embarrass it; its adaptability is practically infinite.

The beliefs which we have just described tended for many centuries to become more and more general. They were taught in that *Ritual of the Dead* which, although certain of its parts date from the most ancient times, did not take its complete and definite form until the Theban epoch. Being more spiritual and less material, they were less opposed to the subdivision of the sepulchre than the more primitive idea; and this subdivision was necessary if the public and commemorative part of the tomb were to receive a splendour and amplitude befitting the exploits of a Thothmes, a Seti, or a Rameses. Dayr-el-Bahari proves that the change had already been made under the eighteenth dynasty, but it was not until the nineteenth that it became definitely adopted. The progress of ideas and of art had then advanced so far, that more ambitious desires could be satisfied, and the country filled with magnificent edifices, which, like the temples of the two Rameses, were original in so far as they belonged at one and the same time to religious and funerary architecture. We should call them cenotaphs, were it not that the Egyptians, like all the other races of antiquity, believed in the real presence of their dead in the buildings erected in their honour.

FIG. 178.—Entrance to a royal tomb. (*Description de l'Égypte*, ii., pl. 79.)

The other division of the tomb is that which contains the well and the mummy-chamber, the eternal dwelling-place of the illustrious dead. The second half of the royal sepulchre had to be as sumptuous and luxurious in its way as the first, but the problem placed before the architect was diametrically opposed to that which he had to solve in the other part of his task. In constructing and decorating the funerary temple upon the plain, he was working before the eyes of the public, for their benefit and for that of the remotest posterity.

But the task of hewing out the tomb was a very different one. For long years together he pursued his enterprise in the mystery and shadow of a subterranean workshop, to which all access was no doubt forbidden to the curious. He and his assistants cut and carved the living rock by the light of torches, and his best ingenuity was taxed to devise means for preserving from the sight of all future generations those works of the best artists of Egypt with which the walls were to be covered. Those prodigies of patience and skill were executed for the benefit of the deceased alone. Important though it was that the sepulchre of a great man should be ornamented to the greatest extent possible, it was of still greater moment that his last resting-place should not be troubled by the visits of the living; and the more completely the mummy was concealed, the greater were the deserts of the faithful servant upon whom the task had been placed.

In order that this blessing of undisturbed peace in his eternal dwelling should be secured, the royal tomb seems to have been constructed without any such external show as would call attention to its situation. The tombs of private individuals usually had a walled courtyard in front of them to which access was obtained by a kind of porch, or tower, with inclined sides and crowned by a small pyramid. But the explorers, Belzoni, Bruce and others, who disengaged the entrances to the royal tombs, found them without propylæa of any kind.[246] The doorway, cut vertically in the rock, is of the utmost simplicity, and we have every reason to suppose that, after the introduction of the mummy, it was carefully masked with sand and rocky *débris*.[247]

The existence of the temples in the plain made it unnecessary that the tombs themselves should be entered after that final operation had been performed. Some words of Diodorus are significant in this direction. "The priests say that their registers attest the existence of forty-seven royal tombs, but that at the time of Ptolemy the son of Lagus, only seventeen remained."[248] This assertion cannot be accepted literally, because twenty-one tombs have already been discovered in the Bab-el-Molouk, some of them in a state of semi-completion, besides four in the ravine which is called the *Valley of the West*, which makes twenty-five in all. What the priests meant when they spoke to Diodorus was no doubt, that at the time of the Ptolemies, no more than seventeen of their entrances had been discovered. If through the plans made for their construction and preserved in the national archives there were some who knew their situation, they preserved the secret. We know, by the inscriptions upon their walls, that fifteen of the tombs which are now accessible, were open in the time of the Ptolemies; several of them seem to have been shown, to the Roman and other travellers who visited Egypt, as national objects of interest.[249]

The precautions taken to hide and obstruct the openings of the royal tombs were thus successful in many cases. Some of these have only been discovered in our own times, through the ardour and patience which characterize modern research, and we have still good reason to suppose that there are others which yet remain to be found. In 1872 Professor Ebers discovered a beautiful private tomb, that of Anemenheb, which, although situated close to one of the most frequented paths in the necropolis, had been previously unknown. It was open, but the opening had been carefully concealed with rough pieces of rock and general rubbish by the fellahs, who used the tomb as a hiding-place from the recruiting officers of the viceroy. They would remain concealed in it for weeks at a time until the officers had left their village. The royal cemetery of the Ramessides has possibly much more to tell us before its secrets are exhausted.

The entrance to the tomb always ran a certain chance of being discovered and freed from its obstacles. It was difficult, of course, to prevent the survival of some tradition as to the whereabouts of the burial-places of those great sovereigns whose memory was a consolation to Egyptian pride in the days of national abasement and decay. Provision had to be made, as in the case of the pyramids, against a forced entry into the gallery either by an enemy or by some robber in search of treasure, and we find that the precautions adopted were similar to those which we have described in noticing the royal tombs at Memphis. Let us take as an example the finest and most complete of all the tombs of the Ramessides, that of Seti I. After descending two flights of steps, and traversing two long and richly decorated corridors, Belzoni arrived, without discovering either sarcophagus or anything that looked like the site of a sarcophagus, at an oblong chamber 13 feet 6 inches by 12 feet. A wide and deep well, which here barred the passage, seemed to indicate that the extremity of the excavation had been reached. Belzoni caused himself to be lowered into the well. The walls were everywhere hard and firm, and without resonance, and there was no sign of a passage, either open or concealed, by which access to a lateral chamber, or to a second series of galleries might be obtained. But Belzoni was too old an explorer to be deceived by such appearances. On his first arrival at the edge of the well he had perceived in the wall on the farther side of it a small opening, about two feet wide, and two feet and a half high. This had been made, at some unknown period, in a wall covered with stucco and painted decorations. Across the well a beam was still lying, which had served the purpose of some previous visitor to the tomb. A cord hung from this beam, and it was after discovering that the well ended in nothing that the screen of masonry on the other side had been pierced. Belzoni had therefore only to follow the road opened for him by earlier explorers. A plank bridge was thrown across the well, the opening was enlarged, and a new series of galleries and chambers was reached, which led at last to the sarcophagus-chamber itself.[250]

Belzoni remarked that throughout the whole course of the excavation the doors of the chambers showed evidence of having been walled up, and that upon the first steps of one of the staircases a heap of stone rubbish had been collected, as if to discourage any one who might penetrate beyond the well and pierce the barrier beyond its gaping mouth. It seems likely that the first violator of the tomb knew the secret of all these arrangements, and consequently that its first opening took place in very ancient times, and was the work of some native Egyptian robber.

In the sarcophagus-chamber Belzoni discovered a contrivance of the same kind as that which had failed to stop him almost upon the threshold of the tomb. The sarcophagus of oriental alabaster was in place, but empty; the lid had been raised and broken.[251] From the sound given out by the floor when struck the explorer perceived that there must be a hollow space under the base of the sarcophagus. He cut a hole and brought to light the first steps of a staircase, which led to an inclined plane by which the interior of the mountain was deeply penetrated. A wall had been raised at the foot of these steps, beyond which a settlement of the superincumbent rock put an end to all advance after a distance of fifty-one yards had been traversed. Is it not possible that Belzoni only discovered a false sarcophagus, placed to deceive unbidden visitors like himself, and that the mummy was deposited, and still lies, in a chamber at the end of this corridor? The point at which the fallen rock arrested his progress is four hundred and eighty-three feet from the external opening, and about one hundred and eighty below the level of the valley. At such a depth, in these narrow and heated galleries, where there is no ventilation and where the smoke of the torches rapidly becomes stifling, it is not astonishing that, in spite of his admirable perseverance, Belzoni held his hand before completing the exploration.[252]

These subterranean tombs are hardly less astonishing than the colossal masses of the pyramids for the sustained effort which they imply; if we take the trouble to reflect upon the peculiarly difficult conditions under which they were constructed, they may even impress our imaginations more profoundly than the artificial mountains of Cheops and Chephren. We have already mentioned a figure which gives some idea of the surprising length of their passages; and although no one of the other tombs quite equals that of Seti, many approach it in dimensions. The tomb of Rameses III. is 416 feet long, that of Siptah 370 feet, and others varied between 200 and 270 feet. For the construction of such places an enormous number of cubic yards of rocky *débris* had to be cut from the interior of the mountain, and carried up by narrow and steep corridors to be "shot" in the open air. Still more surprising is the elegance and completeness of the decoration. In the tombs of Seti and of Rameses III. there is not a single surface, whether of walls, piers, or ceilings, which is not covered with the work of the chisel and the brush, with ornamental designs, with the figures of gods and genii, of men and animals. These figures are far too numerous to count. They swarm like ants in an anthill; a single chamber often contains many hundreds. Colour is everywhere; here it is used to give salience to the delicate contours of the figures in relief, there it is laid flat upon the carefully-prepared surfaces of white stucco. In these sealed-up caverns, in which the air is constantly warm and dry, the pictures have preserved their freshness of tint in the most startling fashion. And to obtain all this harmonious effect no light but an artificial one was available. It was by the smoky glare of torches, or by the flickering flame of little terra-cotta lamps, suspended from the roof by metal threads, that the patient artists of Egypt drew these masterly contours, and elaborated the exquisite harmony of their colour compositions. Egyptian art never reached greater perfection than in these characteristic productions of its genius, and yet no human eye was to enjoy them after that day upon which the final touch was to be given to their beauties, upon which they were to be inclosed in a night which, it was hoped, would be eternal.

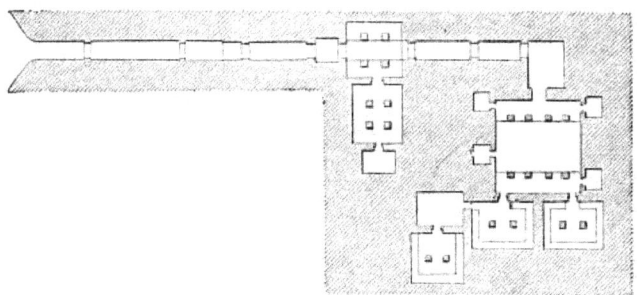

FIG. 179.—Plan of the tomb of Rameses II.; from Prisse.

FIG. 180.—Horizontal section of the same tomb; from Prisse.[253]

But yet all this work was not labour lost. These pictures, in which the details change continually from one tomb to another, were all inspired by a single desire, and all tended to the same end. Like those which we have found in the tombs of the Ancient Empire, they had a sort of magic virtue, a sovereign power to save and redeem. The personages and articles of food represented on the mastabas were shadows of people and shadows of material sustenance, destined for the service and the food of a shadow, the *double* of the defunct proprietor of the tomb. The all-powerful influence of prayer and faith, working through Osiris, turned these shadows into realities.

FIG. 181.—The smaller sarcophagus-chamber
in the tomb of Rameses VI.
(From Horeau, pl. 21.)[254]

Representations of this kind are common enough in the royal tombs of Thebes. It will suffice if we notice those which are still to be seen in the sepulchre of Rameses III., in the series of small chambers in the first two passages. Like the hunting scene which we take from the walls of a private tomb (Fig. 183), these pictures have, beyond a doubt, the same meaning and value as those in the mastaba. But in the Theban tombs their significance is only secondary. Ideas had progressed to some purpose since the days of the Memphite kings. Both in its general arrangement and in the details of its ornamentation, the sepulchres in the Bab-el-Molouk gave expression to the new, more philosophical, and more moral conception which had come to overlie the primitive beliefs.

FIG. 182.—Entrance to the tomb of Rameses III. (From Horeau, pl. 21.)

The first conception was that of the double, inhabiting the tomb, and kept alive in it by sacrifice and prayer. But in time the Egyptians would appear to have realized that the double was not the only thing that remained after the death of a human unit. Their powers of apprehension were quickened, in all probability, by that high moral instinct of which the oldest pages of their literature give evidence. Good or bad, every man had a double, the continuance and prosperity of which depended in no way upon his merits or demerits. Unless the just and the unjust were to come to one and the same end, something more was wanting. This something was the soul (*ba*). Instead of vegetating in the interior of the tomb, this soul had to perform a long and difficult subterranean journey—in imitation of the sun and almost upon his footsteps—during which it had to undergo certain tests and penances. From this period of trial it would emerge with more or less honour, according to its conduct during the few short years passed by it on earth and in company with the body to which it had belonged. It had to appear before the tribunal of Osiris-Khent-Ament, the Sun of Night, around whose seat the forty-two members of the infernal jury were assembled.[255]

FIG. 183.—Hunting scene upon a tomb at Gournah.
(Champollion, pl. 171.)

There, before the "Lords of truth and justice," the soul had to plead its cause, and there it had to repeat, with an amount of assurance and success which would depend upon its conduct in the light, that negative confession which we read in chapter cxxv. of the "*Book of the Dead*," which contains an epitome of Egyptian morality.[256] But those incorruptible judges were not guided solely by the testimony of the *ba* in its own favour. They weighed its actions in a pair of scales and gave judgment according to their weight.[257] The impious soul was flogged, was delivered to storm and tempest, and, after centuries of suffering, underwent a second death, the death of annihilation. The just soul, on the other hand, had to conquer in many a combat before it was admitted to contemplate the supreme verities. During its transit across the infernal regions, hideous forms of evil sprang up before it and did their best to arrest its progress by terrifying threats. Thanks to the help of Osiris and of other soul-protecting gods, such as Anubis, it triumphed in the end over all obstacles, and, as the sun reappears each morning upon the eastern horizon, it arrived surely at last at those celestial dwellings where it became incorporated among the gods.

FIG. 184.—The weighing of actions.
(From an illustrated *Ritual of the Dead* in the British Museum.)

The Egyptian imagination spared no effort to represent with the greatest possible precision those mysterious regions where the soul had to undergo its appointed tests. Such beliefs afforded a wide scope for the individual influence of the artist and the poet, and accordingly we find that they were modified with a rapidity which is unique in Egyptian art. But the Egyptians were accustomed, from such early times, to give a concrete form to all their ideas, that they were sure to clothe the plastic expression of this theme in a richness and brilliancy of colour which we do not find to the same degree in any other people of antiquity. On the other hand, although they did not escape the operation of the eternal law of change, their temperament was sufficiently conservative to give to each of their creations a peculiar fixity and consistency. Their *Hades*, if we may call it so, took on a very definite form, and features which varied but little through a long course of centuries; and this form is practically that which we find in the sepulchres of the great Theban kings and in some belonging to private individuals.

FIG. 185.—Anubis,
in a funerary pavilion;
from a bas-relief.
(*Description de l'Égypte*, i., pl. 74.)

It was through long and gloomy galleries, like those of the σύριγξ, that the perilous voyage of the soul had to be undertaken. A boat carried it over the subterranean river, for in a country which had the Nile for its principal highway, every journey, even that of the sun through space, was looked upon as a navigation. Spacious saloons were imagined to exist among those galleries, chambers where the infernal gods and their acolytes sat enthroned in all the majesty of their office; and so the passages of the tomb were expanded here and there into oblong or square chambers, their roofs supported by pillars left in the living rock. On either side of the audience chambers the imagination placed narrow passes and defiles, in which the walls seemed to close in upon the soul and bar its progress; tortuous corridors and gloomy gulfs were fixed in these defiles, in which the terrible ministers of divine vengeance held themselves in ambush, prepared to harass the march of souls not yet absolved, and to overwhelm with frightful tortures those against whom sentence had already been pronounced. The tomb, therefore, had its snares and narrow passages, its gaping depths and the mazes of its intersecting and twisting corridors. To complete the resemblance nothing more was required than to paint and chisel upon the walls the figures of those gods, genii, and monsters who peopled the regions below. On one side the pious king may be seen, escorted by Amen-Ra and the other divinities whom he had worshipped during life, advancing to plead his cause before Osiris; on the other, the punishment of the wicked helps to give *éclat* to the royal apotheosis by the contrasts which it affords.

Thus the tombs of the Theban period embody the Egyptian solution of the problem which has always exercised mankind. Their subterranean corridors were a reproduction upon a small scale of the leading characteristics of the under world, and we should commit a great mistake were we to look upon the series of pictures which decorate its walls as mere ornament resulting from a desire for luxury and display. Between the ideal models of these pictures and the pictures themselves the Egyptians established one of those mutual confusions which have always been readily accepted by the faithful. Nothing seemed more natural to the Egyptian, or to the Ethiopian who was his pupil, than to ascribe the power of speech and movement to the images of the gods, even when they had painted or carved them with their own hands. This M. Maspero has shown by an ingenious collation of various texts.[258] The chisel which created such tangible deities gave them something more than the appearance of life. Each god exercised his own proper function in that tomb which was a reproduction in small of the regions of the other world. His gestures and the written formulæ which appeared beside him on the walls, each had their protective or liberating power. To represent the king in his act of self-justification before Osiris was in some measure to anticipate that justification. The reality and the image were so intimately commingled in the mind of the believer that he was unable to separate one from the other.

Did the royal tombs contain statues of the defunct? None have been found in any of those already opened, and yet there is a chamber in the tomb of Rameses IV. which appears from its inscriptions to have been called the *Statue chamber*, while another apartment in its neighbourhood is reserved for the funerary statuettes. The tombs of private individuals contained statues; why then should none have been put in those of the sovereigns? The commemorative sanctuary, the external funerary temple, was adorned with his image often repeated, which in order that it might be in better keeping with the magnificence of its surroundings, and should have a better chance of duration, was colossal in its proportions. In the inclosures of the temples of the two Rameses and upon the site of the Amenophium, the remains of these huge figures are to be counted by dozens, most of them are of rose granite from Syene; the smallest are from 24 to 28 feet high, and some, with their pedestals, are as much as from 55 to more than 60 feet. The two colossi of

Amenophis III., the Pharaoh whom the Greeks called Memnon, reached the latter height. Flayed, mutilated, dishonoured as they have been, these gigantic statues are still in place. They should be seen in autumn and from a little distance as they raise their solitary and imposing masses above the inundated plain, when their size and the simplicity of their lines will have an effect upon the traveller which he will never forget (Fig. 20, and Plate vi.).

In the royal tombs at Thebes, as in those at Memphis, the approach to the mummy-chamber is not by a well, but by an inclined plane. The only wells which have been discovered in the tombs of the Bab-el-Molouk are, if we may use the term, false wells, ingeniously contrived to throw any would-be violator off the right scent. We have already mentioned one of these false wells as existing in the tomb of Seti. In the pyramids the corridor which leads to the mummy-chamber is sometimes an ascending plane, but in the Theban tomb it is always descending. At the end of the long descent the mummy-chamber is reached with its sarcophagus, generally a very simple one of red granite, which has hitherto, in every instance, been found empty.

It is doubtful whether the sarcophagus-chamber was closed by a door or not. It is known that tombs were sometimes thus closed; some of the doors have been found in place,[259] and in a few of the texts mention is made of doors, [260] but not the slightest vestige of one has yet been discovered in the royal sepulchres at Thebes. "All the doorways have sills and grooved jambs, as if they had been closed, but no trace of hinges or of the leaves of a door itself have been found."[261] It is possible that they were never put in place. The exact and accurate spirit which marks all the work of Egyptian artists would lead them to prepare for the placing of a door at the entrance to each chamber; but at the same time it is obvious that a few panels of sycamore would do little to stop the progress of any one who should attempt to violate the royal sepulchre. This latter consideration may have caused them to abstain from expending time and trouble upon a futile precaution.

These tombs seem to have varied greatly in size from reasons similar to those which determined the dimensions of the pyramids, namely, the length of reign enjoyed by their respective makers. Cheops, Chephren, and Mycerinus continually added to the height and mass of their tombs until death put an end to the work. In the same way, Seti and Rameses never ceased while they lived to prolong the quarried galleries in the Bab-el-Molouk. As these galleries were meant to be sealed from the sight of man, this prolongation was caused, no doubt, by the desire to develop to the utmost possible extent those pictures which were to be so powerful for good over the fortunes of the defunct in the under world.

Apart from the question of duration, reigns which were glorious would give us larger and more beautiful tombs than those which were obscure and marked by weakness in the sovereign. The three great Theban dynasties included several of those monarchs who have been called the Louis the Fourteenths and the Napoleons of Egypt,[262] and it was but natural that they should employ the crowd of artificers and artists which their enterprises gathered about them, for the excavation and decoration of their own tombs. Either for this reason or for some other, there is an extraordinary difference between king and king in the matter of their tombs. Even when we admit that a certain number of royal sepulchres have so far escaped discovery, it is difficult to find place for all the sovereigns of the nineteenth and twentieth dynasties in the two *Valleys of the Kings*. Many things lead us to believe that several of those princes were content with very simple tombs; some of them may have been merely buried in the sand. Thus Mariette discovered, at *Drah-Abou'l-Neggah*, the mummy of Queen Aah-hotep, of the nineteenth dynasty, some few feet beneath the surface. The mummy chamber consisted of a few ill-adjusted stone slabs. Like other mummies found on the same place, it seemed never to have been disturbed since it had been placed beneath the soil. It was gilt all over, and was decorated with jewels which now form some of the most priceless treasures of the Boulak Museum.

The private tombs in the Theban necropolis, which are much more numerous than those of kings, do not, like the latter, belong to a single period in the national history. The most ancient among them date back to the eleventh dynasty. There are some also of the Sait period, and a few contemporary with the Ptolemies and the Roman emperors. But by far the greater number belong to that epoch which saw Thebes promoted to be the capital of the whole country, to the centuries, namely, between Amosis, the conqueror of the Hyksos, and the last of the Ramessides.

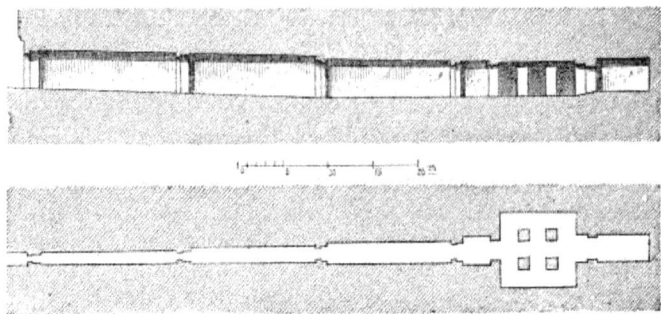

FIG. 186.—Plan and section of a royal tomb.
(*Description de l'Égypte*, vol. ii., pl. 79.)

These tombs are distinguished by great variety, but, before noticing the principal types to which they may be referred, the points which distinguish them from the royal burying-places should be indicated. The private sepulchre is never subdivided like those of the kings. This subdivision is to be explained by the exceptional position of the sovereign mid-way between his subjects and the national deities. A funerary chapel cut in the sides of the mountain would obviously be too small for the purposes to which the commemorative part of the tomb of a Rameses or a Seti would be put. On the other hand, no private individual could hope to receive royal honours nor to associate his memory with the worship of the great Egyptian gods. We find that for him the chapel always remains closely connected with the mummy chamber. Sometimes it is in front of it, sometimes above it, but in neither case does it ever fail to form an integral part of the tomb, so that the latter preserves at once its traditional divisions and its indissoluble unity.

We may say the same of the well, which plays the same part in the private tombs of the New Empire as in the Mastaba and the *Speos* of the Ancient and Middle Empires. In almost every instance the mummy chamber is reached by a well, whether the tomb be constructed in the plain or in the side of the mountains. It is seldom so deep as those of Gizeh or Sakkarah; its depth hardly exceeds from 20 to 30 feet; but its arrangement is similar to those in the early necropolis. The mummy chamber opens directly upon it. Sometimes there are two chambers facing each other at the foot of the well, and of unequal heights.[263] After the introduction of the corpse, which was facilitated by notches cut in two faces of the well, the door of the mummy chamber was built up—the well filled in. In a few exceptional instances, the tombs of private individuals seem to have had no well, and the innermost chamber, as in the case of royal tombs, received the mummy.[264] In such cases it is very necessary to make sure that explorers have not been deceived by appearances. In these dusty interiors the carefully sealed opening might easily escape any but the most careful research; and as for a sarcophagus, when one is found in such a chamber, it may have been placed there long after the making of the tomb. Such usurpations are by no means unknown. [265] In the time of the Ptolemies, influential people, such as priests and military functionaries, made them without scruple. The venerable mummies, dating from the time of Rameses, were thrown into a corner; their cases were made use of, sometimes for the mummy of the usurper, sometimes for more ignoble purposes. In more than one of these usurpations the new comer has been placed in a chamber constructed for some other object.

The well and mummy chamber in the rock are, then, found almost universally, but the form of the rest of the tomb varies according to its date and site. Those in the plain are arranged differently to those in the hill sides. But it must be understood that when we speak of the plain in connection with the Theban tombs, we do not mean the space over which spread the waters of the Nile. We mean the gentle sandy slopes which lie between the foot of the cliffs and the cultivated fields, a narrow band which widens a little between the long spurs which the mountains throw out towards the river. In these land-gulfs the rock crops up here and there, and nowhere is it covered by more than a thin layer of sand. Such a soil, being above the reach of the annual inundation, was marvellously well-fitted both for the construction of the tomb and for the preservation of the mummy.

FIGS. 187, 188.—Theban tombs from the bas-reliefs.
(From Wilkinson, ch. xvi.)

In this, which may be called the level part of the necropolis, the tombs have left but slight and ill-defined traces. Their superstructures have almost entirely disappeared, and yet some which have now completely vanished were seen by travellers to Thebes in the first half of the present century. By comparing what they tell us with the figured representations in bas-relief and manuscript, we may form some idea of the aspect which this part of the cemetery must formerly have presented. The tombs which it contained were built upon the same principles as those of Abydos; a square or rectangular structure with slightly sloping walls was surmounted by a small pyramid. There was, however, an essential difference between the two. At Abydos the nature of the subsoil compelled the architect to contrive the mummy chamber in the interior of his own structure; at Thebes, on the other hand, there was nothing to prevent him from being faithful to a tradition which had manifest advantages, and to intrust the corpse to the keeping of the earth, at a depth below the surface which would ensure it greater safety both from violence and from natural causes of decay. At Thebes the rock was soft enough to be cut with sufficient ease, and yet firm enough to be free from all danger of settlement or disintegration. The soil of all this region is honeycombed with mummy pits, which have long ago been pillaged and are now filled up with sand. The superstructure was built above the well and inclosed the funerary chapel. Sometimes it was surmounted by a small pyramid; sometimes it was a quadrangular mass standing upon a surbase, with a pilaster at each angle and a boldly projecting cornice at the top. The oldest of the known tombs of Apis may be taken as specimens of this latter class, which must also have been represented at Thebes. These are contemporary with the eighteenth dynasty, and were discovered by M. Mariette at Sakkarah.[266]

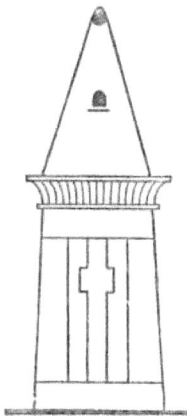

FIG. 189.—Theban tomb from a bas-relief. (From Wilkinson, ch. xvi.)

These little monuments have either been destroyed since 1851 or covered by the sand (see Fig. 190).

The other type is that of the *Speos*. We have here seen that it dates from the Ancient Empire, but came into general employment and obtained its full development under the First and Second Theban Empires. We have already given some idea of the architectural character and of the decoration of the royal sepulchres, we must now indicate the peculiarities which in these respects distinguish the tombs of the kings from those of their subjects.

One of the points of difference has already been noticed; the employment of vertical wells instead of inclined planes as approaches to the mummy chamber. The most extensive of all the Theban catacombs is that of a private individual, the priest Petamounoph (Fig. 191).[267] In this the galleries have not less than 895 feet of total length, besides which there are a large number of chambers, the whole being covered with painted reliefs. But this tomb is quite exceptional. The great majority, those of Rekhmara, for instance, and others excavated in the hill of *Sheikh-Abd-el-Gournah*, are composed of two or three chambers at most, united by corridors. The mummy pit opens sometimes upon the corridor between two of the chambers, sometimes upon the innermost chamber, sometimes upon a corridor opening out of the latter. Rhind tells us that he followed one of these corridors for about 300 feet beyond the chamber without arriving at the mummy pit, the air then became too bad for further progress.[268]

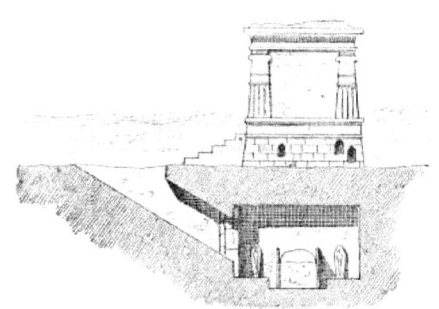

FIG. 190.—A tomb of Apis. From Mariette.

The chamber for the funerary celebration is easily recognized by its decorations. It is sometimes the first, but more often the second in order, in which case the first acts as a sort of vestibule. A considerable number of tombs are very simple in arrangement. The door gives access to a rectangular chamber, from 6 to 10 feet high and 10 to 12 wide, which extends, in a direction parallel to the wall, for from 12 to 24 feet. This chamber is the funerary chapel. From its posterior wall a passage opens which is nearly equal in height and width to the chamber. It has a gentle slope and penetrates into the rock to a distance of some 25 to 35 feet, terminating, in some cases, in the mummy chamber itself, but more frequently in a small apartment containing the opening of a mummy pit.[269]

FIG. 191.—The tomb of Petamounoph.
Drawn in perspective from the plans and elevations of Prisse.

It must not be imagined that all the tombs were decorated; there are many which have received neither painted nor carved ornament, and in others the ornament has never been carried beyond the first sketch. But even in those which are quite bare, the walls are, in nearly every instance, covered with a coat of white stucco.

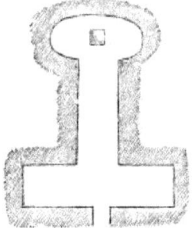

FIG. 192.—The most simple form of Theban tomb; from Rhind.
FIG. 193.—Tomb as represented upon a bas-relief; from Rhind.

As the funerary chapel was contained in the tomb itself, no effort could be made to mask or conceal the entrance, which accordingly was taken advantage of for the display of ornament. But no attempt was made to cut architectural façades in the cliffs like those at Beni-Hassan; not more than one or two sepulchres have yet been discovered which have façades made up of those columns which have been called *protodoric*. The makers of these tombs were usually content with dressing the surface of the rock above and around the entrance. The latter, with its sloping lintel above a cornice, stands in the centre of an almost perpendicular wall which acts as its frame or background. In the uninjured state of the sepulchre this wall was more or less concealed by a construction similar to those which we have described in speaking of the tombs in the plain. According to all appearances, one of these little buildings, a cube of masonry crowned by a pyramidion, was placed before the doorway of every tomb. It is difficult to say whether it was of sufficient size to contain a funerary chamber or not. It may have been no more than a solid erection of small size, meant only to mask the entrance and to indicate its situation to those concerned. The wealthy, indeed, may have been only too pleased to thus call public attention to the position of their gorgeously decorated sepulchres.

The little pyramids of crude brick which we find upon the irregular rocky slopes of the *Kournet-el-Mourrayi*, above the little window-shaped openings with which the rock is honeycombed, probably answered a similar purpose. Of these some are still standing, and others have left unmistakable traces upon, the slope. They seem to have existed in great numbers in this part of the necropolis, which seems to have been set apart, about the time of the eighteenth dynasty, for the priests.

FIG. 194.—Stele in the Boulak Museum, showing tombs with gardens about them. From Maspero.

Although they hardly varied from the two or three types consecrated by custom, these little buildings could easily have been made to present slight differences one from another. When they existed in their entirety, they must have given a very different aspect to the cemetery from that which it presents with its rocky slopes burnt by the sun into one harsh and monotonous tint, varied only by the black and gaping mouths of the countless tombs. The sides which they turned to the city and the river were adorned with those brilliant colours of which the Egyptian architects were so fond, and, spaced irregularly but never very far apart, they were sprinkled over the ground from the edge of the plain to the topmost ridges of the hills. Nearly all of them ended in a pyramid, but the varying dimensions of their bases and their different levels above the plain, gave diversity to the prospect, while here and there the slender apex of an obelisk rose above the private tombs and signalized the sleeping-place of a king. It has been very justly remarked, that the best idea of an Egyptian cemetery in its best time is to be gained by a visit to one of those Italian *Campo-Santos*, that of Naples, for example, where the tombs of many generations lie closely together under a blazing sun.[270] There, too, many sepulchral façades rise one above another upon the abrupt slope of a hill into which the graves are sunk. A comparison with the cemetery of Père-Lachaise, or with that at Constantinople, would not be just because no trees could flourish in the Theban rocks, at least in the higher part of the necropolis. In those districts which border closely upon the irrigation channels, the tombs seem to have had their gardens and fountains. Palms and sycamores appear to have been planted about them, and here and there, perhaps, the care of survivors succeeded in rearing flowers which would shed their perfumes for the consolation of the dead.[271]

FIG. 195.—The sarcophagus of a royal scribe, 19th dynasty. Louvre.

Were there statues in the courtyards by which many of these tombs were surrounded? There is no doubt that such statues were placed in the rock-cut sepulchres; all the museums of Europe have specimens which come from the Theban tombs. The latter were opened and despoiled, however, at such an early period that very few of these figures have been found in place by those who have visited the ruins of Egypt for legitimate motives. We have, however, the evidence of explorers who have penetrated into tombs which were practically intact. They tell us that the statue of the deceased, accompanied often by that of his wife and children, was placed against the further wall of the innermost chamber.[272] In some tombs, a niche is cut in the wall for this purpose,[273] in others a dais is raised three or four steps above the floor of the chamber.[274] Here, too, is found the sarcophagus, in basalt when the defunct was able to afford such a luxury, and the canopic vases, which were sometimes of stone, especially alabaster, sometimes of terra cotta, and now and then of wood, and were used to hold the viscera of the deceased. These vases were four in number, protected respectively by the goddesses Isis, Nephtys, Neith, and Selk (Fig. 196).

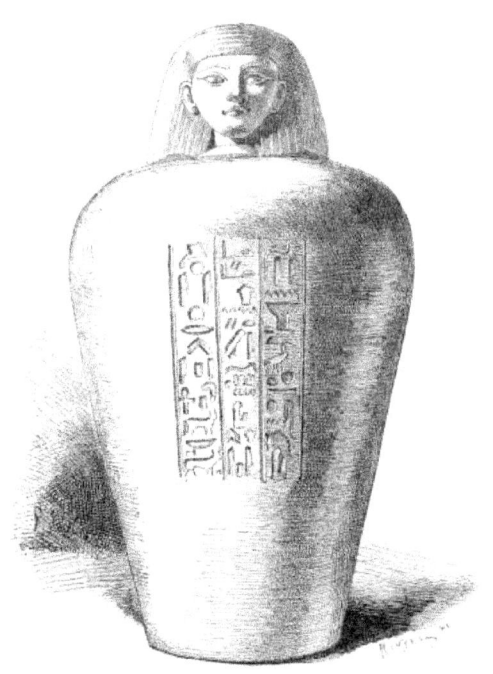

FIG. 196.—Canopic vase of alabaster. Louvre.

During the period of which we have just been treating, the taste for these huge rock-cut tombs was not confined to Thebes and its immediate vicinity; we find obvious traces of them in the city which then held the second place in Egypt, namely, in Memphis, where a son of the sovereign resided as viceroy. It was in the reign of Rameses II., that the fourth of his hundred and seventy children began what is now called the little Sérapeum, in the neighbourhood of the Great Pyramids.[275] Until then each Apis bull had had a tomb apart, a tomb in which everything was of small dimensions. This royal prince was especially vowed to the worship of Ptah and Apis, for whom he inaugurated new rites. He began the excavation of a grand gallery, and lined it on each side with small chambers which were increased in number as each successive Apis died and required a sepulchre. This gallery and its chambers served for 700 years (see Figs. 197 and 198).

FIG. 197.—View of the grand gallery in the Apis Mausoleum; from Mariette.

The funerary architecture of the Saït epoch seems to have had an originality of its own, but we are unable to form an opinion from any existing remains. Not a trace is extant of those tombs in which the princes of the twenty-sixth dynasty were, according to Herodotus, placed one after another. Here are the words of the Greek historian: ὁί δέ (the Egyptians), μιν (Apries) ἀπέπνιξαν, καὶ ἔπειτα ἔθαψαν ἐν τῇσι πατρῴῃσι ταφῇσι--αἱ δέ εἰσι ἐν τῷ ἰρῷ τῆς Ἀθηναίης, ἀγχοτάτω τοῦ μεγάρου ἐσιόντι ἀριστερῆς χερός--ἔθαψαν δὲ Σαΐται πάντας τοὺς ἐκ νομοῦ τούτου γενομένους βασιλέας ἔσω ἐν τῷ ἰρῷ. καὶ γὰρ τὸ τοῦ Ἀμάσιος σῆμα ἐκαστέρω μέν ἐστι τοῦ μεγάρου ἢ τὸ τοῦ Ἀπρίεω καὶ τῶν τούτου προπατόρων· ἔστι μέντοι καὶ τοῦτο ἐν τῇ αὐλῇ τοῦ ἰροῦ, παστὰς λιθίνη μεγάλη, καὶ ἠσκημένη στύλοισί τε φοίνικας τὰ δένδρεα μεμιμημένοισι, καὶ τῇ ἄλλῃ δαπάνῃ. ἔσω δὲ ἐν τῇ παστάδι διξὰ θυρώματα ἕστηκε· ἐν δὲ τοῖσι θυρώμασι ἡ θήκη ἐστί.[276]

Preceding centuries afford no example of a tomb placed within a temple like this.[277]

First of all the royal mummy was entombed in the bowels of an artificial mountain, secondly, under the Theban dynasties, in those of a real one; but at Saïs, it rests above the soil, in the precincts of a temple, where curious visitors come and go at their will, and nothing but a pair of wooden doors protects it from disturbance. Such an arrangement seems inconsistent with all that we know of the passionate desire of the Egyptians to give an eternal duration to their mummies. We have every reason to believe that this desire had shown no diminution at the time of the twenty-sixth dynasty, and we can hardly admit that Psemethek and his successors were less impelled by it than the meanest of their subjects.

The explanation of the apparent anomaly is to be found, we believe, in the peculiar nature of the soil of Lower Egypt. The Sait princes were determined to leave their mummies in the city which they had filled with magnificent buildings and had turned into the capital of all Egypt. Both *speos* and mummy pit, however, were out of the question. Sais was built in the Delta; upon an alluvial soil which was wetted through and through, as each autumn came round, by the water of the Nile. Neither hill nor rock existed for many miles in every direction. It was, therefore, absolutely necessary that the tomb should be a constructed one upon the surface of this soil. It would seem that the pyramid would have been the best form of tomb to ensure the continued existence of the mummy, but, to say nothing of the difficulty of finding a satisfactory foundation for such a structure upon a soft and yielding soil, the pyramid had, for many ages, been completely out of fashion. Egyptian art was entirely occupied with richer and more varied forms, forms which admitted of the play of light and shade, and of all the splendour of carved and painted decoration. The pyramid being rejected, no type remained but that of a building which should inclose both mummy chamber and funerary chapel under one roof, or, at least, within one bounding wall. There was also, it is true, the Abydos type of sepulchre, with its mummy chamber hidden in the thickness of its base; but it was too heavy and too plain, it was too nearly related to the pyramid, and it did not lend itself readily to those brilliant compositions which distinguish the last renascence of Egyptian art. But the hypostyle hall, the fairest creation of the national genius, was thoroughly fitted to be the medium of such picturesque conceptions as were then required, and it was adopted as the nucleus of the tombs at Sais. A hall divided, perhaps, into three aisles by tall shafts covered with figures and inscriptions, afforded a meeting-place and a place of worship for the living. The mummy chamber was replaced by a niche, placed, doubtless, in the wall which faced the entrance, and the well, the one essential constituent of an early Egyptian tomb, was suppressed. Such arrangements as these afforded much less security to the mummy than those of Memphis or Thebes, and to compensate in some measure for their manifest disadvantages, the tomb was placed within the precincts of the most venerable temple in the city, and the security of the corpse was made to depend upon the awe inspired by the sanctuary of Neith. As the event proved, this was but a slight protection against the fury of a victorious enemy. Less than a year after the death of Amasis, Cambyses tore his body from its resting-place, and burnt it to ashes after outraging it in a childish fashion.[278]

FIG. 198.—Sepulchral chamber of an Apis bull; from Mariette.

The tombs of these Sait kings, consisting of so many comparatively small buildings in one sacred inclosure, remind us of what are called, in the modern East, *turbehs*, those sepulchres of Mohammedan saints or priests which are found in the immediate neighbourhood of the mosques. Vast differences exist, of course, between the Saracenic and Byzantine styles and that of Ancient Egypt, but yet the principle is the same. At Sais, as in modern Cairo or Constantinople, iron or wooden gratings must have barred the entrance to the persons while they admitted the glances of visitors; rich stuffs were hung before the niche, as the finest shawls from India and Persia veil the coffins which lie beneath the domes of the modern burial-places. Perhaps, too, sycamores and palm-trees cast their shadows over the external walls.[279] The most hasty visitor to the Bosphorus and the Golden Horn can hardly fail to remember the suburb of Eyoub, where the *turbehs* of the Ottoman princes stand half hidden among the cypresses and plane trees.

The material condition which compelled the Sait princes to break with the customs of their ancestors, affected the tombs of private individuals also. Throughout the existence of the Egyptian monarchy the inhabitants of the Delta were obliged to set about the preservation of their dead in a different fashion to that followed by their neighbours in Upper Egypt; their mummies had to be kept out of reach of the inundation. Isolated monuments, like those of Abydos, would soon have filled all the available space upon artificial mounds, such as those upon which the cities of the Delta were built. The problem to be solved was, however, a simple one. Since there could be no question of a lateral development, like that of the Theban tombs, or of a downward one, like that of the Memphite mummy pits, it was obvious that the development must be upwards. A beginning was made by constructing, at some distance from a town, a platform of crude brick, upon which, after its surface had been raised above the level of the highest floods, the mummies were placed in small chambers closely packed one against another. As soon as the whole platform was occupied, another layer of chambers was commenced above it. Champollion discovered the remains of two such cemeteries in the immediate neighbourhood of Sais. The larger of the two was not less than 1,400 feet long, 500 feet wide, and 80 feet high; an enormous mass "which resembled," he said, "a huge rock torn by lightning or earthquake."[280] No doubt was possible as to the character of the mass; Champollion found among the débris both canopic vases and funerary statuettes. Within a few years of his death Mariette undertook some fresh excavations in the same neighbourhood; they led to no very important results, but they confirmed the justice of the views enunciated by Champollion. Most of the objects recovered were in a very bad state of preservation; the materials had been too soft, and in time the dampness, which had impregnated the base of the whole structure, had crept upwards through the porous brick, and turned the whole mass into a gigantic sponge.

These tombs resemble those of the kings in having no well; and as for the funerary chapel we do not as yet know whether it existed at all, how it was arranged, or what took its place. Perhaps each of the more carefully constructed tombs was divided into two parts, a chamber more or less decorated and a niche contrived in the masonry, like the rock-cut ovens of the

Phœnician catacombs. As soon as the mummy was introduced, the niche was walled up, while the chamber would remain open for the funerary celebrations. In order that the tombs situated at some height above the level of the soil, and in the middle of the block of buildings, should be reached, a complicated system of staircases and inclined planes was necessary. In the course of centuries the tombs of the first layer and especially those in the centre of the mass, were overwhelmed and buried from sight and access by the continual aggregation above and around them. The families to which they belonged, perhaps, became extinct, and no one was left to watch over their preservation. Had it not been for the infiltration of the Nile water, these lower strata of tombs would no doubt have furnished many interesting objects to explorers. In any case it would seem likely that, if deep trenches were driven through the heart of these vast agglomerations of unbaked brick, many valuable discoveries would be made.[281] Such a system left slight scope to individual caprice; space must have been carefully parcelled out to each claimant, and the architect had much less elbow room than when he was cutting into the sides of a mountain or building upon the dry soil of the desert. In the royal tombs alone, if time had left any for our inspection, could we have found materials for judging of the funerary architecture of Sais, but, as the matter stands, we are obliged to be content with what we can gather from Theban and Memphite remains as to the prevailing taste of the epoch.

Upon the plateau of Gizeh, to the south of the Great Pyramid, Colonel Vyse discovered and cleared, in 1837, an important tomb to which he gave the name of Colonel Campbell, then British Consul-General in Egypt. The external part of the tomb had entirely disappeared, but we may conclude that it was in keeping with the subterranean portion. The maker of the tomb had taken the trouble to define its extent by a trench cut around it in the rock. The external measurements of this trench are 89 feet by 74. A passage had been contrived from one of its faces to the well, which had been covered in all probability by an external structure. The well opens upon a point nearer to the north than the south, and its dimensions are quite exceptional. It is 54 feet 4 inches deep, and 31 feet by 26 feet 8 inches in horizontal section; it terminates in a chamber which is covered by a vault 11 feet 2 inches thick. It was not however in this chamber, but in small lateral grottos that several sarcophagi in granite, basalt, white quartz, &c., were found. The remains of two other wells were traced. This tomb dates from the time of Psemethek I.

FIG. 199.—Section in perspective of "Campbell's tomb," from the plans and elevations of Perring.

FIG. 200.—Vertical section in perspective of the sarcophagus chamber of the above tomb; compiled from Perring.

In the necropolis of Thebes there is a whole district, that of the hill *El Assassif*, where most of the tombs belong to the twenty-sixth dynasty. Their external aspect is very different from that of the Theban sepulchres. The entrance to the subterranean galleries is preceded by a spacious rectangular courtyard, excavated in the rock to a depth of 10 or 12 feet. This court was from 80 to 100 feet long and from 40 to 80 feet wide; it was surrounded by a stone or brick wall, and reached by a flight of steps. A pylon-shaped doorway gave access to the courtyard from the side next the rock, another door of similar shape opened upon the plain; "but some tombs are entirely closed (see Fig. 201) except towards the mountain, from which side they may be entered by one or two openings."

FIG. 201.—A Tomb on El-Assassif
(drawn in perspective from the plans and elevations of Prisse).

The subterranean part of these tombs varies in size. In some of them a gallery of medium length leads to a single chamber. In others, and these form the majority, there is a suite of rooms connected by a continuous gallery. To this latter group belongs the largest of all the subterranean Theban tombs, that of Petamounoph (Fig. 191). We have already noticed the extraordinary dimensions of its galleries; there are also two wells which lead to lower sets of chambers. All the walls of this tomb are covered with sculptured reliefs. In the first chambers these are in very bad condition, but they improve as we advance, and in the farthest rooms are remarkable for their finish and good preservation. The exterior of this sepulchre is worthy of the interior. The open court, which acts as vestibule, is 100 feet long by 80 wide. An entrance, looking towards the plain, rises between two massive walls of crude brick, and, to all appearance, was once crowned by an arcade; within it a flight of steps leads down into the court. Another door, pierced through the limestone rock, leads to a second and smaller court which is surrounded by a portico. From this peristyle a sculptured portal leads to the first subterranean chamber, which is 53 feet by 23, and once had its roof supported by a double range of columns. The next chamber is 33 feet square. With a double vestibule and these two great saloons there was no lack of space for gatherings of the friends and relations of the deceased.

Neither at Memphis nor at Thebes do the tombs of this late period contain any novel elements, but they are distinguished by their size and the luxury of their decoration. In some, the wells are much wider than usual; in others it is upon the external courts and upon those double gateways which play a part similar to that of the successive pylons before a Theban temple, that extra care is bestowed. Vaults are frequently employed and help to give variety of effect. Private tombs become as large as those of sovereigns, and similar tendencies are to be found in the sculpture. The Egyptian genius was becoming exhausted, and it endeavoured to compensate for its want of invention and creative imagination by an increase in richness and elegance.

A chronological classification is only possible in the cases of those tombs which bear inscriptions and figures upon their walls. At Memphis, as at Thebes, the remains of thousands of tombs are to be found which give no indication of their date. Sometimes they are deep mummy pits, slightly expanding at the bottom; sometimes, as at Thebes, the rock is honeycombed with graves between the border of the cultivated land and the foot of the Libyan chain. In the mountains themselves there are hundreds of small chambers, with bare walls and often extremely minute in size, cut in the sides of the cliffs. Finally, there are the vast catacombs, in each chamber of which the mummies of labourers and artisans were crowded, often with the instruments of their trade by their sides.[282] Pits full of mummified animals are also found among the human graves. Rhind saw some hundreds of the mummies of hawks and ibises taken from a tomb at the foot of the Drah-Abou'l-Neggah. They were each enveloped in bandages of mummy cloth, and beside them numerous small boxes, each with a carefully embalmed mouse inside it, were found. The lids of these boxes had each a wooden mouse upon it, sometimes gilt.[283]

We have endeavoured to notice all that is of importance in the funerary architecture of Egypt, because the Egyptian civilization, as we know it through the still existing monuments, carries us much farther back than any other towards the first awakening of individual thought and consciousness in mankind. The primitive conceptions of those early periods were, of course, different enough from those to which mankind was brought by later reflection, but nevertheless they were the premises, they contained the germ of all the development that has followed; and to thoroughly understand the origin and constitution of this development it was necessary to follow it up to its source, to the clearness and transparency of its springs.

The art of Egypt is the oldest of all the national arts, and the oldest monuments of Egypt are its tombs. By these alone is that earliest epoch in its history which we call the Ancient Empire known to us.

In later ages the country was covered with magnificent temples and sumptuous palaces, but, even then, the tomb did not lose its pre-eminent importance. The chief care of the Egyptian in all ages was his place of rest after death. Rich or poor, as soon as he arrived at full age he directed all his spare resources towards the construction and decoration of his tomb, his happy, his eternal "dwelling," with which his thoughts were far more preoccupied than with that home in the light, upon which, whether it were a miserable mud hut or a vast edifice of brick or wood, he looked with comparative indifference, regarding it as an encampment for a day or a mere hotel for a passing traveller. The tombs, when not hollowed from the living rock, were built with such solidity and care that they have survived in thousands, while the palaces of great sovereigns have perished and left no trace, and the temples which have been preserved are very few in number.

Being mostly subterranean and hidden from the eye of man, sepulchres preserved the deposits entrusted to them much better than buildings upon the surface. Those among the latter which were not completely destroyed, were, in very remote times, damaged, pillaged, stripped, and mutilated in a thousand ways. All that subsists of their decoration—shattered colossi and bas-reliefs often broken and disfigured—tells us nothing beyond the pomps and triumphs of official history. The tombs have suffered much less severely. The statues, bas-reliefs, and paintings which have been found in them, seem, in many instances, to have been the work of the very men whose footprints were found in the sand which covered their floors when they were opened. [284] The pictures offered to our eyes by the walls of the private tombs are very different from those which we find in the temples. All classes of the people appear in them in their every-day occupations and customary attitudes. The whole national life is displayed before us in a long series of scenes which comment upon and explain each other. Almost all that we know concerning the industrial arts of Egypt has been derived from a study of her tomb-houses. In every hundred of such objects which our museums contain at least ninety-nine come from those safe depositories.

In order to give a true idea of the national character of the Egyptians and to enable the originality of their civilization to be thoroughly understood, it was necessary to show the place occupied in their thoughts by the anticipation of death; it was necessary to explain what the tomb meant to them, to what sentiments and beliefs its general arrangements and its principal details responded; it was necessary to follow out the various modifications which were brought about by the development of religious conceptions, from the time of the first six dynasties to that of the Theban Empire.

The brilliant architectural revival which distinguished the first and second Theban Empires was mainly due to this development of religious thought. Almost all the peculiarities of the Memphite tomb are to be explained by the hypotheses with which primitive man is content. But when mature reflection evolved higher types for the national gods, when polytheism came to be superimposed upon fetishism, the hour arrived for the temple to take its proper place in the national life, for majestic colonnades and massive pylons to be erected on the banks of the life-giving river. The temple was later than the tomb, but it followed closely upon its footsteps, and the two were, in a fashion, united by those erections on the left bank of the Nile, under the Theban necropolis, which partook of the character of both. The temple is the highest outcome of the native genius during those centuries which saw Egypt supreme over all the races of the East, supreme partly by force of arms, but mainly by the superiority of her civilization.

CHAPTER IV.

THE SACRED ARCHITECTURE OF EGYPT.

§ 1. *The Temple under the Ancient Empire.*

No statue of a god is known which can be confidently referred to the first six dynasties. Hence it has sometimes been asserted that at that early period the Egyptian gods were not born, if we may use the expression, that the notions of the people had not yet been condensed into any definite conception upon the point. Some writers incline to believe that Egyptian thought had not yet reached the point where the polytheistic idea springs up, that they were still content with those fetishes which retained no slight hold upon their imaginations until a much later period. Others affirm that the absence of gods is due to the fact that the Egyptian people were so near to the first creation of mankind that they had not yet forgotten those religious truths which were revealed to the fathers of our race. They believe that Egypt began with monotheism, and that its polytheistic system was due to the gradual degradation of pure doctrine which took place among all but the chosen people.

We shall not attempt to discuss the latter hypothesis in these pages. It is a matter of faith and not of scientific demonstration. But to the first hypothesis we shall oppose certain undoubted facts which prove it to be, at least, an exaggeration, and that Egypt was even in those early days much farther advanced, more capable of analysis and reflection, than is generally imagined. M. Maspero, in his desire for enlightenment upon this point, searched the epitaphs of the ancient empire, and found in their nomenclature most of the sacred names which, in later phases of the national civilization, designate the principal deities of the Egyptian pantheon.[285] The composite proper names often seem to express individual devotion to some particular deity, and to indicate some connection between the latter and the mortal who bore his name and lived under his protection. These divinities must, then, have already been in existence in the minds of the Egyptians. The most that can be said is that they had not yet arrived at complete definition; art, perhaps, had not yet given them those unchanging external features and characteristics which they retained to the last days of paganism. It is quite possible that they were, more often than not, represented by those animals which, in more enlightened times, served them for symbols.

If the inscription and the figured representations still existing upon a certain stele which was found a short distance eastward of the pyramid of Cheops[286] are to be taken literally, we must believe that that monarch restored the principal statues of the Egyptian gods and made them pretty much what we see them in monuments belonging to times much more recent than his. The upper part of the stele in question shows the god of generation, Horus, Thoth, Isis in several different forms, Nephthys, Selk, Horus as the avenger of his father, Harpocrates, Ptah, Setekh, Osiris, and Apis. These statues would seem to have been in gold, silver, bronze and wood. Mariette, however, is inclined to think that this stele does not date from the time of Cheops, that it is a restoration made during the middle, or, perhaps, even during the New Empire. On attempting to restore so venerable a relic of the author of the greatest architectural work in their country, the scribes may have allowed themselves to add figures treated in the style of their own day to the ancient text. It is equally doubtful, moreover, whether the text itself dates back to the earlier period, and we need, perhaps, accept as fact only this: that Cheops restored an already existing temple, assigned to it certain sacred offerings as revenues, and restored the statues of gold, silver, bronze, and wood, which adorned the sanctuary.

It may be that the divine effigies were abundant even in those early days, but that they have failed to survive to our day. The portraits of so many private individuals have been preserved because, in their desire to afford a proper support to their *double*, they multiplied their own images to as great an extent as their means would allow. Between the third and the sixth dynasties the multiplication of these portrait statues went on at a prodigious rate, and their number may be judged from the fact that twenty were taken from the *serdab* alone of the tomb of Ti. The greater their number, the greater was the chance that one of them would escape destruction.

The ingenuity of man combined with the process of nature to preserve these figures to generations in the remote future, to a time when they could excite interest enough to save them from destruction and to ensure them a chance of eternal existence. To the thick walls of the mastabas, to the well-concealed serdabs, and, more than all, to the constantly increasing mask of sand laid upon the cemeteries of Gizeh and Sakkarah by the winds from the desert, did they owe their preservation through the troublous times which were in store for Egypt.

In their more exposed situations in the temples and private houses, the images of the gods ran far greater risks than the private statues. The material of those which were of gold, silver, or bronze, would excite dangerous cupidity, while the wooden ones were pretty sure, sooner or later, to be destroyed or damaged by fire. The stone statues might be overthrown and broken and replaced by others of a later fashion, besides which a vast number of them have perished in the lime-kilns.

We see, then, that supposing Cheops and Chephren to have paid their devotions before statues of Isis and Osiris, Ptah and Hathor, there is nothing very astonishing in the total disappearance of those figures. To argue from their absence that in those early days the gods of the Egyptians were not yet created, and consequently that there were no temples erected in their honour, is to hazard a gratuitous assertion which may at any time be disproved by some happy discovery, such as that which gave us, twenty years ago, the statue of Chephren now in the Boulak Museum. Before that statue was found it might similarly have been contended that the series of royal effigies only commenced with the first Theban Empire.

We possess, moreover, at least one divine effigy which, in the opinion of all contemporary archæologists, dates from the time of the ancient monarchy, namely, the great Sphinx at Gizeh (Fig. 157). We learn from epigraphic writings that this gigantic idol, combining the body of a crouching lion with the head of a man, represents Hor-em-Khou, or 'Horus in the shining Sun,' corresponding to the Harmachis, or rising sun, of the Greeks. According to the stele above quoted, it was carved, long before the time of Cheops, out of a natural rock which reared its head above the sand in this part of the necropolis; here and there the desired form was made out by additions in masonry.[287]

As primitive Egypt had gods she must have had temples. Few traces of them are to be found, however, and their almost total disappearance is mainly owing to causes which merit careful notice.

Before they began to erect stone buildings, the early Egyptians made constant use of wood for many ages. Various bas-reliefs and paintings prove that this latter material was never entirely abandoned, but after stone and brick came into general use it was reserved for special purposes; it was usually employed in those lighter and more ephemeral edifices in which rapidity of construction was the chief point required. When, in the remains of the early dynasties, we see the characteristics of wooden constructions so closely imitated in stone, we are constrained to believe that wood then played a much more important part than under the Theban princes. Either brick or stone was absolutely necessary for a tomb, because they alone had sufficient durability, but it is quite possible that most of the temples were of wood. With the help of colour and metal, wood could be easily made to fulfil all the conditions of a temple. The shrine which enclosed either a statue or some symbolic object, the portico which surrounded the inner court, the furniture, the doors, the high palisade which enclosed the sacred precinct, might all have been of wood. When destroyed by accident or damaged by time, such a structure could be quickly and easily restored.

We may admit, however, that from the epoch of the Pyramids onwards, such cities as Thinis, Abydos, Memphis, and others, constructed their temples of stone, which, in the then state of architectural skill, they could have done without any serious difficulty. The chief cause of the disappearance of the early temples was the construction of those that came after them. The national taste changed with the centuries, and the time came when the comparative simplicity of the primitive erections was unable to satisfy the longing of the people for magnificence and splendour. New temples, more vast and sumptuous than the old, were constructed, and the substance of their predecessors was, as a matter of course, employed in their construction. Sometimes a fragmentary inscription or a piece of sculpture betrays the restoration; and, here and there, inscriptions on the later building go so far as to preserve the name of the architect of the first. An instance of this occurs at Denderah. Champollion discovered that the Ptolemaic temples almost always replaced structures dating from the great Theban or Sait dynasties. The island of Philæ, however, affords an exception to this rule.[288] These temples he calls "second editions." But in some cases they were third or even fourth editions.

But in spite of all these rearrangements and restorations, a few sacred buildings of the early period were still in existence during the Roman occupation of the country, and were then shown as curiosities. This we may gather from a passage in Strabo. After having described, with much precision, the disposition of certain buildings which are easily recognized as temples built under the princes of the New Empire, he adds: "At Heliopolis, however, there is a certain building with several ranges of columns, which recalls, by its arrangement, the barbarous style; because, apart from the great size of the columns, their number and their position in several long rows, there is nothing graceful in the building, nothing that shows any power of artistic design; effort, and impotent effort, is its most striking characteristic." [289] Lucian, too, was thinking of the same building in his treatise upon the Syrian goddess, when he said that the Egyptians had, in ancient times, temples without sculptured decorations.[290]

One of these 'barbarous' temples, as Strabo calls them, is supposed to have been discovered in the small building disinterred by Mariette in 1853, at about 50 yards distance from the right foot of the Sphinx in a south-easterly direction. Mariette cleared the whole of the interior, and by means of a flight of steps well protected from the sand, he provided easy access to it. But he left the external walls buried as he found them, and so they still remain.

The entrance is by a passage about 66 feet long and 7 wide, which runs almost in an easterly direction through the massive masonry which constitutes the external wall. About midway along this passage two small galleries branch off; that on the right leads to a small chamber, that on the left to a staircase giving access to the terrace above. At the end of the passage we find ourselves at one of the angles of a hall, running north and south, and about 83 feet long by 23 wide. The roof is supported by six quadrangular piers. These are monoliths 16 feet 6 inches high and 3 feet 4 inches by 4 feet 8 inches in section. Several of their architraves are still in place. These are stones about 10 feet in length.[291] From the eastern side of this hall another opens at right angles. This second hall is about 57 feet long and 30 wide, and its roof was supported by ten columns similar to those we have already mentioned.

Fig. 202.—The Temple of the Sphinx (from an unpublished plan by Mariette).

From the south-west angle of the first hall there is a short corridor which leads to six deep niches in the masonry, arranged in pairs one above the other, and apparently intended for the reception of mummies. In the middle of the eastern wall of this same large chamber there is a short and wide passage which leads to a third and last hall, parallel to the one with six columns; it has no supporting pillars, but there is, in the centre of the floor, a deep well which Mariette cleared from the sand with which it was filled. There had been water in it, because it was sunk below the level of the Nile. At the bottom nine broken statues of Chephren were found; they were not copies, one from the other, but represented the king at different periods of his life. Several stone cynocephali were also found.

At each end of this hall there is a small chamber communicating with it by short corridors. One of these, that in the northern angle of the temple, seems to have communicated with the outward air by an irregular opening in the masonry.

Fig. 203.—Interior of the Temple of the Sphinx (from a sketch by M. Ernest Desjardins).

The materials employed in the interior of this building are rose granite and alabaster. The supporting piers are of granite, the lining slabs of the walls and the ceiling, alabaster. Both these materials are dressed and fixed with care and knowledge, but in no part of the temple is the slightest hint at a moulding or at any other sort of ornament to be found. The pillars are plain rectangular monoliths; the walls are without either bas-reliefs or paintings, and there is not a trace of any inscription on any part of the building. The external walls are constructed of the largest limestone blocks which are to be found in Egypt. In these days none of their outward faces are visible, but according to Mariette, who, doubtless, had inspected them by means of temporary excavation, nothing is to be seen but "smoothly polished surfaces, decorated with long vertical and horizontal grooves skilfully interlaced; in one corner there is a door, the only one, and that very small."[292]

For the last thirty years there has been much controversy as to the true character of this curious monument. Mariette himself allows us to see that he could not convince himself of its real meaning: "It cannot be doubted that this building dates from the time of the pyramids; but is it a temple or a tomb? Its external appearance is, it must be confessed, more that of a tomb than of a temple. From a distance it must have looked not unlike a mastaba from Sakkarah or Abousir, which it but slightly excelled in size. The six deep niches which exist in the interior recall the internal arrangements of the pyramid of Mycerinus and the Mastabat-el-Faraoûn, and the general plan resembles that of several other tombs in the neighbourhood. It appears, therefore, that the hypothesis which would make it a sepulchre might be upheld without violating the rules which should guide the archæologist.... On the other hand it may, very naturally, be asserted that, as the Sphinx is a god, it must be the Temple of the Sphinx."[293]

This latter hypothesis seems to have found most favour with Mariette. The rectangular niches, which at first seemed to him to be intended for funerary purposes, were accounted for in another way. "May they not be here," he asks, "what the crypt is at the temple of Denderah?" And he does not hesitate to employ the terms *Temple of the Sphinx*, and *Temple of Harmachis*. He does not give his reasons, but to some extent we can supply them. Every mastaba of any importance has funerary representations upon it, and inscriptions containing both the name of the deceased and those magical formulæ which we have already explained; the walls display his portrait and the whole course of his posthumous life. The humblest of these tombs shows at least a stele upon which the name of the defunct is inscribed together with the prayer which is to insure him the benefit of the funerary offerings mentioned upon it. The tomb is thus consecrated to the use of some particular person, of an individual whose name is placed upon it, and who is exclusive owner of it and its contents to all eternity. In this temple there is no sign of such individual appropriation. Its total size is rather in excess of that of the largest mastaba yet discovered; its materials are finer and its construction more careful. The bareness of the walls, therefore, can hardly be attributed to want of means on the part of the proprietor.

It is true that in many tombs the decorative works have never advanced beyond the sketch stage; but here, although the building is in a good state of preservation, not the slightest sign is to be discovered that any funerary ornamentation had ever been attempted. It is difficult to see how such an anomaly is to be accounted for except by the supposition that this is not a tomb, and was never intended to be one.

An examination of the well leads to the same conclusion. In the mastaba the well is simply a vertical corridor of approach to the mummy chamber. Here there is neither sarcophagus nor any place to put one; no enlargement of the well of any kind. But of the three parts into which the typical Egyptian tomb may be divided, the most important is the mummy chamber. It is the only one of three which is absolutely indispensable. It could, in itself, furnish all the necessary elements of a place of sepulture, because it could ensure the safety and repose of the corpse entrusted to it. Where there is no mummy chamber there can hardly be a tomb, strictly speaking.

The anomalous character of these arrangements, supposing the building to be a tomb, disappears when it is looked upon as a temple. Its bareness and simplicity agree entirely with the descriptions given by Plutarch and the pseudo-Lucian of those early Egyptian temples which the one saw with his own eyes and the other knew by tradition. A well for providing the water required by the Egyptian ritual and by the ablutions of the priests would be in its proper place in such an edifice, while the similarity between its general arrangements and those of the mastabas may easily be accounted for by the inexperience of the early architect. The forms at his command were too few and too rigid to enable him to mark, with any certainty, the different purposes of the buildings which he erected. The architect of this temple seems, however, to have done his best to express the distinction. In none of the Memphite mastabas do we find such spacious chambers or so many large and well-wrought monolithic columns.

Many hypotheses have been put forward in the attempt to reconcile these two explanations of the "Temple of the Sphinx," but we cannot discuss them here. "Why," asks Mariette, in his recently published memoir, "should not the temple of the Sphinx be the tomb of the king who made the Sphinx itself?" This question we may answer by two more: Why did not that king decorate the walls of his tomb? and why did he have neither sarcophagus nor sarcophagus chamber? Others have seen in it the chapel in which the funerary rites of Chephren were performed;[294] a theory which was of course suggested by the discovery of that king's statues in the well. These statues, we are told, must formerly have been arranged in one of the chambers, and, in some moment of political tumult, they must have been cast into the well either by foreign enemies or by the irritated populace.

In all probability we shall never learn the true cause of this insult to the memory of Chephren, and it seems to us to be hazarding too much to affirm that, because the statues of that king were found in it, the building we are discussing must have been his funerary chapel. It is very near the Sphinx, and it is a considerable distance from the second pyramid,[295] which, moreover, had a temple of its own. According to all analogy, the funerary chapel would be in the immediate neighbourhood of the mummy for whose benefit it was erected.

In the absence of any decisive evidence either one way or the other, the most reasonable course is to look upon this building as the temple in which the worship of the neighbouring Colossus was carried on: as the temple of Harmachis, in a word. This solution derives confirmation from the following facts mentioned by Mariette: "The granite stele, erected by Thothmes IV. to commemorate the works of restoration undertaken by him, was placed against the right shoulder of the Sphinx, that is to say, at the point nearest to the building which we are discussing. In later years this stele and some others representing scenes of adoration which were added by Rameses II., were combined into a sort of small building, which almost directly faced any one coming out of the temple."[296] One of Mariette's favourite projects was to clear the sphinx down to its base, to clear all the space between it and the temple (see Fig. 204), and finally to build a wall round the whole group of sufficient height to keep it free from sand in the future. In Mariette's opinion such an operation could hardly fail to bring to light more than one monument of great antiquity, of an antiquity greater, perhaps, than that of the pyramids. In any case it would lay open the material connection between the great idol and its temple, and would help us to reconstitute the most ancient group of religious buildings in existence.

Those structures which are generally called the *temples of the pyramids* belong to the same class of architecture (Fig. 127). We have already mentioned them, and explained how they are to the pyramids what the funerary chamber is to the mastaba. We must return to them for a moment in their capacity as temples. The deceased kings in whose honour they were erected were worshipped within their walls even down to the time of the Ptolemies. They are in a much worse state of preservation than the Temple of the Sphinx. Unlike the latter they were not protected by the sand, and their materials could readily be carried away for the construction of other buildings. Nothing remains but the lower courses of the walls and their footings, so that no exact agreement has yet been come to even as to their ground plan. We shall quote, however, the description given by Jomard of the temple belonging to the third pyramid. The French *savants*, whose visit to Egypt took place nearly a century ago, saw many things which have disappeared since their time.

"The building situated to the east of the third pyramid is remarkable for its arrangement, its extent, and the enormous size of the blocks of which it is composed. In plan it is almost square, being 177 feet by 186. On its eastern side there is, however, a vestibule or annexe 103 feet long and 46 wide.... Outside the vestibule there is a vast courtyard with two lateral openings or posterns; beyond this there are several spacious saloons, five of which are still in existence; the farthest of these is the same size as the vestibule, and is exactly opposite to the centre of the pyramid, from which it is but 43 feet distant. But I could see no opening in that part of the wall which faced the pyramid.

"The general symmetry of the arrangement, however, suffices to prove the connection between the two buildings.

"After having studied the construction and the materials of the Theban edifices, I was astonished by the size of the stones here made use of, and the care with which they were fixed. The walls are 6 feet 9 inches thick; a thickness which is determined by that of the stones employed. Their length varies from 12 to 23 feet. At first I took these blocks for the face of the rock itself, elaborately worked and dressed, and I might not have discovered my mistake but for the cemented joints between the courses.

"The eastward prolongation or annexe is formed of two huge walls, which are not less than 13 feet 4 inches thick. It may well be asked why such walls should have been constructed, seeing that had they been of only half the thickness they would have been quite as durable and solid.

"This building forms, as it were, the continuation of an enclined plane or causeway laid out at right angles to the base line of the third pyramid, and leading up to it."[297]

Jomard appears to have found no traces of pillars in any part of the edifice; but Belzoni, whose description is, however, both short and confused, seems to have found them in the temple of the second pyramid. He speaks of a *portico*, and he adds that some of its blocks were 24 feet high,[298] or about the same height as the monoliths in the Temple of the Sphinx. Such blocks would, of course, be the first to be carried off and used elsewhere.

In spite of this difference many of the peculiar arrangements of the sphinx temple are repeated in these buildings. There is the same squareness of plan, the same multiplicity of internal chambers, the same employment of huge masses of stone and the same care and skill in dressing and fixing them. It is now impossible to say whether these buildings, when complete, were decorated or not; it is certain that at the present day no sign of any ornamentation, either carved or painted, is to be found upon them.

We see, then, that the religious architecture of the early empire is represented by a very small number of monuments, of which only one is in a good state of preservation. When we recall the texts which we have quoted, when we compare the temple of the Sphinx with tombs like the pyramids or the sepulchre of Ti, we must acknowledge that the energies of the Egyptians during the early dynasties were mainly directed to their resting-places after death, that the worship of the dead held the largest place in their religious life. Their temples were small in size, insignificant in height, and severe in their absence of ornament. They give slight earnest of the magnificent edifices which the country was to rear some ten or fifteen centuries afterwards at the command of the great Theban pharaohs. The monolithic pillars, however, of which we have spoken, give some slight foretaste of a feature which was to reach unrivalled majesty in the hypostyle halls of Karnak and Luxor.

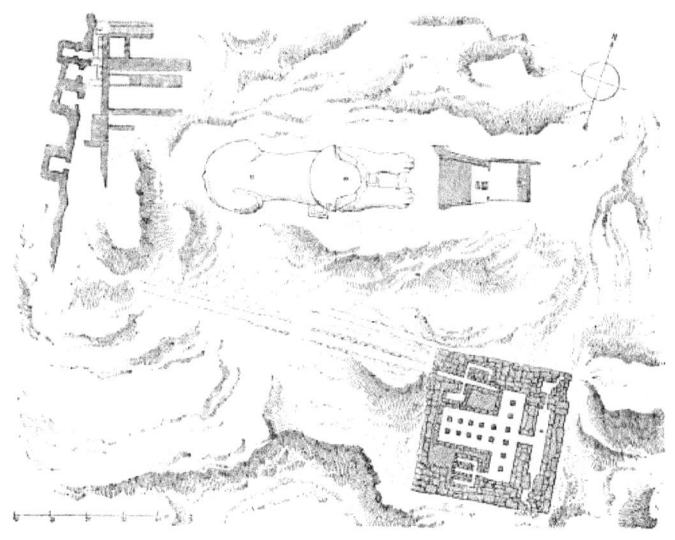

Fig. 204.—The Temple of the Sphinx, the Sphinx, and the neighbouring parts of the Necropolis.

§ 2. *The Temple under the Middle Empire.*

No temples constructed under the first Theban empire are now in existence; and yet the Egyptians had then generally adopted the worship of all those deities whose characters and attributes have been made known to us through the monuments of the New Empire. The Theban triad received the homage of the Ousourtesens and Amenemhats; its principal personage, Amen, or Ammon, identified with Ra, already showed a tendency to become a supreme deity for the nation as a whole. To him successful sovereigns attributed their successes both of peace and war. As the god of the king and of the capital, Amen acquired an uncontested superiority throughout the whole valley of the Nile, which affected, however, neither the worship of the local deities, nor the homage paid by every man and woman in Egypt to Osiris, the god to whom they looked for happiness beyond the grave.

Art, at this period, had advanced so far that there was no longer any difficulty in marking the distinction between the temple and the tomb. In the sepulchres at Beni-Hassan which date from the twelfth dynasty, we find two very different kinds of support, and there was nothing to prevent the forms employed in these rock-cut chambers from being made use of in constructed buildings, seeing especially how skilful the Egyptians had shown themselves to be in working the excellent materials provided for them by nature. The architect could, if he had chosen, have multiplied to infinity those stone supports which his distant predecessors had employed, apparently with some inkling of their future possibilities. The obelisk set up by Ousourtesen at Heliopolis, proves that the cutting and polishing of those monoliths was understood in his time, and as the obelisk seems always to have been closely combined with the pylon, it is not improbable that the religious edifices of the time of Ousourtesen were prefaced by those huge pyramidoid masses. The hypostyle halls, the pylons, and the obelisks of the New Empire differed from those of the Middle Empire rather in their extent and in the magnificence of their decoration, than in their general arrangement.

Of all the temples then constructed, the only one which has left any apparent traces is that which was erected at Thebes by the princes of the twelfth dynasty to the honour of Amen. It forms the central nucleus around which the later buildings of Karnak have been erected. The name of Ousourtesen is to be read upon the remains of the polygonal columns which mark, it is believed, the site of the sanctuary properly speaking, between the granite chambers and the buildings of Thothmes III.; these columns, like those at Beni-Hassan, are hexagonal in section.[299]

Of many other buildings erected at this period, nothing is left to us beyond tradition and the mere mention of them in various texts. This, however, is sufficient to prove their existence. We shall choose examples of them from the two extremities of Egypt. Nothing has been found of that great temple at Heliopolis which all the Greek travellers visited and described, but we know that a part, at least, of its buildings dated from the time of the first Theban empire, because a MS. at Berlin, published by Herr Ludwig Stern in 1873, narrates the dedication of a chapel by Ousourtesen. It is probable that the obelisk was in the portion then built and consecrated to the god Ra.

At Semneh, in Nubia, the fortress on the left bank of the river contains a temple of Thothmes III., which, according to the pictures and inscriptions which cover its walls, is no more than a restoration of one built, in the first instance, in honour of Ousourtesen III. This latter prince was deified at Semneh after his death, and his worship continued for more than ten centuries. His temple, which had fallen into ruin during the first reigns of the eighteenth dynasty, was reconstructed by Thothmes, and that prince is represented doing homage to the local deities, among whom Ousourtesen may be discovered presenting his pious successor to the other gods.

Many more instances might be given, but the monuments of the second Theban empire demand our attention. A Thothmes or an Amenophis, a Seti or a Rameses, could dispose of all the resources of a rich country and of an aged civilization for the construction of their edifices, edifices so great and splendid that they ran no risk of being destroyed in later times for the sake of constructing others still more sumptuous; besides which they were built at the zenith of the national greatness, at the moment when, in the Egyptian character, all the energy of an unconquered people was combined with the knowledge and experience resulting from an old and complex social system. In the later ages of the monarchy a few unimportant additions were made, an obelisk or a pylon here, there a court, a colonnade, or a few chambers; but the great temples of the New Empire have come down to us with few modifications beyond those caused by the three thousand years through which they have existed, and we have little difficulty in restoring them, on paper, to the condition in which they were left by the great monarchs of the eighteenth, nineteenth, and twentieth dynasties. The later additions, although they render the ground-plans more complicated, fail to hide or materially affect the general characteristics of the buildings, and in no way prevent us from recognizing and defining the spirit and originality of their conception.

§ 3. *The Temple under the New Empire.*

Before we cross the threshold of the great Theban temples and attempt to evolve order out of their complexity of courts, halls, porticos and colonnades, it may be convenient to describe their approaches. Each temple had its external and accessory parts which had their share in the religious ceremonies of which it was the theatre, and it would be difficult to make its economy understood unless we began by noticing them in detail.

FIG. 205.—Ram, or *Kriosphinx*, from Karnak.

One of the first signs which denoted to visitors the proximity of an Egyptian temple was what the Greek travellers called a δρόμος, that is to say a paved causeway bordered on each side with rams or sphinxes, their heads being turned inwards to the road. These avenues vary in width, that at Karnak is 76 feet between the inner faces of the pedestals;[300] within the precincts of the sacred edifice, between the first and second pylon, this width underwent a considerable increase. The space between one sphinx and another on the same side of the causeway was about 13 feet. The *dromos* which led from Luxor to Karnak was about 2,200 yards long; there must, therefore, have been five hundred sphinxes on each side of it. At the Serapeum of Memphis the sphinxes which Mariette found by digging 70 feet downwards into the sand were still nearer to one another;[301] the dromos which they lined was found to be 50 feet wide and about 1,650 yards long.

Following our modern notions we should, perhaps, expect to find these causeways laid out upon an exactly rectilinear plan. They are not so, however. It has sometimes been said that one of the characteristic features of Egyptian architecture is its dislike, or rather hatred, of a rigorous symmetry. Traces of this hatred are to be found in these avenues. The very short ones, such as those which extend between one pylon and another, are straight, but those which are prolonged for some distance outside the buildings of the temple almost always make some abrupt turns. The Serapeum *dromos* undergoes several slight changes of direction, in order, no doubt, to avoid the tombs between which its course lay. We find the same thing at Karnak, where the architect must have had different motives for his abandonment of a straight line. At the point where the man-headed sphinxes of Horus succeed to those sphinxes without inscriptions the date of which Mariette found it impossible to determine, the axis of the avenue inclines gently to the left.

These avenues of sphinxes are always outside the actual walls of the temple, from which it has been inferred that they were merely ornamental, and without religious signification.[302]

Some of the great temples have several of these avenues leading up to their different gates. It is within these gates only that the sacred inclosure called by the Greeks the τέμενος commences. The religious ceremonies were all performed within this space, which was inclosed by an encircling wall built at sufficient distance from the actual temple to allow of the marshalling of processions and other acts of ritual.

These outer walls are of crude brick. At Karnak they are about 33 feet thick, but as their upper parts have disappeared through the perishable nature of the material, it is impossible to say with certainty what their original height may have been.[303] Their summits, with their crenellated parapets, must have afforded a continuous platform connected with the flat tops of the pylons by flights of steps.

"These inclosing walls served more than one purpose. They marked the external limits of the temple. They protected it against injury from without.

When their height was considerable, as at Denderah, Sais, and other places, they acted as an impenetrable curtain between the profane curiosity of the external crowd and the mysteries performed within; and when they had to serve their last named purpose they were constructed in such a fashion that those without could neither hear nor see anything that passed.

"It is probable that the walls of Karnak served all three purposes. There are four of them, connected one with another by avenues of sphinxes, and all the sacred parts of the building, except a few chapels, are in one of the four inclosures.... Their height was at least sufficient to prevent any part of the inside from being overlooked from any quarter of the city, so that the ceremonies in the halls, under the colonnades, or upon the lakes could be proceeded with in strict isolation from the outer world.[304] We may therefore perceive that, on certain occasions, these inclosures would afford a sanctuary which could not easily be violated, while they would keep all those who had not been completely initiated at a respectful distance from the holy places within."[305]

These walls were pierced in places by stone doorways, embedded in the masses of crude brick, whose highest parts always rose more or less above the battlements of the wall (Fig. 206). At those points where the sphinx avenues terminated, generally at the principal entrance of the temple but sometimes at secondary gateways, these portals expanded into those towering masses which by their form as well as their size, so greatly impress the traveller who visits the ruins of ancient Egypt. These masses have by common consent been named *pylons*. They seem to have been in great favour with the architects of Egypt, who succeeded by their means in rendering their buildings still more original than they would have been without them.[306]

FIG. 206.—Gateway and boundary wall of a temple; restored by Ch. Chipiez.

The pylon is composed of three parts intimately allied one with another; a tall rectangular doorway is flanked on either hand by a pyramidal mass rising high above its crown. Both portal and towers terminate above in that hollow gorge which forms the cornice of nearly all Egyptian buildings. Each angle of the towers is accentuated by a cylindrical moulding, which adds to the firmness of its outlines. This moulding bounds all the flat surfaces of the pylon, which are, moreover, covered with bas-reliefs and paintings. It serves as a frame for all this decoration, which it cuts off from the cornice and from the uneven line which marks the junction of the sloping walls with the sandy soil. From the base of the pylon spring those vertical masts from whose summits many coloured streamers flutter in the sun.[307] In consequence of the inclination of the walls, these masts, being themselves perpendicular, were some distance from the face of the pylon at its upper part. Brackets of wood were therefore contrived, through which the masts passed and by which their upright position was preserved; without some such support they would either have been liable to be blown down in a high wind, or would have had to follow the inclination of the wall to which they were attached, which would have been an unsightly arrangement. The interiors of the pylons were partly hollow; they inclosed small chambers to which access was obtained by narrow staircases winding round a central square newel. The object of these chambers seems to have been merely to facilitate the manœuvring of the masts and their floating banners, because when the latter were in place, the small openings which gave light to the chambers were entirely obscured.

If the pylons had been intended for defensive purposes, the doors in their centres would have been kept in rear of the flanking towers, as in more modern fortifications. But instead of that being the case they are slightly salient, which proves conclusively that their object was purely decorative.

The pylon which we have taken as a type of such erections, is one of those which inclose a doorway opening in the centre of one of the sides of the brick inclosure, it may be called an external pylon, or a *pro-pylon*, to make use of the word proposed by M. Ampère, but in all temples of any importance several pylons have to be passed before the sanctuary is reached. At Karnak, for instance, in approaching the great temple from the temple of Mouth, the visitor passes under four pylons, only one of which, the most southern, is connected with the inclosing wall. So, too, on the west. After passing the pylon in the outer wall, another has to be passed before the hypostyle hall is reached, and a third immediately afterwards. Then, behind the narrow court which seems to cut the great mass of buildings into two almost equal parts, there are three more at very slight intervals. Thus M. Mariette counts six pylons, progressively diminishing in size, which lie in the way of the visitor entering Karnak by the west and passing to the east. At Luxor there are three.

A glance at our general view of the buildings of Karnak will give a good idea of the various uses to which the Egyptian architect put the pylon.[308] There is the pro-pylon; there are those pylons which, when connected with curtain walls, separate one courtyard from another; there are those again, which, placed immediately in front of the hypostyle halls, form the façades of the temples properly speaking. The temple is always concealed behind a pylon, whose summit rises above it while its two wings stretch beyond it laterally until they meet the rectangular wall which incloses the sanctuary.

The dimensions of pylons vary with those of the temples to which they belong. The largest still existing is the outer pylon of the great temple of Karnak. It was constructed in Ptolemaic times. Its two chief masses are 146 feet high, or about equal to the Vendôme column in Paris. This pylon is 376 feet wide at the widest part and 50 feet thick. The first pylon at Luxor, which was built by Rameses II., is less gigantic in its proportions than this; it is, however, 76 feet high, each of its two great masses is 100 feet wide, and the portal in the middle is 56 feet high (see Fig. 207).

In those temples which were really complete, obelisks were erected a few feet in front of the pylons, and immediately behind the obelisks, in contact with the pylons themselves, were placed those colossal statues by which every Egyptian monarch commemorated his connection with the structures which were reared in his time. The obelisks are generally two in number, the colossi vary from four to six for each pylon, according to the magnificence of the temple. The obelisks range in height from about 60 to 100 feet, and the statues from 20 to 45 feet.[309] Obelisks and colossal statues seem to have been peculiarly necessary outside the first, or outer, pylon of a temple. This produced an effect upon the visitor at the earliest moment, before he had entered the sacred inclosure itself. But they are also to be found before the inner pylons, a repetition which is explained by the fact that such temples as those of Karnak and Luxor were not the result of a single effort of construction. Each of the successive pylons which met the visitor during the last centuries of Egyptian civilization had been at one time the front of the whole edifice.

To complete our description of the external parts of the temple we have yet to mention those small lakes or basins which have been found within the precincts of all the greater temples. Their position within the inclosing walls suggests that they were used for other purposes beyond such ablutions as those which are prescribed for all good Mohammedans. If nothing but washing was in view they might have been outside the inclosure, so that intending worshippers could discharge that part of their duty before crossing the sacred threshold; but their situation behind the impenetrable veil of such walls as those we have described, suggests that they had to play a part in those religious mysteries which could not be performed within sight of the profane. Upon certain festivals richly decorated boats, bearing the images or emblems of the gods, were set afloat upon these lakes. As the diurnal and nocturnal journeys of the sun were looked upon as voyages by navigation across the spaces of heaven and through the shadows of the regions below, it may easily be understood how a miniature voyage by water came to have a place in the worship of deities who were more or less solar in their character.

We have now arrived upon the threshold of the temple itself, and we must attempt to describe and define that edifice, distinguishing from each other its essential and accessory parts.

When we cast our eyes for the first time either upon the confused but imposing ruins of Karnak themselves, or upon one of the plans which represent them, it seems a hopeless task to evolve order from such a chaos of pylons, columns, colossal statues and obelisks, from such a tangled mass of halls and porticos, corridors and narrow chambers. If we begin, however, by studying some of the less complex structures we soon find that many of these numerous chambers, in spite of their curious differences, were repetitions of one another so far as their significance in the general plan is concerned. When a temple was complete in all its parts any monarch who desired that his name too should be connected with it in the eyes of posterity, had no resource but to add some new building to it, which, under the circumstances supposed, could be nothing but a mere *replica* of some part already in existence.[310] They took some element of the general plan, such as the hypostyle hall at Karnak, and added to it over and over again, giving rise to interesting changes in the proportion, arrangement and decoration.

FIG. 207.—Principal façade of the temple of Luxor; restored by Ch. Chipiez.

One of the most intelligent of the ancient travellers, namely, Strabo, attempted the work of discrimination which it is now our duty to undertake. He wrote for people accustomed to the clear and simple arrangements of the Greek temple, and he attempted to give them some idea of the Egyptian temple, such as he found it in that Heliopolis whose buildings made such an impression upon all the Greeks who saw them.[311]

His description is, perhaps, rather superficial. It says nothing of some accessory parts which were by no means without their importance, and those details which most strongly attracted the author's attention are not mentioned in their natural order, which would seem to be that in which the visitor from without would meet them in his course from the main door to the sanctuary. But Strabo had one great advantage over a modern writer. He saw all these great buildings in their entirety, and could follow their arrangement with an easy certainty which is impossible in our day, when so many of them present nothing but a confused mass of ruins, and some indeed, such as the temple at Luxor, are partly hidden by modern ruins. We shall, then, take Strabo for our guide, but we shall endeavour to give our descriptions in better sequence than his, and to fill up some of the gaps in his account by the study of those remains which are in the best state of preservation. In our descriptions we shall advance from simple buildings to those which are more complex. We should soon lose the thread of our argument if we were to begin by attacking temples which are at once so complicated and so mutilated as those of Karnak and Luxor. The character of each of the elements of an Egyptian temple of this period will be readily perceived if we begin our researches with one which is at once well preserved, simple in its arrangements, and without those successive additions which do so much to complicate a plan.

Of all the ruins at Thebes the *Temple of Khons*, which stands to the southwest of the great temple at Karnak, is that which most completely fulfils these conditions.[312] Time has not treated it very badly, and, although the painted decoration may be the work of several successive princes, we are inclined to believe from the simplicity of the plan that most of the architectural part of the work was begun and completed by Rameses III.

The advanced pylon, or propylon, which stands some forty metres in front of the whole building and was erected by Ptolemy Euergetes, may be omitted from our examination. The really ancient part of the structure begins with the rows of sphinxes which border the road behind the propylon. They lead up to a pylon of much more modest dimensions than that of Ptolemy. In front of this pylon there is no trace of either obelisks or colossal figures. As the whole temple is no more than about 233 feet long and 67 feet wide, it may not have been thought worthy of such ornaments, or perhaps their small size may have led to their removal. In any case, Strabo appears to have seen religious edifices in front of which there were neither obelisks nor the statues of royal founders.

Immediately behind this pylon lay a rectangular court surrounded by a portico of two rows of columns standing in front of a solid wall. In this wall and in the columns in front of it we recognise the wings of which Strabo speaks; the *two walls of the same height as those of the temple, which are prolonged in front of the pronaos*. There is but one difficulty. Strabo says that the space between these walls diminishes as they approach the sanctuary.[313]

His court must therefore have been a trapezium with its smallest side opposite to the pylon, rather than a rectangle. We have searched in vain for such a form among the plans of those pharaonic temples which have been measured. In every instance the sides of the peristylar court form a rectangular parallelogram. It must, apparently, have been in a Ptolemaic temple that Strabo noticed these converging sides, and even then he was mistaken in supposing such an arrangement to be customary. The Ptolemaic temples which we know, those of *Denderah, Edfou, Esneh*, have all a court as preface to the sanctuary, but in every case those courts are rectangular. In the great temple of Philæ alone do we find the absence of parallelism of which Strabo speaks,[314] the peristylar court which follows the second pylon is rather narrower at its further extremity than immediately behind the pylon. In presence of this example of the trapezium form we may allow that it is quite possible that in the temples of Lower and Middle Egypt, which have perished, the form in question was more frequently employed than in those of Upper Egypt, where, among the remains of so many buildings, we find it but once.

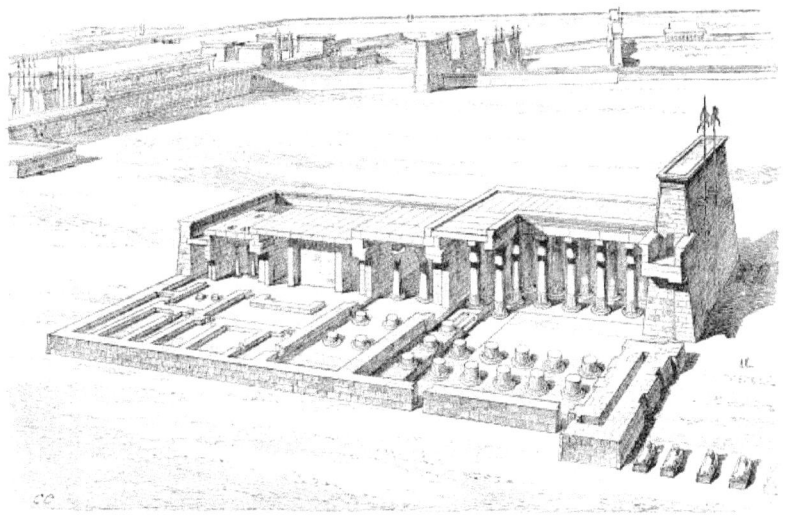

FIG. 208.—The temple of Khons; horizontal and vertical section showing the general arrangements of the temple.

To return to the Temple of Khons. From the courtyard of which we have been speaking, a high portal opens into a hall of little depth but of a width equal to that of the whole temple. The roof of this hall is supported by eight columns, the central four being rather higher than the others.[315] It is to this room that the name of hypostyle hall has been given. We can easily understand how Strabo saw in it the equivalent to the *pronaos* of the Greek temples. We know how in the great peripteral buildings of Greece and Italy, the *pronaos* prefaced the entrance to the *cella* with a double and sometimes a triple row of columns. Except that it is entirely inclosed by its walls, the Egyptian hypostyle had much the same appearance as the Greek *proanos*. Its name in those texts which treat of its construction is the *large hall*; but it is also called the *Hall of Assembly* and the *Hall of the Appearance*, terms which explain themselves. Only the kings and priests were allowed to penetrate into the sanctuary for the purpose of bringing forth the emblem or statue of the god from the tabernacle or other receptacle in which it was kept. This emblem or figure was placed either in a sacred boat or in one of those portable wooden tabernacles in which it was carried round the sacred inclosure to various resting places or altars. The crowd of priests and others who had been initiated but were of inferior rank awaited the appearance of the deity in the hypostyle hall, in which the *cortége* was marshalled before emerging into the courts.

FIG. 209.—The *bari*, or sacred boat; from the temple of Elephantiné.

The second division of the temple, for Strabo, was the sanctuary, or σηκός. In this Temple of Khons it was a rectangular chamber, separated by a wide corridor running round its four sides from two smaller chambers, which filled the spaces between the corridor and the external walls. In this hall fragments of a granite pedestal have been discovered, upon which either the *bari* or sacred boat, which is so often figured upon the bas-reliefs (Fig. 209), or some other receptacle containing the peculiar emblem of the local divinity, must have been placed. Strabo was no doubt correct in saying that the σηκός differed from the *cella* of the Greek temple in that it contained no statue of the divinity, but nevertheless it must have had something to distinguish it from the less sacred parts of the building. This something was a kind of little chapel, tabernacle, or shrine, closed by a folding door, and containing either an emblem or a statue of the divinity, before which prayers were recited and religious ceremonies performed on certain stated days. Sometimes this shrine was no more than an inclosed niche in the wall, sometimes it was a little edifice set up in the middle of the sanctuary. In those cases in which it was a structure of painted and gilded wood, like the ark of the Hebrews, it has generally disappeared and left no trace behind. The tabernacle in the Turin Museum (Fig. 210) is one of the few objects of the kind which have escaped complete destruction. In temples of any importance the shrine was hollowed out of a block of granite or basalt. A monolithic chapel of this kind is still in place in the Ptolemaic temple of Edfou; it bears the royal oval of Nectanebo I.[316] Examples are to be found in all the important European museums. One of the finest belongs to the Louvre and bears the name of Amasis; it is of red granite and is entirely covered with inscriptions and sculpture (Fig. 211).[317] It must resemble, on a smaller scale, the tabernacle prepared in the Elephantiné workshops, under Amasis, for the temple of Neith, at Sais, which so greatly excited the admiration of Herodotus.[318]

The doors of the shrine were kept shut and even sealed up. The king and the chief priest alone had the right to open them and to pay their devotions before the image or symbol which they inclosed. This seems clearly proved by the following passage from the famous stele discovered by Mariette at *Gebel-Barkal*, upon which the Ethiopian conqueror Piankhi-Mer-Amen celebrates his victories and the occupation of Egypt from south to north. After noticing the capture of Memphis he tells us that he stopped at Heliopolis in order that he might sacrifice to the gods in the royal fashion: "He mounted the steps which led to the great sanctuary in order that he might see the god who resides in Ha-benben, face to face. Standing alone, he drew the bolt, and swung open the folding doors; he looked upon the face of his father Ra in Ha-benben, upon the boat Mad, of Ra, and the boat Seket, of Shou; then he closed the doors, he set sealing clay upon them and impressed it with the royal signet."[319]

FIG. 210.—**Portable tabernacle of painted wood, 19th dynasty. In the Turin Museum.**

From the description of Strabo we should guess that the Egyptian temple ended with the sanctuary. Such was not the case however. Like most of the Greek temples, the Egyptian temple had its further chambers which served nearly the same purposes as the ὀπισθόδομοι of the Greeks. Thus in the Temple of Khons, the sanctuary opens, at the rear, into a second hypostyle hall which is smaller than the first and has its roof supported by only four columns instead of eight. Upon this hall open four small and separate chambers which fill up the whole space between it and the main walls.

FIG. 211.—Granite tabernacle: in the Louvre.

Similar general arrangements to those of the Temple of Khons are to be found in even the largest temples. The second hypostyle hall is however much larger and the chambers to which it gives access much more numerous. It is not easy to determine the object of each of these small apartments; in the Pharaonic temples they are usually in very bad condition, but in some of the Ptolemaic buildings, such as the temples of Edfou and Denderah, they are comparatively well preserved. In the last named the question is complicated by the existence of numerous blind passages contrived in the thickness of the walls. The stone which stopped the opening into these passages seems to have been manipulated by some secret mechanism.[320] Some of the sacred images and such emblems as were made of precious materials were kept in these hiding places. Their absolute darkness and the coolness which accompanied it, were both conducive to the preservation of delicately ornamented objects in such a climate as that of Egypt.

It was this part of the temple, then, that the Greeks called the treasure-house. It inclosed the material objects of worship. Some of its chambers, however, were consecrated to particular divinities and seem to have had somewhat of the same character as the apsidal chapels of a Roman Catholic Church. They are material witnesses to the piety of the princes who built them and who wished to associate the divinities in whose honour they were raised with the worship of the god to whom the temple as a whole had been dedicated.

Whether store-rooms or chapels, these apartments might be multiplied to any extent and might present great varieties of aspect. At Karnak, therefore, where they communicate with long and wide galleries, they are very numerous. One of them was that small chamber which was dismantled thirty years ago by Prisse d'Avennes and transported to Paris. It is known as the *Hall of Ancestors*. In it Thothmes III. is, in fact, represented in the act of worshipping sixty kings chosen from among his predecessors on the Egyptian throne.

The last feature noticed by Strabo in the small temple taken by him as a type, was the sculpture with which its walls were lavishly covered. These works reminded him of Etruscan sculpture and of Greek productions of the archaic period, but we can divine from the expressions[321] of which he makes use, that he perceived the principles which governed the Egyptian sculptor to be different from those of the Greeks. The Greek architect reserved certain strictly circumscribed places for sculpture, such as the friezes and pediments of the temples, while in Egypt it spreads itself indiscriminately over every surface. In the temple of Khons, as in every other building of the same kind at Thebes, we find this uninterrupted decoration. Mariette has shown the interesting nature of these representations and their value to the historian.

We have still to notice, always keeping the same edifice in view, two original points in the characteristic physiognomy of the Egyptian temple which seem to have escaped the attention of the Greek traveller.

In the Greek temple there is no space inclosed by a solid wall but that of the *cella*, which, by its purpose, answers to the σηκός of the Egyptian buildings. Both the peristyle and the pronaos are open to the air and to the view of all comers; the statues of the pediments, the reliefs of the friezes are all visible from outside, and the eye rejoices freely both in masterpieces of sculpture and in the long files of columns, which vary in effect as they are looked at from different points of view.

The appearance of the Egyptian temple is altogether dissimilar. The peristylar court, the hypostyle hall, the sanctuary and its adjuncts, in a word the whole combination of chambers and courts which form the temple proper, is surrounded by a curtain wall which is at least as high as the buildings which it incloses. Before any idea of the richness and architectural magnificence of the temple itself can be formed, this wall must be passed. From the outside nothing is to be seen but a great rectangular mass of building, the inclined faces of which seem to be endeavouring to meet at the top so as to give the greatest possible amount of privacy and security to the proceedings which take place within. The Egyptian temple may, in a word, be compared to a box (Fig. 61), and in such buildings as that dedicated to Khons, the box is a simple rectangular one. The partitions which separate its various halls and chambers are kept within the main wall. But in larger buildings the box is, partially at least, a double one. When we examine a plan of the great temple at Karnak, we see that all the back part of the vast pile, all that lies to the west of the open passage and the fourth pylon, is inclosed by a double wall. A sort of wide corridor, open to the sky, lies between the outer wall and that which immediately surrounds the various chambers. This outer wall is absent only on the side closed by the inner pylon. In some temples, especially in those of the Ptolemaic period, the hypostyle hall is withdrawn some distance behind the courtyard, and the sanctuary behind the hypostyle hall. This arrangement is repeated in the position of the two walls. The inner one embraces the chambers of the temple and follows their irregularities; the other describes three sides of a rectangle leaving a wider space at the back of the temple than at the sides. The pylon, as we have said, supplies the fourth side. This outer wall has no opening of any kind. It is true that at Karnak lateral openings exist in the hypostyle hall and in the courtyard, but those parts were less sacred in their character than the inner chambers to which they gave access. From the point where the wall becomes double, that is from the posterior wall of the hypostyle hall, there are no more external openings of any kind. To reach the presence of the deity the doors of the fourth and fifth pylons had to be passed. The high and thick wall, without opening of any kind, which inclosed the sanctuary and its dependencies like a cuirass, was no doubt intended to avert the possibility of clandestine visits to the holy place.

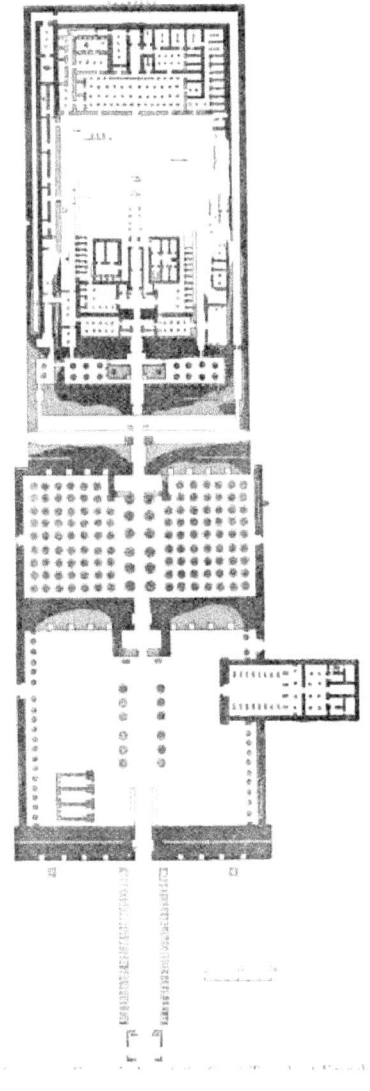

FIG. 212.—General plan of the Great Temple at Karnak.

The evident desire of the architect to hide his porticos and saloons behind an impenetrable curtain of limestone or sandstone suffices to prove that shadow rather than sunshine was wanted in the inner parts of the temple. When the slabs which formed the roofs of the temple of Khons were all in place—they are now mostly on the ground—it must have been very dark indeed. The hypostyle hall communicated directly and by an ample doorway with the open courtyard, which was bathed in the constant sunlight of Egypt; besides which there were openings just under the cornice and above the capitals of the columns. When the door was open, therefore, there would be no want of light, although it would be softened to a certain extent. The sanctuary was much darker. The light which came through the door was borrowed from the hypostyle hall. The hall with the four supporting columns and the chambers which surrounded it were still worse provided than the sanctuary; the first named was feebly illuminated by small openings in the stone roof, the latter were in almost complete darkness. The only one which could have enjoyed a little light was that which lay on the central axis of the building. A few feeble rays may have found their way to this chamber when the doors of the temple were open, but, as a rule, they seem to have been closed. Marks of hinges have been found in the Egyptian temples, and it is certain that the sanctuary was permanently closed in some fashion against the unbidden visits of the curious.[322]

We shall return elsewhere to the illumination of the Egyptian temples, and shall discuss the various methods made use of to ensure sufficient light for the enjoyment of the sumptuous decorations lavished upon them; here, however, it will be sufficient if we indicate their general character, which is the same in all the religious edifices in the country.

The largest and best lighted chambers are those nearest to the entrance. As we leave the last pylon behind and penetrate deeply into the temple, the light gradually becomes less and the chambers diminish in size, until the building comes to an end in a number of small apartments in which the darkness is unbroken. There are even some temples which become gradually narrower and lower from front to back; this is especially the case with those which have a double wall round their more sacred parts.

This progressive diminution is even more clearly marked in a vertical section than in one taken horizontally. The pylon is much higher than any other point in the building. After the pylon, in the temple of Khons, comes the portico which surrounds the courtyard. Next come in their order the columns of the hypostyle hall, the roof of the sanctuary, the roof of the chamber with four columns, and the roof of the last small apartment which rests upon the inclosing wall. Between the large hypostyle hall and the smaller one there is a difference in height amounting to a quarter of the whole height of the former.

In the most important temples, such as those of Karnak, Luxor, and the Ramesseum, the same *law of constant diminution in height from front to rear* holds good, with the exception that in their cases it is the hypostyle hall which is the highest point in the building after the pylons. In this hall their architects have raised the loftiest columns, and it is after these that the progressive diminution begins. The longitudinal section of the temple of Luxor (Fig. 213) and the general view of Karnak (plate v.) illustrate this statement.

As the roofs of the temple chambers are gradually lowered, their carefully paved floors are raised, but not to an equal degree. In the temple of Khons four steps lead up from the court to the hypostyle hall, and one step from the hall to the sanctuary. Similar arrangements are found elsewhere. At Karnak a considerable flight is interposed between the courtyard and the vestibule of the hypostyle hall. At Luxor the level of the second court is higher than that of the first. In the Ramesseum there are three flights of steps between the first and second hypostyle hall.

All these buildings are provided with staircases by which their flat roofs may be reached. These roofs seem to have been freely opened to the people. The interiors of the temples were only to be visited by the priests, except on a few stated days and in a fashion prescribed by the Egyptian ritual; but the general public were allowed to mount to the roofs, just as with us they are allowed to ascend domes and belfries for the sake of the view over the surrounding buildings and country. The numerous *graffiti*, some in the hieroglyphic, others in the demotic character, which are still to be seen upon the roof of the temple of Khons, attest this fact.

We thus find the characteristic features of Egyptian architecture united in a single building in this temple of Khons; but, even at Thebes, no such similarity between one building and another is to be found as in the great temples of Greece. In passing from the Parthenon to the temple of Theseus or to that of Jupiter Olympius, from a Doric to an Ionic, and from an Ionic to a

Corinthian building, certain well marked variations, certain changes of style, proportion and decoration are seen. But the differences are never sufficient to embarrass the student of those buildings. The object of each part remains sufficiently well defined and immutable to be easily recognised by one who has mastered a single example. In Egypt the variations are much greater even among buildings erected during a single dynasty and by a single architect. After the attentive study of some simple and well marked building, like the temple of Khons, the visitor proceeds to inspect the ruins of Karnak, Luxor, the Ramesseum, Medinet-Abou or Gournah, and attempts to restore something like order in his mind while walking among their ruins. But in vain are the rules remembered which were thought to apply to all such buildings; they are of little help in unravelling the mazes of Karnak or Luxor, and at each new ruin explored the visitor's perplexities begin anew.

GENERAL VIEW OF EXISTING BUILDINGS AT KARNAK RESTORED BY CHARLES CHIPIEZ

The variations are, in fact, very great, but they are not so great as they seem at the first glance. They are generally to be explained by those developments and repetitions of which Egyptian architects were so fond. We shall endeavour to demonstrate this by glancing rapidly at each of the more celebrated Theban buildings in turn. Our purpose does not require that we should describe any of them in detail, as we have already done in the case of the temple of Khons, and we shall be content with noticing their variations upon the type established by our study of the minor monument.

FIG. 213.—Longitudinal section of the Temple of Luxor. Restored by Ch. Chipiez.

Let us take Karnak first. This, the most colossal assemblage of ruins which the world has to show, comprises no less than eleven separate temples within its four inclosing walls of crude brick. The longest axis of this collection of ruins is that from north to south; it measures about 1,560 yards; its transverse axis is 620 yards long. The whole circuit of the walls is nearly two English miles and a half.[323]

The first thing that strikes us in looking at a general map of Karnak is that Egyptian temples were not oriented.[324] The Great Temple is turned to the west, that of Khons to the south, that of Mouth to the north. There is some doubt as to the name which should be given to several of these buildings. Two of the most important are consecrated to those deities who, with Amen, form the Theban triad. The highest and largest of them all, that which is called the *Great Temple*, is dedicated to Amen-Ra.

We are here concerned with the latter building only. We reproduce, on a much larger scale and in two parts (Fig. 214 on page 363, and Fig. 215 on page 367), the plan given on page 358 (Fig. 212). A few figures will suffice to give an idea of the several dimensions. From the external doorway of the first western pylon to the eastern extremity of the building, the length, over all, is 1,215 feet. Its greatest width is that of the first pylon, namely 376 feet. The total circumference of the bounding wall is about 3,165 feet. The outside curtain wall of brick is from 2,500 to 2,700 yards in length, which corresponds closely to the 13 stadia said by Diodorus to be the circumference of the oldest of the four great Theban temples.[325]

After passing the first pylon (No. 1 on the plan) we find ourselves in a peristylar court answering to that in the temple of Khons. On our right and left respectively we leave two smaller temples, one of which (C on plan) cuts through the outer wall and was built by Rameses III.; Seti II. was the author of the other (D). Those two buildings are older than the court and its colonnades. When the princes of the twenty-second dynasty added this peristyle to the already constructed parts of the great temple, they refrained from destroying those monuments to the piety of their ancestors. We also may regard these temples as mere accidents in the general arrangement. We may follow the path marked out down the centre of the court by the remains of an avenue of columns which dates from the times of the Ethiopian conquerors and of the Bubastide kings (E). After the second pylon (2) comes the hypostyle hall, the wonder of Karnak, and the largest room constructed by the Egyptians (F). It is 340 feet long by 170 wide.[326] One hundred and thirty-four colossal columns support, or rather did once support, the roof, which, in the central portion, was not less than 76 feet above the floor; in this central portion, twelve pillars of larger proportions than the others form an avenue; these columns are 11 feet 10 inches in diameter and more than 33 feet in circumference, so that, in bulk, they are equal to the column of Trajan. They are, without a doubt, the most massive pillars ever employed within a building. From the ground to the summit of the cube which supports the architrave, they are 70 feet high. Right and left of the central avenue the remaining 122 columns form a forest of pillars supporting a flat roof, which is lower than that of the central part by 33 feet. The cathedral of Notre Dame, at Paris, would stand easily upon the surface covered by this hall (see Plate V.).

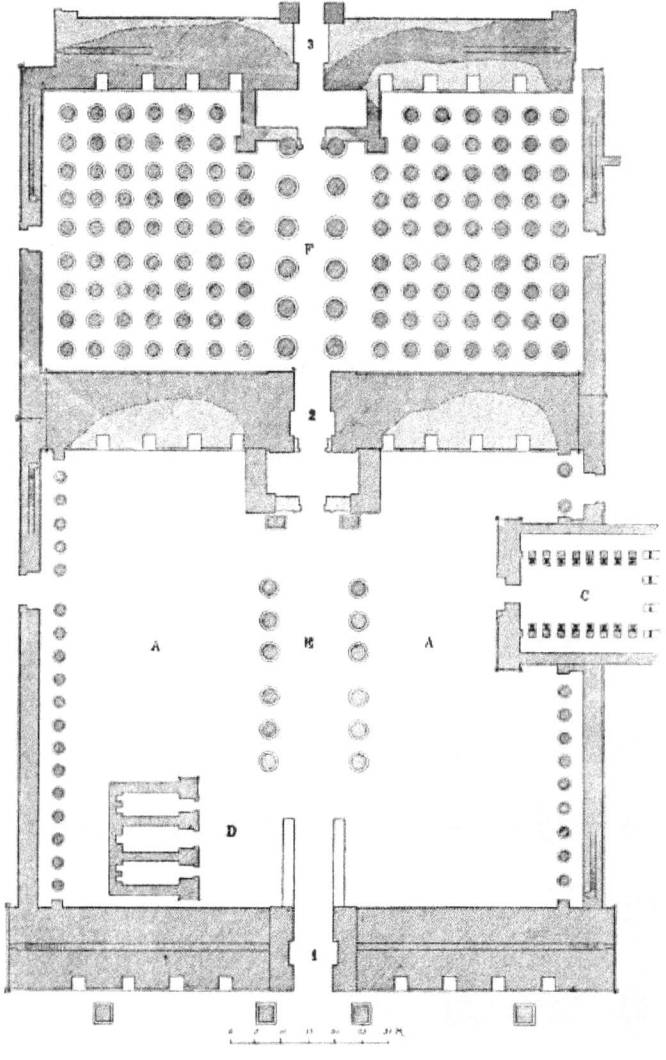

Fig. 214.—Plan of the anterior portion of the Great Temple at Karnak. From the plan of M. Brune.

Its proportions are very different from those of the corresponding chamber in the little temple of Khons, but yet it fills the same office in the general conception, it is constructed on the same principle and lighted in the same fashion. To use the expression of Strabo, we have here a real *pronaos* or *ante-temple*, because a passage, open to the sky, intervenes between it and that part of the building which contains the sanctuary. The four doorways[327] with which this vast hall is provided seem to indicate that it was more accessible than the parts beyond the passage just mentioned.

We cannot pretend to determine the uses of all those chambers which encumber with their ruins the further parts of the great building. It is certain however that between them they constitute the *naos*, or temple properly speaking. They are surrounded by a double wall and there is but one door by which they can be reached—precautions which suffice to prove the peculiarly sacred character of this part of the whole rectangle. In which of these chambers are we to find the σηκός? Was it, as the early observers thought, in those granite apartments which are marked H on the plan? This locality was suggested by the extra solicitude as to the strength and beauty of those chambers betrayed by the use of a more beautiful and costly material upon them than upon the rest of the temple. Moreover, the chamber (H) which is situated upon the major axis of the temple bears a strong resemblance in shape as well as position, to the sanctuary of the temple of Khons, in the case of which no doubt was possible. Or must we follow Mariette when he places the sanctuary in the middle of the eastern court (I in plan)? All traces of it have now almost vanished, but Mariette based his opinion upon the fact that in the ruins of this court alone are to be found any traces of the old temple dating back to the days of the Amenemhats and Ousourtesens of the twelfth dynasty. He does not attempt to account, however, for those carefully built granite apartments which seem to most visitors to be the real sanctuary, or, at least, the sanctuary of the temple as reconstructed and enlarged by the princes of the second Theban Empire.

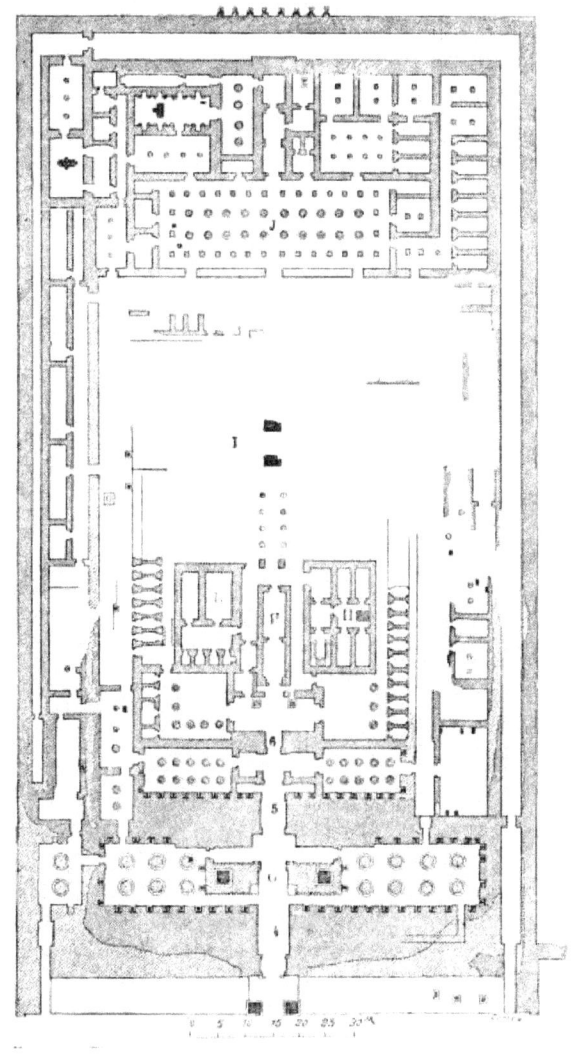

Fig. 215.—The Great Temple at Karnak; inner portion; from the plan of M. Brune.

In the actual state of the ruins the doubts on this point are, perhaps, irremovable. But the final determination of the question would be of no particular moment to our argument. For our purposes it is sufficient to note that in the Great Temple, as in the Temple of Khons, the sanctuary was surrounded and followed by a considerable number of small apartments. In the Great Temple these chambers are very numerous and some of them are large enough to require central supports for their ceilings in the form of one or more columns. In other respects they are similar to those in the Temple of Khons.

INTERIOR OF THE HYPOSTYLE HALL AT KARNAK

The resemblance between the two temples is completed by the existence in both of a minor hypostyle hall behind the sanctuary. The hall of four columns of the smaller building corresponds to the large saloon called the *Hall of Thothmes*, in the Great Temple (J). The roof of this saloon is supported by twenty columns disposed in two rows and by square piers standing free of the walls. It is 146 feet wide, and from 53 to 57 feet deep. Immediately before the granite apartments, and between the fifth and sixth pylons, another hall, also with two ranges of columns but not so deep as the last, is introduced. Its position shows it to be meant for a vestibule to the naos properly speaking.

The fine *Court of the Caryatides* with its Osiride pillars, the first chamber entered by the visitors who penetrate into the temple proper, seems to have been designed for a similar purpose (G).

FIG. 216.—**Karnak as it is at present.
The ruins of a pylon and of the hypostyle hall.**

If we wish, then, to evolve some order out of the seeming chaos of Karnak; if we wish to find among its ruins the essential characteristics, the vital organs, if we may put it so, of the Egyptian temple, we have only to apply the method of analysis and reduction suggested by examination of simpler monuments, and to take account of the long series of additions which resulted in the finally stupendous dimensions of the whole mass.[328] These additions may be distinguished from one another by their scale of proportions and by their methods of construction. When rightly examined the gigantic ruins of the great temple of Amen betray those simple lines and arrangements, which form, as we have shown, the original type.

The same remark may be applied to the other great building on the left bank of the river, the Temple of Luxor. There, too, the architecture is, to use the words of Champollion, the "architecture of giants." From the first pylon to the innermost recesses of the sanctuary the building measures about 850 feet.

No traveller can avoid being deeply impressed by the first sight of its lofty colonnades, by its tall and finely proportioned pillars rearing their majestic capitals among the palms and above the huts of the modern village. These columns belong to the first hypostyle hall, and, were they not buried for two-thirds of their height, they would be, from the ground up to the base of their capitals, rather more than 50 feet high; the capitals and the cubes above them measure about 18 feet more.

The plan of Luxor is more simple than that of Karnak; it was built in two "heats" only, to borrow an expression from the athletes, under Amenophis III. and Rameses II. In later periods it underwent some insignificant retouches, and that is all. It is narrower than its great neighbour, and covers a very much less space of ground, neither has it so many chambers, and yet we are in some respects more at a loss in attempting to assign their proper uses to its apartments and in finding some equivalent for them in the elementary type from which we started, than we were in the larger temple.

It is true that the proper character of the *naos* is better marked at Luxor than elsewhere. The sanctuary may be determined at a glance. It consists of a rectangular chamber standing in the middle of a large square hall; it is the only chamber in the whole building for which granite has been used; it has two doors, one in each end, exactly upon the major axis of the building. The hall in which it is placed is preceded by a vestibule, and surrounded by those small chambers which are always found in this part of a temple. So far, then, there is nothing to embarrass us; everything is in conformity with the principles which have been laid down.

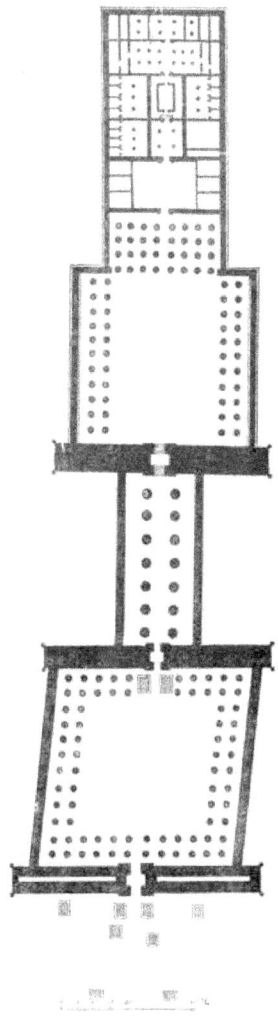

FIG. 217.—Plan of the Temple of Luxor.

The real difficulty begins when we look round us for the *pronaos*, and examine the hypostyle halls. Here, as elsewhere, there is a hall of modest dimensions beyond the sanctuary. It is supported by twelve columns. There is another, much wider and deeper, in front of the naos; it has thirty-two of those lofty columns of which we have already spoken. By its design, situation, and the spacing of its columns, it reminds us of the hypostyle hall of Karnak. It differs from it in being open, without any external wall towards the court; so that it may be called a portico with four ranges of columns. Moreover, again unlike the Karnak hall, it is by no means the most imposing feature of the whole edifice. The greatest elevation and the most imposing proportions, so far as the interior of the building is concerned, are to be found in the great gallery which leads from the first to the second court, from the second to the third pylon. This gallery is in effect a hypostyle hall, but it differs profoundly from the superb edifice which bears that name at Karnak. It is long and narrow and looks more like a mere covered corridor than an ample hall in which the eager crowd could find elbow-room.

The place occupied by this hall in the whole composition is equally singular. It has been ascertained that the first pylon and the peristylar courtyard behind it date from the time of Rameses II., while all the rest of the building, from what is at present the second pylon inwards, was built by Amenophis III. The doorway in the second pylon leads immediately into the grand gallery, some 176 feet long, of which we have been speaking.

We can hardly tell, therefore, where to look for the true pronaos at Luxor. In that part of the ground plan where it is generally found there is nothing but an open portico, which is considerably lower than the highest parts of the building. The great colonnade, again, is separated from the naos by an open court, so that it ought, perhaps, to be classified as what the Greeks called a propylæum; but yet it is a hall, inclosed and covered, of great size and height, and richly decorated, like the hypostyle halls which we have already described and others which we have yet to notice.[329]

FIG. 218.—Bird's-eye view of Luxor, as restored by M. Ch. Chipiez.

Another peculiarity of Luxor is its change of axis. The first pylon, that of Rameses, is not parallel with the two built by Amenophis; the angle at which they stand is a very perceptible one. Neither is the doorway of this pylon in alignment with the other doorways on the major axis of the building. No justification or even explanation of this irregularity, which is unique among the Theban temples, has been discovered.

If we cross the Nile and land upon the plain which stretches between the river and the Libyan hills, we find ourselves in the presence of those temples, the Ramesseum, Medinet-Abou, and Gournah, whose funerary destination we have already noticed. These are royal chapels erected in connection with the royal tombs in their neighbourhood, they are cenotaphs filled with the memories of the great Theban princes, and with representations of their exploits. Consequently we do not find in them those complications which, in the great temples of the right bank, mark the successive dynasties to which their final form was due. But yet the difference in general appearance is not great; there is however, one distinction which, as it goes far to prove the peculiar character of these buildings, should be carefully noticed. In no one of them, if we may judge from plans which have been made, has any chamber or structure been found which corresponds to the sanctuary or σηκός, of the temples of Amen or Khons. The absence of such a chamber might easily be explained by our supposition that these buildings were funerary chapels; as such they would require no depository for those mysterious symbols of this or that deity which the temples proper contained: they were the lineal descendants of the upper chambers in the mastabas, in which no rudiment of such a thing is to be found. On the other hand, we have reason to believe that the great Theban divinities were associated in the worship paid to deceased kings. If that were so these funerary temples might well have been arranged like those of the right bank. The inner portions of the Ramesseum and of Medinet-Abou are so ruinous that the question cannot be settled by the examination of their remains.

The Ramesseum certainly appears to have been the monument described by Diodorus as the *Tomb of Osymandias*, a name which has never been satisfactorily explained.[330] It is also called by the *Institut d'Égypte*, the Palace of Memnon and the Memnonium, upon the faith of Strabo's identification of Ismandes and Memnon.[331] It is to Champollion that this building owes the restoration of its true title, under which it is now generally known.

Without being so colossal as Karnak, the size of the Ramesseum would astonish us anywhere but in Egypt. When it was complete, it must have been as large as Luxor before the additions of Rameses II. were made, if not larger. The first pylon was 226 feet wide; the whole of its upper part is destroyed. [332] Immediately behind this pylon comes a vast peristylar court, almost square on plan (186 feet by 173). On the left the remains of a double colonnade exist, which must at one time have extended along at least two sides of the quadrangle. At the further end of this court and directly facing the back of the pylon, was a colossal statue of Rameses. Although seated, this statue was more than 56 feet high; its fragments now cover a considerable amount of the courtyard. A grand doorway, pierced through the centre of the wall upon which the defeat of the Khetas is painted, leads to a second court, a little less extensive than the first. Right and left there are porticos, each with a double range of columns. On the side of the entrance and on that opposite to it there are single ranges of Osiride figures. Many of these figures are still standing; they are 31 feet high.

THEBES

Three flights of steps lead up from this court into a vestibule ornamented with two colossal busts of Rameses and with a row of columns. From this vestibule the hypostyle hall is reached by three doorways of black granite. It measures 136 feet wide and 103 deep. Its roof is supported by forty-eight columns, in eight ranges of six each, counting from front to rear. Five of these eight ranges are still standing and still afford support to a part of the ceiling. This latter is painted with golden stars upon a blue ground, in imitation of the vault of heaven. The side walls have entirely disappeared.
[333]

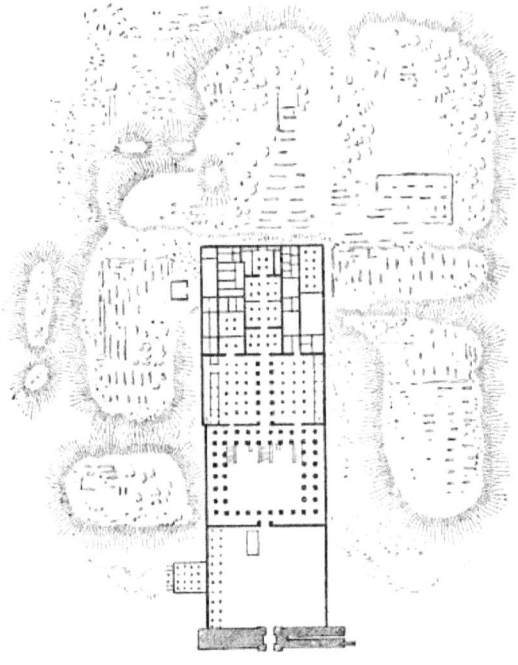

FIG. 219.—Plan of the Ramesseum (from Lepsius.)

This hall resembles that at Karnak, both in its plan and in its general appearance. The mode of lighting is the same; the arrangement is the same; there is in both a wide passage down the centre, supported by columns thicker and higher than the rest, from which they are also distinguished by the nobility of their bell-shaped capitals. At Karnak the hall was begun by Rameses I. and Seti; Rameses II. did no more than carry on the work of his predecessors. He heard the chorus of admiration with which the completion of such a superb building must have been hailed, and we can easily understand that he was thereby incited to reproduce its happy arrangement and majestic proportions in the great temple which he was erecting in his own honour on the left bank of the river.

Ambitious though he was, Rameses II. could not attempt to give the colossal dimensions of the great temple of Amen to what was, after all, no more than the chapel of his own tomb. The great hall at Karnak required three reigns, two of them very long ones, for its completion. In the Ramesseum an attempt was made to compensate for inferior size by extra care in the details and by the beauty of the workmanship. The tall columns of the central nave were no more than thirty-six feet high, including base and capital, the others were only twenty-five feet; but they surpassed the pillars at Karnak by the elegance of their proportions.

The admiration excited in us by the ruins of Karnak is mingled with astonishment, almost with stupefaction, but at the Ramesseum we are more charmed although we are less surprised. We see that, when complete, it must have had a larger share than its rival of that beauty into which merely colossal dimensions do not enter.[334]

Beyond the hall there are wide chambers, situated upon the major axis of the building, and each with its roof supported by eight columns. Beyond them again there is a fourth and smaller chamber which has only four columns. Round these rooms a number of smaller ones are gathered; they are all in a very fragmentary state, and among them no vestige of anything like a *secos* has been found. On the other hand, the bas-reliefs in one of the larger rooms seem to confirm the assertion of Diodorus, in his description of the *Tomb of Osymandias*, that the library was placed in this part of the building.[335]

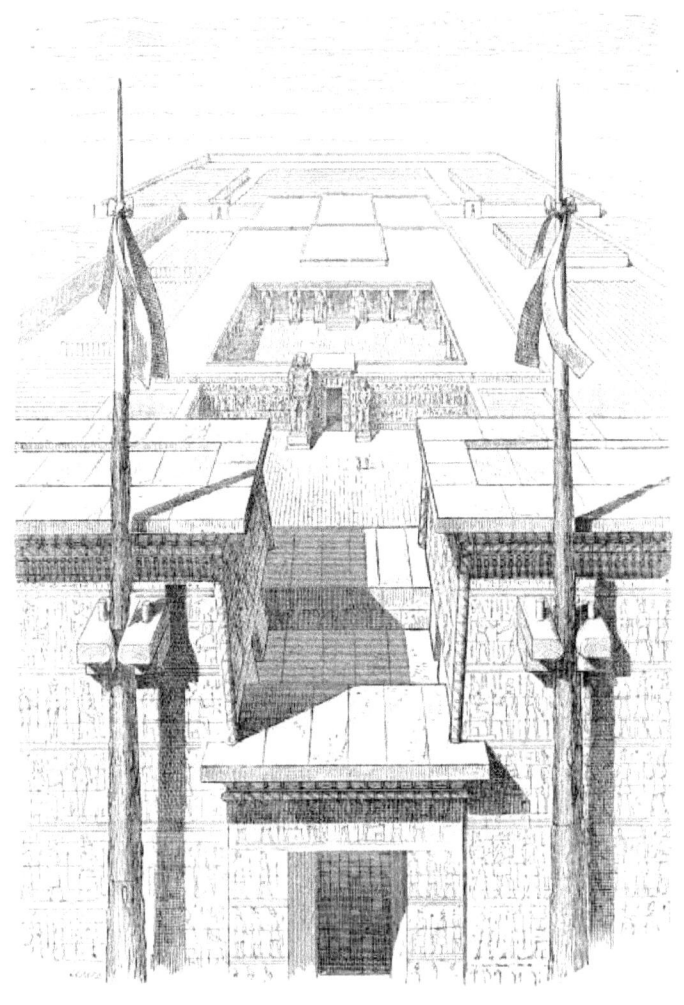

FIG. 220.—The Ramesseum.
Bird's-eye view of the general arrangement,
restored by M. Ch. Chipiez.

The Ramesseum was formerly surrounded by brick structures of a peculiar character, some of which are yet to be found in good preservation at about 50 metres from the north face of the building. They consist of a double range of vaults closely abutting on each other, numbering from ten to twelve in each range, and surmounted by a platform. If it be true that a library was included in the building, these curious structures, which are situated within the outer bounding wall of the temple, may have contained rooms for lodging and instructing students, as well as chambers for the priests. In that case Rameses would deserve the credit of having founded, like the Mussulman sovereigns, a *médressé*, or sort of university, by the side of his *turbeh* and *mosque*. Additional probability is given to this conjecture both by certain discoveries which have been made in tombs near the Ramesseum and by the evidence of several papyri.[336] But for these texts we should be inclined to believe that these remains are the ruins of storehouses.

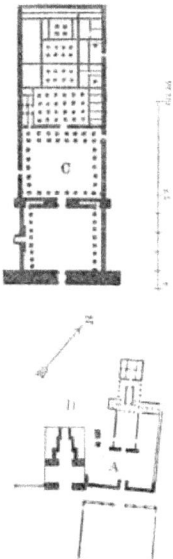

Fig. 221.—General plan of the buildings at Medinet-Abou.

About a thousand yards south-west of the Ramesseum rises the group of buildings which is known by the name of the modern village of Medinet-Abou. It was not until the second half of the present century had commenced that they were cleared from the *débris* and modern huts which concealed many of their parts. The group is composed of three distinct buildings in one enclosure. The oldest is a temple built by Thothmes II. and Thothmes III. and afterwards enlarged by the Ptolemies and the Roman Emperors (A on plan). The other two date from the time of Rameses III., the founder of the twentieth dynasty. They both lie upon the same axis, they are connected by a sphinx avenue, and they must certainly be considered as two parts of one whole. The first of the three which we encounter in approaching the group from the river is known as the Royal Pavilion or Pavilion of Rameses III. (B). Ninety yards farther to the north we come upon the great temple, the funerary character of which we have already explained (C). It is a second *Ramesseum*, and to avoid confusion it is generally known as the *Great Temple of Medinet-Abou*. We shall return to the Royal Pavilion presently, and, as for the Temple of Thothmes, which was consecrated to Amen, its really ancient portion is of too little importance to detain us long. It consists merely of an isolated secos surrounded on three sides by an open gallery upheld by square piers and, upon the fourth, by a block containing six small chambers (Fig. 222).

The great temple, however, whose picturesque ruins attract every visitor to Thebes, deserves to be carefully considered even in our summary review.[337] It bears a striking resemblance to the Ramesseum. Their dimensions are nearly the same. The first pylon at Medinet-Abou is 210 feet wide. The two courts which follow and isolate the second pylon are severally 113 feet by 140, and 126 feet by 136. The plan of Medinet-Abou does not differ (223) in any very important points from that of the Ramesseum. Upon two of its sides only, those which are at right angles to the face of the pylon, the first quadrangle has colonnades. One of these colonnades, that on the right of a visitor entering the temple, consists of a row of pillars faced with caryatides of Osiris. These Osiride piers are repeated in the second court, where a double colonnade, five steps above the pavement, leads to the pronaos. The latter seems too small for the two peristyles. It has only twenty-four supporting columns, in four rows of six each, counting from front to back of the building. These columns are smaller in section than those of the peristyles, and the eight which constitute the central nave do not differ from their companions.[338] This hypostyle hall lacks, therefore, some of the remember the suburb of Eyoub, where the *turbehs* of the Ottoman princes stand half hidden among the cypresses and plane trees.

The material condition which compelled the Sait princes to break with the customs of their ancestors, affected the tombs of private individuals also. Throughout the existence of the Egyptian monarchy the inhabitants of the Delta were obliged to set about the preservation of their dead in a different fashion to that followed by their neighbours in Upper Egypt; their mummies had to be kept out of reach of the inundation. Isolated monuments, like those of Abydos, would soon have filled all the available space upon artificial mounds, such as those upon which the cities of the Delta were built. The problem to be solved was, however, a simple one. Since there could be no question of a lateral development, like that of the Theban tombs, or of a downward one, like that of the Memphite mummy pits, it was obvious that the development must be upwards. A beginning was made by constructing, at some distance from a town, a platform of crude brick, upon which, after its surface had been raised above the level of the highest floods, the mummies were placed in small chambers closely packed one against another. As soon as the whole platform was occupied, another layer of chambers was commenced above it. Champollion discovered the remains of two such cemeteries in the immediate neighbourhood of Sais. The larger of the two was not less than 1,400 feet long, 500 feet wide, and 80 feet high; an enormous mass "which resembled," he said, "a huge rock torn by lightning or earthquake."[280] No doubt was possible as to the character of the mass; Champollion found among the débris both canopic vases and funerary statuettes. Within a few years of his death Mariette undertook some fresh excavations in the same neighbourhood; they led to no very important results, but they confirmed the justice of the views enunciated by Champollion. Most of the objects recovered were in a very bad state of preservation; the materials had been too soft, and in time the dampness, which had impregnated the base of the whole structure, had crept upwards through the porous brick, and turned the whole mass into a gigantic sponge.

These tombs resemble those of the kings in having no well; and as for the funerary chapel we do not as yet know whether it existed at all, how it was arranged, or what took its place. Perhaps each of the more carefully constructed tombs was divided into two parts, a chamber more or less decorated and a niche contrived in the masonry, like the rock-cut ovens of the extended to the sanctuary and its dependencies in the rear. The last of the great Theban Pharaohs certainly drew much of his inspiration from the work of his illustrious predecessors. In their present state of mutilation it is impossible to decide which was the finer of the two in their complete state. To the fine hypostyle hall of the Ramesseum, Medinet-Abou could oppose the Royal Pavilion which rose in front of the temple and grouped itself so happily with the first pylon, affording one of the most effective compositions in the whole range of Egyptian architecture.

e mummy was introduced, the niche was
would remain open for the funerary
s situated at some height above the level
: block of buildings, should be reached, a
nd inclined planes was necessary. In the
he first layer and especially those in the
med and buried from sight and access by
d around them. The families to which they
t, and no one was left to watch over their
ie infiltration of the Nile water, these lower
iave furnished many interesting objects to
em likely that, if deep trenches were driven
agglomerations of unbaked brick, many
ade.[281] Such a system left slight scope to
have been carefully parcelled out to each
much less elbow room than when he was
intain or building upon the dry soil of the
if time had left any for our inspection, could
ging of the funerary architecture of Sais, but,
liged to be content with what we can gather
iains as to the prevailing taste of the epoch.

the south of the Great Pyramid, Colonel Vyse
37, an important tomb to which he gave the
then British Consul-General in Egypt. The
entirely disappeared, but we may conclude that
iterranean portion. The maker of the tomb had
extent by a trench cut around it in the rock. The
; trench are 89 feet by 74. A passage had been
:es to the well, which had been covered in all
icture. The well opens upon a point nearer to the
dimensions are quite exceptional. It is 54 feet 4
oy 26 feet 8 inches in horizontal section; it
ch is covered by a vault 11 feet 2 inches thick. It
iamber, but in small lateral grottos that several
:, white quartz, &c., were found. The remains of
This tomb dates from the time of Psemethek I.

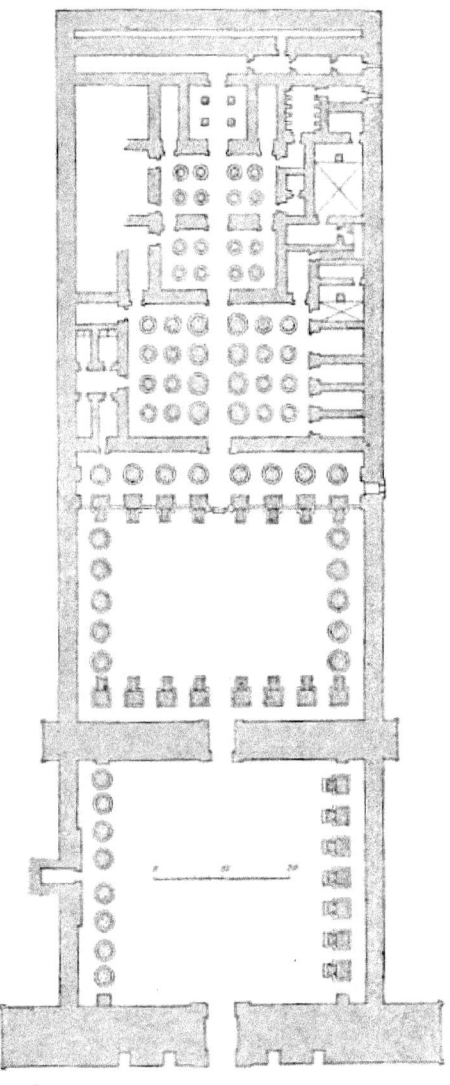

FIG. 223.—**Plan of the great Temple at Medinet-Abou. (Communicated by M. Brune.)**

The rest of the temples in this neighbourhood and within the enclosures at Karnak are all more or less intimately allied to the type we have established, and need not be noticed in detail.[339]

We have good reason to believe that the type of temple which we have described was a common one in other parts of Egypt than Thebes. The temples of Memphis, of Heliopolis and of the Delta cities, have perished and, practically, left no trace behind; but the great buildings constructed by the Theban conquerors outside the limits of Egypt proper, in Nubia, are in comparatively good preservation. One of these, the Temple of *Soleb*, built by Thothmes III. and reconstructed by Amenophis III., must have borne a strong resemblance to the Ramesseum, so far as can be judged through the discrepancies in the available plans of the first-named building. Cailliaud only allows it one peristylar court, while Hoskins and Lepsius give it two. According to Cailliaud, its hypostyle hall, which must have been a very beautiful one, contained forty-eight columns. After it came another hall, with a roof supported by twelve columns. This was surrounded by small chambers, the remains of which are very confused. In the plan given by Lepsius there are two hypostyle halls with a wall between them, an arrangement which is also found at Abydos. The outer one must have had twenty-four columns, the largest in the building, and the second forty, of rather less diameter; the remainder of the temple has disappeared.[340]

We find analogous arrangements in the great temple of Napata (*Gebel-Barkal*). Built by Amenophis III. when Napata was the seat of an Egyptian pro-consul, and repaired by Tahraka when Ethiopia became supreme over Egypt, this temple resembles the Theban buildings in its plan. From a peristylar court enclosed between two pylons, we pass into a hypostylar hall containing forty-six columns; behind this hall comes the sanctuary, in its usual position, with its *entourage* of small chambers. We may call this the *classic type* of Egypt.

The temples which we have hitherto examined are chiefly remarkable for the simplicity of their plan. A single sanctuary forms the centre and, so to speak, the heart of the whole composition. Pylons, peristylar courts and hypostylar halls, are but anterooms and vestibules to this all important chamber; while the small apartments which surround it afford the necessary accommodation for the material adjuncts of Egyptian worship. In the great temple at Karnak, the anterior and posterior dependencies are developed to an extraordinary extent, but this development is always in the direction of the length, or to speak more accurately, of the depth of the building. The smaller faces of the whole rectangle are continually carried farther from each other by the additions of fresh chambers and architectural features, which are distributed, with more or less regular alternation, on the right and left of the major axis which always passes through the centre of the *secos*. The building, therefore, in spite of many successive additions always contrives to preserve the unity of its organic constitution.

But all the great buildings in Egypt which were constructed for the service of religion were not so simply designed. A good instance of a more complex arrangement is to be found in the great temple at Abydos (Fig. 224). It was begun by Seti I. and finished by Rameses II. Mariette freed it from the *débris* and modern hovels which encumbered it, and, thanks to his efforts, there are now few monuments in Egypt whose inner arrangements can be more clearly and certainly perceived.

Its general shape is singular. The courts and the pronaos compose a narrow and elongated rectangle, with which the parts corresponding to the sanctuary and its dependent chambers form a right angle (see Fig. 224). This salient wing has no corresponding excrescence on the other side. We might consider the building unfinished, but that there is no sign whatever that the architect meant to complete it with another wing at the opposite angle. The Egyptians were never greatly enamoured of that exact symmetry which has become one of the first artistic necessities of our time.

Still more surprising than the eccentricity of its plan, are the peculiar arrangements which are to be found in the interior of this temple. As at Medinet-Abou and the Ramesseum, there are two courts, each preceded by a pylon. After these comes the pronaos. The courts differ from those at Thebes in having no peristyles or colonnades. The only thing of the kind is a row of square pillars standing before the inner wall of the second court (see plan). This is a poor equivalent for the majestic colonnades and files of caryatides which we have hitherto encountered.

The suppression of the portico has a great effect upon the appearance of these two courts. It deprives them of the rich shadows cast by the long colonnades and their roofs of the Theban temples, and the long walls must have seemed rather cold and monotonous in spite of the bas-reliefs and paintings which covered them. Their absence, however, is not allowed to affect the general lines of the plan.

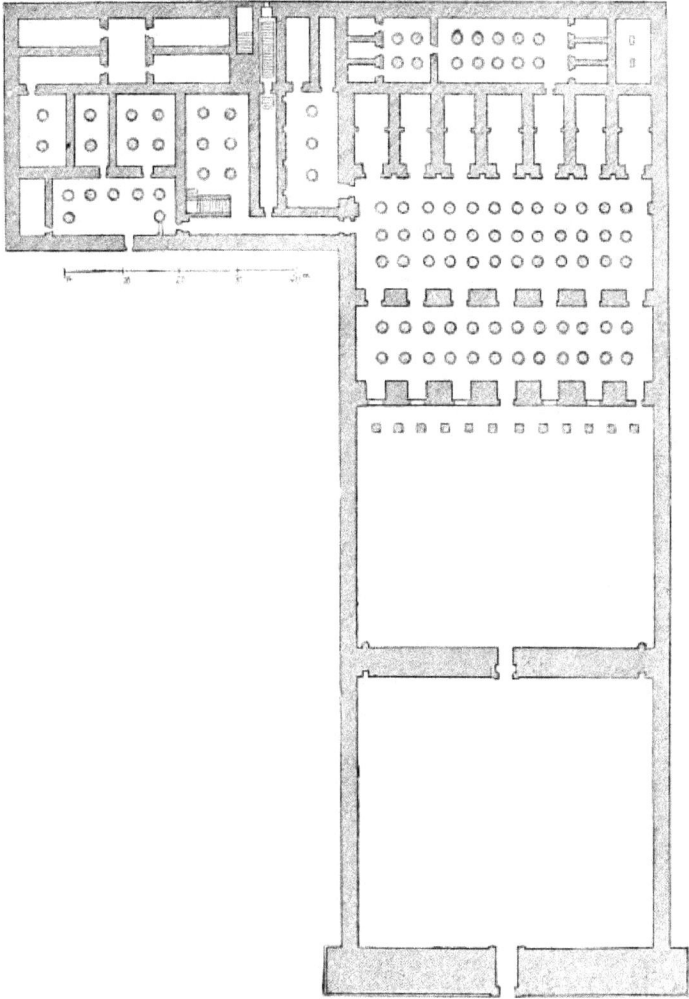

Fig. 224.—Plan of the Temple at Abydos (from Mariette).

We have given neither an elevation nor a section of the temple at Abydos, because neither the one nor the other was to be had. The building was hardly known until Mariette freed it from the *débris* with which it was engulphed. He, too, studied rather as an egyptologist than as an architect, and was content with making known its internal arrangements by a plan. This plan does not appear to be minutely exact. A little farther on we shall have to speak of a peculiarity which exists at Abydos, but which is not hinted at in the adjoining plan; some of the columns are coupled in the first hypostyle hall. We take this fact from the *Description*, where the measurements are given in a fashion which forbids all doubt of their fidelity.

It is when we arrive at the pronaos that we fail to recognize the disposition to which we have grown accustomed. There is no central nave, with its columns of extra size and more careful design, leading to the closed door of the sanctuary. There are two hypostyle halls, the first supported by twenty-four, the second by thirty-six columns. They are separated by a wall pierced with seven doorways, each doorway corresponding to one of the aisles between the columns. In the farther wall of the second of these halls, there are seven more doorways, corresponding to the last named, and opening upon seven oblong vaulted saloons, all of one size and completely isolated one from another.

By their situation on the plan, by their form, and by the decoration of their walls, these vaulted chambers declare themselves to be so many sanctuaries. Each one of them is dedicated to some particular deity, whose name and image appear in the decorations of the chamber itself and also upon the lintel of the door outside. These names and images are again repeated upon all the surfaces presented by the aisle which leads up to the door.

The seven deities thus honoured, beginning at the right, are Horus, Isis, Osiris, Amen, Harmachis, Ptah, and Seti himself, whom we thus find assimilated with the greatest of the Egyptian gods. Each chamber contains a collection of thirty-six pictures, which are repeated from one to another with no changes beyond those rendered necessary by the substitution of one god for another. These pictures deal with the rites which would be celebrated by the king in each of the seven sanctuaries.

Behind this septuple sanctuary there is a secondary hypostyle hall, just as we find it behind the single *secos* of the ordinary temple. Its roof was supported by ten columns, and access to it was obtained through the third sanctuary, that of Osiris. This part of the temple is in a very fragmentary condition. Very little is left of the bounding walls, but it has been ascertained that several of these chambers were dedicated to one or other of the deities between whom the naos was apportioned. Thus one of the chambers referred to was placed under the protection of Osiris, another under that of Horus, and a third under that of Isis.

The decoration of the southern wing of the temple seems never to have been completed. It contains a long corridor, a rectangular court with an unfinished peristyle, several small chambers with columns, and a flight of steps leading up on to the flat roof. A dark apartment or crypt, divided into two stories by a floor of large stone slabs, may have been used as a storehouse.

FIG. 225.—Seti, with the attributes of Osiris, between Amen, to whom he is paying homage, and Chnoum.

These farthest apartments seem to have been arranged in no sort of order. We shall not here enter into such matters as the construction of the seven parallel vaults in the naos; for that a future opportunity will be found;[341] at present our business is to make the differences between the temple at Abydos and that of Khons and its congeners, clearly understood. The distinction lies in the seven longitudinal subdivisions, beginning with the seven doors in the façade of the hypostyle hall, and ending in the vaulted chambers which form the same number of sanctuaries. Seen from outside, the temple would not betray its want of unity; it was surrounded by a single wall, the complex naos was prefaced by courts and pylons in the same fashion as in the temples of Thebes which we have already noticed, and it would not be until the building was entered and explored that the fact would become evident that it was seven shrines in one, seven independent temples under one roof.[342]

At Thebes also we find a temple which, by its internal arrangements, resembles that of Abydos. It is called sometimes the *Palace* and sometimes the *Temple of Gournah*; in the inscriptions it is called the *House of Seti*. Two propylons, one about fifty yards in front of the other, form an outwork to the main building, with which they are connected by an avenue of sphinxes. It is probable that they were originally the doorways through brick walls, now demolished, which formed successive enclosures round the temple. The dromos led up to the pronaos, which was reached by a few steps. The front of the naos is a portico of simple design, consisting of ten columns between two square pilasters, the whole being 166 feet long by 10 feet deep. Eight of these line columns are still erect. The wall at the back of the portico is pierced by three doorways, to which three distinct compartments or divisions of the interior correspond (see plan, Fig. 226).

The only feature in which these compartments resemble one another is their independence. They are isolated from one another by walls which run from front to back of the naos. The most important and elaborate of the three compartments is the middle one. Its entrance doorway opens directly upon a hall which is the largest in the whole temple. It is eighteen metres long, its roof is supported by six columns similar to those of the portico already mentioned, and ranged around it are nine small chambers, the pictures in which illustrate the apotheosis of Seti, who, often indued with the attributes of Osiris, is sometimes shown doing homage to the Theban triad of gods, and more especially to Amen-Ra, sometimes as himself the object of worship. The central one of these chambers opens upon a hall where the roof is supported by four square pillars, and upon this hall again four small apartments open. These can hardly be mere storehouses, but they have suffered so greatly that no certain opinion can be formed as to their real purposes.

The right-hand compartment is in a very bad state, but enough of it remains to show that its arrangements were quite different from those of its neighbour and much less complex. So far as we can judge, the larger part of it was taken up with a peristylar court or hall seventy-six feet long and forty-six wide. Behind this the site of three rectangular chambers may be distinguished. Every wall which is still standing bears representations of Rameses II. paying his devotions to the Theban gods.

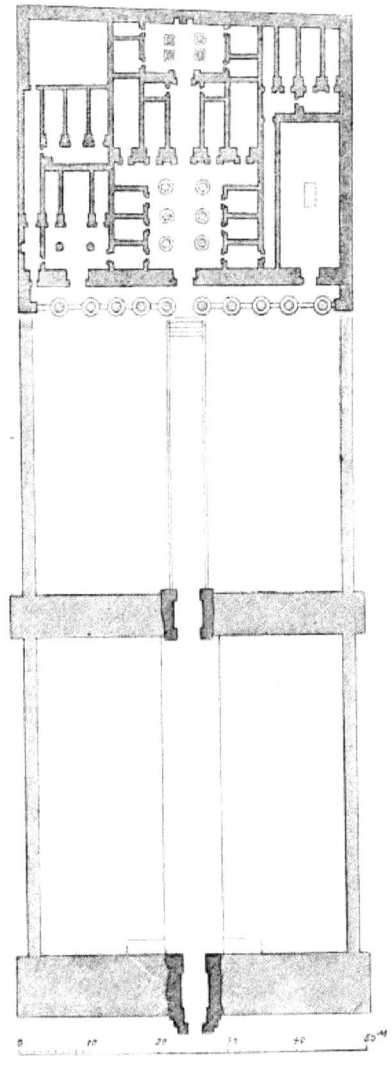

Fig. 226.—Plan of the Temple of Gournah.

The left compartment is in better preservation than the right, and its arrangements are more like those of the central part of the naos. It is not so large, however, and it contains no hypostyle hall. It has six chambers placed in two sets of three, the one set behind the other. Here we find Rameses I., the founder of the dynasty, honoured by his son Seti I. and his grandson Rameses II.

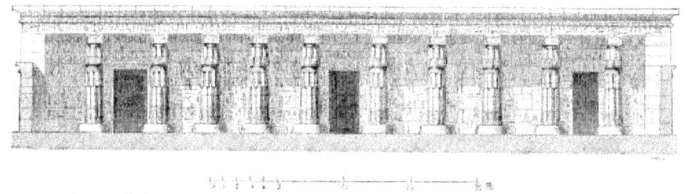

FIG. 227.—Façade of the *naos* of the Temple of Gournah
(from the *Description de l'Égypte, Antiquités*, vol. ii. pl. 42).

FIG. 228.—Longitudinal section of the Temple of Gournah,
from the portico of the *naos* to the back wall
(from Lepsius's *Denkmæler*, part i. pl. 86).

The great temples of Abydos and Gournah were built by the same sovereigns, Seti I. and Rameses II. Perhaps, too, their plans were traced by the same architect. The resemblance between them is so great that they may be looked upon as variants of one type, of a type which is distinguished by the juxtaposition of similar parts grouped laterally one by the side of the other. Each of the chapels which we have described was self-contained, the subsidiary chambers which were required for the routine of worship were grouped round it, either on one side, as at Abydos, or in the angles of the sanctuary itself, as at Gournah. With such slight differences of detail as this, the two buildings were built upon the same principle. At Gournah the division is tripartite, and the three compartments vary in their arrangements; at Abydos they are seven in number, and exactly similar in design. A temple thus cut into three parts, or seven, reminds us of the seed-pods of certain plants, in which the fertilizing grain is divided between several cells. But whether these are numerous or few, the naos never has any great depth. It seems as if the absence of a true organic centre arrested the development of the building; we find no signs of an edifice which, like the temple of Amen at Karnak, might be developed almost to infinity without losing its unity.

On the other hand, there were a few temples in which a severe and extreme unity was the distinguishing characteristic. In Upper Egypt and Nubia a few examples of the class are still to be seen. As a rule they date from the eighteenth dynasty, but there were a few temples of the same kind erected under the Ptolemies.[343] It seems probable, therefore, that they were common to all the periods of Egyptian history, and to the conquered provinces, as well as to Egypt proper. They were erected within, and in the neighbourhood of, those cities whose importance was not sufficient to demand such great monumental works as the temples of Thebes or Abydos, of Memphis or Sais. We might call them chapels, raised either to the honour of the local deities, or for the purpose of commemorating the passage of some conquering prince and the homage paid by him to the deity to whom he looked for protection and victory.

In these chapels there are neither internal peristyles nor hypostyles; there are none of those subsidiary chambers among which it is sometimes so easy to lose our way. There is, in fact, nothing but a rectangular chamber and a portico about it, and, in most cases, it would appear that a short dromos, consisting of a few pairs of sphinxes, lent dignity to the approach.

The best proportioned and perhaps the most interesting building of this class is the little sandstone temple built by Amenophis III. at Elephantiné, upon the southern frontier of Egypt. It was discovered at the end of the last century by the draughtsmen of the French Expedition, and named by them the *Temple of the South*.[344] This little building no longer exists. It was destroyed in 1822 by the Turkish Governor of Assouan, who had a mania for building. Happily the plans and drawings, which we reproduce, seem to have been made with great care.

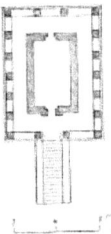

FIG. 229.—**Plan of the Temple of Elephantiné.**
(*Description de l'Égypte*, i. 35.)

The total area of the temple, at the floor level of the cella, was 40 feet by 31. It was raised upon a well-built rectangular base of almost the same lateral dimensions,[345] and 7 feet 6 inches high to the pavement of the portico. From the earth level to the top of the cornice the temple was 21 feet 6 inches in height. A flight of steps, enclosed between two walls of the same height as the stylobate, led up to the portico. The portico itself was composed of square piers and round columns. Two of the latter were introduced in the centre of each of the smaller faces of the building, while the side galleries were enclosed by seven square piers, inclusive of those at the angles. A dwarf wall about three feet in height bounded the gallery on the outside, and afforded a base for the piers; the circular columns on each side of the entrance alone stood directly upon the pavement of the gallery, and were thus higher by about three feet than either the piers or the columns in the corresponding façade at the rear. The oblong chamber enclosed by this portico had two entrances, one at the top of the steps, the other at the back.[346] The first named was indicated as the true entrance to the building by the slight salience of its jambs and lintel, by the increased size of the columns in front of it, and by its position with regard to the steps.

One more peculiarity must be noticed. Neither in piers nor in walls do we find that inward slope which is almost universal in Egyptian exteriors. The lines are vertical and horizontal. This is not the effect of caprice; the architect had a good reason for neglecting the traditions of his profession. By avoiding the usual inclination towards the centre, he gave to his small creation a dignity which it would otherwise have missed, and, in some degree, concealed its diminutive size.

FIG. 230.—View in perspective of the Temple of Elephantiné (from the *Description de l'Égypte*, i. 35).

In spite of its modest dimensions, this temple was without neither beauty nor grandeur. Its stylobate raised it well above the plain, while the steps in front gave meaning and accent to its elevation. The wide spacing of the columns in front allowed the richly decorated doorway to be seen in effective grouping with the long perspectives of the side galleries. The piers on the flanks were more closely spaced than the columns of the *façade*, and the contrast was heightened by the simplicity of their form. The dignity of the entablature and the bold projection of the cornice added to the effect of the whole, and emphasized the well-balanced nature of the composition. The Egyptian architects never produced a building better calculated to please modern tastes. Its symmetry and just proportion appeal directly to those whose artistic ideas are founded upon the creations of the Greeks and Romans.

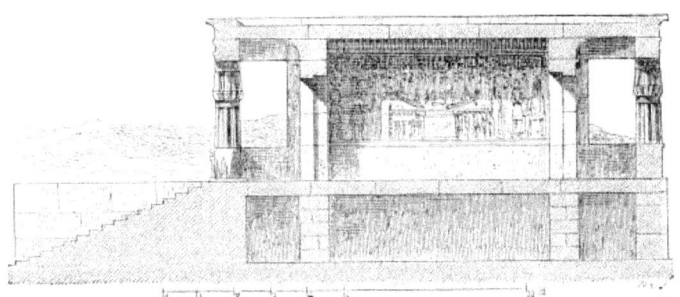

FIG. 231.—Longitudinal section of the Temple of Elephantiné (from the *Description*, i. 35).

This sympathy was conspicuously felt by those who discovered the little monument. "The arrangement," says Jomard, "is a model of simplicity and purity.... The Temple of Elephantiné is pleasing as a whole, and commands our attention." But the purity and harmony of its lines are not its only claims to our admiration. The pleasure which it causes us to feel is partly the result of its resemblance to a well-known and much admired type, that of the Greek temple. In all essentials the arrangements are the same, a cella raised upon an important base and surrounded by a colonnade.

The general arrangement of the Elephantiné structure has even its name in the technical language of the Greek architects, they would call it a *peripteral* temple, because the colonnade goes completely round it. Nowhere else do we find such a striking resemblance between Greece and Egypt. But for the mouldings, the sculptured decorations, and the inscribed texts, we should be tempted to see in it a building of the Ptolemaic period, Greek in conception and plan, but decorated in the Egyptian taste. Such a mistake would, however, be impossible in these days, and even at the end of the last century. The French *savants* knew enough to prevent them falling into such an error. They were unable to read the hieroglyphics, but the general physiognomy of the building told them that it could boast of a venerable antiquity. In coming to this conclusion they were right, but they should have stopped there instead of attempting to establish a direct connection, as cause and effect, between the Egyptian building and the temples of Greece. We shall not here discuss the delicate question of the indebtedness of Greek artists to those of Egypt, but we may allow ourselves to make two observations. In the first place, the temples built upon this plan were very small, and must have attracted very little notice indeed from strangers dazzled by the wonders of Sais, Memphis, and Thebes; and the buildings in those great cities did not offer the peculiar characteristics which, we are asked to believe, inspired the early Greek architects. In the second place, if there had been any direct imitation of an Egyptian model, we should have found in the copy at least some passing trace of those square piers which were so continually and successfully used by the Egyptian architects; but in the Greek peripteral temples the external colonnades are always made up exclusively of circular columns. The Greek architect hardly ever made use of the square pier, except in the form of a pilaster, to give strength to the extremities of a wall.

Would it not be much simpler to admit that we have here one of those coincidences which are so frequent in the history of the arts? Human nature is pretty much the same all over the world. When human skill has been employed at different times and in different countries, in supplying similar wants and solving almost identical problems, it has been led to results which vary only in the minor details. These variations are more or less marked according to race characteristics or material surroundings. When examined closely the circumstances of mankind are never found unchanged from one period or one race to another, but a superficial resemblance is enough to ensure that their artistic creations shall have many important points in common. In no pursuit does the human mind turn in a narrower circle than in architecture. The purpose of the building on the one hand, and the qualities of the material on the other, exercise a great influence upon form. But the purposes for which important buildings are erected are very few, neither are the materials at the command of the architect very many. The possible combinations are therefore far from numerous. Take two races placed in conditions of climate and civilization which may fairly be called analogous; put the same materials in the hands of their architects and give them the same programme to carry out; is it not almost certain that they would produce works with many features in common, and that without any knowledge of each other's work? From this point of view only, as it seems to us, should the type of building just described be regarded. If the temple at Elephantiné had possessed no other interest but that belonging to it as an example of Egyptian temple building, we might have omitted all mention of it, or at least devoted but a few words to it. And yet such types are scarce. The French explorers found a second temple of the same class not far from the first; now, however, it exists only in their drawings.[347] A third has been discovered in Nubia, which must resemble the two at Elephantiné very strongly; we mean the temple constructed by Thothmes III. on the left bank of the river, at Semneh. Although it has suffered greatly, traces of a portico are to be found about the cella, and it has been ascertained that this portico consisted both of square piers and columns.[348] Finally, at El-kab (Eilithya), in Upper Egypt, there is a temple constructed upon the same plan; it differs from that at Elephantiné in having only two circular columns, those upon the façade; all the rest of the peristyle consists of square piers.[349] The oldest part of the temple built by Thothmes II. and Thothmes III. at Medinet-Abou presents an analogous arrangement. The sanctuary is there surrounded on three sides by a portico of square piers (Fig. 222).

There is nothing to forbid the supposition that these temples were once much more numerous in the valley of the Nile, but it appears certain that they were always of small dimensions. If like those of Sais and Memphis, the temples of Thebes had vanished and left no trace behind, we might have been led to believe that some of the great religious buildings of the Egyptians had been in this form; but we have Luxor and Karnak, Medinet-Abou and the Ramesseum, Gournah and Abydos; we have several important temples built in Ethiopia by Egyptian conquerors, and others erected by the Ethiopian sovereigns in imitation of Egyptian architecture.[350] When we compare these remains with one another and call to mind the words of Strabo and of other ancient travellers as to the monuments which have been destroyed, we are forced to this general conclusion, that it was within the high external walls of their buildings, around courts open to the sky or as supports for wide and lofty halls, that the Egyptians loved to group their mighty piers and columns. When the portico was outside it was so placed because there was no room for it within. When the temple was reduced to a single narrow chamber, so small that there was no room for columns and that the walls could support the roof without help, the colonnade was relegated to the exterior, where it served to give importance to the cella, and to clothe and beautify it.

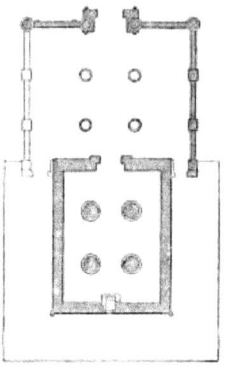

FIG. 232.—Temple of Amenophis III. at Eilithyia; from Lepsius.

The peripteral arrangement, which is a constant principle in Greek architecture, is no more than a rare accident in that of Egypt. But in spite of this difference the similarity, which might be called a chance likeness, if the word chance had any place in history, is full of interest for the historian of art.

The following facts are sufficient to prove that it was the small size of these peripteral temples that first suggested the external situation of their colonnades. As long as the cella was large enough to admit supports of the ordinary diameter without encumbering the space or destroying its proportions, we find the columns inside. Of this the temple of Amenophis III. at Eilithyia, a plan and section of which we take from Lepsius (Figs. 232 and 233),[351] is an instance. It is prefaced by a chamber, very ruinous, and wider than it is deep. It is now difficult to say whether this was an uncovered court or a hypostyle hall.[352] Immediately abutting upon it comes the naos, a rectangular chamber measuring internally 28 feet by 22 feet 6 inches. The roof might very possibly have been supported by the four columns, as their bases were 4 feet in diameter. A niche contrived in the further wall of the naos acted the part of a *secos*.

Here too we find a very simple form of temple, but the naos being large enough to admit, and even to demand, the use of internal columns, it never entered the architect's head to surround it with a portico externally. Thus arranged, the chapel, as we have called these buildings, was nothing more than an epitome of the temple, and there is no need for insistance upon the variations which it presents upon a single theme, upon a first principle which sometimes was developed into a colossal structure like that at Karnak, sometimes reduced until it resulted in buildings where a few paces carry the visitor from one extremity to the other.

We may say the same of those subterranean temples which are called *speos* or *hemi-speos*, *grotto*, or *half-grotto*, according to whether they are entirely rock cut, or prefaced by architectural constructions. They are chiefly found in Lower Nubia, a fact which has sometimes been explained by the natural configuration of the soil. In that portion of the Nile Valley the river is embraced so closely by the rocks between which it flows that it would, we are told, have been difficult to find a site for a constructed temple. In this, however, there is some exaggeration. If we examine a map of Nubia we shall find many places where either one or the other of the two chains of hills fall back from the river far enough to allow a considerable intervening fringe of level ground. This is cropped and tilled by little groups of natives, who live, as a rule, at the mouth of those *wadis*, or dry torrent beds, which intersect the mountains. These strips of arable land are always either level or of a very gentle slope. It would, therefore, not be very difficult to obtain a site for such little oratories as were required for the scanty population, for the soldiers in the nearest military post, for the engineers and workmen in some neighbouring quarry. Even supposing that it pleased the king to choose some deserted site in a conquered province for the erection of some durable memorial of his prowess, no very large building would be required. Great temples were reserved for populous cities, in which the king, the military commanders, and the priest resided, in which the popular ceremonies of religion were performed.

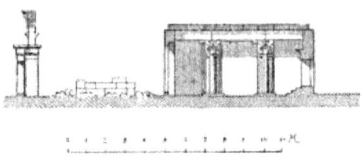

FIG. 233.—Temple of Amenophis III. at Eilithyia; longitudinal section, from Lepsius.

The Egyptian architect did not hesitate to cut away part of the side of a mountain when it was the only means open to him of obtaining a level site for building. In this fashion Seti obtained a site for his great temple at Abydos. The same thing might have been done, at much less cost, for these little Nubian temples. It would always have been easy with pick and chisel to adapt some ridge or cornice of the cliffs for their reception, or to cut a sort of courtyard in the slope of the hill, in which a small temple might have been erected. We must not seek, then, for a reason for the multiplication of these rock temples in the Nubian section of the Nile Valley either in natural conditions or in the want of architectural resource. Even in Egypt proper there are chapels cut in the flanks of the hills; near Beni-Hassan there is the *Speos Artemidos*, and near Assouan, close to the quarries of Gebel Silsilis, [353] there is another. Below the first cataract, however, these grottos are as rare as they are numerous on the other side of the frontier, where, indeed, they sometimes rise to a magnificence of which nothing else in Egypt, unless it be the finest of the sepulchral excavations at Thebes, can give an idea. How are we to account for this difference, or rather contrast?

This question is more easily asked than answered. The following explanation seems to us, however, the most probable.

Ethiopia was not Egypt. Although they were closely connected as early as the sixth dynasty, the former never lost its character of a conquered province. In Ethiopia men did not feel so sure of the morrow as in Egypt proper. Between the sixth and the eleventh dynasty the hold of Egypt upon Ethiopia had been lost at least once. Reconquered by the kings of the first Theban period, it regained its independence during the domination of the

Hyksos; the eighteenth dynasty had, therefore, to begin the work of subjugation all over again, and it did its work more thoroughly than any of its predecessors. Then, when the Egyptian sceptre ruled as far south as Napata and the great bend of the Nile, the governors of the southern provinces must have been continually employed in repelling the incursions of the negroes from Upper Ethiopia, and in suppressing the warlike tribes who lived within the conquered frontier. At such times the king himself must often have been compelled to take the field and lead his armies in person. A constructed temple, especially when of small size, would be in great risk of destruction in a country exposed to the repeated incursions of savage tribes; columns and piers would soon be overturned by their ruthless arms. But chambers cut in the living rock would offer a much stouter resistance; the decorations might be scraped down or daubed over, but the time and patience required for any serious attack upon the limestone or granite sides and piers would not be forthcoming. Such damage as could be done in a short time and by the weapons of the invaders could readily be repaired when the raid was over.

We think it probable, therefore, that subterranean architecture was preferred throughout this region because the political condition of the province was always more or less precarious, rather than because the configuration of the country required it. Where security was assured by the presence of a strong and permanent garrison, as at Semneh and Kumneh, we find constructed temples just as we do in Egypt. They are found, too, in those localities— Soleb and Napata for instance—where there was a large urban population, and therefore fortifications and troops for their defence. Everywhere else it was found more convenient to confide the temple to the guardianship of its own materials, the living rock, and to bury it in faces of the cliffs. This kind of work, moreover, was perfectly easy to Egyptian workmen. For many centuries they had been accustomed, as we have seen, to hollow out the flanks of their mountains, and to decorate the chambers thus obtained, for the last resting-places of their dead. In the execution of such works they must have arrived at a degree of practised skill which made it as easy for them to cut a speos like the great temple at Ipsamboul, as to build one of the same size. This fact probably had its weight in leading the conquerors of Nubia to fill it with underground temples. Such a method of construction was at once expeditious and durable, a double advantage, which would be greatly appreciated in the early years of the occupation of the province. When security was established, the same process continued to be used from love for the art itself. When Rameses II. cut those two caves in the rock at Ipsamboul, whose façades, with their gigantic figures, have such an effect upon the travellers of to-day, it was neither because he was pressed for time, nor because he was doubtful of the tenure of his power. The military supremacy of Egypt and the security of her conquests seemed to be assured. The Egyptian monarch carved the cliffs of Ipsamboul into gigantic images of himself because he wished to astonish his contemporaries and their posterity with the boldness and novelty of the enterprise. At Thebes he had built, on the right hand of the river, the hall of Karnak and the pylons of Luxor; on the left bank, the *Temple of Seti* and the Ramesseum. For these he could have imagined no pendant more original or more imposing than the great temple carved from a natural hill, in front of which statues of the sovereign, higher than any of those which adorned the courtyards at Thebes, would see countless generations of Egyptians pass before their feet in their journeys up and down the Nile. The hypostyle hall at Karnak was a marvel of constructed architecture, the great temple at Ipsamboul was the masterpiece of that art which had been so popular with the Egyptians from the earliest periods of their civilization, the art which imitated the forms of a stone building by excavations in the living rock.

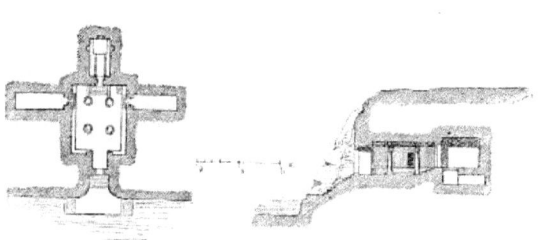

FIG. 234.—The speos at Addeh; plan from Horeau.
FIG. 235.—The speos at Addeh. Longitudinal section; from Horeau.

Subterranean architecture had, of course, to go through a regular course of development before it was capable of such works as the tomb of Seti, at Thebes, and the temples of Ipsamboul. In the necropolis of Memphis, and in that of the First Theban Empire, its ambition was more easily satisfied. So, too, the first rock-cut temples were of very modest dimensions. They date from the eighteenth dynasty. Two of them are to be found in the neighbourhood of Ipsamboul but on the other side of the river, one near the castle of Addeh, the other at Feraïg. The latter was cut by the king Harmhabi (or Armaïs). It is composed—as also is that of Addeh—of a hall supported by four columns, two lateral chambers, and a sanctuary. There is an equally small *speos* in Egypt which dates from the same period; it is the grotto at Beni-Hassan, which, ever since antique times, has been known as the *Speos Artemidos*. The goddess Sekhet, to which it was consecrated, had been identified with the Greek Artemis. It was begun by Thothmes III., carried on by Seti I., and seems never to have been finished. The temple proper is prefaced by a kind of portico of square pillars cut, with the roof which they support, from the limestone rock. A narrow passage about nine feet deep leads to the naos, which is a quadrangular chamber about thirteen feet square, with a niche in the further wall in which an image of the lion-headed goddess probably stood.[354] The most important of the rock-cut chapels of Silsilis was also inaugurated by Harmhabi and restored and embellished by Rameses II.[355] The hemispeos at Redesieh, in the same district, is a work of Seti I.[356]

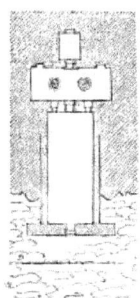

FIG. 236.—Plan of speos
at Beit-el-Wali;
from Prisse.

Only one subterranean temple later than the nineteenth dynasty is known to us, namely, that which is cut in the flanks of the Gebel-Barkal at Napata.

[357] It is called the *Typhonium*, on account of the grimacing figures which stand before the piers. It dates from the time of Tahrak, and was one of the works with which the famous Ethiopian decorated his capital in the hope that it might become a formidable rival to those great Egyptian cities which he had taken and occupied.[358] All the other rock-cut temples were the work of Rameses II.; they are, as we ascend the Nile, Beit-el-Wali, near Kalabcheh (Figs. 236 and 237); Gherf-Hossein, or Gircheh, Wadi-Seboua, Dayr, and Ipsamboul.

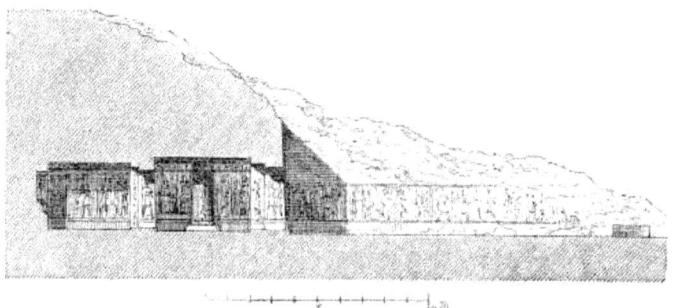

FIG. 237.—Longitudinal section of the speos at Beit-el-Wali; from Prisse.

We may give Gherf-Hossein as a good example of the hemispeos (Figs. 238 and 239). It was approached from the river by a broad flight of steps, decorated with statues and sphinxes, of which but a few fragments now remain. A pylon gave access to a rectangular court, on the right and left sides of which stood five piers faced with colossal statues of Rameses II. These statues were about twenty-six feet high. Next, and at a slightly higher level, came a hypostyle hall; its roof was supported by twelve square piers, those forming the central avenue being of caryatid form and higher than the others. The subterranean part of the temple begins with a passage cut in the rock on the further side of this hall. This passage leads to a long transverse vestibule, from which open two lateral chambers, and three from its further side. The furthest chamber on the major axis of the whole building was the sanctuary. This is proved by its position, its shape, and the niche which is cut in its further wall. Four deities are sculptured in this niche, and in spite of the ill-usage to which they have been subjected, one of them can still be identified as Ptah, the chief god of the temple.[359]

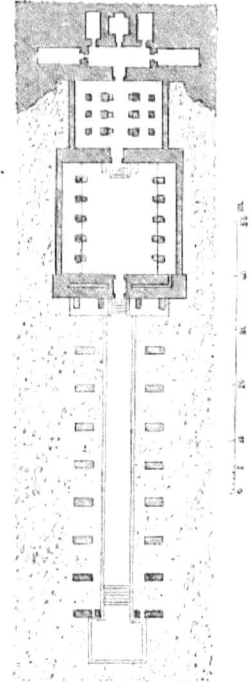

FIG. 238.—Plan of the hemispeos of Gherf-Hossein; from Prisse.

We find almost the same arrangements in the hemispeos of Wadi-Asseboua. [360] That of Derri (Figs. 240 and 241) is more simple. There are neither dromos nor pylon, properly speaking, and only four caryatid pillars; but there is an open court with a hypostyle hall and a sanctuary cut in the rock. At the back of the sanctuary there is a stone bench upon which three statues were seated.

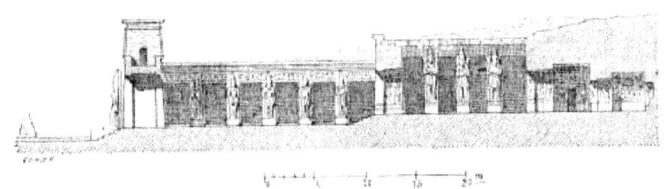

FIG. 239.—Gherf-Hossein, longitudinal section; from Prisse.

The two temples of Ipsamboul are so well known and have been so often illustrated and described, that they need not detain us long. The chief thing to be noticed here is that they are without any external and constructed part, and that from their position, high above the river and close to it, it was impossible that they could have any dromos; and yet between the doorway of the speos and the river bank there were steps which are now either worn away by the action of the floods or hidden by the *débris* from the cliffs. The façades of these temples were, however, as richly decorated and as monumental in their way as those of the most sumptuous buildings in Thebes.

FIG. 240.—Plan of the hemispeos of Derri; from Horeau.
FIG. 241.—Longitudinal section, Derri; from Horeau.

The prototype of these façades is the Theban pylon. They have the same trapeziform surfaces covered with figures and inscriptions, circumscribed by a moulding and crowned by a cornice in bold relief; they are inclined from the perpendicular, and they afford a background to the statues of the king who caused them to be made. The chief difference is in the situation of these statues. In the case of a built temple they are monoliths, brought from a distance and erected in front of the pylon. But space was wanting for such an arrangement at Ipsamboul; besides which it was better, for many reasons, that the whole edifice should be homogeneous, and that the statues should be carved in the rock from which its chambers were to be cut. The way to do this was obvious. The colossi had but to recede a pace or two so as to be incorporated in the substance of the pylon itself.

At Ipsamboul there are, as we have seen, two temples close to one another. Their façades, though conceived in the same spirit, executed by the same processes, and having a good deal in common in their design, are yet by no means similar. That of the temple of Hathor, generally called the *Smaller Temple,* is on a smaller scale than the *Great Temple,* but perhaps its design is the happier and more skilful of the two. The front is 90 feet wide and nearly 40 high. It is ornamented by six colossal upright statues, four of them Rameses himself, the other two his wife Nefert-Ari. These statues, which are about 34 feet high, are separated one from another by eight buttresses, two of them acting as jambs for the door, above which they unite and become a wide band of flat carving marking the centre of the façade. The gentle salience of these buttresses forms a framework for the statues (see Fig. 242), which are chiselled with great care and skill in the fine yellow sandstone of which the mountain consists.

The façade of the Great Temple is much larger. It is about 130 feet wide by 92 high. It is not divided by buttresses like the other, but it has a bold cornice made up of twenty-two cynocephalic figures seated with their hands upon their knees. Each of these animals is sculptured in the round, and is only connected with the face of the rock by a small part of its posterior surface. They are not less than seven feet high. A frieze, consisting of a dedicatory inscription carved in deep and firmly drawn hieroglyphs runs below the cornice. Above the doorway a colossal figure of Ra is carved in the rock, and on each side of him Rameses is depicted in low relief, in the act of adoration. This group occupies the middle of the façade. But the most striking feature of the building is supplied by the four colossi of Rameses placed two and two on either side of the door. They are the largest in Egypt. From the sole of the feet to the apex of the pschent which the king bears on his head, they are about sixty-five feet in height. Rameses is seated, his hands upon his thighs, in the pose ordinarily made use of for the royal statues at the entrances of the temples. In spite of these enormous dimensions the workmanship is very fine. The countenance, especially, is remarkable for its combination of force and sweetness, an expression which has been noticed by all the travellers who have written upon Ipsamboul.

FIG. 242.—Façade of the smaller temple at Ipsamboul.

FIG. 243.—Plan of the smaller temple.
FIG. 244.—Perspective of the principal chamber in the smaller temple; from Horeau.

 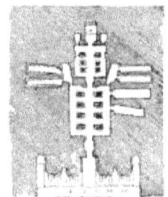

FIG. 245.—Longitudinal section of the smaller temple; from Horeau.
FIG. 246.—Plan of the Great Temple.

The interiors of the two temples are still more different than the exteriors, and, in this instance, the variations are entirely in favour of the greater monument. The total depth of the smaller edifice is about ninety feet. A single hall, supported by six square Hathor-headed pillars, precedes the sanctuary. The latter is nothing but a narrow gallery, in the middle of which a small chamber or niche is cut, in which the rock-carved cow of Hathor may be seen with a statue between its legs. The other temple is a great deal larger. Its total length is about 180 feet. The first hall is 60 feet long and 53 wide; the roof is supported by eight pillars, against each of which a colossal figure 33 feet high is placed. A doorway in the middle of the further side leads to a second chamber not quite so large as the first, and supported by four thick square pillars. Three openings in its furthest side lead to a third chamber, as wide as the second, but only 10 feet deep. Through this the innermost parts of the speos are reached; they consist of three small chambers, those on the left and right being very small indeed, while that in the centre, the adytum, is about 13 feet by 23. In the middle of this chamber was an altar, or table for offerings; at the back of it a bench with four seated statues. The walls of both temples are covered with pictures like those of Luxor, Karnak, and the Ramesseum. They represent the battles and triumphs of Rameses, and the king seated upon the laps of goddesses, who act as the tenderest of nurses.

FIG. 247.—**Perspective of the principal hall in the Great Temple; from Horeau.**

Besides the halls which form the main body of the temple, the plan shows eight lateral chambers, some perpendicular to the major axis of the building, others falling upon it obliquely. Several of these do not seem to have been finished. There are indications that they were utilized as depositories for the objects worshipped in the temple.

FIG. 248.—Façade of the Great Temple at Ipsamboul.

We have now briefly noticed the principal rock-cut temples in Egypt and Nubia. Neither in plan nor in decoration do they materially differ from the temples of wrought masonry. The elements of the building are the same, and they are arranged in the same order—an avenue of sphinxes when there is room for it, colossi before the entrance, a colonnaded court, a hypostyle hall acting as a *pronaos*, a *naos* with its *secos*, or sanctuary; but sometimes one, sometimes many of these divisions are excavated in the living rock. Sometimes only the sanctuary is subterranean, sometimes the hypostyle hall is included, and at Ipsamboul the whole temple is in the mountain, from the *secos* to those colossal statues which generally form the preface to the pylon of the constructed temple.

FIG. 247.—**Perspective of the principal hall in the Great Temple; from Horeau.**

Besides the halls which form the main body of the temple, the plan shows eight lateral chambers, some perpendicular to the major axis of the building, others falling upon it obliquely. Several of these do not seem to have been finished. There are indications that they were utilized as depositories for the objects worshipped in the temple.

FIG. 248.—Façade of the Great Temple at Ipsamboul.

We have now briefly noticed the principal rock-cut temples in Egypt and Nubia. Neither in plan nor in decoration do they materially differ from the temples of wrought masonry. The elements of the building are the same, and they are arranged in the same order—an avenue of sphinxes when there is room for it, colossi before the entrance, a colonnaded court, a hypostyle hall acting as a *pronaos*, a *naos* with its *secos*, or sanctuary; but sometimes one, sometimes many of these divisions are excavated in the living rock. Sometimes only the sanctuary is subterranean, sometimes the hypostyle hall is included, and at Ipsamboul the whole temple is in the mountain, from the *secos* to those colossal statues which generally form the preface to the pylon of the constructed temple.

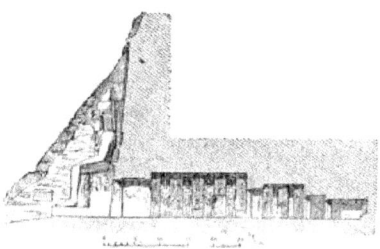

FIG. 249.—Longitudinal section of the Great Temple; from Horeau.

Except in the case of the peristylar court, the interior of the rock-cut temple did not differ so much in appearance from that of the constructed edifice as might at first be imagined. We have already explained how scantily lighted was the interior of the Egyptian temple; its innermost chambers were plunged in almost complete darkness, so that the absolute night which was involved in their being excavated in the heart of a mountain was no very great change from the obscurity caused by the thick walls and heavy roofs of the edifices in the plain. In the case of a hemi-speos the internal effect must have been almost identical with that of any other religious building. In the great temple of Ipsamboul the daylight does not penetrate beyond the second hall; from that point onwards artificial light is necessary to distinguish objects, but the Egyptians were so thoroughly accustomed to a mysterious solemnity of shadow, to a "dim religious light," in their temples, that the darkness of the speos would seem no drawback in their eyes.

The column occurs very seldom in these subterranean temples.[361] Even those chambers which correspond to the hypostyle hall by their places in the excavation and the general characteristics of their form, are hardly ever supported by anything but the rectangular piers in use in the early ages of the monarchy; but these piers are often clothed with an elaborate decoration which is unknown in the works of the primitive architects. This preference for the pier is easily to be explained by the necessity for having supports of sufficient strength and solidity to bear the weight of the superincumbent mountain.

Another and more constant peculiarity of the underground temples, is the existence in them of one or more seated statues carved from masses of rock expressly left in the furthest recesses of the excavation. These statues, which represent the presiding deity of the place and his acolytes, do not occur in the constructed temples. In the latter the tabernacle which stood in the *secos* was too small to hold anything larger than a statuette or emblem. We think that the cause of this difference may be guessed. At the time these rock temples were cut, the Pharaohs to whom they owed their existence no doubt assigned a priest or priests to each. But their position, sometimes in desert solitudes, as in the case of the *Speos Artemidos*, sometimes in places only inhabited for an intermittent period, in the quarries at Silsilis for instance, or in provinces which had been conquered by Egypt and might be lost to her again, rendered it impossible that they could be served and guarded in the ample fashion which was easy enough in the temples of Memphis, Abydos and Thebes. All these considerations suggested that, instead of a shrine containing some small figure or emblem, statues of a considerable size, from six to eight or ten feet high, should be employed, and that they should be actually chiselled in the living rock itself and left attached to it by the whole of their posterior surfaces. By their size and by their incorporation with the rock out of which both they and their surroundings were cut, such statues would defend themselves efficiently against all attempts on the part of enemies. In spite of their age several of these statues came down to us in a sufficiently good state of preservation to allow Champollion and his predecessors to recognize with certainty the divine personages whom they represented. During the last fifty years they have suffered as much at the hands of ignorant and stupid tourists as they did in the whole of the many centuries during which they were exposed to all the vicissitudes of Egyptian history.[362]

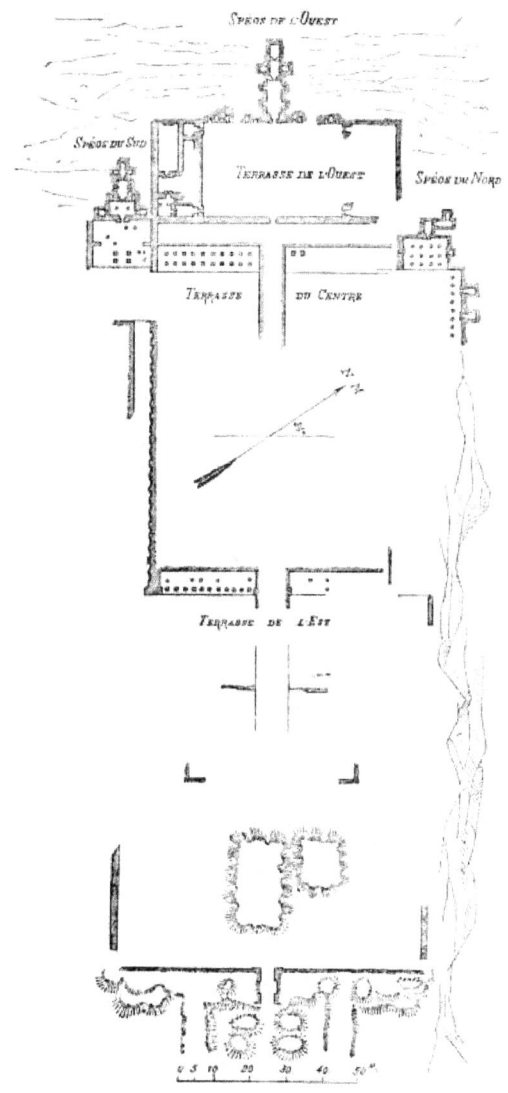

Fig. 250.—Dayr-el-Bahari; according to M. Brune.

Our study of the Egyptian temple would not be complete without a few words upon the buildings called *Dayr-el-Bahari*.[363] By their extent, their picturesqueness, and the peculiar nature of their situation, these ruins have always had a great effect upon foreign visitors. Those who know Thebes will, perhaps, be surprised at our having said so little about them hitherto, especially as they are older than most of the buildings over which we have been occupied. We have not yet described them because they do not belong to any of the categories which we have been treating; they form a class by themselves; their general arrangement has no parallel in Egypt, and therefore we have reserved them to the last.

The building in question is situated at the foot of the Libyan chain, in a deep amphitheatre hollowed out by nature in the yellow limestone rocks which rise on the north-west of the necropolis. On two sides, on the right and at the back, it rests against perpendicular walls of rock cut by the pickaxe and dominating over the built part of the temple. On the left this natural wall is absent and is replaced by an inclosure of bricks (Figs. 250 and 251).

Under such conditions we need feel no surprise at finding part of the temple subterranean. In backing his work against the mountains in this fashion the architect must have been partly impelled by a desire to make use of the facilities which it afforded. The mausoleum of Hatasu, unlike the other funerary chapels at Thebes, is, then, a triple hemispeos. At a point immediately opposite to the door in the external pylon, but at the other extremity of the building, a chamber about sixty-five feet deep was excavated in the rock. This must have acted the part of a sanctuary. Right and left of it, and at a shorter distance from the entrance, there are two more groups of rock-cut apartments. The whole arrangement may be compared to the system of three apsidal chapels which is so common at the east end of European cathedrals.

In approaching this temple from the river bank, a dromos of sphinxes had to be traversed of which very scanty traces are now to be found, but in the time of the *Institut d'Égypte* there were still two hundred of them to be distinguished, a few of the last being shown in the restoration figured upon the opposite page (Fig. 251). At the end of the dromos, upon the spot where a few traces of the bounding walls still remain, we have placed a pylon with a couple of obelisks in front of it. We have done so not only because nearly all the important temples had such a preface, but also because Sir Gardner

Wilkinson says that he saw the foundations of two obelisks and of a doorway. After passing the pylon, a first courtyard was entered, which communicated with a second by an inclined plane stretching almost across its width.[364] Here the arrangements which constituted the real originality of Dayr-el-Bahari began. The whole interior of the temple, between the pylon and the commencement of the speos, consisted of four courtyards, rising in terraces one above another like the steps of a gigantic staircase. The walls upon which these inclined planes and terraces were constructed are still to be traced in places. In order to furnish the vast courts, we have supposed them to contain seated statues at regular intervals along the inner faces of their walls; in such matters of decorative detail a little conjecture may perhaps be allowed.[365] As for the portico which ornamented the further side of the second court, its remains were visible even before the excavations of Mariette.[366]

FIG. 251.—Restoration in perspective of Dayr-el-Bahari, by Ch. Chipiez.

Those excavations have since 1858 led to the discovery of the porticos of the third court. There seems to have been only a plain wall on the left of this court, while on the right there was a long colonnade which masked a number of chambers cut in the rock which rose immediately behind it. Facing the entrance to the court there was also a colonnade which was cut in two by the steps leading to the fourth and highest terrace. In the middle of this terrace a line doorway leading to the principal speos was raised. While all the rest of the temple was of limestone, this doorway was built of fine red granite, a distinction which is to be explained by its central situation, facing the gateway in the pylon though far above it, and forming the culminating point of the long succession of terraces and inclined planes. The attention of the visitor to the temple would be instantly seized by the beauty and commanding position of this doorway, which, moreover, by its broad and mysterious shadows, suggested the secos hidden in the flanks of the mountains, to which all the courts were but the prelude.

These terraced courts have surprised all visitors to the cenotaph of Hatasu. "No one will deny," says Mariette, "that the temple of Dayr-el-Bahari is a strange construction, and that it resembles an Egyptian temple as little as possible!"[367] Some have thought foreign influence was to be traced in its arrangements. "Are we to consider it an accident, asks Ebers, that the stepped building at Dayr-el-Bahari was built shortly after an Egyptian army had, under Thothmes, trodden the soil of Mesopotamia for the first time, and found monumental buildings constructed in terraces in its great cities? Why did the Egyptians, who as a rule were so fond of repeating themselves that they became almost incapable of inventing new forms, never imitate the arrangements of this imposing building elsewhere, unless it was because its forms reminded them of their foreign enemies and therefore seemed to be worthy of condemnation?"[368]

We are content with asking the question and with calling attention to its interest. The materials are wanting for a definite answer but the suggestion of Professor Ebers is probable enough. Twelve or thirteen centuries later the Persians, after their conquest of Egypt, carried back with them the notion of those hypostyle halls which gave to the buildings of Persepolis so different an aspect from those of Assyria, although the decorative details were all borrowed from the latter country. So too the Egyptians, in spite of the pride which they felt in their ancient civilization, may have been unable to control their admiration when they found themselves, in the wide plains of Persia, before those lofty towers with their successive terraces, to which access was obtained by majestic flights of steps. It seems by no means unlikely that one of their architects should have attempted to acclimatize an artistic conception which was so well calculated to impress the imaginations of the people; and none of the sovereigns of Egypt was better fitted to preside over such an attempt than the high spirited and enterprising Hatasu, the queen who reared two obelisks in the temple of Karnak, one of them being the highest that has remained erect; who made the first recorded attempt at acclimatization;[369] and who was the first to launch a fleet upon the waters of the Red Sea.

Whether Hatasu's architect was inspired by those artistic creations of the Chaldees which, as time went on, were multiplied over the whole basin of the Euphrates and even spread as far as northern Syria, or whether he drew his ideas entirely from his own brain, his work was, in either case, deserving of high praise. In most parts of the Nile Valley sites are to be found which lend themselves readily to such a building. The soil has a gentle slope, upon which the erection of successive terraces would involve no architectural difficulties, and there is no lack of rocky walls against which porticoes could be erected, and in which subterranean chambers could be excavated. Upon a series of wide platforms and easy gradients like these, the pompous processions, which played such an important part in the Egyptian ritual, could defile with great effect, while under every portico and upon every landing place they could find resting places and the necessary shelter from the sun. Why did such a model find no imitators? Must we seek for the reason in the apparent reaction against her memory which followed the death of Hatasu? "The Egyptian people chose to look upon her as an usurper; they defaced the inscriptions which celebrated her campaigns; they effaced her cartouches and replaced her titles with those of her brothers."[370]

It is certain that nowhere in Egypt has any building of considerable dimensions been discovered in which the peculiar arrangements of Dayr-el-Bahari are repeated. At most it may be said that something of the same kind is to be found in those rock-cut temples of Nubia which are connected with the river bank by a dromos and flights of steps. When the princes of the nineteenth dynasty wished to raise funerary temples to their memory in their own capital, it would have been easy, had they chosen, to find sites upon the slopes of the western chain similar to that which Hatasu had employed with such happy results; but they preferred a different combination. They erected their cenotaphs in the plain, at some distance from the hills, and they chose a form which did not essentially differ from that of the great temples on the opposite bank of the Nile.

The religious architecture of Egypt, in all its richness and variety, is known to us only through the monuments of the second Theban Empire, through the great works of the kings belonging to the eighteenth and nineteenth dynasties. We are tempted, however, to believe that the architects of the Sait period must have introduced fresh beauties into the plans, proportions, and decorations of those temples which the princes of the twenty-sixth dynasty, in their desire that their capital and the other cities of the Delta should rival or excel the magnificence of Memphis and Thebes, confided to their skill. Both the statues and the royal tombs of the Sait period have characteristics which distinguish them from those of earlier epochs. In all that we possess from this last period of artistic activity in Egypt, there is a new desire for elegance, for grace, carried sometimes to an extreme which is not free from weakness and affectation. It is probable that the same qualities existed in the religious architecture of Sais.

Unhappily all the buildings constructed in Memphis and Lower Egypt during the Sait supremacy have disappeared leaving hardly a trace behind, and the Greek writers have left us nothing but vague accounts to supply their place. Herodotus goes into ecstasies over the propylæa, that is, the pylons and outer courts, which Amasis added to the temple of Neith at Sais, and over the enormous size of the stones employed. He describes in great detail a chapel carved out of a single block of Syene granite, which Amasis transported from the quarries at great cost in order that it might be erected in the sanctuary of the said temple; unhappily it was so much injured on the journey that his intention had to be abandoned.[371]

All that we learn from the historian is that the Sait princes made use of colossal stones in their buildings without much regard to their appropriateness, but simply to impress their contemporaries with an exaggerated idea of their wealth and power. The contractors of an earlier age were also in the habit of employing blocks which seem astonishing to us from their length and size, but they were never used except when they were required, to cover a void or some other purpose; the earlier architects never made the mistake of seeking for difficulties merely to show how cleverly they could overcome them.

It is to be regretted that we know so little of the monument attributed by Herodotus to Psemethek, and described by him in the following terms: —"Having become master of the whole of Egypt, Psammitichos constructed those propylæa of the temple of Hephaistos which lie to the south of that building. In front of these propylæa he also caused to be constructed an edifice in which Apis was nourished as soon as he had manifested himself. It was a peristyle ornamented with figures. Colossal statues, twelve cubits high, were employed as supports, instead of columns."[372] We may assume that these colossi were, as in other Egyptian buildings, placed immediately in front of the real supports, and did not themselves uphold an entablature. Herodotus was not an architect, and, in taking account merely of the general effect, he doubtless used an expression which is not quite accurate.

The most important point to be noticed in this short extract from the Greek historian is the hint it contains of the attempts at originality made by the later generations of Egyptians, by "men born too late in too old a century," and of the means by which they hoped to rival their predecessors. The architect of Psemethek borrowed a motive which had long been disused, of which, however, there are many examples at Thebes, and employed it under novel conditions.

The caryatid form of pier is generally found, in temples, in the peristyles of the fore-courts or the hypostyles of the pronaos. Psemethek made use of it for the decoration of what was no more than a cattle stable.[373] The stable in question had, it must be confessed, a god for its inhabitant, and so far it might be called a temple; but it was a temple of a very peculiar kind, in which the arrangements must have been very different from those required in the abode of an inanimate deity. In it the god was present in flesh and blood, and special arrangements were necessary in order to provide for his wants, and to exhibit him to the crowd or conceal him, as the ritual demanded. The problem was solved, apparently, in a method satisfactory to the Egyptians, as the guide who attended Herodotus called his attention to the building with an insistance which led the historian to pay it special attention.

Herodotus does not tell us what form the caryatides took in this instance. It is unlikely that they were Osiride figures of the king, as in the Theban temples, but as Apis was the incarnation of Ptah, the great deity of Memphis, they may very possibly have been carved in the image of that god.

Between the days of Cambyses and those of Alexander, Egypt temporarily recovered her independence more than once. The art of that period—during which numerous works were carried out and many others restored—was a prolongation of the art of the Sait princes. Its aims, methods, and taste were entirely similar. We may, therefore, in spite of the limits which we have imposed upon ourselves, mention a work carried out no more than fifty years before the Greek conquest, in the reign of Nectanebo I. We mean the small building which is sometimes called the southern temple, in the island of Philæ. It is the oldest building upon the island, all the rest being Ptolemaic or Roman.

Its arrangements are different to anything we have hitherto encountered in religious architecture. There are no internal subdivisions of any kind, nothing which resembles a secos. According to all the plans which have been published, it contained only one hall, or rather rectangular court, inclosed by fourteen graceful columns and a low, richly-decorated wall, which forms a kind of screen between the lower part of the columns. This screen does not extend quite half-way up the columns; these latter support an entablature, but there has never been a roof of any kind. There can be no doubt that the building was consecrated to Isis, whose image is carved all over it; but could an edifice thus open to the outward air and to every prying eye be a temple? Ebers is disposed to look upon it as a waiting-room.[374] Close to it the remains of a wide staircase are to be traced, against which boats were moored, and upon which they discharged their loads. Thus the faithful who came to be present at the rites of Isis would assemble in the waiting-hall, whence they would be conducted by the priests to that sanctuary which became the object of so many pilgrimages in the later years of the Egyptian monarchy.

Certain peculiarities in the management of the column, which grew into frequent use in the Ptolemaic epoch, are here encountered for the first time. This is not the place for its detailed consideration, but one must point it out as a second result of the desire shown by the architects of the period to achieve new developments without breaking the continuity of the national traditions. Here, as in the monumental cattle-shed at Memphis, there is no invention of new forms; all the architectural elements introduced are to be found in earlier buildings. It is the general aspect and physiognomy of the building that is new. Whatever we may call it, the edifice erected by Nectanebo at the southern point of the island is certainly novel in form; we have found nothing like it either in Egypt or in Nubia, but the repetition of its forms in a much later generation proves that it answered to a real change in the national taste and to new aspirations in the national genius. Painting, engraving, and photography have given us countless reproductions of the picturesque building which rises on the eastern shore of the island, amid a bouquet of palm-trees. It has been variously called the *bed of Pharaoh*, the *eastern temple*, the *great hypæthra*, the *summer-house of Tiberius*, &c. It is nothing more than a replica of Nectanebo's creation; it is larger and its proportions are more lofty, but its plan is quite similar.[375] In the sketch lent to us by M. Hector Leroux, the eastern temple is seen on the right, while the left of the drawing is filled up with the pylons of the great temple of Isis (Fig. 252).

FIG. 252.—The ruins on the Island of Philæ; from a sketch by Hector Leroux.

If we knew it better, we should probably find that the architecture of the Sait period formed the transition between that of the second Theban empire and that of the Ptolemies. We should find in it at least hints and foreshadowings of those original features of which we shall have to speak when we arrive at the Græco-Egyptian temples. Unhappily, as none of the temples built by Psemethek, Amasis, and their successors have been recovered from the sands of Egypt, we shall be reduced to conjecture on this point. But must all hope of recovering something from the ruins of Sais be abandoned? Mariette himself made some excavations upon its site, and confessed that he was discouraged by their result, or rather by their want of result. Perhaps, however, deeper and more prolonged excavations might bring to light sufficient indications of the ordonnance and plans of the more important buildings to permit of some attempt at restoration being made.[376]

§ 4. General Characteristics of the Egyptian Temple.

We have now conducted our history of the Egyptian temple from the most ancient monument to which that title can be given to the period when Greek art, introduced into the country by the Macedonian conquest, began to have an influence upon many of the important details, if not upon the general aspects of the national architecture. The reader will not be surprised to find that before we conclude our study we wish to give a *résumé* of the leading ideas which seem to be embodied in the temple, and to define the latter as we see it in its finest and most complete expression, in the buildings of the great Theban Pharaohs. We cannot do better for our purpose than borrow the words of Mariette upon the subject. No one has become more thoroughly acquainted with the temples of the Nile valley. He visited them all at his leisure, he explored their ruins and sounded most of them down to their foundations, and he published circumstantial descriptions of Abydos, Karnak, Dayr-el-Bahari, and Denderah. In these monographs and in the *Itinéraire de la Haute-Égypte*, he returned to his definition again and again, in a continual attempt to improve it, to make it clear and precise. We shall freely extract from his pages all those expressions which seem to us to give the best rendering of their author's ideas, and to bring out most clearly the originality which belongs to the monuments of which he treats.[377]

"The Egyptian temple must not be confused with that of Greece, with the Christian church, or with the Mohammedan mosque. It was not a place for the meeting of the faithful, for the recital of common prayers; no public ritual was celebrated within it; no one was admitted to it except the priests and the king. The temple was a kind of royal oratory, a monument reared by the king in token of his own piety, and in order to purchase the favour of the gods.

"The elaborate decoration with which all the walls of the temples are covered is only to be explained by admitting this point of departure. The essential element of this decoration is the picture; many pictures are arranged symmetrically side by side, and tiers above tiers of pictures cover the walls from floor to ceiling. This arrangement never varies, and the same may be said of the general significance of the pictures: on the one hand, the king, on the other, one or more deities; these are the subjects of all the compositions. The king makes an offering (meats, fruits, flowers, emblems) to the god and asks for some favour at his hands; in his answer the deity grants the favour demanded. The whole decoration of a temple consisted therefore in an act of adoration on the part of the monarch repeated in various forms. The temple was therefore the exclusive personal monument of the prince by whom it was founded and decorated. This fact explains the presence of those precious representations of battles which adorn the external walls of certain temples. [378] The king ascribed all his successes in the field to the immediate protection of the gods. In combating the enemies of Egypt, in bringing them by thousands to the capital, in employing them upon the construction of their temples, he was performing an act as agreeable to the gods as when offering incense, flowers, and the limbs of the animals sacrificed. By such deeds he proved his piety and merited the continuation of those favours for which the erection of a temple was meant to be an acknowledgment."

The piety and gratitude of the monarch also found expression in the splendour of the great festivals of which the temple was the scene several times in the course of the year. "The ceremonies consisted for the most part of great processions, issuing from the sanctuary to be marshalled in the hypostyle hall, and afterwards traversing the open courts which lay between the buildings of the temple and the great wall which incloses the whole. They perambulated the terraced roofs, they launched upon the lake the sacred barque with its many-coloured streamers. Upon a few rare occasions the priests, with the sacred images, sallied from the inclosure which ordinarily shielded their rites from profane eyes, and, at the head of a brilliant flotilla, directed their course to some other city, either by the Nile or by the waterway which they called 'the sacred canal.'"[379]

"The ensigns of the gods, the coffers in which their effigies or symbolic representations were inclosed, their shrines and sacred barques were carried in these processions, of which the kings were the reputed conductors. At other times all these objects were deposited in the naos. Upon the occurrence of a festival, the priest to whom the duty was delegated by the king entered the naos and brought out the mysterious emblem which was hidden from all other eyes; he covered it with a rich veil, and it was then carried under a canopy."

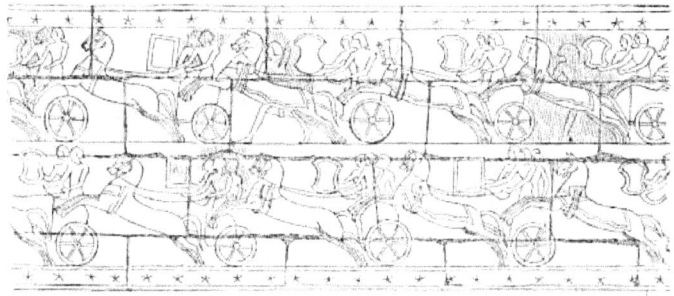

FIG. 253.—The battle against the Khetas, Luxor.
(From Champollion, pl. 328.)

A ritual to which so much "pomp and circumstance" was attached required material appliances on a great scale. The preservation of so much apparatus required extensive store-rooms, which, like the sanctuary itself, had to be kept in almost total darkness in order to preserve the sacred vestments and other objects from the deteriorating effects of sun, dust, heat, and the insects which they engender. There is nothing in the texts which seems to hint at the celebration of any rites in the dark parts of the temple by artificial light, and no trace of the discoloration caused by smoke has been found upon the walls. There seems to have been no necessity for anything beyond the most subdued daylight within the chambers of the temple. All the important part of the ritual was performed in the open air, and the few liturgical acts in the naos were short and took place before a very restricted audience. They consisted of a few prayers said by the king or by the chief priest, and in the presentation of the traditional offerings. The cares of maintenance and of preparation for the periodical festivals had also to go on in that part of the temple. Such duties, however, could be readily discharged by the practised and disciplined priests in the half light of the sanctuary, and even the almost total darkness of the apartments which were ranged behind it.

FIG. 254.—Rameses II. returning in triumph from Syria.
On the external face of the northern wall of the Great Temple at Karnak.
(From Champollion, pl. 292.)

"The temples show no trace of dwelling-places for the priests, nor of places for initiation, nor of any contrivance for divination or the giving of oracles. There is nothing to lead us to suppose that, except the king and the priests, any of the public were admitted into the building," at least beyond the hypostyle hall. Certain privileged individuals or classes were admitted into the latter on the occasion of a festival; others, less fortunate, were compelled to wait in the courtyards. It was their right to be the first to see the god as he emerged from the sanctuary on the shoulders of the priests. But in spite of their vast dimensions, these halls would have been ill fitted for the uses to which the spacious naves of a church or mosque are put. The huge and closely spaced columns would embarras the movements and intercept the view of those who crowded about their bases. It was only in the central aisle that sufficient space was left for the easy passage of a procession. The hypostyle hall was lofty and wide in order that it might be a vestibule worthy of the god who dwelt in the sanctuary beyond it, and in order that it might bear witness by its magnificence to the piety, wealth, and power of the king who constructed it. It offered no place in which the faithful could assemble to listen to religious discourses, to unite in the expression of their faith and hope, to sing and pray in common.

In virtue of the sanctuary which was its nucleus, the temple was the dwelling of the god, the terrestrial resting-place to which the king, his son and the nursling of the goddesses, came to offer him thanks and to do homage in return for the protection and support which he received. The temple was also, in virtue of those numerous chambers which surrounded the sanctuary, a place for the preparation, consecration, and preservation of holy objects; a huge sacristy to which access was forbidden to all but those who were specially attached to the service of the god and charged with the custody of the sacred furniture.

Such being the origin and purpose of the temple, we need feel no surprise at the triple fortification behind which it was entrenched. This fortification consisted, in the first place, of the brick wall which formed the outermost inclosure; secondly, of the wall of masonry which embraced the temple proper, leaving a narrow passage only wide enough for the walk of a sentry; thirdly, of the wall which divided the really secret parts of the building from the pronaos. Now that the line of the external wall is only indicated by a gentle swell of the ground, now that the best preserved of the inner walls are broken down in many places, and now that all the roofs and ceilings have fallen and encumbered the floors, it is difficult enough to form a true idea of the former appearance of the Egyptian temples. Could we see them as they left their architects' hands, we should be struck by the jealous severity of their isolation, by the austere monotony of the screen of stone which was interposed between the eyes of the people and the internal splendours of the building. In this we should find the chief point of distinction between the temples of Egypt and those great religious edifices of our own times with which we half involuntarily compare all other works of the kind.

But the Greek temple was no more a church than its Egyptian rival. It was not a place of assembly for public praise or religious teaching. Its cella was an inclosed chamber, illuminated only by the door and by a few openings contrived in the roof, and reserved for the god who inhabited it. The two architects in fact, Egyptian and Greek, had the same points of departure; the problems which they had to solve strongly resembled each other, and yet they created types which differed very greatly. The Greek temple was not isolated and hidden behind a stone curtain; it could be seen from all sides in its commanding position; its encircling bands of porticos seemed to invite all comers to the shelter of their galleries, while they charmed all eyes with the play of light and shadow afforded by their alternate voids and solids. The colonnades reserved by the Egyptian for the decoration of courts and halls were placed by the Greek upon the external faces of his temples, and although the task of both architects was to fulfil almost identical requirements, this transposition of the elements employed was sufficient to cause a profound difference in the outward expression, in the physiognomy, of their several works.

FIG. 255.—**The goddess Anouké suckling Rameses II., Beit-Wali; from Horeau.**

Another and perhaps still more characteristic difference is to be found in the fact that the Greek temple is not susceptible, like that of Egypt, of almost infinite extension. Greece never produced anything like Karnak or Luxor; even in the centuries when the taste for the colossal eclipsed the love for the great, she never dreamed or imagined anything of the kind. The Greek temple had the unity of a living organism. Given the main dimensions, the elements of which it was to be composed could only vary within very narrow limits. In accordance with the degree of luxury desired, the cella would be either surrounded by a simple wall or would be encircled by a portico, but this portico would only be a kind of adornment, a vesture which would be more or less rich and ample according to circumstances. Behind the long files of columns on either side, behind the double or triple rows which veiled the two façades, the body of the temple could always be discerned, just as the modelling of the human form may be distinguished under the drapery of a statue, in spite of the folds which cover it. The cella was proportioned to the sacred figure which was to be its inhabitant, which, again, afforded a standard by which the proportions and subjects of the groups which filled the pediments, and of the bas-reliefs of the frieze, as well as the height of the columns and the projection of the entablature, were determined. Between all these parts there was an intimate and clearly defined connection.

When a plant is seen bursting from the seed, we are able, if we know the species to which it belongs, to say beforehand what its leaves, its flower, and its fruit will be like, and to foretell the limits of its height. It is the same, to a great extent, with the Greek temple. The trench dug to receive the footing stones of the cella walls is the hole into which the seed is thrown from which the whole temple is to spring. These walls rise above the level of the ground, the building progresses to completion, but from the day upon which the seed was sown, from the day upon which the foundation was laid, the temple had been virtually complete. Like an organic body, the Greek temple inclosed within itself the principle of its own growth, the law which governed its development, and forbade it in advance to exceed certain definite limits.

Such was not the case with the Egyptian temple. In those of small or moderate dimensions this unity and simplicity of plan exists to a certain extent. The peripteral temple of Elephantiné and even the temple of Khons may be given as instances of this; in them there is much with which the most exclusive philo-Greek can sympathize. The impression received from the ruins of Abydos or Gournah, still more from those of Karnak or Luxor, is very different. There we find several sanctuaries closely wedged together, all of the same size and decorated in the same fashion, in one place the architect has built seven in a row, and there was nothing to prevent him doubling the number if he had chosen to do so. In another we find a succession of courts, of hypostyle halls and chambers, of forests of columns. Sometimes it requires considerable search to pitch upon the sanctuary, which, again, is not the loftiest part of the building, being dominated by hypostyle hall and pylons.

When Egypt had arrived at the summit of her greatness and wished to erect temples to her gods which should be worthy both of herself and of them, she found herself obliged either to sacrifice the unity of the temple by dividing it up into distinct naves and sanctuaries, or to hide the main parts by the accessories in such a fashion that the sanctuary seems to be lost among the annexes which envelop it in front and rear. The vestibule and other subsidiary parts mask the real dwelling of the god. We are sometimes at a loss to decide the uses of all the chambers of so vast and complex a structure, because our knowledge of the circumstances of ancient Egyptian worship is still far from complete. It is significant that even among such an imposing pile of buildings as those of Karnak, egyptologists have found it impossible to agree as to the situation of the heart and organic centre of the whole. That centre exists; it existed before all those sumptuous additions of which it was the cause. But it would seem that its influence failed to make itself felt beyond a certain distance. The temple was enlarged by additions made at its two extremities, in the manner of an inorganic body, so that no limit could be logically assigned to its development. Karnak, as it was left by the Pharaohs and their successors, is the most colossal work of architecture which has come down to us from antiquity, and yet our imagination can give to it even greater dimensions than it actually possessed without injury to its artistic expression. If the worship of which it was the scene had endured a few centuries longer, it would have been easy to add new pylons, new courts, and new hypostyle halls to those already existing; but had the worship of Athene endured through as many ages as that of Ptah or Amen, it would have been impossible to make additions to the Parthenon as it left the hands of Ictinus and Phidias.

END OF VOL. I.

FOOTNOTES:

[1] Page 92, Vol. I.

[2] Our national library at the British Museum is, perhaps, the only one which does not deserve this reproach.—ED.

[3] *Geschichte der bildenden Kunst*, 2nd ed., corrected and augmented, with wood engravings in the text, 8 vols. 8vo. 1865-1873. The first edition consisted of 7 vols., and appeared between 1843 and 1864.

[4] Germany had long felt the want which Schnaase attempted to satisfy. As early as 1841 Franz Kugler published his *Handbuch der Kunstgeschichte*, which embraces the whole history of art from the earliest times down to our own day. The book was successful; the fourth edition, revised and corrected by Wilhelm Lübke (2 vols. 8vo. 1861, Stuttgart), lies before us, but to give an idea of its inadequacy as a history of ancient art, it is enough to say that the whole of the antique period, both in Greece and Asia, occupies no more than 206 pages of the first volume. The few illustrations are not very good in quality, and their source is never indicated; the draughtsman has taken little care to reproduce with fidelity the style of the originals or to call attention to their peculiarities; finally, the arrangements adopted betray the defects of a severely scientific method. The author commences with Celtic monuments (dolmens and menhirs), and then passes to the structures of Oceania and America; before commencing upon Egypt he takes us to Mexico and Yucatan. Lübke, whilst still occupied with the work of Kugler, wished to supply for the use of students and artists a book of a more elementary character; he therefore published in 1860 an 8vo volume which he called *Grundriss der Kunstgeschichte*; the antique here occupies 208 pages out of 720. His plan seems to us to be open to the same objection as that of Kugler; he follows a geographical instead of an historical arrangement; he begins with the extreme east; he puts the Assyrians and the Persians before Egypt, and India before Assyria. His illustrations are sometimes better than those of Kugler, but many of the cuts are common to both works.

Under the title *Geschichte der Plastik*, Overbeck and Lübke have each written a comprehensive history of sculpture. [The word "comprehensive" must here be understood in a strictly limited sense.—ED.] The word *Plastik* in the language of German critics has this special and restricted meaning—it comprises sculpture only. The work of Overbeck, far superior to that of Lübke, deserves the success which has attended it; the third edition, which contains the results of the searches at Olympia and at Pergamus, is now in course of publication.

[5] Winckelmann's History of Ancient Art should be read in connection with his Remarks upon the History of Art, which is a kind of supplement to it, and takes the place of that new edition of which the author's premature and tragic death deprived the world. It is an answer to the objections which made themselves heard on every side; the preface to *Monumenti inediti* (Rome, 1867, 2 vols. in folio, with 208 plates) should also be read. The method of Winckelmann is there

most clearly explained. Finally, the student of the life and labours of Winckelmann may consult with profit the interesting work of Carl Iusti, *Winckelmann, sein Leben, seine Werke, und seine Zeitgenossen*, which will give him a clear idea of the state of archæology at the time when the German *savant* intervened to place it upon a higher footing.

[6] Zoëga busied himself greatly with Egypt, and in inaugurating the study of Coptic prepared the way for Champollion. But the work which gave him a place among the chief scholars of Winckelmann is unfinished; the *Bassirilievi antichi di Roma* (Rome, 2 vols. 4to. 1808) only contains the monuments in the Villa Albani, engraved by Piroli, with the help of the celebrated Piranesi. A volume containing most of his essays was given to the world by Welcker in 1817 (*Abhandlungen herausgegeben und mit Zusätzen begleitet*, 8vo. Göttingen), who also published his life and a volume of his correspondence (Zoëga, *Sammlung seiner Briefe und Beurtheilung seiner Werke*, 2 vols. 8vo. Stuttgart, 1819).

[7] *Il Museo Pio-Clementino*, Visconti, vol. i. 1782; by Enn. Quir. Visconti, vols. ii. to vii. Rome, 1784-1807. *Museum Worsleyanum*, 2 vols. folio. London, 1794. *Monumenti Gabini della Villa Pinciana*, Visconti, 8vo. 1797. *Description des Antiques du Musée Royal*, begun by Visconti and continued by the Comte de Clarac. 12mo. Paris, 1820. For the collection of the materials and the execution of the plates in the *Iconographie Grecque et Romain*, Visconti took advantage of his opportunities as director of the *Musée Napoléon*, into which the art treasures of all Europe, except England, were collected at the beginning of this century.

[8] They were discovered in 1811 amid the ruins of one of the temples at Ægina, by a company of excavators presided over by Mr. Cockerell. They were bought by Prince Louis of Bavaria in 1812, and Thorwaldsen was occupied during several years in putting together and restoring them. They were first exhibited in the Glyptothek of Munich in 1820.

[9] The *débris* of the temple at Bassæ was explored by the same company in the year 1812, and a whole frieze was found, which was bought by the British Museum in 1815.

[10] *The Antiquities of Athens, Measured and Delineated by J. Stuart and N. Revett.* Folio. London, 1761.

[11] *Expédition scientifique de Morée, ordonnée par le Gouvernement Français. Architecture, Sculpture, Inscriptions, mesurées, dessinées, recueillies et publiées, par* A. Blouet, A. Ravoisié, Alph. Poirot, F. Trézel, et Fr. de Gournay. Paris, 1831-7.

[12] The restoration of the temple of Athenè Polias and of the Parthenon, by Ballu and Paccard, dates from 1845. Since that time the students of the French Academy have drawn and restored all the most important monuments of Greece.

[13] One temple at Baalbec was restored in 1865 by M. Moyau; the Mausoleum of Halicarnassus by M. Bernier in 1878, and the temple of Athenè at Priene by M. Thomas in 1879.

[14] In 1872 this collection consisted of sixty-one restorations, comprising 691 original drawings upon a very large scale, and forming fifty-two bound volumes.

Thanks to M. Jules Simon, then Minister of Public Instruction, and M. Charles Blanc, Director of Fine Arts, the publication of the series in its entirety was resolved upon. A commission, with M. Ernest Vinet as secretary, was appointed to superintend the expenditure of an annual grant of 20,000 francs voted by the Chamber. But the work progresses very slowly. In 1881 only five sections had appeared, the most important being the *Restauration des Temples de Pæstum*, by Labrouste.

[15] F. C. PENROSE, *An Investigation of the Principles of Athenian Architecture*. Folio, with plates. London, 1851.

[16] J. J. HITTORF, *Restitution du Temple d'Empédocle à Sèlinonte; ou, l'Architecture polychrome chez les Grecs*, 4to. and plates in folio. Paris, 1851.

[17] See upon this subject M. Wolfgang Helbig's *Untersuchungen ueber die Campanische Wandmalerei*. Leipsic, 1873. M. Boissier has summed up the leading opinions in this matter in an interesting article in the *Révue des Deux Mondes*, entitled *Les Peintures d'Herculaneum et de Pompéi* (October 1, 1879).

[18] *Rapporto intorno i Vasi Volcenti* (*Annali dell' Instituto di Corrispondenza Archeologica*, vol. iii. p. 5).

[19] One of the first antiquaries to whom it occurred that the examination of these little objects might lead to profitable results was the Comte de Caylus, a *savant* who is in some danger of being forgotten, and who deserves that his claims to our gratitude should be recalled to the public mind. The work in which he has brought together the fruits of a long life spent in travelling, in collecting, and in examining the technical processes of the ancients, both by himself and with the help of specialists, may be consulted with advantage (*Recueil d' Antiquites égyptiennes, étrusques, grecques, et romains*, 6 vols. 4to. 1752-64. Supplement, 1 vol. 4to. 1767).

[20] *Recherches sur les Figures de Femmes voilées dans l'Art Grec*, 4to. Paris, 1873. *Recherches sur un Groupe de Praxitèle, d'après les Figurines de terre cuite*, 8vo. Paris, 1875. *Les Figurines antiques de terre cuite du Musée du Louvre*, 4to. 1878, Morel.

[21] For the history of the *Instituto Archeologico*, the notice written for the celebration, in 1879, of the fiftieth anniversary of its foundation, may be consulted. It is from the pen of Michaëlis, one of the most learned of modern German archæologists, and bears the following title: *Storia dell' Instituto Archeologico Germano, 1829-1879, strenna pubblicata nell' occasione della festa del 21 Aprile, 1879, dalla direzione centrale dell' Instituto Archeologico*, 8vo. Roma, 1879. It was also published in German. An article by M. Ernest Vinet in the volume entitled *L'Art et l'Archéologie* (pp. 74-91, 8vo. Didier, 1874), upon the origin and labours of the *Instituto*, will also be found interesting.

[22] LÉO JOUBERT, *Essais de critique et d'histoire* (Paris, Firmin-Didot, 1 vol. 1863, p. 4). We shall never cease to regret that politics have deprived literature of this judicious and widely instructed critic.

[23] *Kunstarchæologische Werke*. Berlin, Calvary, 18 mo. 1873.

[24] *Handbuch der Archæologie der Kunst*, 1 vol. 8vo.

[25] The French translation, from the pen of M. P. Nicard, forms three volumes of the collection of handbooks known under the name of the *Encyclopédie Roret*. It appeared in 1841, so that the translator was unable to make use of the additions and corrections with which Welcker enriched the edition of 1848. But M. Nicard's edition has one great advantage over the German versions in the complete tables with which it is provided. The best English translation is that by J. Leitch, the second edition of which appeared in 1850.—ED.

[26] Stark died at Heidelberg in October, 1879. The title of his work was identical with that of Müller: *Handbuch der Archæologie der Kunst*. The first 256 pages of the first volume were published in 1878 with the sub-title: *Einleitender und grundlegender Theil* (Leipsic, Engelmann, 8vo). A second instalment appeared in 1880, by which the introduction was completed. The entire work, which will not be continued, was to have formed three volumes. We explained its plan and made some remarks upon the part already published in the *Revue Critique* of July 14, 1879.

[27] *Journal of a Tour in Asia Minor, with Comparative Remarks on the Ancient and Modern Geography of that Country* (1 vol. in 8vo. London, Murray, 1821, pp. 31-33).

[28] *A Description of some Ancient Monuments with Inscriptions still existing in Lydia and Phrygia*. London, 1842, in folio.

[29] *Timæus*, p. 22.

[30] *Dictionnaire archéologique de la Gaule*, vol. i., Cavernes, figure 28. Al. BERTRAND, *Archéologie celtique et gauloise* (1 vol. 8vo. Didier, 1876, p. 68).

[31] SCHLIEMANN, *Mycenæ*, see figs. 33 and 213; CESNOLA, *Cyprus*, see pls. 44 and 46.

[32] *Archæological Survey of India*, 3 vols. 1871-73.

[33] *Archæologische Zeitung*, 1876, p. 90. *Die Griechische Kunst in Indien*.

[34] The Louvre has lately acquired some curious examples of this art.

[35] *Histoire de l'Art*; Huber's preface to his translation, p. xxxii.

[36] The word "plastic" is used throughout this work in its widest significance, and is not confined to works "in the round."—ED.

[37] HERODOTUS, ii. 7.

[38] MARIETTE, *Itineraire de la haute Égypte*, p. 10 (edition of 1872, 1 vol. Alexandria, Moures).

[39] The river should rise to this height upon the Nilometer at Cairo if there is to be a "good Nile." In upper Egypt the banks of the river are much higher than in middle Egypt. In order to flow over those banks it must rise to a height of some eleven or twelve metres, and unless it rises more than thirteen metres it will not have a proper effect.

[40] This work of Champollion's, to which we are greatly indebted, is entitled: *Monuments de l'Égypte et de la Nubie*, 4 vols. folio. It contains 511 plates, partly coloured, and was published between the years 1833 and 1845. The drawings for the plates were made by members of the great scientific expedition of which Champollion was the head. Many of those drawings were from the pencil of Nestor L'Hôte, one of those who have most sympathetically rendered the Egyptian monuments.

[41] This advantage was thoroughly appreciated by the ancients. Diodorus Siculus, speaking of the Egyptians, says that "At the beginning of all things, the first men were born in Egypt, in consequence of the happy climate of the country and the physical properties of the Nile, whose waters, by their natural fertility and their power of producing various kinds of aliment, were well fitted to nourish the first beings who received the breath of life.... It is evident that from the foundation of the world Egypt was, of all countries, the most favourable to the generation of men and women, by the excellent constitution of its soil" (i. 10).

[42] In all ages the rod has, in Egypt, played an important part in the collection of the taxes. In this connection M. Lieblein has quoted a passage from the well-known letter from the chief guardian of the archives of Ameneman to the scribe Pentaour, in which he says: "The scribe of the port arrives at the station; he collects the tax; there are agents with rattans, and negroes with branches of palm; they say 'Give us some corn!' and they are not to be repulsed. The peasant is bound and sent to the canal; he is driven on with violence, his wife is bound in his presence, his children are stripped; as for his neighbours, they are far off and are busy over their own harvest." (*Les Récits de Recolte dans l'ancienne Égypte, comme Éléments chronologique*, in *Recueil de Travaux relatifs à la Philologie et à l'Archéologie égyptiennes et assyriennes*, t. i. p. 149).

[43] ROBIOU, *Histoire ancienne des Peuples de l'Orient*, ch. v.

[44] HERODOTUS, ii. 4.

[45] MASPERO, *Histoire ancienne des Peuples de l'Orient*, pp. 6 and 7. In such general explanations as are unavoidable we shall content ourselves with paraphrasing M. Maspero.

[46] Their exceptional breadth of shoulder has been confirmed by an examination of the skeletons in the mummies. See on this subject a curious note in BONOMI's *Some Observations on the Skeleton of an Egyptian Mummy* (*Transactions of the Society of Biblical Archæology*, vol. iv. pp. 251-253).

[47] MASPERO, *Histoire ancienne*, p. 16.

[48] *Notice des principaux Monuments exposés dans les Galeries provisoires du Musée d'Antiquités égyptiennes de S. A. le Vice-Roi, à Boulaq* (1876), No. 492. The actual statue holds the *bâton* in its left hand.

[49] *Notice des principaux Monuments exposés dans les Galeries provisoires du Musée d'Antiquités égyptiennes de S. A. le Vice-Roi, à Boulaq* (1876), p. 582. With the exception of a few woodcuts from photographs the contents of the museums at Cairo and Boulak have been reproduced from drawings by M. J.

Bourgoin. The Boulak Museum will be referred to by the simple word Boulak. The reproductions of objects in the Louvre are all from the pencil of M. Saint-Elme Gautier.

[50] MASPERO, *Histoire ancienne*, p. 17.

[51] *Histoire des Langues sémitiques*, Book i. ch. ii. § 4.

[52] See LEPSIUS, *Ueber die Annahme eines sogenannten prehistorischen Steinalters in Ægypten* (in the *Zeitschrift für Ægyptische Sprache*, 1870, p. 113, et seq.).

[53] MASPERO, p. 18.

[54] *Histoire ancienne des Peuples de l'Orient*, p. 53. We believe that the division proposed by M. Maspero is, in fact, the best. It is the most suggestive of the truth as to the successive displacements of the political centre and the movement of history. We shall, however, have no hesitation in making use of the terms *Ancient, Middle*, and *New Empire*, as occasion arises.

[55] MARIETTE, *Aperçu de l'Histoire d'Égypte*, p. 66.

[56] BRUGSCH-BEY, *Histoire de l'Égypt*, pp. 6 and 7. Maspero's *Histoire ancienne*, p. 382, may also be consulted upon the character of the Ethiopian kingdom and the monuments of Napata. A good idea of this process of degradation may be gained by merely glancing through the plates to part v. of Lepsius's *Denkmœler*; plate 6, for example, shows what the caryatid became at Napata.

[57] MASPERO, *Histoire ancienne*, p. 58. This affiliation of the king to the god was more than a figure of speech. In an inscription which is reproduced both at Ipsamboul and at Medinet-Abou, Ptah is made to speak in the following terms of Rameses II. and Rameses III. respectively: "I am thy father, as a god I have begotten thee; all thy members are divine; when I approached thy royal mother I took upon me the form of the sacred ram of Mendes" (line 3rd). This curious text has lately been interpreted by E. Naville (*Society of Biblical Archæology*, vol. vii. pp. 119-138). The monarchy of the Incas was founded upon an almost identical belief.

[58] See the account of the visit to Heliopolis of the conquering Ethiopian, Piankhi-Mer-Amen; we shall quote the text of this famous inscription in our chapter upon the Egyptian temple.

[59] FR. LENORMANT, *Manuel d'Histoire ancienne*, t. 1, pp. 485-486. The most celebrated of these is the famous *Chamber of Ancestors* from Karnak, which is now preserved in the *Bibliothèque Nationale* at Paris.

[60] The beaters for the great hunts which took place in the Delta and the Fayoum were procured in the same fashion. These hunts were among the favourite pleasures of the kings and the great lords. See MASPERO, *Le Papyrus Mallet*, p. 58 (in *Recueil de Travaux*, etc. t. 1).

[61] The work to which we here refer is the *Histoire de l'Art Égyptien d'après les Monuments*, 2 vols. folio. Arthus Bertrand, 1878. As the plates are not

numbered, we can only refer to them generally.

[62] "The foundations of the great temple at Abydos, commenced by Seti I. and finished by Rameses II., consist of but a single course of generally ill-balanced masonry. Hence the settling which has taken place, and the deep fissure which divides the building in the direction of its major axis."—MARIETTE, *Voyage dans la Haute-Égypte*, p. 59. The same writer speaks of Karnak in a similar strain: "The Pharaonic temples are built, as a rule, with extreme carelessness. The western pylon, for instance, fell because it was hollow, which made the inclination of the walls a source of weakness instead of strength."—*Itineraire*, p. 179.

[63] HERODOTUS, ii. 172. For an earlier epoch, see the history of a certain Ahmes, son of Abouna, as it is narrated upon his sepulchral inscription, which dates from the reign of Amosis, the founder of the eighteenth dynasty (DE ROUGÉ, *Mémoire sur l'Inscription d'Ahmes, Chef des Nautoniers*, 4to. 1851, and Brugsch, *Histoire d'Égypte*, t. i. p. 80). Starting as a private soldier for the war against the Shepherds, undertaken for the re-conquest of Avaris, he was noticed by the king for his frequent acts of gallantry, and promoted until he finally became something in the nature of high admiral.

[64] Louvre, c. i. Cf. MASPERO, *un Gouverneur de Thèbes au temps de la douzième dynastie*.

[65] Quoted by MASPERO, *Conférence sur l'Histoire des Âmes dans l'Égypte ancienne, d'après les Monuments du Musée du Louvre* (*Association scientifique de France, Bulletin hebdomadaire*, No. 594; *23 Mars, 1879*).

[66] Translated by MASPERO (*la Grande Inscription de Beni-Hassan* in the *Recueil de Travaux relatifs à la Philologie et à l'Archéologie égyptienne et assyrienne* (t. i. pp. 173-174)).

[67] BRUGSCH-BEY, *Histoire d'Égypte*, pp. 14, 15.

[68] The saying of one of the characters of Petronius might be applied to Egypt: "This country is so thickly peopled with divinities that it is easier to find a god than a man." The place held by religious observances in the daily life of Egypt is clearly indicated by HERODOTUS (ii. 37): "The Egyptians," he says, "are very religious; they surpass all other nations in the adoration with which they regard their deities."

[69] MASPERO, *Histoire ancienne*, pp. 26, 27.

[70] This formula frequently occurs in the texts. To cite but one occasion, we find upon a Theban invocation to Amen, translated by P. PIERRET (*Recueil de Travaux relatifs à la Philologie et à l'Archéologie égyptienne et assyrienne*, t. i. p. 70), at the third line of the inscription: "Sculptor, thou modelest thine own members; thou begettest them, not having thyself been begotten."

[71] See the fine hymns quoted and translated by M. Maspero in his *Histoire ancienne*, pp. 30-37.

[72] Several of the bronzes which we reproduce may belong to the Ptolemaic epoch; but they are repetitions of types and attributes which had been fixed for

many centuries by tradition. It is in this capacity chiefly that we reproduce them, as examples of those forms which seemed to the Egyptian imagination to offer the most satisfactory emblems of their gods.

[73] In his work entitled *Des deux Yeux du Disque solaire*, M. GRÉBAUT seems to have very clearly indicated how far we are justified in saying that Egyptian religious speculation at times approached monotheism (*Recueil de Travaux, etc.*, t. i. p. 120).

[74] HERODOTUS, ii. 75-86.

[75] We do not mean to say that the higher qualities of the Egyptian religion were then altogether lost. In Roman Egypt the fetish superstitions were no doubt predominant, but still it had not lost all that theological erudition which it had accumulated by its own intellectual energy. In an inscription cut in the time of Philip the Arab, we find an antique hymn transcribed in hieroglyphs upon the wall of a temple. We find abstract and speculative ideas in all those Egyptian books which have come down to us, in a form which betrays the last two centuries of the Empire. Alexandria had its Egyptian Serapeum by the side of its Greek one. Monuments are to be found there which are Egyptian in every particular. Gnosticism was particularly successful in Egypt, which was predestined to accept it by the whole of its past. Certain doctrines of Plotinus are thus best explained. More than one purely Egyptian notion may be found interpreted in the works of Alexandrian philosophers and in the phraseology of Greek philosophy. The principal sanctuaries did not allow their rites and ceremonies to fall into disuse. Although Thebes was nothing but a heap of ruins, a dead city visited for its relics of the past, the worship of Vulcan, that is of Ptah, at Memphis, was carried on up to the establishment of Christianity. That of Isis, at Philæ, lasted until the time of Justinian. Diocletian negotiated a treaty with the Blemmyes, those people of Nubia who were at one time such redoubtable soldiers, which guaranteed to them the free use of that temple. It was not converted into a church until after the destruction of the Blemmyes by Silco and the Christian kings of Ethiopia.

The old religion and theology of the Egyptians did not expire in a single day. It was no more killed by the Roman conquest than it was by that of the Ptolemies. But although its rites did not cease, and some of its elaborate doctrines still continued to be transmitted, its vitality had come to an end. It exercised some remains of influence only on condition of being melted down and re-modelled in the crucible of Greek philosophy. A little *coterie* of thinkers set themselves to complete this transfusion, but the great mass of the people returned to simple practices which had been sanctified by thousands of years, and formed nearly the whole of their religion.

[76]

> Porrum et cæpe nefas violare et frangere morsu.
> O Sanctas gentes, quibus hæc nascuntur in hortis
> Numina!—JUVENAL, xv. 9-11.

[77] CLEMENS ALEXANDRINUS, quoted by Maspero, *Histoire ancienne*, p. 46.

[78] This was perceived by the President de Brosses, a *savant* with few advantages but a bold and inquiring spirit, to whom the language is indebted for the use of the term *fetishism* as a name for a definite state of religious conception. We can still read with interest the book which he published anonymously in 1760, under the title: *Du Culte des Dieux fétiches; ou, Parallèle de l'Ancienne Religion de l'Égypte avec la Religion actuelle de Nigritie* (12mo). The study of the fetish elements of the Egyptian religion has been resumed lately with competent knowledge and talent by a German egyptologist, Herr Pietschmann, in an essay which appeared in 1878 in the *Zeitschrift für Ethnologie*, which is published in Berlin under the direction of M. Virchow. It is called *Der Ægyptische Fetischdienst und Götterglaube—Prolegomena zur Ægyptischen Mythologie* (28 pp. 8vo). A great many judicious observations and curious facts are to be found in it; the realistic and materialistic character of the Egyptian conceptions are very well grasped; it is perhaps to be regretted that the author has not endeavoured to make the creeds to which he gives this name of *fétichisme* somewhat clearer, and to show by what workings of the mind they were adopted and abandoned. With regard to the Egyptian religion, we shall find treated, in the excellent *Manuel de l'Histoire des Religions*, by Tiele, which M. Maurice Vernes has just translated from the Dutch (1 vol. 12mo, Ernest Leroux, 1880), views much the same as those which we have just described. The author denominates the religious state which we call fetishism *animism*, but he points out the fact that this class of conceptions had a perennial influence over the Egyptian mind. "The Egyptian religion," he says, "like the Chinese, was nothing to begin with but an organised *animism*." He finds traces of this *animism* in the worship of the dead, the deification of the kings, and the adoration of animals. From his point of view the custom of placing a symbol of the divinity rather than an image in the temple, must be traced to fetishism (pp. 44 and 45 of the French version).

[79] Pierret, *Dictionnaire d'Archéologie Égyptienne.*

[80] See in *L'Oiseau* the chapter-headed *L'Épuration*. With his genius for history and poetry Michelet has well understood the sentiment which gave birth to these primitive forms of worship, forms which have too long provoked unjust contempt. The whole of this beautiful chapter should be read; we shall only quote a few lines: "In America the law protects these public benefactors. Egyptian law does still more for them—it respects them and loves them. Although they no longer enjoy their ancient worship, they receive the friendly hospitality of man as in the time of Pharaoh. If you ask an Egyptian fellah why he allows himself to be besieged and deafened by birds, why he patiently suffers the insolence of the crow perched upon the horn of the buffalo, on the hump of a camel, or fighting upon the date-trees and shaking down the fruit, he will say nothing. Birds are allowed to do anything. Older than the Pyramids, they are the ancients of the country. Man's existence depends upon them, upon the persevering labour of the ibis, the stork, the crow and the vulture."

[81] Maspero, *Notes sur différents Points de Grammaire et d'Histoire dans le Recueil de Travaux relatifs à la Philologie et à l'Archéologie égyptienne et assyrienne*, vol. i. p. 157.

[82] Herodotus, ii. 42.

[83] JAMES DARMESTETER, *Le Dieu suprême dans la Mythologie indo-européenne* (in the *Revue de l'Histoire des Religions*, 1880).

[84] τὴν αὐτὴν δὲ τέχνην ἀπειργασμένα, etc. Laws, 656. D. E. [We have quoted from Professor Jowett's English version, p. 226, vol. v.—ED.]

[85] *Cours d'Archéologie*, 8vo. 1829, pp. 10, 11. This critic's ideas upon Egyptian art were both superficial and false. "Egyptian art," he says, "never attempted any realistic imitation." We even find sentences utterly devoid of meaning, such as, for instance, "The fundamental principle of Egyptian art was the absence of art." (p. 12.)

[86] See the *Revue des Deux Mondes* of April 1, 1865.

[87] *Voyage dans la Haute Égypte*, vol. i.

[88] M. MELCHOIR DE VOGÜÉ, *Chez les Pharaons* (*Revue des Deux Mondes* of Jan. 15, 1877).

[89] DIODORUS, i. 98, 7, 8.

[90] *Denkmæler aus Ægypten und Æthiopien* (from drawings of the expedition sent into Egypt in 1842, which remained there till 1845), 12 vols. folio. Berlin, no date.

[91] *Histoire de l'Art égyptien d'après les Monuments depuis les Temps les plus reculés jusqu'à la Domination romaine*, 2 vols. Paris, Arthus Bertrand, 1878. The text (1 vol. 4to.), published after the death of Prisse, has this great inconvenience, that it is not always easy to distinguish what belongs to the editor, M. Marchandon de la Faye, from the contributions of Prisse, who was one of the most practical and experienced of egyptologists. The papers, sketches, and drawings left by Prisse became the property, in 1880, of the Bibliothèque Nationale; when they are classified and published we shall probably find among them several interesting documents; we have only been able hurriedly to look through them, when the illustrations to this work were already prepared. It is desirable that a complete inventory of these collections should be made as soon as possible.

[92] *Lois générales de l'Inclinaison des Colonnes dans la Construction des Temples grecs de l'Antiquité*, dedicated to his Majesty, Otho I., by CHARLES VILLEROI, engineer. Athens, 1842, 8vo.

[93] Egyptian landscape is well characterised in these lines of M. CH. BLANC, taken from the *Voyage de la Haute Égypte* (p. 116): "Pour le moment, notre plaisir se borne à regarder un paysage simple, monotone, mais grand par sa simplicité même et par sa monotonie. Ces lignes planes qui s'allongent et se prolongent sans fin, et qui s'interrompent un instant pour reprendre encore leur niveau et se continuer encore, impriment à la nature un caractère de tranquillité qui assoupit l'imagination et qui apaise le cœur. Par une singularité peut-être unique au monde, les variétés qui viennent rompre de distance en distance la vaste uniformité de la terre égyptienne se reproduisent toujours les mêmes." [We have refrained from translating this piece of word painting, lest its suggestive rhythm should vanish in the process.—ED.]

[94] Similar notions are expressed by M. CH. BLANC in his *Grammaire des Arts du Dessin* (Book i. ch. viii.). "The wide-spreading base is the distinguishing characteristic of the Egyptian monuments. Wall, pier, and column, all the constructive members of Egyptian architecture, are short and thick set. To add to this appearance of solidity the relative size of the base is increased by that tendency towards the pyramid which is to be found in every Egyptian building. The pyramids of Memphis, one of them the greatest building upon earth, stand upon enormous bases. Their height is far less than their largest horizontal diameter. The pyramid of Cheops, for instance, is 233 metres along one side of its base, and only 146 in height, *i.e.*, its base is to its height as 8 to 5. All Egyptian monuments, even the most lofty, are more remarkable for the ground they cover than for their height [except the monoliths!—ED.], and this extension of their bases gives them an appearance of absolutely eternal durability."

[95] This illustration has been compiled in order to give a general idea of the more persistent characteristics of the Egyptian temple.

[96] We know but one or two exceptions to this rule. It will suffice to quote the Royal Pavilion of Medinet-Abou, which is crowned by a row of battlements.

[97] From the work of the Abbé Uggeri, entitled: *Le Détail des Matériaux dont se servaient les Anciens pour la Construction de leurs Bâtiments* (Rome, oblong folio, 1800, pl. v.).

[98] The only granite quarries that were worked in antiquity were those of Syene now Assouan, in Upper Egypt, upon the right bank of the Nile.

[99] Sandstone was chiefly obtained from two localities, Djebel-Ahmar, near Cairo, and Djebel-Silsili in Upper Egypt.

[100] The Arab Chain is almost entirely calcareous. Near the sites of all the ancient cities it shows numerous excavations bearing witness to the activity of the ancient builders. The most celebrated of these quarries is that at Mokattam, near Cairo. The stone of which the body of the pyramids is composed was drawn from it.

[101] The alabaster quarries of to-day are all in the Arab Chain, between the southern slopes of the mountain Mahsarah, near Cairo, and the springs of the Wady-Siout, opposite the town of that name.

[102] The obelisk of Queen Hatasu, at Karnak, is 105 ft. 8 in. high; the statue of Rameses II. at Thebes, on the left bank of the river, is a monolith 55 ft. 5 in. high, and weighing about 1,200 tons. [The obelisk which still remains at Syene, never having been completely detached from the rock in which it was quarried, is nearly 96 ft. high and 11 ft. 1-1/2 in. diameter at its base.—ED.]

[103] We find this construction in the so-called Temple of the Sphinx, near the Great Pyramid.

[104] The vertical support and the architrave form the two vital elements of an Egyptian building, which is therefore enabled to dispense with those buttresses and other lateral supports which are necessary to give stability to the edifices of many other nations.

[105] We may here remark that the modest dwellings of the Egyptian fellah are often covered by vaults of pisé, that is to say, of compressed and kneaded clay. None of the ancient monuments of Egypt possess such vaults, which are of much less durability than those of stone or brick. We are, however, disposed to believe that they were used in antique times.

[106] Another explanation has been given of the employment of the vault in subterranean work. Mariette believed the arch to be symbolic, to signify the canopy of heaven, the heaven of Amen. One objection to this is the fact that the vault was not universal in tombs; some of those at Beni-Hassan have flat ceilings, others have coves.

[107] In this respect there is a striking resemblance between Egyptian carpentry (see Fig. 83), and much of the joinery of the modern Japanese.—ED.

[108] In this figure we have attempted to give some notion of what a wooden building must have been like in ancient Egypt, judging from the imitations of

assembled construction which have been found in the tombs and sarcophagi of the ancient empire.

[109] We here speak of the fauna as a whole, disregarding particular genera and species. It may be said that some particular plant which is to be found both in France and Norway, is much brighter in colour when it grows in the neighbourhood of the pole than in our temperate climate, but this apparent exception only confirms the rule which we have laid down. The plant whose whole season of bloom is comprised between a late spring and an early autumn develops itself much more rapidly than with us, and, granting that it has become so hardened that it is able to resist the long and hard frosts of winter, it receives, during the short summer, much more light and sun than its French or German sister. During those fleeting summers of the north, whose strange charm has been so often described, the sun hardly descends below the horizon; the nights are an hour long, and not six or seven. The colour of flowers is therefore in exact proportion to the amount of light which they receive.

[110] This was perceived by Goethe. In art, as in natural science, he divined beforehand some of the discoveries of our century by the innate force of his genius. He was not surprised by the discovery that the temples of classic Sicily were painted in brilliant tones, which concealed the surface of their stone and accentuated the leading lines of their architecture. He was one of the first to accept the views of Hittorf and to proclaim that the architects who had found traces of colours upon the mouldings of Greek buildings were not deceiving themselves and others.

[111] We borrow these expressions from M. CH. BLANC, who, when in Egypt, was very much struck with this phenomenon. "Those villages which approach in colour to that Nile mud of which they are composed, hardly stand out at all against the background, unless that be the sky itself or those sunny rocks which reflect the light in such a fashion that they fatigue the most accustomed eyes. I notice here, as I did in Greece, at Cape Sunium, that cupolas and round towers have their modelling almost destroyed by the strong reflections." (*Voyage de la Haute Égypte*, 1876, p. 114).

[112] WILKINSON thought there was always a layer of stucco, even upon the beautiful granite of the obelisks (*Manners and Customs of the Ancient Egyptians*, 2nd ed., 1878, vol. ii. p. 286.) His statement must be treated with great respect. During his long sojourn in Egypt he examined the remains of the ancient civilisation with great care and patience, but yet we think his opinion upon this point must be accepted with some reserve. There are in the Louvre certain sarcophagi and other objects in hard stone, upon which traces of colour are clearly visible on the sunk beds of the figures and hieroglyphics, while not the slightest vestige of anything of the kind is to be found upon the smooth surface around those carvings. But it is certain that granite was often stuccoed over. MARIETTE has verified that it was so on the obelisk of Hatasu at Thebes; both from the inscription and the appearance of the monument itself he came to the conclusion that it had been gilded from top to bottom, and that the gold had been laid upon a coat of white stucco. "The plain surface," he says, "alone received this costly decoration. It had been left slightly rough, but the hieroglyphs, which had their beds most carefully polished, preserved the colour

and surface of the granite." (*Itinéraire*, p. 178.) As for buildings of limestone or sandstone, like the temples of Thebes, they are always coated.

[113] *Apropos* of the Temple of Khons, JOLLOIS and DEVILLIERS (*Description générale de Thébes*, ch. ix.) remark: "It was upon this coat that the hieroglyphs and figures were sculptured.... The contour of the figures is sometimes marked upon the stone beneath, because the depth of the cutting is greater than the thickness of the stucco."

[114] "*Conférence sur l'Histoire des Âmes dans l'Égypte ancienne, d'après les Monuments du Musée du Louvre*," in the *Bulletin hebdomadaire de l'Association scientifique de France*, No. 594. M. Maspero has often and exhaustively treated this subject, especially in his numerous lectures at the Collège de France. Those lectures afforded the material for the remarkable paper in the *Journal asiatique* entitled, "*Étude sur quelques Peintures et sur quelques Textes relatifs aux Funérailles*" (numbers for May, June, 1878, for December-June, and November, December, 1879, and May-June, 1880). These articles have been republished in a single volume with important corrections and additions (Maisonneuve, 1880).

[115] Or *ba*.—ED.

[116] *Conférence*, p. 381. Mr. Herbert Spencer, in the first chapters of his *Principles of Sociology*, has given a curious and plausible explanation of how this conception of a *double* was formed. He finds its origin chiefly in the phenomena of sleep, of dreams, and of the faintness caused by wounds or illness. He shows how these more or less transitory suspensions of animation led men to suppose that death was nothing but a prolonged interruption of life. He also thinks that the actual shadow cast by a man's body contributed to the formation of that belief. But had it no other elements which belonged to the general disposition of humanity in those early periods of intellectual life? Into that question we cannot enter here further than to say that Mr. Spencer's pages make us acquainted with numerous facts which prove that the beliefs in question were not confined to a single race, but were common to all humanity.

[117] This expression, which is very common in the Egyptian texts, seems to have made a great impression upon the Greek travellers. The following passage of DIODORUS is well known: "This refers to the beliefs of the natives, who look upon the life upon earth as a thing of minor importance, but set a high value upon those virtues of which the memory is perpetuated after death. They call their houses hotels, in view of the short time they have to spend in them, while they call their tombs their *eternal dwellings*" (i. 51).

[118] The dead were put under the protection of, and, as it were, combined with, Osiris; they talked of *the Osiris so and so* in naming one who was dead.

[119] Εἴδωλα καμόντων (*Il.* xxiii. 72; *Od.* xi. 476; xxiv. 14).

[120] This belief is clearly stated in a passage from Cicero quoted by Fustel: "Sub terrâ censebant reliquam vitam agi mortuorum" (*Tusc.* i. 16). This belief was so strong that it subsisted even after the universal establishment of the custom of burning the bodies of the dead.

[121] Texts to this effect abound. FUSTEL brought the more remarkable of them together in his *Cité antique* (p. 14). We shall be content with quoting three: "Son of Peleus," said Neoptolemus, "take this drink which is grateful to the dead; come and drink this blood" (Hecuba, 536). Electra says when she pours a libation: "This drink has penetrated the earth; my father has received it" (Choephorœ, 162). And listen to the prayer of Orestes to his dead father: "Oh my father, if I live thou shalt have rich banquets; if I die thou wilt have no portion of those smoking feasts which nourish the dead" (Choephorœ, 482-484). Upon the strange persistence of this belief, traces of which are still found in Eastern Europe, in Albania, in Thessaly, and Epirus, the works of HEUZEY (*Mission archéologique de Macédoine*, p. 156), and ALBERT DUMONT (*le Balkan et l'Adriatique*, pp. 354-356), may be consulted. Some curious details relating to the funeral feasts of the Chinese are to be found in the *Comptes rendus de l'Académie des Inscriptions*, 1877, p. 325. There are some striking points of resemblance between the religion of China and that of ancient Egypt; in both one and the other the same want of power to develop may be found. Taking them as a whole, both the Chinese and the Egyptians failed to emerge from the condition of fetichism.

[122] In the eleventh book of the Odyssey it is only after "they have drunk deep draughts of black blood" that the shades are capable of recognising Ulysses, of understanding what he says and answering. The blood they swallowed restored their intelligence and powers of thought.

[123] The speeches of the Greek orators are full of proofs that these beliefs had a great hold upon the popular mind, even as late as the time of Demosthenes. In contested cases of adoption they always laid great stress upon the dangers which would menace the city if a family was allowed to become extinct for want of precautions against the failure of the hereditary line; there would then be some neglected tomb where the dead never received the visits of gift-bringing friends, a neglect which would be visited upon the city as a whole as the accomplice in such abandonment. Such an argument and others like it may not seem to us to be of great judicial value, but the talent of an Isæus understood how to make it tell with an audience, or we should not find it so often repeated in his pleadings (see G. PERROT, *L'Éloquence politique et judiciare à Athènes. Les Précurseurs de Demosthène*, pp. 359-364).

[124] Seventh edition, Hachette, 18mo., 1879.

[125] Mr. Herbert Spencer, in his ingenious and subtle analysis of *primitive ideas* draws our attention to their frequent inconsistencies and even positive contradictions; but he shows us at the same time that the most highly civilised races in these modern days admit and combine ideas which are logically quite as irreconcilable as those which seem to us so absurdly inconsistent when we think of the beliefs of the ancients or of savage races. Custom renders us insensible to contradictions which we should perceive at once were we removed to a distance from them. (*The Principles of Sociology*, vol. i. pp. 119, 185).

[126] The texts also bear witness to the ideas with which the complicated processes of embalming were undertaken. See P. PIERRET, *Le Dogme de la la Résurrection*, &c., p. 10. "It was necessary that no member, no substance, should be wanting at the final summons; resurrection depended on that." "*Thou countest*

thy members which are complete and intact." (Egyptian funerary text.) "Arise in To-deser (the sacred region in which the renewal of life is prepared), thou august and coffined mummy. Thy bones and thy substance are re-united with thy flesh, and thy flesh is again in its place; thy head is replaced upon thy neck, thy heart is ready for thee." (Osirian statue in the Louvre.) The dead took care to demand of the gods "*that the earth should not bite him, that the soil should not consume him.*" (MARIETTE, *Feuilles d'Abydos*.) The preservation of the body must therefore have been an object of solicitude at the earliest times, but the art of embalming did not attain perfection until the Theban period. Under the ancient empire men were content with comparatively simple methods. Mariette says that "more examples would have to be brought together than he had been able to discover before the question of mummification under the ancient empire could be decided. It is certain, first, that no authentic piece of mummy cloth from that period is now extant; secondly, that the bones found in the sarcophagi have the brownish colour and the bituminous smell of mummies.

"Not more than five or six inviolate sarcophagi have been found. On each of these occasions the corpse has been discovered in the skeleton state. And as for linen, nothing beyond a little dust upon the bottom of the sarcophagus, which might be the *débris* of many other things than of a linen shroud." (*Les Tombes de l'Ancien Empire*, p. 16.)

[127] PASSALACQUA gives the following description of the mummy of a young woman which he discovered at Thebes: "Her hair and the rotundity and surprising regularity of her form showed me that she had been a beauty in her time, and that she had died in the flower of her youth." He then gives a minute description of her condition and ornaments, and concludes by saying that "the peculiar beauty of the proportions of this mummy, and its perfect preservation, had so greatly impressed the Arabs themselves that they had exhumed it more than once to show to their wives and neighbours." (*Catalogue raisonné et historique des Antiquités découvertes en Égypte*, 8vo. 1826.)

[128] RHIND describes several mummy-pits in the necropolis of Thebes which receive the water of the Nile by infiltration; but, as he himself remarks, this is because those who dug them did not foresee the gradual raising of the valley, and, consequently, of the level attained in recent ages by the waters of the Nile. It is doubtless only within the last few centuries that the water has penetrated into these tombs. (*Thebes, its Tombs and their Tenants*, p. 153.)

[129] MASPERO, *Conférence*, p. 381.

[130] MASPERO, *Notes sur différentes Points de Grammaire et d'Histoire*, p. 155. (In the *Recueil de Travaux relatifs à la Philologie et à l'Archéologie Égyptienne et Assyrienne*, vol. i.)

[131] Jars, which seem to have been once filled with water, are found in many tombs of all epochs. Different kinds of dates are also found, together with the fruit of the sycamore, corn, cakes, &c. See the *Catalogue* of PASSALACQUA, pp. 123, 151, and elsewhere. Quarters of meat have also been found in them, which are easily recognised by their well-preserved bones.

[132] MASPERO, *Études sur quelques Peintures funéraires*, in the *Journal Asiatique*, May-June, 1880, p. 387, *et seq.*

[133] In one of the great inscriptions at Beni-Hassan, recently translated anew both by M. Maspero and Professor Birch, Chnoumhotep speaks thus: "I caused to prosper the name of my father. I completed the existing temples of the Ka. I served my statues at the great temples. I sacrificed to them their food, bread, beer, water, vegetables, pure herbs. My priest has verified (I chose a priest for the Ka,—Maspero). I procured them from the irrigation of my work-people (I made him master of fields and slaves,—Maspero). I ordered the sepulchral offerings of bread, beer, cattle, fowl, in all the festivals of Karneter, at the festivals of the beginning of the year, the opening of the year, increase of the year, diminution of the year (little year,—Brugsch and Maspero), close of the year, at the great festival, at the festival of the great burning, at the festival of the lesser burning, the five intercalary days, at the festival of bread making (of the entry of grain,—Maspero) at the twelve monthly and half monthly festivals, all the festivals on the earth (plain), terminating on the hill (of Anubis). But should my sepulchral priest or men conduct them wrongly may he not exist, nor his son in his place."—BIRCH, *Records of the Past*, vol. xii. p. 71.—ED.

[134] In each opening of the serdab in the tomb of Ti, at Sakkarah, people, probably relatives of the deceased, are represented in the act of burning incense in a contrivance which resembles in form the θυμιατήριον of the Greek monuments. (MARIETTE, *Notice des principaux Monuments de Boulak*, p. 27, note 1.)

[135] See the paper by M. MASPERO upon the great inscription at Siout, which has preserved for us a contract between Prince Hapi-Toufi and the priests of Ap-Môtennou, by which offerings should be regularly made to the prince's statue, which was deposited in a temple at Siout. (*Transactions of the Society of Biblical Archæology*, vol. vii. pp. 1-32.)

[136] It was the same in the case of a still older king, Seneferu, the founder of the fourth dynasty. (DE ROUGÉ, *Recherches sur les Monuments que l'on peut attribuer aux six premières Dynasties de Manéthon*, p. 41.)

[137] *Tombes de l'Ancien Empire*, p. 87.

[138] HERODOTUS, iv. 71, 72.

[139] In a few rare cases the objects destined for the nourishment of the *double* are represented in the round instead of being painted upon the wall. In the tomb of the personage called Atta, a wooden table, supporting terra-cotta vases and plucked geese carved in calcareous stone, has been found. (MARIETTE, *Tombes de l'Ancien Empire*, p. 17.) The vases must have been full of water when they were placed in the tomb; the stone geese may be compared to the *papier-mâché* loaves of the modern stage.

[140] All Egyptian collections contain coffers of painted wood, often decorated in the most brilliant fashion, which served to hold these statues when they were placed in the tomb. The size and the richness of their ornament depended upon the wealth of the deceased for who they were made.

[141] PIETSCHMANN (*Der Egyptische Fetischdienst*, &c., p. 155), has well grasped the character and significance of these statuettes. Conf. PIERRET, *Dictionnaire d'Archéologie égyptienne*, vol. v. See also, in connection with the

personality attributed to them and to the services which were expected from them, a note by M. MASPERO, *Sur une Tablette appartenant à M. Rogers*. (*Recueil de Travaux*, vol. ii. p. 12.)

[142] DE ROUGÉ, *Mémoire sur les Monuments des six premières Dynasties* (p. 80 *et seq.*). Conf. MASPERO, *Histoire Ancienne*, pp. 88-92.

[143] See MARIETTE, *Tombes de l'Ancien Empire*, p. 88.

[144] This word, σύριγξ (flute), was employed by the Greeks to designate those long subterranean galleries cut in the rock of the necropolis at Thebes, in the valley called the *Valley of the Kings*; modern egyptologists apply it in a more general sense to all tombs cut deeply into the flanks of the mountain. For the reason which led the Greeks to adopt a term which now seems rather fantastic, see PIERRET, *Dictionnaire d'Archéologie égyptienne*. The chief passages in ancient authors in which the term is applied either to the subterranean excavations of Egypt or to other galleries of the same kind, are brought together by Jomard in the third volume of the *Description* (*Antiquités*, vol. iii. pp. 12-14).

[145] *Journal asiatique*, May-June, 1880, pp. 419, 420.

[146] See above, Figs. 87 and 91.

[147] We borrow the translation of this inscription, as well as the reflections which precede it, from M. MASPERO (*Conférence*, p. 382). According to M. de Rougé, it dates from about the twelfth dynasty. An invocation of the same kind is to be found in another epigraph of the same period, the inscription of Amoni-Amenemhaït, hereditary prince of the nome of Meh, at Beni-Hassan. See MASPERO, *La Grande Inscription de Beni-Hassan*, p. 171 (*Recueil de Travaux*, etc., vol. i. 4to.).

[148] MASPERO, *Conférence*, p. 282.

[149] Among the cemeteries of the right bank we may mention that of Tell-el-Amarna; where the tombs would have been too far from the city had they been dug in the Libyan Chain. The cemeteries of Beni-Hassan and of Eilithyia (*El-Kab*) are also in the Arab Chain. In spite of these exceptions, however, the west was the real quarter of the dead, their natural habitation, as is proved by the tearful funeral songs translated by M. MASPERO: "The mourners before the ever-to-be praised Hor-Khom say, 'O chief, as thou goest toward the West, the gods lament thee.' The friends who close the procession repeat, 'To the West, to the West, oh praiseworthy one, to the excellent West!'" MASPERO, *Étude sur quelques Peintures funéraires* (*Journal asiatique*, February-April, 1881, p. 148).

[150] "It is so," says Mariette, "four times out of five." (*Les Tombes de l'Ancien Empire*, in the *Revue archéologique*, new series, vol. xix. p. 12.)

[151] "In the further wall of the chamber, and *invariably facing eastwards*, is a stele." (*Ibidem*, p. 14.)

[152] MARIETTE, *Abydos*, vol. ii. p. 43.

[153] The tombs in the Arab Chain form, of course, an exception to this rule. The unusual circumstances which took them eastward of the river forced them

also to neglect the traditional law.

[154] The symbolic connection established by man between the course of the sun and his own life was well understood by Champollion, who used it to explain the paintings in the royal tombs at Thebes. (See his remarks on the tomb of Rameses V. on the 185th and following pages of his *Lettres d'Égypte*, &c.)

[155] Upon the papyrus known as the *Papyrus Casati*, mention is made of a priest who is charged to watch over a whole collection of mummies.

"This is the list of bodies belonging to Osorvaris:—
"Imouth, son of Petenefhotep, his wife and children;
"Medledk, the carpenter, his wife and children;
"Pipee, his wife and children, from Hermouth;
"The father of Phratreou, the fuller;
"Aplou, the son of Petenhefhotep the boatman, his wife and children, from Thebes;
"Psenmouth, the carpenter, his wife and children;
"Psenimonthis, the mason;
"Amenoth, the cowherd."

There are many more lists of the same kind. The above is cited from M. E. LE BLANT (*Tables égyptiennes à Inscriptions grecques*, p. 6, 1875, 8vo.).

[156] See in the interesting work of Mr. H. RHIND (*Thebes, its Tombs and their Tenants*, London, 1862, 8vo.), the chapter headed *A Burial-place of the Poor*.

[157] MARIETTE, *Tombes de l'Ancien Empire*, p. 83. See also the great inscription of Beni-Hassan, the first lines of which run thus: "The hereditary chief ... Khnumhotep ... has made a monument for the first time to embellish his district; he has sculptured his name for ever; he has embellished it for ever by his chamber of Karneter; he has sculptured the names of his household; he has assigned their place. The workmen, those attached to his house, he has reckoned amongst his dependants of all ranks." [BIRCH, *Records of the Past*, vol. xii. p. 67. —ED.] It was, no doubt, in order to conform to the Egyptian custom that Antony and Cleopatra commenced in their lifetime that tomb which Augustus ordered to be finished after their death (SUETONIUS, *Augustus*, 17). "To be laid to rest in the tomb which he had made for himself and furnished with every necessary was the greatest good which the gods could insure to an Egyptian. In Papyrus IV. at Boulak we find the following phrases: 'Be found with thy dwelling finished in the funerary valley: in every enterprise which thou meditatest *may the morning when thy body shall be hid be present to thee.*'" (From the French of M. MASPERO, *Journal asiatique*, 7th series, t. xv. p. 165, note 1.)

[158] *Briefe aus Ægypten*, p. 23 *et seq.* Before the Prussian commission left Middle for Upper Egypt they had studied 130 private tombs, of which the principal ones are figured in the *Denkmæler*.

[159] Lexicographers do not seem to know the origin of this word; they believe it to be foreign, perhaps Persian.

[160] Vol. xix. (1869), pp. 1-22 and 81-89.

[161] EBERS (*Ægypten*, p. 137) gives this necropolis a length of more than forty-five miles, but in making it extend to Meidoum he seems to be exaggerating.

[162] Upon the plateau which, at Sakkarah, extends westwards of the stepped pyramid the manner in which the necropolis was developed can be readily seen. In walking eastwards, that is, from the pyramid towards the cultivated land, we pass a first zone of tombs which date from the Ancient Empire, a second which possesses sculptures of the twenty-sixth dynasty, and a third which dates from the Greek period.

[163] We may quote as an interesting example of such usurpation the Theban tomb first opened by a Scottish traveller, HENRY RHIND, to whose interesting work (*Thebes, its Tombs and their Tenants, Ancient and Present, with a Record of Excavations in the Necropolis*, Longman, 1862, 8vo.) we shall often have to refer. This tomb seems to have been made in the reign of Amenophis III. by a brother and sister whose statues were found in it, but it also contained Sebau, son of Menkara, a high official of the time of the Ptolemies, with his wife and all his family (c. iv.).

[164] MARIETTE (*Voyage dans la haute Égypte*, p. 32) thought that the word Sakkarah was an ancient name derived from *Socharis*, a Memphite form of *Osiris*.

[165] The way in which the mastabas were arranged with respect to each other is well shown in plates xiv. and xviii. of Lepsius's first volume (map of the pyramids of Gizeh and panorama taken from the summit of the second pyramid).

[166] The general aspect of this city of the dead, and the regularity of its monuments, made a great impression upon the members of the "Institut d'Égypte." The following are the words of JOMARD (*Description*, vol. v. p. 619): "From the top of the building one sees an infinite quantity of the long rectangular structures extending almost to the Pyramids. They are carefully oriented, and exactly aligned one with another. I counted fourteen rows of them, in each direction, on the west of the Great Pyramid, and as many on the east, making nearly four hundred in all. The sand under which many of them are buried leaves their forms easily distinguishable." Since the time of Jomard many of the mastabas have been changed by the excavations into mere formless heaps of *débris*, and yet the general arrangement can still be clearly followed.

[167] One of these exceptions is furnished by the tomb of Ti, of which we shall often have to speak (Fig. 114). The large public hall near the entrance to the tomb was separated from the two chambers farther in by a corridor closed at two points by doors, some remains of which were found in place when the tomb was opened.

[168] This is a word of Persian origin adopted by the Arabs. Its strict meaning is a dark subterranean opening, cave, or passage.

[169] The tomb of Ti had two serdabs as well as three chambers; one of these was close to the door, the other in the innermost part of the mastaba. In the latter several statues of Ti were found, the best preserved being now in the museum at Boulak.

[170] In a Theban tomb described by M. MASPERO (*Étude sur quelques Peintures funéraires*) the tenant, Harmhabi, is made to speak thus: "I have come, I have received my bread; joining the embalmed offerings to my members, I have breathed the scent of the perfumes and incense." It is also possible that this conduit may have been intended to permit of the free circulation of the *double*, to allow it to pass from its supporting statues to the chapel in which it is honoured. This curious idea, that the spirit of the dead can pass through a very small hole, but that it cannot dispense with an opening altogether, is found among many nations. The Iroquois contrived an opening of very small diameter in their tombs, through which the soul of the dead could pass and repass. See HERBERT SPENCER, *Principles of Sociology*, vol. i. p. 192.

[171] There is an example of this in a mastaba at Gizeh (Fig. 120). See No. 95 of LEPSIUS (*Denkmæler*, vol. i. p. 29; vol. iii. pl. 44).

[172] This figure is a composition by Mariette for the purpose of showing the relation between the subterranean and constructed parts of the tomb. (*Notice des principaux Monuments*, p. 22.) [It shows, however, the well opening from the floor of the upper chamber, an arrangement which is not characteristic of the mastaba.—ED.]

[173] The broken up and decayed remains of wooden boats have been found in two or three mummy pits (MARIETTE, *Les Tombes de l'Ancien Empire*, p. 17). They originally formed part, perhaps, of the boats upon which the corpse was transported across the Nile to the nearest point of the western bank to the tomb. There can be no doubt that, in placing them in the well, the survivors believed that they were serving the deceased. Both the bas-reliefs in the tomb and the *Ritual* contain many representations of the soul navigating the regions of Ament (see the upper section of Fig. 98). In certain Theban tombs, models of fully rigged boats have been found; there are some of them in the Louvre (*Salle Civile*, case K). [There are two in the British Museum, and one, a very fine one, in the museum at Liverpool.—ED.]

[174] *Description de l'Égypte*, vol. v. p. 647, and *Atlas, Ant.* vol. v. pl. 16, Figs. 3, 4, and 5.

[175] *History of Egypt* (English version, Murray, 1879), vol. i. pp. 72, 73.

[176] FIALIN DE PERSIGNY, *De la Destination et de l'Utilité permanente des Pyramides d'Égypte et de Nubie contre les Irruptions sablonneuses du Désert, Développements du Mémoire adressé à l'Académie des Sciences le 14 Juillet, 1844*, suivie d'*une nouvelle interprétation de la Fable d'Osiris et d'Isis*. Paris, 1845, gr. in-8.

[177] HERODOTUS, ii. 127.

[178] DIODORUS, l. 64, 4.

[179] STRABO, xvii. p. 1161, C.

[180] MARIETTE, *Itinéraire de la Haute-Égypte*, pp. 96, 97. [An excellent translation of this work into English, by M. Alphonse Mariette, has been published (Trübner, 1877, 8vo.)—ED.]

[181] The existence of the passage leading to the mummy chamber was not unknown to STRABO. He says: "Very nearly at the middle of their sides, as to height, the pyramids had a stone which could be moved away; when this is done, a winding passage appears, which leads to the coffin" (xvii. p. 1161, C).

[182] This pyramid was opened on February 28, 1881. Circumstantial accounts of the discoveries to which it led have not yet been published. The *Moniteur Égyptien* of March 15, 1881, contains a short account of the opening. [Since this note was written, a full account of the entrance and exploration of this pyramid, together with the texts discovered, has been published by M. MASPERO in the *Recueil de Travaux*, vol. iii. liv. 3 and 4, 1882.—ED.]

[183] VYSE (Howard), *Operations carried on at the Pyramids of Gizeh in 1837, with an Account of a Voyage into Upper Egypt, and an Appendix*. (London, 1840, 3 vols. 8vo.)

[184] PERRING (J. L.), *The Pyramids of Gizeh, from Actual Survey and Admeasurement, illustrated by Notes and References to the Several Plans, with Sketches taken on the Spot by J. Andrews*. (3 parts, large oblong folio. London, 1839-42.)

[185] The base of the great pyramid at Sakkarah is a rectangle, measuring 390 feet from north to south, and 347 from east to west. The three great pyramids at Gizeh like most of these structures, are built upon a base which is practically square.

[186] MARIETTE, *Itinéraire de la Haute-Égypte*, p. 96.

[187] This method of construction may be easily recognized in the Pyramid of Meidoum. That curious structure was built in concentric layers round a nucleus. These layers are by no means equal in the excellence either of the workmanship or of the materials employed. Some show supreme negligence; in others we find the builders of the Ancient Empire and their materials both at their best. The same fact has been observed in regard to the Stepped Pyramid and the pyramids at Abousir. It would seem that the work was assigned in sections to different *corvées*, whose consciences varied greatly in elasticity. (MARIETTE, *Voyage de la Haute-Égypte*, p. 45.)

[188] LEPSIUS, *Briefe aus Ægypten*, pp. 41, 42 (in speaking of the Pyramid of Meidoum, from which he received the first hint of this explanation). See also his paper entitled *Ueber den Bau der Pyramiden*, in the *Monatsbericht* of the Berlin Academy, 1843, pp. 177-203.

[189] *Ægypten*, First part, 1878, p. 341.

[190] It has been suggested by Mr. Cope Whitehouse that the nucleus of rock under the great pyramids was originally much more important than is commonly supposed. During his expedition in March, 1882, he ascertained that a profile from the Mokattam across the Nile valley into the western desert would present the contours shown in the annexed woodcut. He concludes that a large part of the material of those pyramids was obtained upon their sites, and quarried above the level at which the stones were finally placed. He cites HERODOTUS (ii. 125) as conveying in an imperfect form the tradition that the pyramids were "constructed from above."

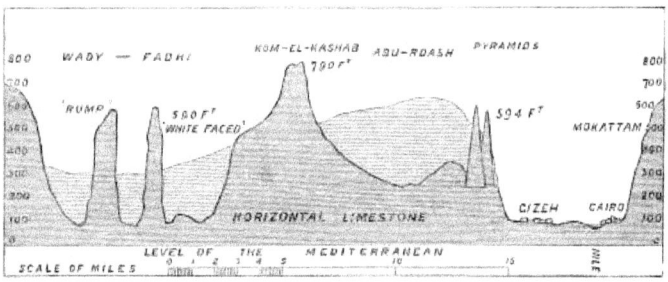

[191] The weight of this stopper is about four tons, and it has long been a puzzle to egyptologists how it, and others like it, could be raised and lowered. M. Perrot's words must not, therefore, be taken too literally.—ED.

[192] ARTHUR RHONÉ, *L'Égypte à petites Journées*, p. 259.

[193] There are other stepped pyramids besides that at Sakkarah. Jomard describes one of crude and much crumbled brick at Dashour. It is, he says, about 140 feet high. Its height is divided into five stages, each being set back about 11 feet behind the one below. These steps are often found, he adds, among the southern pyramids, and there is one example of such construction at Gizeh. (*Description de l'Égypte*, vol. x., p. 5.) At Matarieh, between Sakkarah and Meidoum, there is a pyramid with a double slope like that at Dashour.

[194] Fig. 5 of his paper, *Ueber den Bau der Pyramiden.*

[195] Fig. 8 of his paper, *Ueber den Bau der Pyramiden.*

[196] *Voyage au Temple de Jupiter Amman et dans la Haute-Égypte.* (Berlin, 1824, 4to. and folio; Pl. xxvii. Fig. 3.)

[197] BÆDEKER, *Egypt*, part i. 1878. The pages dealing with the monumental remains were edited in great part by Professor Ebers.

[198] *Voyage dans la Haute-Égypte*, vol. i. p. 45.

[199] *Voyage dans la Haute-Égypte*, vol. i. p. 34.

[200] LEPSIUS, *Denkmæler*, part i. pl. 94. RHIND, *Thebes, its Tombs and their Tenants*, p. 45. MARIETTE, *Voyage dans la Haute-Égypte*, vol. ii. p. 80.

[201] Thus the Great Pyramid was 482 feet high, while the length of one side at the base is 764 feet. On the other hand, the "third pyramid" at Gebel-Barkal (Napata) is 35 feet square at the base and 60 feet high; the "fifth" is 39 feet square at the base and nearly 50 feet high. Their proportions are not constant, but the height of the Nubian pyramids is always far greater than the length of one side at its base.

[202] HERODOTUS, ii. 124.

[203] DU BARRY DE MERVAL, *Études sur l'Architecture Égyptienne*, pp. 129, 130.

[204] The discovery of these chambers was interesting from another point of view. The name of Choufou was found continually repeated upon the blocks of which they are formed. It was written in red ochre, and, in places, it was upside down, thus proving that it must have been written before the stones were put in place. It cannot therefore have been traced after the tradition which assigned the pyramid to Cheops, that is, to Khoufou, arose; and so it affords conclusive corroboration of the statements of Herodotus.

[205] This is no exaggeration. JOMARD expresses himself to the same effect almost in the same terms. (*Description de l'Égypte*, vol. v. p. 628.)

[206] The extremity of this gallery appears on the right of Fig. 152.

[207] The presence of this lining in the "Queen's Chamber" also led to its being dubbed a funerary chamber, for no trace of a sarcophagus was found in it. If we had any reason to believe that the pyramid was built in successive wedges, we should look upon this as a provisional chamber, made before it was certain that

the pyramid would attain its present dimensions. As the work went on, it would be decided that another, larger, and better defended chamber should be built. In this case the first may never have been used, and may always have been as empty as it is now.

[208] These observations are to be found in one of the early works of Letronne. Their presence is in no way hinted at by the title, which is: *Recherches Géographiques et Critiques sur le Livre 'De mensura orbis terræ'* (8vo. 1844). The treatise, Περὶ τῶν ἑπτὰ θεαμάτων, may have been written either by Philo of Heraclea or Philo of Byzantium. They both belonged to the third century before our era, but the bombastic style and numerous errors incline us to believe that the little work must have been from the pen of some unknown rhetorician of a later date.

[209] These are the words of Philo, which we have translated rather freely:—
Ποικίλαι δὲ καὶ πορφυραὶ λίθων φύσεις ἀλλήλαις ἐπιδεδόμεναι, καὶ τὰ μέν ἐστιν ἡ πέτρα λευκὴ καὶ μαρμαρίτης· τῇ δὲ Αἰθιοπικὴ καὶ μέλαινα καὶ μετὰ ταύτην ὁ καλούμενος αἱματίτης λίθος· εἶτα ποικίλος καὶ διάχλωρος ἀπὸ τῆς Ἀραβίας κεκομισμένος, p. 2,259, A.

[210] According to the calculations of Letronne, the Great Pyramid must have been 482 feet high when it was complete. In the time of Diodorus it was slightly over 480 feet; in that of Abd-ul-Latif it measured 477 feet 3 inches. In 1795 it was only 456 feet and a few inches, so that it lost about 24 feet in the course of eighteen centuries. This lowering of the summit was mainly caused by the destruction and removal of the outer casing. Since it disappeared the Arabs have been in the habit of loosening the stones on the top and launching them down the sides for the amusement of travellers; the smooth casing alone could prevent such outrage as this. The common idea that the Pyramid of Cheops is the highest building in the world is erroneous. Even if we take its height when complete, it is surpassed by at least two modern buildings, as may be seen by the following table of the most lofty buildings now existing:—

	Feet.
Spires of Cologne Cathedral	533
Flèche of the Cathedral at Rouen	500
Spire of St. Nicholas, Hamburg	480
Dome of St. Peter's, Rome	476
Spire of Strasbourg Cathedral	473
Pyramid of Cheops	456
Spire of St. Stephen's, Vienna	450
Spire of St. Martin's, Landshut	443
Spire of the Cathedral of Freiburg, Breisgau	417
Spire of Antwerp Cathedral, not including the cross	411
Spire of Salisbury Cathedral	404
Dome of Cathedral at Florence	396
Dome of St. Paul's, London	371
Flèche of Milan Cathedral	363

Tower of Magdeburg Cathedral	344
Victoria Tower, Westminster	336
Rathhaus Tower, Berlin	293
Spire of Trinity Church, New York	287
Pantheon, Paris	266
Towers of Nôtre Dame, Paris	226

[211] DIODORUS, i. 63, 64.

[212] HERODOTUS, ii. 49.

[213] M. MASPERO has given in the *Annuaire de l'Association pour l'Encouragement des Études Grecques* and elsewhere, several extracts from a commentary upon the second book of Herodotus, which we should like to see published in its entirety. We may point out more particularly his remarks upon the text of the Greek historian in the matter of the 1,600 talents of silver which, he says, was the value of the onions, radishes, and garlic consumed by the workmen employed upon the Great Pyramid (ii. 125). He has no difficulty in showing that Herodotus made a mistake, for which he gives an ingenious and probable explanation. (*Annuaire de 1875*, p. 16.)

[214] HERODOTUS, ii. 148. DIODORUS (l. 89) speaks of the same and STRABO, who also appears to have seen it, asserts its funerary character (p. 1165, C). He says it was four plethra (393 feet) both in width and height. This last dimension is obviously exaggerated, because in all the Egyptian pyramids that are known to us the shortest diameter of the base is far in excess of the height.

[215] If the passage in which Herodotus makes the statement here referred to be taken in connection with the remarks of Diodorus, a probable explanation of the old historian's assertion may be arrived at. Diodorus says that the king ὀρύττων ταύτην (λίμνην sub.) κατέλιπεν ἐν μέσῃ τόπον, ἐν ᾧ τάφον ᾠκοδόμησε καὶ δύο πυραμίδας, τὴν μὲν ἑαυτοῦ, τὴν δὲ τῆς γυναικός, σταδιαίας τὸ ὕψος. By this it would appear that, in excavating the bed, or a part of the bed, of the famous lake, a mass of earth was left in order to bear future witness to the depth of the excavation and the general magnitude of the work. This mass would probably be reveted with stone, and, in order that even when surrounded and almost hidden by water, its significance should not be lost, the pyramids raised upon it were made exactly equal to it in height.—ED.

[216] *Notice sommaire des Monuments Égyptiens exposés dans les Galeries du Louvre* (4th edition, 1865, p. 56).

[217] Ἐξεποιήθη δ' ὧν τὰ ἀνώτατα αὐτῆς πρῶτα, μετὰ δὲ τὰ ἐπόμενα τούτων ἐξεποίευν ... (ii. 125).

[218] Σύναρμον δὲ καὶ κατεξεσμένον τὸ πᾶν ἔργον, ὥστε δοκεῖν ὅλου τοῦ κατασκευάσματος μίαν εἶναι πέτρας συμφυίαν, p. 2,259, A. So, too, the elder Pliny, though with rather less precision: "Est autem saxo naturali elaborata et lubrica" (*Nat. Hist.* xxxvi. 12).

[219] According to Jomard, the casing stones of the Great Pyramid were "a compact grey limestone, harder and more homogeneous than those of the body

of the building" (*Description de l'Égypte*, t. v. p. 640); but according to Philo, this casing was formed, as we have already said, of various materials, so we need feel no surprise if blocks of granite or other rock are shown to have formed part of it.

[220] *Journal des Savants*, August, 1841.

[221] BÆDEKER, *Egypt*, part i. p. 338 (ed. of 1878). Herodotus (ii. 127) says that the first course of the Great Pyramid was built of a parti-coloured Ethiopian stone (ὑποδείμας τὸν πρῶτον δόμον λίθου Αἰθιοπικοῦ ποικίλου). By Ethiopian stone we must understand, as several illustrations prove, the granite of Syene. The Greek historian seems to have thought that the whole of the first course, throughout the thickness of the pyramid, was of this stone. His mistake was a natural one. In his time the pyramid was in a good state of preservation, and he never thought of asking whether or no the core was of the same material as the outer case.

[222] On the other hand, these awkwardly shaped prisms offered less inducement to those who looked upon the pyramids as open quarries than the easily squared blocks of Cheops, while their position in the angles of the internal masonry enabled them to keep their places independently of the lower courses of the casing.—ED.

[223] The determination to use a concrete such as that described affords a good reason for the prismatic shape of the granite blocks used in the lower courses. It would evidently be easy enough to cover the pyramid with a coat of cement—working downwards—if its surface did not greatly overpass the salient angles of the steps, while the difficulty would be enormously increased if the coat were to have a considerable thickness of its own independently of the pyramid, like the casing shown in Fig. 155.—ED.

[224] *Description de l'Égypte, Antiquités*, vol. v. p. 7.

[225] G. CHARMES, in the *Journal des Débats*, February 8, 1881.

[226] *Moniteur Égyptien*, March 15, 1881.

[227] The causeway which led to the Pyramid of Cheops still exists for some 400 yards of its length; here and there it rises as much as eighty-six feet above the surface of the plateau. A similar causeway is to be distinguished on the eastern side of the Third Pyramid. At Abou-Roash, at Abousir, and elsewhere, similar remains are to be found.

[228] *Description de l'Égypte*, vol. v. p. 643. See also in the plates, *Antiquités*, vol. v. Pl. xvi. Fig. 2. According to Jomard, the surbase of the second pyramid was in two parts—a stylobate, 10 feet high and 5 feet thick, and a plinth about 3 feet high.

[229] HERODOTUS, ii. 126.

[230] Jomard remarks that the upper part of the second pyramid still reflects the rays of the sun. "It still possesses," he says, "a portion of its polished casing, which reflects the rays of the sun and declares its identity to people at a vast distance."

[231] *Description de l'Égypte, Antiquités*, vol. v. p. 597.

[232] PSEUDO-PLUTARCH, *On Isis and Osiris*, c. xx. M. Maspero finds, however, no confirmation of this statement in the monuments themselves. "All the tombs which have yet been discovered at Abydos," he says (*Revue Critique*, January 31, 1881), "are those of Egyptians domiciled at Abydos. But the author from whom this Plutarch derived his inspiration must have known the ancient fiction according to which the soul could only pass into the next world by betaking itself to Abydos, and thence through the opening to the west of that town which gave access to the regions of Ament. Hence the voyage of the dead to Abydos which we find so often represented on tombs; an imaginary voyage, as the mummy would be reposing safely at Thebes or Memphis (Fig. 159). At all events, the family, after the death of its head, or any Egyptian during his own life, could deposit upon the *ladder of Osiris* a stele, upon which the tomb actually containing his body could be represented and unmistakably identified with its original by the formula inscribed upon it."

[233] MARIETTE, *Abydos, Description des Fouilles exécutées sur l'Emplacement de cette Ville*, folio, vol. i. 1869; vol. ii. 1880. Mariette thought that the sacred tomb was probably in the immediate neighbourhood of the artificial mound called *Koum-es-Soultan*, which may cover its very site. In the article which we quote above, M. Maspero has set forth the considerations which lead him to think that the staircase of Osiris, upon which the consecrated steles were placed, was the flight of steps which led up to the temple of that god. Consequently the tomb of Osiris, at Abydos as at Denderah, would be upon the roof of his temple.

[234] MARIETTE, *Voyage dans la Haute-Égypte*, vol. i. 1879.

[235] *Ibidem.*

[236] All these steles are figured in the last work published by MARIETTE, the *Catalogue général des Monuments d'Abydos, découverts pendant les Fouilles de cette Ville*, 1 vol. 4to. Paris, 1880.

[237] MARIETTE, *Voyage dans la Haute-Égypte*, vol. i. p. 51.

[238] MASPERO, *Rapport sur une Mission en Italie* (in the *Recueil de Travaux*, vol. ii. p. 166). The Abbott Papyrus gives a list of these little pyramids.

[239] Fig. 172 reproduces only a part of the long plate given in Wilkinson. In order to bring the more important groups within the scope of one page, we have been compelled to omit the central portion, which consists principally of columns of hieroglyphs.

[240] See the description of the Valley of the Kings in the *Lettres d'Égypte et de Nubie* of CHAMPOLLION (p. 183 of the second edition).

[241] EBERS, indeed, found something of the same kind in the temple of Abydos. He found there a cenotaph consecrated to his own memory by Seti I. This cenotaph was near the tomb of Osiris, while the king himself was buried in the Theban necropolis. (*Ægypten*, pp. 234, 235.)

[242] The beautiful little temple of Dayr-el-Medinet, begun by Ptolemy Philopator and finished by his successors, especially by Physco, has often been

considered a funerary monument. It is alleged that the situation of the temple in the necropolis, and the nature of the subjects represented in the interior, particularly in the Western Chamber, prove that it was so. If we accept this opinion, we must look upon the temple as a mere freak of fancy, suggested to Ptolemy Philopator by a journey to Thebes. The Greek prince was interred far from it, and it could have formed no part of his tomb.

[243] MARIETTE, *Deir-el-Bahari*, § 1. (Atlas, folio, Leipsic, 1877, with 40 pages letterpress, 4to.)

[244] DIODORUS, i. §§ 47-49.

[245] This must have been the structure which STRABO calls the *Memnonium*, and near to which he seems to place the two colossi (xvii. p. 816). The true name of the author of both temple and colossi might easily be confused with that of the mythical Greek personage which the Hellenic imagination persisted in discovering everywhere in Egypt, and the similarity of sound must have helped to perpetuate the mistake among all the foreign travellers who visited the country. A curious passage in PAUSANIAS (*Attica*, 42) shows us, however, that the Egyptian scholars of his time knew how properly to convey the name of the prince represented in the colossi to foreigners: "I was less struck by that marvel," he says, in speaking of some sonorous stone which was shown to him at Megara, "than by a colossal statue which I saw beyond the Nile in Egypt, not far from the *pipes*. This colossus is a statue of the sun, or of Memnon, according to the common tradition. It is said that Memnon came from Ethiopia into Egypt, and that he penetrated as far as Susa. But the Thebans themselves deny that it is Memnon. They declare that it represents Phamenoph (Φάμενοφ), who was born in their own country...." The story told by PHILOSTRATUS (*Life of Apollonius*, l. vi. p. 232) of the visit of the sorcerer to Memnon, shows that in his time the colossus was surrounded by nothing but ruins, such as broken columns and architraves, fragmentary walls and shattered statues. Even then the monumental completeness of the "Amenophium" had vanished.

[246] In many cases the sites are wanting for such external constructions. The fine tomb of Seti I., for instance, opens upon a ravine which is filled with the waters of a mountain torrent at certain seasons.

[247] When Belzoni's workmen found the entrance to the tomb of Seti, they declared that they could not advance any farther, because the passage was blocked with big stones to such an extent as to be impracticable (*Narrative of the Operations and Recent Discoveries within the Pyramids, &c., in Egypt and Nubia*, 1820, 4to.). Mariette also believed that as soon as the mummy was in place, the external door was closed and earth heaped against it in such a way as effectually to conceal it. It is thus that the clashing between the tomb of Rameses III. and another is accounted for. The workmen did not see the entrance of the latter, and were, in fact, unaware of its existence until they encountered it in the bowels of the rock. (*Voyage dans la Haute-Égypte*, t. ii. p. 81.)

[248] DIODORUS, i. 46.

[249] "Above the Memnonium," says STRABO (xvii. 46), "there are royal tombs cut in the living rock to the number of forty; their workmanship is excellent and well worthy of attention."

[250] BELZONI, *Narrative of Operations, &c.*, pp. 233 et seq.

[251] This beautiful sarcophagus is now in the Soane Museum.—ED.

[252] Belzoni believed that this passage led again into the open air; that it was, in fact, another entrance to the tomb. "I have," he says, "reasons to think so;" but he does not give his reasons.

[253] The tomb of Seti having been so often reproduced, we have thought it better to give the plan and section of that of Rameses II., which is less generally known. The general arrangements are pretty much the same as those of Seti's tomb, but the plan is a little more complicated.

[254] *Panorama de l'Égypte et de la Nubie*, folio.

[255] This belief in the appearance of the dead before Osiris and his assessors gave rise to one of the most curious errors made by the Greeks in speaking of Egypt. The scene in question is figured upon many of the tombs visited by the Greek travellers, and in many of the illustrated papyri which were unrolled for their gratification. In the fragments of some funerary inscription or of some of these manuscripts, hastily translated for them by the accompanying priests, they found frequent allusions to this act of trial and judgment. They were greatly struck by the importance attached by the Egyptians to the sentence of this tribunal, but, always in a hurry, and sometimes not especially intelligent, they do not seem to have always understood what the dragoman, without whom they could not stir from the frontier, told them as to this matter. They believed that the judges in question were living men, and their tribunal an earthly one, and that they were charged to decide whether sepulture should be granted to the dead or not. One of the early travellers, we do not know which, gave currency to this belief, and we know how it has served as the foundation for much fine writing, from the time of Diodorus to that of Bossuet. We can find nothing either in the figured monuments or in the written texts which hints at the existence of such a custom. Ever since the key to the hieroglyphics was found, egyptologists have been agreed upon this point. Every Egyptian was placed in a sepulchre befitting his station and fortune; his relations and friends had to ask no permission before they placed him in it; it was in the other world that he was brought up for judgment, and had to fear the sentence of an august tribunal.

[256] MASPERO gives a translation of it into French in his *Histoire Ancienne*, pp. 44 and 45.

[257] This weighing of the actions of the deceased was represented in the illustrated specimens of the *Ritual of the Dead* and upon the walls of the tombs, and perhaps upon those monuments decorated with Egyptian motives which were sprinkled by the Phœnicians over the whole basin of the Mediterranean. Coming under the eyes of the Greeks, it was modified by their lively imaginations into that ψυχοστασία, or *weighing of souls*, which we find in the Iliad (xxii. 208-212), where success in a combat between two heroes depends

upon the result of that operation. (See ALFRED MAURY, *Revue archéologique*, 1844, pp. 235-249, 291-307; 1845, pp. 707-717, and DE WITTE, *ibidem*, 1844, pp. 647-656.)

[258] *Recueil de Travaux*, vol. i. pp. 155-159.

[259] One was found in a Theban tomb opened by RHIND (*Thebes*, &c., pp. 94 and 95). In the tomb of Ti easily recognized traces of a door were found (BÆDEKER, *Unter-Ægypten*, p. 405); nothing but a new door was required to put the opening in its ancient state.

[260] See one of the great inscriptions at Beni-Hassan, interpreted by M. MASPERO (*Recueil*, etc. vol. i. p. 168).

[261] *Description de l'Égypte*, (*Antiquités*, vol. iii. p. 35).

[262] A. RHONÉ, *l'Égypt à petites journées*, p. 104.

[263] PASSALACQUA describes a tomb of this kind in detail in his *Catalogue raisonné et historique des Antiquités découvertes en Égypte* (8vo., 1826). This tomb had been visited and pillaged at some unknown epoch. One of the two chambers had been opened and stripped, but the second, which opened lower down the well, and on the other side, escaped the notice of the violators (pp. 118-120). In the tomb opened by RHIND (*Thebes, its Tombs*, etc. pl. 5, v.), the well gave access to four chambers of different sizes arranged round it like the arms of a cross.

[264] *Description de l'Égypte*, (*Antiquités*,) plates, vol. ii. p. 78.

[265] RHIND describes one of the most curious of these substitutions in his chapter IV. In that case an usurper of the time of Ptolemy established himself and all his family in the mummy chambers at the foot of the well, after relegating the statues and mummies of the rightful owner and his people to the room above.

[266] *Athenæum Français*, 1855, p. 55 (*Renseignements sur les soixante quatre Apis trouvés dans le Sérapeum de Memphis*).

[267] This view is obtained by a series of horizontal and vertical sections in the rock to the right of the galleries. By this operation we are enabled to show the subterranean parts of the tomb.

[268] RHIND, *Thebes*, etc. p. 43.

[269] RHIND, *Thebes*, etc. pp. 56, 57.

[270] RHIND, *Thebes*, etc. p. 55.

[271] MASPERO, *Recueil de Travaux*, vol. ii. p. 105. The formula which is generally found upon the funerary steles of the eighteenth and nineteenth dynasties hints at this: "That I may walk daily upon the border of my fountain; that my soul may rest upon the branches of the funerary garden which has been made for me, that each day I may be out under my sycamore!" These desires may be taken literally, as is proved by two steles in the museums of Turin and

Boulak, which bear representations of tombs upon their lower portions. The latter, which we reproduce, comes from the Theban necropolis.

[272] Most of these statues were of calcareous stone, but in the *Description de l'Égypte* (*Antiquités*, vol. iii. p. 34) two granite ones are mentioned.

[273] In the tomb of Amenemheb, for instance, discovered by Professor Ebers. See also *Description de l'Égypte*, vol. iii. p. 41.

[274] *Description de l'Égypte* (*Antiquités*, vol. iii. p. 34).

[275] It is no part of our plan to describe this discovery, which did so much honour both to the perspicacity and the energy of Mariette. We refer all those who are interested in the matter to the article contributed by M. E. Desjardins to the *Revue des Deux-Mondes* of March 15, 1874, under the title: *Les Découvertes de l'Égyptologie française, les Missions et les Travaux de M. Mariette*. Many precious details will also be found, some of them almost dictated by Mariette, in the *L'Égypte à petites Journeés* of M. ARTHUR RHONÉ (pp. 212-263). This work includes two plans, a general plan and a detailed plan of the subterranean galleries, which were supplied by the illustrious author of the excavations himself; views of the galleries are also given, and reproductions of various objects found in the course of the exploration. We may also mention the *Choix des Monuments du Sérapéum*, a collection of ten engraved plates published by Mariette, and the great work, unfortunately incomplete, which he commenced under the title: *Le Sérapéum de Memphis* (folio, Paris, Gide, 1858). In the second volume of *Fouilles et Découvertes* (Didier, 8vo., 1873, 2 vols.) BEULÉ has given a very good description of the bold but fortunate campaign which, begun in the month of October, 1850, brought fame to a young man who had, until then, both open enmity and secret intrigue to contend against.

[276] HERODOTUS, ii. 169. "The Egyptians strangled Apries, but, having done so, they buried him in the sepulchre of his fathers. This tomb is in the temple of Athenè (*Neith*), very near the sanctuary, on the left hand as one enters. The natives of Sais buried all the kings which belonged to their nome within this temple, and, in fact, it also contains the tomb of Amasis, as well as that of Apries and his family, but the former is not so close to the sanctuary as the former, but still it is within the buildings of the temple, in a large chamber constructed of stone, with columns in the shape of the trunks of palm-trees, and richly decorated besides, which incloses a kind of niche or shrine with folding doors, in which the mummy is placed." This is one of the most difficult passages in Herodotus, and has given much trouble to translators and commentators. See Larcher's note (ii. 565), and the passage in Stobæus (serm. xli. p. 251), which he cites in justification for the sense which is here given to the word θυρώματα. STRABO is content with but a line on this subject: "Sais," he says, "especially worships Athenè (Neith). The tomb of Psammitichos is in the very temple of that goddess" (xvii. 18).

[277] HERODOTUS affirms (ii. 129-132) that Mycerinus caused the body of his daughter to be inclosed in the flank of a wooden cow, richly gilt, and he says that "the cow in question was never placed in the earth." In his time it was exposed to the view of all comers in a magnificently decorated saloon of the royal palace of Sais. We may be allowed to suggest that Herodotus was mistaken in the name of

the prince; Mycerinus is not likely to have so far abandoned all the funerary traditions of his time, or to have entombed the body of his daughter in a spot so distant from his own pyramid at Gizeh. There is one hypothesis, however, which may save us from the necessity of once again accusing the Greek historian of misunderstanding what was said to him; in their desire to weld together the present with the past, and to collect into their capital such national monuments as might appeal to the imaginations of their subjects, the Sait princes may have transported such a curiously shaped sarcophagus either from the pyramid of Mycerinus or from some small pyramid in its neighbourhood.

[278] HERODOTUS, iii. 16. Upon this subject see an interesting article by M. EUGÈNE REVILLOUT, entitled: *Le Roi Amasis et les mercenaires Grecs, selon les Donnés d'Hérodote et les Renseignements de la Chronique Démotique de Paris.* (*Revue Égyptologique*, first year; p. 50 *et seq.*)

[279] There are two passages in HERODOTUS (ii. 91, and 138) from which we may infer that the Egyptians were fond of planting trees about their temples.

[280] *Lettres Écrites d'Égypte et de Nubie*, 2nd edition, 1868, p. 41.

[281] Similar structures exist in lower Chaldæa, and have furnished many inscriptions of great interest and value to assyriologists.

[282] RHIND, *Thebes*, etc. p. 51. BELZONI, *Narrative of the Operations*, etc. p. 167.

[283] RHIND, p. 52. Among the mummified animals found at Thebes, Wilkinson also mentions monkeys, sheep, cows, cats, crocodiles, etc. See BELZONI, *Narrative*, p. 187.

[284] When Mariette discovered the tomb of the Apis which had died in the twenty-sixth year of the reign of Rameses II., the fingers of the Egyptian mason who laid the last stone of the wall built across the entrance to the tomb were found marked upon the cement, and "when I entered the sarcophagus-chamber I found upon the thin layer of dust which covered the floor the marks made by the naked feet of the workmen who had placed the god in his last resting place 3,200 years before." (Quoted by RHÔNÉ in *L'Égypte à Petites Journées*, p. 239.)

[285] We may take a few of those in the Boulak Museum at random: Ra-Hotep (No. 590), Hathor-En-Khéou (588), Ra-Nefer (23), Ra-Our (25), Sokar-Kha-Ca-u (993), Noum-Hotep (26), Hathor-Nefer (41), Ptah-Asses (500), Ptah-Hotep, &c. The names of several deities are to be found in the inscription upon the wooden coffin or mummy-case of Mycerinus, now in the British Museum. (MASPERO, *Histoire Ancienne*, p. 75). A priest of Apis is mentioned upon a tomb of the fourth dynasty; Osiris is invoked in the steles of the sixth dynasty. (Boulak Catalogue, No. 41.)

Amen, or Ammon, is never mentioned on the monuments of the Ancient Empire; his first appearance is contemporary with the twelfth dynasty. (GRÉBAULT, *Hymne à Ammon-Ra*, Introduction, part iii. p. 136.) This is natural enough. Amen was a Theban god, and Thebes does not seem to have existed in the time of the Ancient Empire.

[286] *Notice des principaux Monuments exposés dans les Galeries provisoires du Musée d' ntiquités Égyptiennes à Boulak.* (Edition of 1876, No. 582.)

[287] The total height of the Sphinx is 66 feet; the ear is 6 feet 4 inches high; the nose is 6 feet, the mouth 7 feet 9 inches, wide. The greatest width of the face across the cheeks is 14 feet 2 inches. If cleared entirely of sand the Sphinx would thus be higher than a five-storied house. For the history of the Sphinx, the different restorations which it has undergone, and the aspect which it has presented at different epochs, see MARIETTE, *Questions relatives aux nouvelles Fouilles.* Our plan (Fig. 204) shows the wide flight of steps which was constructed in the time of Trajan to give access to a landing constructed immediately in front of the fore-paws. Between these paws a little temple was contrived, where the steles consecrated by several of the Theban kings in honour of the Sphinx were arranged. Caviglia was the first to bring all these matters to light, in 1817, but the *ensemble*, as it now exists, only dates back to the Roman epoch. It is curious that neither Herodotus, nor Diodorus, nor Strabo, mention the Sphinx. Pliny speaks of it (N. H. xxxvi. 17); some of the information which he obtained was valuable and authentic, but it was mixed with errors; it was said to be, he tells us, *the tomb of the king Armais*, but he knows that the whole figure was painted red. The *Denkmæler* of Lepsius (vol. i. pl. 30) gives three sections and a plan of the little temple between the paws. The same work (vol. v. pl. 68) contains a reproduction of the great stele of Thothmes relative to the restoration of the Sphinx.

[288] CHAMPOLLION, *Lettres d'Égypte et de Nubie*, pp. 125, 143, and 166. Under both the temples at Ombos, Champollion discovered remains of a building of the time of Thothmes III. The same thing occurred at Edfou and at Esneh. We except Philæ, because there is good reason to believe that in the time of the Ancient Empire that island did not exist, and that the cataract was then at Silsilis.

[289] STRABO, xvii. 128: Οὐδὲν ἔχει χαρίεν οὐδὲ γραφικόν, etc.

[290] LUCIAN, § 3: Ἀξοάνοι νηοί, etc.

[291] The piers are not quite equidistant; their spacing varies by some centimetres. Exact symmetry has been sacrificed in consequence of the different lengths of the stones which formed the architrave.

[292] MARIETTE, *Questions relatives aux nouvelles Fouilles à faire en Égypte.* (*Académie des Inscriptions, Comptes Rendus des Séances de l'Année*, 1877, pp. 427-473.)

[293] *Itinéraire des Invités du Vice-roi*, p. 99.

[294] BÆDEKER, *Guide to Lower Egypt*, p. 350.

[295] The actual distance is about 670 yards.

[296] MARIETTE, *Questions relatives aux nouvelles Fouilles*, etc.

[297] *Description de l'Égypte, Ant.*, vol. v. p. 654.

[298] BELZONI, *Narrative of the Operations*, etc. pp. 261-2.

[299] The little that now remains of the columns and foundations of the ancient temple is marked in the plan which forms plate 6 of Mariette's *Karnak*, Fig. *a*. In plate 8 the remains of all statues and inscriptions which date from the same period are figured. See also pages 36, 37, and 41-45 of the text.

[300] MARIETTE, *Karnak*, p. 4.

[301] We may infer from what Mariette says that they were separated from one another by a distance of 12 feet 4 inches.

[302] MARIETTE, *Karnak*, p. 5. We find, however, that sphinxes were sometimes placed in the interior of a temple. The two fine sphinxes in rose granite which form the chief ornaments of the principal court of the Boulak museum, were found in one of the inner halls of the temple at Karnak. They date, probably, from the time of Thothmes III., to whom this part of the building owes its existence.

[303] *Description*, etc.; *Description générale de Thèbes*, section viii. § 1.

[304] The wall of the principal inclosure at Denderah, that on the north, is not less than 33 feet high, and between 30 and 40 thick at the base. Its surface is perfectly smooth and naked, without ornament of any kind, or even rough-cast. (MARIETTE, *Denderah*, p. 27.) At Karnak the bounding walls are in a much worse state of preservation; they are ten or twelve centuries older than those of Denderah, and those centuries have had their effect upon the masses of crude brick. Our only means of estimating their original height is by comparing, in the representations furnished to us by certain bas-reliefs, the height of walls with that of the pylons on which they abut.

[305] MARIETTE, *Karnak*, pp. 5, 6.

[306] The word πυλών strictly means the place before the door (like θυρών), or rather great door (upon the augmentative force of the suffix ών, ῶνος, see AD. REGNIER, *Traité de la Formation des Mots dans la Langue Grecque*, § 184). Several passages in POLYBIUS (*Thesaurus*, s. v.) show that in the military language of his time the term was employed to signify a fortified doorway with its flanking towers and other defences. We may therefore understand why DIODORUS (i. 47) made use of it in his description of the so-called tomb of Osymandias. STRABO (xvii. 1, 28) preferred to use the word πρόπυλων. Modern usage has restricted the word *propylœum* to Greek buildings, and *pylon* to the great doorways which form one of the most striking features of Egyptian architecture.

[307] We learn the part played by these masts and banners in Egyptian decoration entirely from the representations in the bas-reliefs. The façade of the temple of Khons is illustrated in one of the bas-reliefs upon the same building. That relief was reproduced in the *Description de l'Égypte* (vol. iii. pl. 57, Fig. 9), and is so well known that we refrained from giving it in these pages. It shows the masts and banners in all their details. Another representation of the same kind will be found in CAILLIAUD, *Voyage à Méroé*, plates, vol. ii. pl. 64, Fig. 1. See in the text, vol. iii. p. 298. It is taken from a rock-cut tomb between Dayr-el-Medinet and Medinet-Abou.

[308] This plate (v.) is not a picturesque restoration; it is merely a map in relief. Only those buildings are marked upon it which have left easily traceable remains. No attempt has been made to reconstruct by conjecture any of those edifices which are at present nothing but confused heaps of *débris*.

[309] The obelisk of Ousourtesen at Heliopolis is 20·27 metres, or 67 feet 6 inches, high; the Luxor obelisk at Paris, 22·80 metres, or 76 feet; that in the piazza before St. Peter's in Rome, 83 feet 9 inches; that of San Giovanni Laterano, the tallest in Europe, is 107 feet 2 inches; and that of Queen Hatasu, still standing amid the ruins at Karnak, 32·20 metres, or 107 feet 4 inches. This is the highest obelisk known. [The Cleopatra's Needle on the Victoria Embankment is only 68 feet 2 inches high.—ED.]

[310] At Thebes, still existing inscriptions prove this to be the case, and at Memphis the same custom obtained, as we know from the statements of the Greek travellers. The temple of Ptah—the site of which seems to be determined by the colossal statue of Rameses which still lies there upon its face—must have rivalled Karnak in extent and in the number of its successive additions. According to DIODORUS (i. 50) it was Mœris (Amenemhat III.) who built the southern propylons of this temple, which, according to the same authority, surpassed all their rivals in magnificence. At a much later period, Sesostris (a Rameses) erected several colossal monoliths, from 20 to 30 cubits high, in front of the same temple (DIODORUS, cap. lvii.; HERODOTUS, ii. 140); at the same time he must have raised obelisks and constructed courts and pylons. Herodotus attributes to two other kings, whom he names *Rhampsinite* and *Asychis*, the construction of two more pylons on the eastern and western sides of the temple (ii. 121 and 136). Finally Psemethek I. built the southern propylons and the pavilion where the Apis was nursed after his first discovery. (HERODOTUS, ii. 153.)

[311] STRABO, xvii, 1, 28.

[312] This is the temple which the members of the Egyptian institute call the Great Southern Temple. In the background of our illustration (Fig. 208) the hypostyle hall and the southern pylons of the Great Temple are seen.

[313] Τοῦ δὲ προνάου παρ' ἑκάτερον πρόκειται τὰ λεγόμενα πτερά· ἔστι δὲ ταῦτα ἰσοΰψη τῷ ναῷ τείχη δύο, κατ' ἀρχὰς μὲν ἀφεστῶτα ἀπ' ἀλλήλων μικρὸν πλέον, ἢ τὸ πλάτος ἐστὶ τῆς κρηπῖδος τοῦ νεώ, ἔπειτ' εἰς τὸ πρόσθεν προϊόντι κατ' ἐπινευούσας γραμμὰς μέχρι πηχῶν πεντήκοντα ἢ ἑξήκοντα.— STRABO, xvii, 1, 28.

[314] *Description de l'Égypte, Antiquités*, vol. i. pl. 5.

[315] *Description de l'Égypte*, vol. iii. 55.

[316] According to GAU, there was, in 1817, a well preserved tabernacle in the sanctuary of the temple at *Debout*, in Nubia. (*Antiquités de la Nubie*, 1821, pl. v. Figs. A and B.)

[317] DE ROUGÉ, *Notice des Monuments*, etc. (Upon the ground floor and the staircase.) *Monuments Divers*, No. 29. The term *naos* has generally been applied to these monuments, but it seems to us to lack precision. The Greeks used the

word ναός or νεώς to signify the temple as a whole. Abd-el-Latif describes with great admiration a monolithic tabernacle which existed in his time among the ruins of Memphis, and was called by the Egyptians the *Green Chamber*. Makrizi tells us that it was broken up in 1349. (*Description de l'Égypte, Ant.*, vol. v. pp. 572, 573.)

[318] HERODOTUS, ii. 175.

[319] Translated by MASPERO, *Histoire Ancienne*, p. 385. The whole inscription has been translated into English by the Rev. T. C. Cook, and published in vol. ii. of *Records of the Past*.—ED.

[320] As M. MASPERO has remarked (*Annuaire de l'Association des Études Grecques*, 1877, p. 135), these secret passages remind us of the movable stone which, according to HERODOTUS (ii. 121), the architect of Rhampsinit contrived in the wall of the royal treasure-house which he was commissioned to build. Herodotus's story was at least founded upon fact, as the arrangement in question was a favourite one with Egyptian constructors.

[321] Ἀναγλυφὰς δ' ἔχουσιν οἱ τοῖχοι οὗτοι μεγάλων εἰδώλων (STRABO, xvii, 1, 28).

[322] *Description de l'Égypte, Antiquités*, vol. i. p. 219. The authors of the *Description générale de Thèbes* noticed recesses sunk in the external face of one of the pylons at Karnak, which they believed to be intended to receive the leaves of the great door when it was open (p. 234); they also noticed traces of bronze pivots upon which the doors swung (p. 248), and they actually found a pivot of sycamore wood.

[323] These measurements are taken from MARIETTE, *Voyage dans la Haute-Égypte*, vol. ii. p. 7.

[324] We have not given a general map. In order to do so we should either have had to overpass the limits of our page, or we should have had to give it upon too small a scale. Our fourth plate will give a sufficiently accurate idea of its arrangement. The plan in Lepsius's *Denkmæler* (part i. pl. 74-76) occupies three entire pages.

[325] DIODORUS, i. 46.

[326] These are the figures given by MARIETTE (*Itinéraire de la Haute-Égypte*, p. 135). Other authorities give 340 feet by 177. Diodorus ascribed to the temple of which he spoke a height of 45 cubits (or 69 feet 3 inches). This is slightly below the true height. We may here quote the terms in which Champollion describes the impression which a first sight of these ruins made upon him: "Finally I went to the palace, or rather to the town of palaces, at Karnak. There all the magnificence of the Pharaohs is collected; there the greatest artistic conceptions formed and realised by mankind are to be seen. All that I had seen at Thebes, all that I had enthusiastically admired on the left bank of the river, sunk into insignificance before the gigantic structures among which I found myself. I shall not attempt to describe what I saw. If my expressions were to convey but a thousandth part of what I felt, a thousandth part of all that might with truth be said of such objects, if I succeeded in tracing but a faint sketch, in the dimmest

colours, of the marvels of Karnak, I should be taken, at least for an enthusiast, perhaps for a madman. I shall content myself with saying that no people, either ancient or modern, have had a national architecture at once so sublime in scale, so grand in expression, and so free from littleness as that of the ancient Egyptians." (*Lettres d'Égypte*, pp. 79, 80.)

[327] Including a postern of comparatively small dimensions, there are five doorways to the hypostyle hall.—ED.

[328] A plan of the successive accretions is given in plates 6 and 7 of MARIETTE's work. The different periods and their work are shown by changes of tint. The same information is given in another form in pages 36 and 37 of the text. The complete title of the work is as follows: *Karnak, Étude topographique et archéologique, avec un Appendice comprenant les principaux Textes hiéroglyphiques*. Plates in folio; text in a 4to. of 88 pages (1875).

[329] In presence of this double range of superb columns one is tempted to look upon them as the beginning of a hypostyle hall which was never finished, to suppose that a great central nave was constructed, and that, by force of circumstances unknown, the aisles were never begun, and that the builders contented themselves by inclosing and preserving their work as far as it had gone.

[330] DIODORUS, i. 47-49.

[331] STRABO, xvii. i. 42. In another passage (xvii. i. 46) he seems to place the Memnonium close to the two famous colossi. He would, therefore, seem rather to have had in view an "Amenophium," the remains of which have been discovered in the immediate neighbourhood of the two colossi. The French *savants* suspected this to be the case, but they often defer to the opinions of their immediate predecessors among Egyptian travellers. (*Description générale de Thèbes*, section iii.)

[332] This pylon stands in the foreground of our view (Fig. 220). The face which is here shown was formerly covered—as we may judge from the parts which remain—with pictures of battles; and that we might not have to actually invent scenes of combat for our restoration, we have borrowed the ornamentation of the first pylon of the Temple of Khons. The scale of our cut is too small, however, to show any details.

[333] LEPSIUS, *Denkmæler*, part i. plates 88 and 89. The engineers of the *Institut d'Égypte* fell into an error in speaking of this hall. They failed to notice that it was smaller than the second court, and they accordingly gave it sixty columns. (*Description générale de Thebes*, vol. i. p. 132.)

[334] See EBERS, Ægypten, vol. ii. pp. 309 et seq.

[335] Ibid., p. 312.

[336] EBERS, Ægypten, vol. ii. p. 312.

[337] The plan in the Description de l'Égypte (Antiquités, vol. ii. pl. 4) does not go beyond the back wall of the second court. That of Lepsius goes to the back of the hypostyle hall. (Denkmæler, part i. pl. 92.) Ours is much more comprehensive—it goes three stages farther back; it was communicated to us by M. Brune, who measured the building in 1866.

[338] Here M. Perrot is in error, as may be seen by reference to his own plan. The columns of the central passage of the hypostyle hall are similar in section to those of the two peristyles, except that their bases are flattened laterally in a somewhat unusual fashion.—ED.

[339] A few of these buildings—that, for instance, on the right of the great lake—seem to have been very peculiar in arrangement, but their remains are in such a state of confusion that it is at present impossible to describe their plans.

[340] CAILLIAUD, Voyage à Méroé, plates, vol. ii. pl. 9-14. LEPSIUS, Denkmæler, part i. pl. 116, 117. HOSKINS, Travels in Ethiopia, plates 40, 41, and 42. The plan given by Hoskins agrees more with that of Lepsius than with Cailliaud, but it only shows the beginning of the first hypostyle hall and nothing of the second. These divergences are easily understood when it is remembered that nothing but some ten columns of two different types remain *in situ*, and that the mounds of *débris* are high and wide. In order to obtain a really trustworthy plan, this accumulation would have to be cleared away over the whole area of the temple. All the plans show a kind of gallery, formed of six columns, in front of the first pylon; it reminds us in some degree of the great corridor at Luxor; by its general form, however, rather than its situation.

[341] Full particulars of the more obscure parts of the temple at Abydos will be found in Mariette's first volume.

[342] Upon the funerary character of the great temple at Abydos, see EBERS, Ægypten, vol. ii. pp. 234, 235.

[343] We may cite as a peripteral temple of the Ptolemaic epoch the building at Edfou, called, in the *Description*, the *Little Temple* (Antiquités, vol. i. plates 62-65). It differs from the Pharaonic temples of the same class in having square piers only at the angles, the rest of the portico being supported by columns.

[344] Description de l'Égypte, Antiquités, vol. i. plates 34-38.

[345] This base contained a crypt, no doubt for the sake of economising the material. There seems to have been no means of access to it, either from without or within.

[346] Our plan, etc. shows the temple as it must have left the hands of the architect, according to the authors of the *Description de l'Égypte*. Jomard (pl. 35, Fig. 1) has imported a small chamber into his plan, placing it behind the large hall as a sort of *opisthodomos*; but he bids us remark that it was constructed of

different materials, and in a different *bond*, from the rest of the temple. It showed no trace of the sculptured decoration which covered all the rest of the temple. This chamber was therefore a later addition, and one only obtained at the expense of the continuous portico, the back part of which was enclosed with a wall in which the columns became engaged. According to Jomard, this alteration dates from the Roman period, but however that may be, in our examination of the temple we may disregard an addition which appears to have been so awkwardly managed.

[347] In the *Description de l'Égypte* it is called *The Northern Temple* (see vol. i. pl. 38, Figs. 2 and 3). The only difference noted by Jomard was in the ornamentation of the capitals.

[348] LEPSIUS *Denkmæler*, part i. pl. 113.

[349] *Description, Antiquités*, vol. i. pl. 71, Figs. 1, 2, 3, 4; letterpress, vol. i. ch. vi. This temple is 50 feet long, 31 wide, and 15 feet 8 inches high.

[350] See LEPSIUS for plans of these buildings; *Denkmæler*, part i. plates 125, 127, and 128.

[351] *Denkmæler*, part i. pl. 100.

[352] The internal measurements of this chamber were 26 feet by 33. Lepsius gives it four columns, but at present there are only the remains of one to be found. Almost the same arrangements are to be found in the Temple of *Sedeinga*. (LEPSIUS, *Denkmæler*, part i. pl. 115.)

[353] See, for Gebel Silsilis, LEPSIUS, *Denkmæler*, part i. pl. 102.

[354] *Description de l'Égypte, Antiquités*, vol. iv. pl. 65, Fig. 1. The French draughtsmen thought this building was a disused quarry, and give nothing but a picturesque view of the façade.

[355] LEPSIUS, *Denkmæler*, part i. pl. 102; ROSELLINI (vol. iii. pl. 32, Fig. 3) gives a view of the interior of the Silsilis chapel.

[356] LEPSIUS, *Denkmæler*, part i. pl. 101.

[357] LEPSIUS, *Denkmæler*, part i. pl. 127.

[358] There are also a hemispeos or two of the Ptolemaic period. That, for instance, of which the plans are given in plate 101 of Lepsius's first part, was begun by Ptolemy Euergetes II.

[359] This description has been mainly taken from the plate given by PRISSE (*Histoire de l'Art Égyptien*, vol. i.). There are discrepancies, however, between it and both the inscription of Isambert and the plan of HOREAU (*Panorama d'Égypte et Nubie*), discrepancies which may probably be referred to the bad condition of the structural part of the building. According to Prisse's measurements the dromos, from its commencement to the foot of the first pylon, was about fifty-five yards long, and the rest of the temple, to the back of the niche, was about as much again. The rock-cut part was only about ten yards deep.

[360] The resemblance between Prisse's plan of Gherf-Hossein and Horeau's plan of Wadi-Asseboua is so great as to suggest that one of the two writers may have made a mistake.

[361] There are two polygonal columns resembling those at Beni-Hassan in the small speos at Beit-el-Wali (Fig. 237).

[362] For *Beit-el-Wali* and *Gircheh*, see plates 13, 30 and 31 in GAU, *Antiquités de la Nubie*. It seems that the statues, when they were drawn by him, were in a fairly good state.

[363] These words mean *Convent of the North*. The name is derived from an abandoned Coptic convent which existed among the ruins of the ancient building.

[364] This wide inclined plane agrees better, as it seems to us, with the indications in M. Brune's plan of the actual remains at Dayr-el-Bahari, than the narrow flight of steps given in his restoration; the effect, too, is better, more ample and majestic.

[365] The same idea caused M. Brune to place sphinxes upon the steps between the courts; he thought that some small heaps of *débris* at the ends of the steps indicated their situation; but M. Maspero, who recently investigated the matter, informs us that he found no trace of any such sphinxes.

[366] We must refer those who wish to study the remains of this temple in detail to the work devoted to it by M. Mariette. The plan which forms plate 1 in the said work was drawn, in 1866, by an architect, M. Brune, who is now a professor at the École des Beaux Arts. M. Brune succeeded, by intelligent and conscientious examination of all the remains, in obtaining the materials for a restoration which gave us for the first time some idea of what this interesting monument must have been in the great days of Egypt. Plate 2 contains a restored plan; plate 3 a view in perspective of the three highest terraces and of the hill which forms their support. We have attempted to give an idea of the building as a whole. Our view is taken from a more distant point than that of M. Brune, but except in some of the less important details, it does not greatly differ from his.

[367] MARIETTE, *Dayr-el-Bahari*, letterpress, p. 10.

[368] EBERS, *Ægypten*, p. 285.

[369] MASPERO, *Histoire Ancienne*, pp. 202, 203. The bas-reliefs at Dayr-el-Bahari represent the booty brought back by Hatasu from the expedition into Pount. Among this booty thirty-two perfume shrubs, in baskets, may be distinguished; these shrubs were planted by the orders of Hatasu in the gardens of Thebes. On the subject of Hatasu and her expedition, see MASPERO's paper entitled: *De quelques Navigations des Égyptiens sur les Côtes de la Mer Érythrée* (in the *Revue Historique*, 1878).

[370] MASPERO, *Histoire Ancienne*, p. 203.

[371] HERODOTUS, ii. 175.

[372] HERODOTUS, ii. 153.

[373] Herodotus uses the word αὐλή, of which stable or cattle-shed was one of the primitive meanings.

[374] *Égypte*, etc. p. 406.

[375] The temple of *Kerdasch* or *Gartasse* in Nubia resembles the Eastern Temple at Philæ in plan; its date appears to be unknown.

[376] We have omitted to speak of those little temples known since the time of Champollion as *mammisi* or places for accouchement, because the existing examples all belong to the Ptolemaic period. The best preserved is that of Denderah. It is probable, however, that the custom of building these little edifices by the side of those great temples where a triad of gods was worshipped dated back as far as the Pharaonic period. The mammisi symbolised the celestial dwelling in which the goddess gave birth to the third person of the triad. The authors of the *Description* called them *Typhonia*, from the effigy of a grimacing deity which figures in their decoration. This deity has, however, nothing in common with Set-Typhon, the enemy of Osiris. We now know that his name was Bes, that he was imported into Egypt from the country of the Aromati, and that he presided over the toilette of women. (EBERS, *L'Égypte*, etc., p. 255.)

[377] MARIETTE, *Itinérare*, pp. 13-16, 157-159; *Karnak*, p. 19; *Voyage dans la Haute-Égypte*, vol. i. pp. 15, 16.

[378] The canal figured in front of the Chariot of Rameses, in Fig. 254 was, according to Ebers, the oldest of the Suez Canals, the one dug by Seti I. This canal was defended by fortifications, and is called in inscriptions *the Cutting* (*L'Égypte*, etc.).

[379] To follow these processions was an act of piety. Upon a Theban stele we find the following words addressed to Amen-Ra: "I am one of those who follow thee when thou goest abroad." The stele of Suti and Har, architects at Thebes, translated into French by PAUL PIERRET, in *Recueil de Travaux*, p. 72.

Transcriber's Note:

A mouse hover over Greek text will display English transliteration.

Archaic and inconsistent spelling and punctuation retained.

Most of the coloured plates were too faded to resolve colours.

Some of the figure references appear to be incorrect.

Fig. 460 (Referenced in Fig. 56.) does not exist. It is possible Figure 205 in volume II.

www.ingramcontent.com/pod-product-compliance
Lightning Source LLC
Chambersburg PA
CBHW062020290426
44108CB00024B/2720